PAL FOR PARADOX 4 MADE EASY

PAL FOR PARADOX 4 MADE EASY

Cary Jensen, Ph.D.
and
Loy Anderson, Ph.D.

Osborne McGraw-Hill
Berkeley New York St. Louis San Francisco
Auckland Bogotá Hamburg London Madrid
Mexico City Milan Montreal New Delhi Panama City
Paris São Paulo Singapore Sydney
Tokyo Toronto

Osborne **McGraw-Hill**
2600 Tenth Street
Berkeley, California 94710
U.S.A.

For information on translations or book distributors outside of the U.S.A., please write to Osborne **McGraw-Hill** at the above address.

PAL for Paradox 4 Made Easy

Copyright © 1992 by McGraw-Hill. All rights reserved. Printed in the United States of America. Except as permitted under the Copyright Act of 1976, no part of this publication may be reproduced or distributed in any form or by any means, or stored in a database or retrieval system, without the prior written permission of the publisher, with the exception that the program listings may be entered, stored, and executed in a computer system, but they may not be reproduced for publication.

1234567890 DOC 998765432

ISBN 0-07-881771-4

Publisher
Kenna S. Wood

Acquisitions Editor
Elizabeth Fisher

Associate Editor
Scott Rogers

Editorial Assistant
Hannah Raiden

Technical Editor
Sedge Simons

Copy Editor
K. D. Sullivan

Proofreader
Audrey Johnson

Indexers
Cary Jensen
Loy Anderson

Computer Designer
Lance Ravella

Illustrator
Susie C. Kim

Cover Designer
Bay Graphics Design, Inc.

Information has been obtained by Osborne **McGraw-Hill** from sources believed to be reliable. However, because of the possibility of human or mechanical error by our sources, Osborne **McGraw-Hill**, or others, Osborne **McGraw-Hill** does not guarantee the accuracy, adequacy, or completeness of any information and is not responsible for any errors or omissions or the results obtained from use of such information.

To our friends, John and Robin Spurlino

CONTENTS AT A GLANCE

1	Introduction to PAL	1
2	Scripts and PAL Tools	13
3	Creating Scripts Without Programming	43
4	Expressions	69
5	Commands	103
6	System Control Commands	135
7	Control Structures	149
8	Displaying Information to the User	169
9	Getting Input from the User	199
10	Viewing and Editing Tables	239
11	Manipulating Data	285
12	Procedures and Procedure Libraries	311
13	Events and Event Procedures	343
14	Multiuser Applications	383
A	ASCII Codes and Key Names	405
B	Color Codes	421
C	Error Codes	425
D	Exercise Tables	431
	Index	437

CONTENTS

Acknowledgments xix
Introduction xxi

1 — Introduction to PAL 1
What Is PAL? 2
When to Use PAL 2
Automating Paradox 3
Adding Features to Paradox 3
Developing Applications 4
Why Use PAL to Create Applications? 7
Quick Review 10

2 — Scripts and PAL Tools 13
What Are Scripts? 14
Creating a Script 14
Playing a Script 15
Terminating a Script 16
Script Names 17
PAL Canvases 19
PAL Tools 21
The Scripts Menu 21

The PAL Menu	22
The Paradox 4 Editor	22
Using the Paradox Editor	25
Using the Editor Menu	27
The Paradox 3.5 Script Editor	31
The PAL Debugger	31
Script Error Debugging	33
Debugging Errors in Logic	35
The Debugger Features	36
Other Script Tools	39
Quick Review	40

3 — Creating Scripts Without Programming 43

What Are Recorded Scripts?	44
Using Recorded Scripts	45
Creating a Recorded Script	46
Playing a Recorded Script	47
Stepping Through a Script	48
What Paradox Records	50
Another Recorded Script	52
What Are Instant Scripts?	54
Using Instant Scripts	54
Creating an Instant Script	54
Playing an Instant Script	56
Another Instant Script	56
Playing the Second Instant Script Example	57
Limitations of Recorded and Instant Scripts	58
What Are Saved Queries?	59
Creating a Saved Query	60
Playing a Saved Query	62
Processing a Saved Query	63
Automating a Saved Query	64
Quick Review	66

4 — Expressions 69

Expression Data Types	70
The Elements of Expressions	70

Constants	71
Using Alphanumeric Constants	71
Using Numeric Constants	73
Using Date Constants	74
Using Logical Constants	74
Variables	74
Assigning Values to Variables	75
Choosing Variable Names	78
Arrays	79
Declaring an Array	80
Field Specifiers	82
Using Field Specifiers	86
PAL Functions	89
Using Functions	90
Operators	92
Using the Alphanumeric Operator	96
Using Numeric Operators	96
Using Date Operators	97
Using Logical Operators	97
Quick Review	101

5 Commands — 103

Controlling Paradox	104
Using Keypress Interactions	104
Braced Menu Selections	104
Quoted Strings	106
Using PAL Commands	109
Abbreviated Menu Commands	109
Special Key Commands	113
Programming Commands	117
Command Syntax	121
Understanding Syntax Notation	122
Using Commands in Scripts	124
Arranging Commands	125
Using Blank Spaces	126
Using Comments in Your Scripts	129
Quick Review	133

6 System Control Commands 135
- The RETURN Command 136
  - RETURN Exercise 136
- The SLEEP Command 137
- The DEBUG Command 138
  - DEBUG Exercise 138
- The PLAY Command 139
  - PLAY Exercise 140
- The QUIT Command 142
  - QUIT Exercise 143
- The SETKEY Command 144
  - SETKEY Exercise 145
  - Quick Review 147

7 Control Structures 149
- Control Within Scripts 150
- Branching Control Structures 150
  - Using the IF Command 151
  - IF Exercise 153
  - Using the SWITCH Command 153
- Looping Commands 156
  - Using the FOR Command 156
  - FOR Exercise 158
  - Using the FOREACH Command 159
  - FOREACH Exercise 161
  - Using the WHILE Command 162
  - The SCAN Command 163
- Controlling Loops 164
- Nesting Control Structures 164
  - Quick Review 166

8 Displaying Information to the User 169
- The Desktop, Canvases, and Windows 170
- Controlling Canvas Display 172
  - Controlling the Cursor 173
  - Clearing the Canvas 174
  - Printing Text on the Canvas 176

Text Attributes	182
Echoing the Full-Screen Canvas	186
Canvas Windows	187
Creating a Canvas Window	188
Getting Window Attributes	190
Setting Window Attributes	192
Closing Windows	194
Selecting the Current Canvas	195
The Current Canvas and the Active Window	195
Quick Review	197

9 — Getting Input from the User 199

Using Menus	200
The SHOWMENU Command	202
The SHOWARRAY Command	205
The SHOWTABLES and SHOWFILES Commands	206
The SHOWPOPUP Command	208
The SHOWPULLDOWN Command	210
Getting Keyboard Input	214
The ACCEPT Command	214
The GETCHAR( ) Function	218
Dialog Boxes	222
Creating a Dialog Box	223
Quick Review	236

10 — Viewing and Editing Tables 239

Desktop Management	240
Placing a Table on the Desktop	240
Picking a Form	242
Changing Between Table View and Form View	245
Setting Attributes of Object Windows	246
Keeping the Desktop Clear	247
Desktop Movement	248
Special Key Commands	248

Using Programming Commands	250
Viewing Tables	256
WAITing on a Table	257
Prompting a WAIT	259
Using Retval in a WAIT	261
Reports	264
Printing Reports	264
Using the PRINTERSTATUS( ) Function	265
Previewing Reports	266
Editing Tables	267
Entering Edit Mode	267
Exiting Edit Mode	268
Editing a Table in a WAIT Command	268
Advanced Editing Topics	269
Getting User Confirmation	270
Editing a Specific Record	273
Adding New Records	275
Adding a Record to a Keyed Table	278
Quick Review	282

11 ▬ Manipulating Data   285

Assignment	286
Using Quoted Strings	286
Using the TYPEIN Command	287
Using Direct Assignment	287
Processing at the Record Level	289
Other Editing Commands	291
Giving Feedback	292
Queries	293
Displaying a Query Form	294
Processing Queries	295
Changing a Query Form	298
Checking Fields in Queries	299
Conditions, Calculations, and Operators	300
Creating Example Elements	301
Using Variables in Queries	304

User-Defined Queries	306
Quick Review	308

12 — Procedures and Procedure Libraries 311

Procedures	312
Calling a Procedure	314
Defining a Procedure	314
Using Private Variables	317
Passing Values to a Procedure	319
Returning a Value	321
Releasing a Procedure	322
Procedure Libraries	323
Creating a Library	324
Adding Procedures to a Library	325
Changing Procedures in a Library	327
Listing the Contents of a Library	329
Using Procedures from a Library	330
The READLIB Command	331
The Autolib Variable	332
The Paradox Library	333
Advanced Procedure Topics	334
Using the SETSWAP Command in Paradox 3.5	334
Making Better Use of Memory in Paradox 3.5	335
Using Closed Procedures	336
Using an Error Procedure	338
Quick Review	341

13 — Events and Event Procedures 343

Events	344
Getting Events	345
The Event Dynamic Array	347
Executing an Event	355
SHOWPULLDOWN and GETEVENT	356

Event Procedures	358
Trigger Events	358
Dialog Procedures	360
Building Dialog Procedures	361
Returning from a Dialog Procedure	364
Controlling the Dialog Box	366
Wait Procedures	369
Building a Wait Procedure	370
Returning from a Wait Procedure	375
Controlling the Desktop from a Wait Procedure	376
Creating More Efficient Event Procedures	376
Calling Procedures Within Event Procedures	377
Using Dynamic Arrays to Process Events	377
Quick Review	381

14 ■ Multiuser Applications 383

Table Locking	384
Explicit Table Locking	386
Removing Explicit Locks	387
Managing Table Locks	388
CoEdit Mode	389
Explicit Record Locking	390
Private Directories	395
Declaring Private Tables	396
Other Multiuser Application Topics	396
Using DataEntry in a Multiuser Application	396
Testing Multiuser Applications	398
Adding Security to an Application	398
Quick Review	403

A ■ ASCII Codes and Key Names 405

B ■ Color Codes 421

Color Monitors	422
Monochrome Monitors	423

C Error Codes	....	**425**
D Exercise Tables	....	**431**
Tables	....	432
Customer Table Structure	....	432
Customer Table Contents	....	432
Employee Table Structure	....	433
Employee Table Contents	....	433
Invoice Table Structure	....	433
Invoice Table Contents	....	433
Indetail Table Structure	....	434
Indetail Table Contents	....	434
Product Table Structure	....	434
Product Table Contents	....	434
Creating a Form for the Exercises	....	435
Index	....	**437**

ACKNOWLEDGMENTS

We want to thank all of the individuals whose efforts and support have made this book a reality: In particular, Kenna Wood, Publisher, and Jeff Pepper, Editor-in-Chief, at Osborne/McGraw-Hill, whose support made this project possible. To Scott Rogers, Associate Editor, and Judith Brown, Project Editor, and the many others on the editorial and production staff at Osborne/McGraw-Hill for their hard work. To K.D. Sullivan, for her excellent copyedit, and Susie Kim, for her eye-catching illustration. To Dr. Sedge Simons, for his thorough technical review. To Karen Giles and Nan Borreson of Borland International for their support and encouragement.

To all the Paradox users who implored us to write the predecessor to this book, *PAL Made Easy,* and to those who expressed their appreciation for finally finding an introductory PAL book, thank you for your support. We sincerely hope that this book also lives up to your expectations. Finally, thanks to Liz Fisher, our acquisitions editor at Osborne/McGraw-Hill, for her persistence, hard work, and dedication to this project.

INTRODUCTION

If you are using Paradox, but not using PAL, you are working too hard. Using PAL (the Paradox Application Language) improves the effectiveness and efficiency of your Paradox work dramatically. In fact, there is so much that PAL can do for you, it will become an integral part of your everyday Paradox usage. This is true whether you want to automate parts of your Paradox session, add new features or utilities to Paradox, or create sophisticated database applications.

Paradox earned its name by being powerful yet easy to use. You might say that this is especially true of PAL. On one hand, it is a powerful and full-featured computer programming language, comparable to BASIC, FORTRAN, and Pascal. On the other, it is an extraordinary productivity tool accessible to every Paradox user, even if you have never programmed a computer before.

PAL for Paradox 4 Made Easy is written especially for you, the Paradox user. No assumptions have been made about your previous programming experience. In fact, if you have never programmed a computer before, this book will introduce you to the exciting world of computer programming without resorting to esoteric jargon or obscure terms. Each new concept is explained clearly, and examples are backed up with hands-on exercises that give you immediate experience.

If you do have previous programming experience, this book will provide you with a rapid introduction to writing PAL programs. In addition to the descriptions of PAL properties and principles, you will also find many examples of well-organized PAL scripts. In most cases, you will be able to use these example programs as is, or with slight modifications, to immediately create your own PAL applications. As a result, you will be writing your own PAL programs in no time at all.

We wrote this book with two specific goals in mind. The first is to provide you with a thorough introduction to PAL. After completing *PAL for Paradox 4 Made Easy,* we believe you will experience what we have observed time and time again: PAL users make better Paradox users.

The second goal is to help you make sense of the PAL documentation that comes with Paradox. We feel that those manuals are some of the finest available with any commercial software product—for the experienced programmer, that is. In most cases, the Paradox documentation is not appropriate for people getting started with PAL, or programming for that matter. After reading *PAL for Paradox 4 Made Easy,* you will be prepared to use the Paradox manuals for complete information on PAL.

How This Book Is Organized

The first three chapters of this book provide you with a meaningful introduction to PAL and PAL tools, including the Paradox Editor, the PAL menu, and the PAL Debugger. You also learn how to use Paradox to create PAL programs such as recorded scripts, instant scripts, and saved queries. If you have never used PAL before, these chapters alone will make you a better Paradox user.

Chapters 4 and 5 give you an introduction to basics of computer programming and more specifically, PAL programming. Concepts such as expressions, variables, functions, and commands are described and demonstrated with practical exercises.

Chapters 6 through 14 show you how to create the building blocks of PAL scripts and how to put them together into powerful utilities and applications. In Chapter 6 you learn basic system commands. In Chapter 7, the control structures you use to add intelligence to your scripts are demonstrated. Chapters 8 and 9 teach you how to effectively interact with a user from within a script. In Chapter 10 you learn how to navigate Paradox tables and provide users with controlled access to

Introduction

these tables. Chapter 11 focuses on manipulating data, both through record-level processing and with queries. Chapter 12 shows you how to create faster, shorter, and more flexible applications using procedures and procedure libraries. In Chapter 13 you learn how to take complete control over the interaction between the user and your application with event trapping and event procedures. Finally, Chapter 14 introduces you to the essentials of creating multiuser applications.

This book concludes with four appendixes. The first three give you instant access to ASCII codes, color codes, and error codes. The last appendix contains the tables that you can create to follow along with the exercises in the rest of the book.

Is This Book for You?

Do you use Paradox and now want more? Are you using an application written in PAL and want to learn more about how this was done? Are you considering having an application developed for yourself or your organization and want to know if PAL is the appropriate language for this project? Are you an experienced programmer of one or more other languages and want to learn what all the fuss about PAL is? Are you a current PAL user upgrading to Paradox 4 and want an introduction to the new features? Are you using Paradox 3.5 and want to know if the Paradox 4 features justify upgrading?

If you answered yes to one or more of these questions, this book is for you. *PAL for Paradox 4 Made Easy* provides you with a thorough introduction to the PAL language, what it can do, and how to do it.

Although the main focus of *PAL for Paradox 4 Made Easy* is Paradox 4, the book also covers Paradox 3.5. This is because while every feature of 3.5 is available in Paradox 4, Paradox 4 cannot run on older 8088 and 8086 computers. Consequently, Paradox 3.5 will continue to be a powerful and viable solution to many users' database needs. Also, since Paradox 4 is a superset of Paradox 3.5 features, most of the material in this book applies equally to both products. Topics not available in Paradox 3.5 are clearly marked.

Preparing the Tables

Throughout this book, exercises are provided to give you immediate experience with the many concepts and techniques presented. In order to participate in these exercises, and compare your results to those shown in the book, you must first create the tables described in Appendix D "Exercise Tables." In this appendix, you will find the table structures and sample data that will be referred to again and again.

In addition to the tables, you should also create one form for one of the tables, the Customer table. This form need not be elaborate (although you may be as creative as you like). If you are short on time, you will find step-by-step instructions on how to have Paradox create a default form in Appendix D. All in all, it will only take you a few minutes to make the necessary preparations.

Conventions Used in This Book

The following conventions are used throughout this book:

- ◆ Capitalization of menu selections follows that displayed on the Paradox menus.

- ◆ When you must make a sequence of menu selections, they are displayed in order of selection, separated by slashes. For example, the sequence Scripts/Editor/Open means that you first select Scripts from the Main menu, Editor from the Scripts menu, followed by Open from the next menu displayed.

- ◆ Keys and key combinations are displayed like this: (Enter), (Alt)-(F8). Any key that has a name is followed by its key name in parentheses, for example, (F2) (Do-It!).

- ◆ PAL commands and functions are printed in uppercase letters.

- ◆ Notes, Tips, Warnings, and Cautions specific to one version (3.5 or 4) are clearly identified.

- ◆ Script examples are shown in monospaced type, for example:
  ```
  Menu {TableBand} {Erase} Enter
  ```

CHAPTER

1 INTRODUCTION TO PAL

Paradox is widely regarded as the most powerful and easy-to-use of the microcomputer databases. If you are a typical Paradox user, you have probably found Paradox capable of handling most of your database needs. However, using Paradox interactively, by selecting from its menus, represents only half of its capabilities. Untapped by most Paradox users is the powerful feature called PAL, the Paradox Application Language.

If you have not used PAL before now, you are in for a wonderful surprise. You are standing on a threshold and a door is about to be opened. What you will find is that PAL is fun, PAL is easy, and PAL will make you a better Paradox user. Once you step through the door, there is no going back. PAL will forever be an effective tool entirely at your command.

As you read this chapter you will gain a basic understanding of PAL, including what PAL is and what its uses are. You will explore specific features of PAL in later chapters.

What Is PAL?

PAL is a computer programming language that is completely integrated with Paradox. PAL consists of keywords, which permit you to work with Paradox tables, forms, reports, and queries. These keywords can be incorporated into computer programs, called *scripts,* that can be used to control Paradox.

Even though PAL is a sophisticated programming language, you do not need to be a computer programmer to use it. If you have never programmed a computer before, you will be surprised how easy and how much fun PAL can be. If you do have experience programming computers, however, you will be delighted with the convenience and power of PAL. In addition, you do not have to write scripts to benefit from PAL, since Paradox provides you with features that will write scripts for you.

When to Use PAL

In general, you can use PAL to increase the power and flexibility of Paradox. At the very least, you can use it to automate repetitive tasks you perform in Paradox. Don't be surprised, however, if you go even further, using PAL to customize your everyday Paradox sessions by adding features and utilities that improve your Paradox usage. You might even take it to the limit, using PAL to create advanced database applications. Whether they are for your own use or the use of others, your database applications can control every aspect of the collection, management, manipulation, and reporting of data.

Automating Paradox

One of the simplest ways to use PAL is to record a series of keystrokes you perform routinely. Once you record them, you can play them back again, as many times as you like and as often as you like. For example, you may have a table that you frequently add data to, and you use a form to enter the data. Each time you edit this table, you select Modify/Edit (select Modify from the Main menu followed by Edit from the next menu displayed) and use Image/PickForm to select the desired form. Although this is a simple task in interactive Paradox, it requires a number of keystrokes to achieve. Furthermore, you might have to repeat part of this process if you make a mistake while typing the table name or selecting the form.

Rather than repeating these same steps each time you want to edit the table, you can store the keystrokes that bring up the table and choose the correct form in a PAL script. This script can then be used at a later time to repeat the original keystrokes. These keystrokes will be repeated faster than you can type, and with no errors.

PAL can also save you effort if you need to repeatedly generate the same query. For example, each week you may create a query to track the performance of your sales staff. Instead of constructing this query every time, you can construct it once and then save it in a PAL script. The next time you want to perform the query, you play the script and Paradox automatically creates the query form for you, based on the information you stored in your script.

Adding Features to Paradox

Paradox has many features that assist you in working with data. Using PAL, you can either increase the power of existing features or add entirely new ones. Consider, for example, the [Ctrl]-[D] (Ditto) feature in Paradox. When you add data to a table in Paradox, you can copy the contents of the field in the immediately preceding record into the current field by pressing [Ctrl]-[D] (Ditto). But what if you want to copy the contents of the entire previous record into the current record? Paradox does not support such a feature. You can add this feature using PAL, however. With a minimal amount of PAL programming you can create a new record-copying feature and assign it to the [Alt]-[D] key combination, or any other keys, for that matter.

Another example of a feature you may want to program to improve your Paradox usage involves using the [Del] key while you are editing a table. When you are using Paradox interactively, pressing the [Del] key while you are editing a table deletes a record without asking you for confirmation. Using PAL, you can modify this feature so that when you press [Del], Paradox offers you a menu with Cancel (do not delete) and OK (delete) as the selections.

As you become more familiar with PAL, you will likely add many such features or modifications for use in your everyday Paradox session. Most users who customize their Paradox session in this manner increase their productivity substantially.

Developing Applications

You can use PAL to combine related tasks or features. That combination is called an *application*. You can think of an application as a set of different scripts that perform varied yet integrated functions. For instance, one script can assist you in adding data to a table, while another generates a query to prepare a report.

With PAL, you can design small or large applications, for yourself or for someone else to use.

Applications can be small or large. For example, you can create a small application to summarize and print data from a single table. Or you can create a large application to help manage and automate an entire project or function in your business, such as an inventory management application that tracks inventory, generates orders, and performs accounting functions.

The need for an application is particularly obvious when you want features that are just not available in interactive Paradox. For instance, you may want changes you make to one table to be matched by corresponding changes to other tables. A common example of this is when you want to delete a record in one table and have all of the corresponding detail records in other tables deleted automatically. Although this situation occurs frequently, in interactive Paradox it is up to you to remember to make the changes to the master table and all necessary detail tables. Instead of trying to remember in which detail tables the related records reside however, you can create a PAL application that automatically performs the detail record deletions when the master record is deleted.

Introduction to PAL

As you might imagine, PAL is even more important when you are developing an application that someone other than yourself will use. Designing applications that will be used by others poses a number of challenges, principally in the areas of customization, accuracy of data, and control over who can access the data.

Customization

One feature that makes PAL especially useful is the complete control over the Paradox environment PAL offers you. For example, instead of using the Paradox menu, you can use PAL to display a customized menu that contains selections specific to your particular data. Furthermore, you can create interactive dialog boxes where you specify information that your application can use. An example of such a dialog box is shown in Figure 1-1.

You can determine every facet of your application's "look and feel" (or *user interface*) using PAL. Not only can you specify what the screen looks like when your application is running, you also have complete control over the data. For example, your application can permit other users to add a record to a table only if the addition has a unique entry in the key field(s).

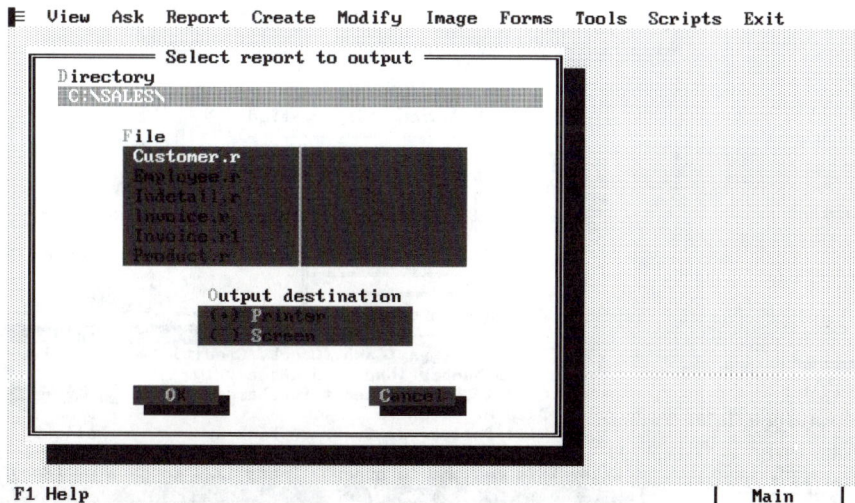

A custom dialog box
Figure 1-1.

Pal for Paradox 4 Made Easy

Data Accuracy

Using PAL you can anticipate data entry or editing errors that might compromise the quality of the data stored in your Paradox tables. Consider an example in which a table contains customer payments for products purchased. When the payment type is Cash, the Credit Card # field should be blank. Likewise, when the payment type is Credit, the credit card number must be entered (an authorization code may also be required). With PAL, you can make sure that a credit card number is supplied whenever the payment type is Credit, and only then. You can also ensure that the beginning date for a service is before the ending date.

You can use PAL to perform these checks and others (as many as necessary) as a part of your application. If one of these anticipated, unacceptable conditions occurs, your PAL program can display a warning and require that corrected data be entered before allowing the user to continue.

Figure 1-2 is an example of how you can use PAL to check for errors and inform users about them. A PAL script was written to make sure that when users enter a credit purchase they also supply the credit card number. In this case, the user failed to supply the credit card number. The figure shows that the PAL script found the error and displayed an error message indicating the problem.

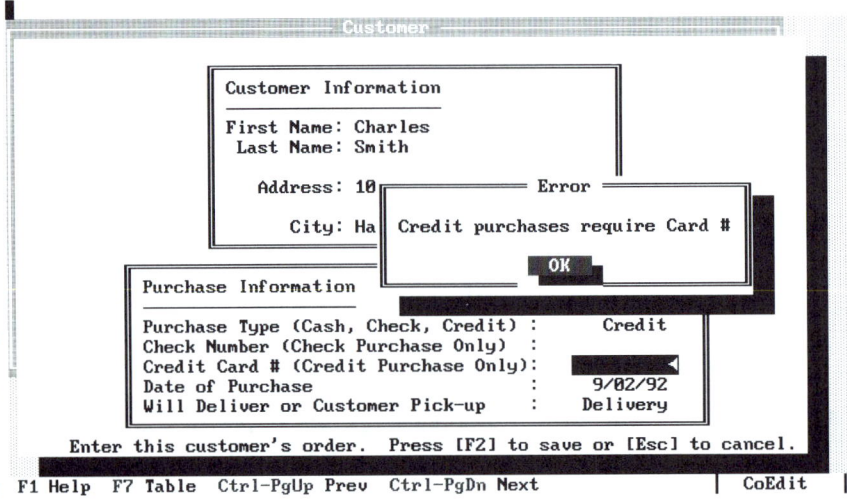

A PAL script reporting a data entry error
Figure 1-2.

Introduction to PAL

PAL can also be used to detect events, such as a user pressing [F1] (Help) during data entry. Using PAL you could design a custom Help screen that will be displayed whenever [F1] is pressed during data entry. (This screen would appear instead of the standard Paradox Help screen.) This allows you to provide specific information to assist the user in entering correct data. An example of a customized Help screen is shown in Figure 1-3.

Data Security

Because your PAL application can be designed to have total control over your Paradox tables, it can restrict access to the data to persons you authorize. For example, your application can test for a valid password before allowing a user to access the application's features. Furthermore, your application can provide two or more levels of authorization. One password could provide limited access, only permitting a user to add new records to a table. A second password might permit a user to edit records in addition to adding them.

Why Use Pal to Create Applications?

With PAL, you can create powerful applications quickly and easily. Other programming languages also permit the development of

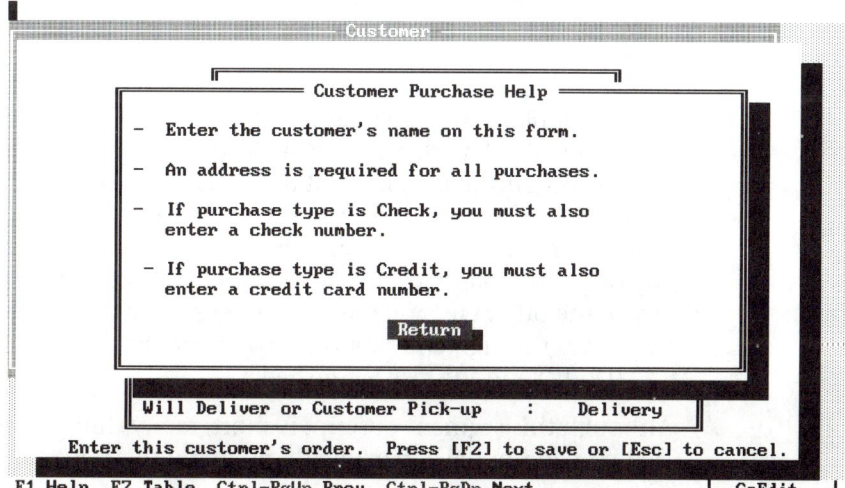

A customized Help screen created with PAL
Figure 1-3.

sophisticated databases. However, PAL's integration with Paradox makes it an especially useful application development tool.

Paradox provides you with many objects that are necessary in a database application. Objects include tables, forms, reports, and queries. Paradox features are also available, such as record sorting, crosstabs, complete multiuser capabilities, and presentation-quality graphs. When you use PAL to write scripts, all these Paradox objects and features are at your disposal. You do not have to write a program to format a screen for entering data, for example, as you must using other programming languages. Instead, you specify in your script that it display a form you previously created in Paradox.

Similarly, you do not have to write a complicated script to format data for output to a printer (although you can do this, if the need arises). Instead, your script can send an existing report to the printer. All you need to do is create the report beforehand using Paradox.

Because your scripts can incorporate Paradox objects and features, your scripts can be short yet feature-filled. Take, for example, the following script segment:

```
EDIT "Customer"
PICKFORM 1
INS
WAIT RECORD
   PROMPT "Enter a new customer record.  "+
          "Press [F2] to continue."
   UNTIL "F2"
DO_IT!
```

This script places the table called Customer on the desktop, enters the Edit mode, displays the table using form 1, inserts a new record, and displays an informative prompt to the user. When this script is played, Figure 1-4 is displayed. (Your screen will vary, depending on the design of your form 1.) With the form displayed, a user can move the cursor to any of the regular fields on the form. However, the user cannot move to any of the other customer records or delete the current record. When the user is through entering the new record, he or she merely presses [F2] (Do-It!) and the task is finished.

Although this segment of script is short, many things happen within it that you do not have to explicitly program; they are managed entirely

Introduction to PAL

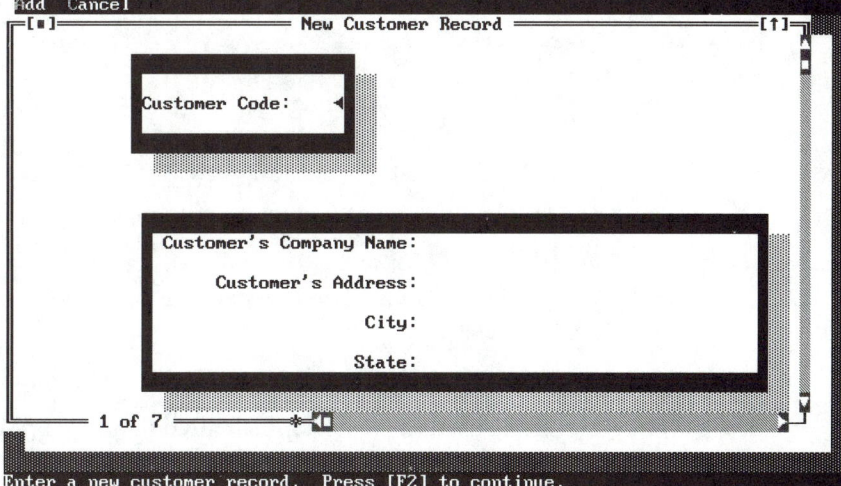

PAL scripts can use Paradox forms
Figure 1-4.

by Paradox. These tasks include the construction of the screen image, navigation of the user's cursor movements on the screen, and prevention of unwanted keystrokes (such as the [Del] key). Your scripts use and manipulate the Paradox objects and provide the overall structure of your application. Paradox, on the other hand, takes care of most of the details.

Quick Review

✦ PAL is a programming language that is completely integrated with Paradox.

✦ Using PAL you can automate repetitive tasks performed in Paradox.

✦ PAL permits you to add features and utilities to Paradox.

✦ PAL can be used to create sophisticated database applications that control all elements of the Paradox environment, including the user interface, data accuracy, and data security.

✦ PAL programs are shorter and more powerful than other computer programs because they have unlimited access to all Paradox's objects, such as tables, forms, reports, and queries. PAL programs can also make use of any Paradox feature, including crosstabs, presentation-quality graphs, and complete multiuser capabilities.

CHAPTER

2 SCRIPTS AND PAL TOOLS

This chapter begins with an introduction to PAL scripts—what they are and what they do. General concepts used in creating, using, and naming scripts are also covered. The remainder of this chapter describes the various PAL tools.

Unlike the material presented in the remaining chapters in this book, the topics in this chapter are presented conceptually, without hands-on examples. Later chapters will reintroduce needed information, so you do not need to memorize the details presented here. However, familiarity with these topics will give you a solid, overall understanding of PAL and a framework in which to place new aspects of PAL as they arise.

As you continue through this book, you will have many opportunities to use the various features described here. Indeed, as your use of PAL increases, many of these concepts and tools will become second nature to you.

What Are Scripts?

A PAL script is a list of instructions. Just as a script for a film or stage play contains instructions to actors, where to move and what to say, PAL scripts contain instructions to Paradox. For instance, a script may instruct Paradox to display a particular table on the Paradox desktop. Your role is that of both playwright and director: you create the script and you tell Paradox to follow it.

Creating a Script

There are four different ways to create a script:

    Creating a recorded script
    Creating a saved query
    Using the Paradox Application Workshop
    Programming the script yourself

A recorded script contains instructions that you record while using Paradox interactively. A recorded script can be created by using either the BeginRecord feature or the Instant Script feature of Paradox. While recording, Paradox stores each menu selection and keystroke you make in a script. These stored instructions can be used later to repeat your original keystrokes and menu selections.

Saved queries are created by using the QuerySave feature in Paradox. After you have constructed a query on the Paradox desktop, you can save it as a script by selecting Scripts/QuerySave (that is, selecting Scripts from the Paradox Main menu followed by QuerySave from the Scripts menu). The saved query script contains the PAL commands that Paradox can use to reconstruct the original query.

Scripts and PAL Tools

The Paradox Application Workshop is a menu-driven tool you use to define the features of an application. These include which menus to display and what actions will occur when menu selections are made. When you have finished defining your application, the Paradox Application Workshop creates a finished application that controls a user's access to the tables, forms, and reports associated with the application.

NOTE: Paradox 3.5 does not include the Application Workshop. Instead it offers the Personal Programmer, which is similar to, though less powerful than the Application Workshop.

The final way to create a script is to write it yourself using the Paradox Editor. Since this method provides you with the greatest flexibility and power, most of this book is dedicated to it.

Playing a Script

In order to have Paradox read the instructions contained in a script, you must *play* the script. When you play a script, Paradox follows the instructions contained in the script until play is complete. At that time control of Paradox returns to you.

How you play a script depends on a number of factors, including how the script was originally created and what its purpose is. For instance, you are likely to use a different method to play a recorded script than one created with the Paradox Application Workshop. Here is a list of ways scripts can be played:

◆ You can select Play from the Scripts menu. This method is a good all-around method for playing a script. There are some scripts, however, that cannot be played this way. These include both recorded scripts and instant scripts that were created while Paradox was in a mode other than Main, such as Report or Form mode.

◆ You can select Play from the PAL menu. Though similar to the previous method, this one is even more flexible since the PAL menu can be accessed from any Paradox mode. Therefore, even recorded scripts created while Paradox was in Report or Form mode can be played this way.

- ◆ You can press Alt-F4 (Instant Script Play) to play an instant script. This method only works with one type of script, the instant script.

- ◆ You can assign one or more instructions to a key or key combination on your keyboard using the PAL command SETKEY. When you press that key or key combination the instructions are played.

- ◆ You can include a script name when starting Paradox to automatically play the script once Paradox is loaded. Use this method when you are playing a script that begins an application. For example, if you want to load Paradox and immediately enter a database created using the Paradox Application Workshop, provide the name of the application script following the command to load Paradox. Thus, if your database script is called Sales, use the following command from the directory where Sales is stored to begin Paradox and start the SALES application:

    PARADOX SALES

NOTE: You cannot use this method if you have a working directory defined in your custom configuration and the startup script is not located in this directory.

- ◆ You can use the PAL command PLAY to play a script from within another script. You will probably only use this method when you have programmed a database application using the Paradox Editor. Nearly every application makes use of more than one script, each one controlling a different element of the application. This control is usually passed by having one script play another. While this method is appropriate for applications you create, you will eventually use called procedures in place of played scripts. You will learn how to create and call procedures in Chapter 12.

Terminating a Script

Paradox normally executes a script until all the instructions have been played. When the last instruction in a script is played, the script

Scripts and PAL Tools

terminates normally and control is returned to Paradox. If the script is one you created using the Paradox Editor, you can also terminate a script using one of several PAL commands. The commands are discussed in Chapter 6. On occasion, however, you may want to terminate a script before it terminates naturally. To do so, hold down the Ctrl key and then press Break. Paradox will display this menu:

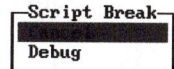

Select Cancel. Alternatively, if you want to enter the PAL Debugger, select Debug. The PAL Debugger is described later in this chapter.

TIP: There are some scripts you cannot terminate with the Ctrl-Break key combination. Specifically, if the script is part of a database application, Ctrl-Break may be unavailable. This is a security measure that prevents unauthorized access to data or scripts being used by the application. More will be said about this feature in Chapter 11.

Script Names

Whenever you create a script, Paradox asks you to provide a name for it. Script names can be up to eight characters in length and can include numbers and letters as well as the following characters:

! @ # $ % ( ) – _ { } ' ~

Script names cannot contain spaces, however. Paradox will save your script in a file using the name you provide and the extension .SC. For example, if you create a script and call it Newtable, Paradox will create a file called NEWTABLE.SC.

It is a good idea to provide your scripts with meaningful names, to the extent that the eight character limit permits. For example, the script name Viewtab would be appropriate for a script that displays a table on the desktop. Similarly, you may want to use the script name Addrec for a script that adds a new record to a table.

There are six script names that have special uses. You should use these names only when you need to achieve specific effects. These special script names are Init, Instant, Mini, Value, Execute, and Savevars.

Init

When you start your Paradox session, Paradox looks at your private directory. If Paradox locates a script in your private directory called Init, it executes the script even before executing any script you name at the DOS prompt when loading Paradox. You can use this feature to customize Paradox to your own specifications. The following are just a few examples of uses for an Init script:

- Changing your current directory from the one where you started Paradox to one in which you store your tables.

- Assigning custom functions to specific keystrokes. For example, if you have created a script that copies the contents of one record in a table to another record in the same table, you could specify that Paradox play that script anytime you press [Alt]-[D].

- Playing an application. This is useful when you normally do not use interactive Paradox, but instead use a database application written in PAL. By loading the application from the Init script, you will never have to tell Paradox to load the application.

- Displaying a greeting. For example, you may always want to begin your Paradox session by displaying the date and time and a friendly *Hello*.

Instant

Paradox uses the script name Instant to store the current instant script. *Do not* use this script name for your own script. If you do, Paradox will replace that script the next time you record another instant script.

Mini, Value, and Execute

Mini and Value are names used for scripts created when you use the MiniScript and Value selections from the PAL menu or the Debugger menu. Execute is a script created when Paradox encounters the PAL command EXECUTE in a script. Since Paradox executes these scripts

Scripts and PAL Tools

from memory and does not write them to disk, you can safely use these as names for your own scripts.

Savevars

Paradox creates the Savevars script when you issue the PAL command SAVEVARS. This script contains a definition of all variables that are defined at the time the SAVEVARS command is executed (variables are described in Chapter 4). As with the Instant script, if you create your own script called Savevars and then issue the PAL command SAVEVARS, your script will be replaced by the one created by Paradox.

PAL Canvases

When you play a script, something rather special happens to the Paradox desktop; you no longer see it. What you see instead is the *full-screen PAL canvas*. Once your script is completed, you will again see the Paradox desktop.

Unless your script uses PAL commands to modify the full-screen canvas, it contains a snapshot of the desktop as it looked the moment you began playing the script. All activity on the desktop is hidden from view by this canvas. This is why the screen appears momentarily frozen when you play a script. When your script is finished playing, the canvas is dropped, and the screen will suddenly shift or change if an object was added or removed from the desktop during execution of the script. For example, your script statements may view a table on the desktop, enter the Edit mode, and select a form. When you play this script, your screen briefly freezes, showing an image of what the desktop looked like when you started playing the script. As soon as the script terminates, the full-screen canvas is dropped and the form becomes visible.

NOTE: The terms *raised* and *dropped* are used to describe the activation and deactivation, respectively, of the full-screen PAL canvas. When the canvas is raised (activated), you no longer see the desktop. Instead you see a captured image of the desktop as it appeared at the moment the canvas was raised. When the canvas is dropped (deactivated), any images that were on the canvas are lost, and the current contents of the desktop appear.

The full-screen canvas is automatically displayed during script play so that Paradox need not spend time updating your screen while following the instructions in the script. This permits the script to execute much faster. Another benefit of the canvas is that it permits you to completely customize what the user sees. When you write your own scripts using the Paradox Editor, you have access to a number of PAL commands that manipulate the PAL canvas. For example, you can erase the image on the canvas, write text, and even paint colors and boxes onto it. In this way, you can make a PAL application take on any look you desire. Figure 2-1 shows an example of a customized screen. While a script is manipulating tables and other Paradox objects on the desktop, PAL commands can be used to paint this thermometer-style indicator on the canvas. This indicator provides the user with assurance that the process is continuing successfully.

In addition to the full-screen canvas, which covers the entire desktop, each window also has a canvas. As with the full-screen canvas, your scripts can use PAL commands to control the individual window canvases, permitting you to hide the contents of the window, display a frozen image of a window while the script is changing the contents, or to paint text or colors on top of the window image. You have a great deal of flexibility concerning how your application looks, and what information it displays.

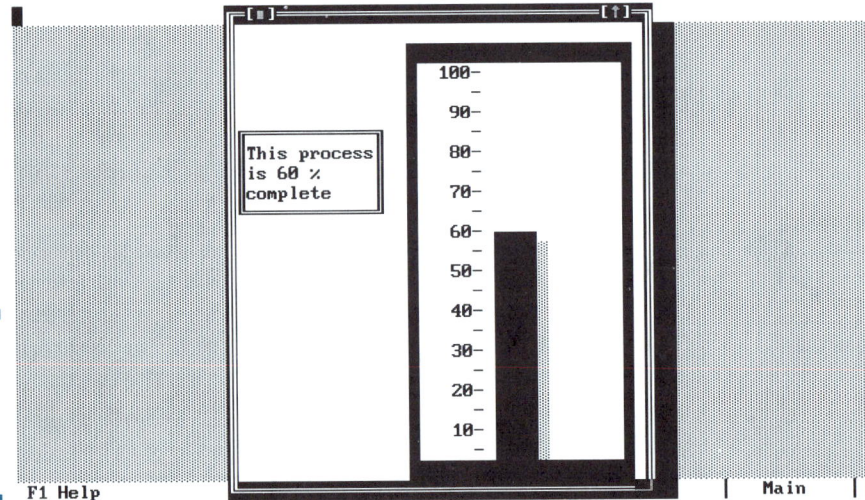

Thermometer-style indicator on the PAL canvas
Figure 2-1.

Scripts and PAL Tools

NOTE: In Paradox 3.5 there is only one canvas. This single canvas is similar to the full-screen canvas in Paradox 4.

PAL Tools

The remaining sections in this chapter describe the various PAL tools available in Paradox. As you work through the later chapters in this book, you will become quite familiar with these tools. The PAL tools are

The Scripts menu
The PAL menu
The Paradox Editor (Script Editor in Paradox 3.5)
The PAL Debugger
Paradox tools for copying, renaming, and deleting scripts

The Scripts Menu

The Scripts menu provides you with access to some basic script features. To access the Scripts menu, select Scripts from the Paradox Main menu. The Scripts menu, shown in Figure 2-2, will be displayed. The Play, ShowPlay, and RepeatPlay selections allow you to play a script. BeginRecord and QuerySave are used to create scripts. Select Editor to use the Paradox Editor. The uses of the individual Scripts menu selections are listed in Table 2-1.

Menu Selection	Description
Play	Plays a script
BeginRecord	Begins recording a recorded script
QuerySave	Creates a script that will rebuild the query on the desktop
ShowPlay	Plays a script without using the PAL canvas
RepeatPlay	Plays a script a specified number of times
Editor	Accesses the Paradox Editor

Scripts Menu Selections
Table 2-1.

Figure 2-2. Scripts menu

The PAL Menu

The PAL menu is a special Paradox menu available from anywhere in Paradox. This is important because it places all PAL's features at your fingertips, regardless of what you are doing in Paradox. (In contrast, the Scripts menu is only available from the Paradox Main menu.) To display the PAL menu, press [Alt]-[F10]. You will see the menu shown in Figure 2-3.

The PAL menu contains many of the same selections found in the Scripts menu. Two selections that are unique to the PAL menu, Value and MiniScript, are among the most useful in all of Paradox. It is these two selections that provide you direct access to PAL during your interactive Paradox sessions. The uses of the individual PAL menu selections are listed in Table 2-2.

The Paradox 4 Editor

The Paradox Editor is an ASCII text editor integrated with Paradox. You use it to create and modify PAL scripts or to edit memo fields in Paradox 4. There are a number of ways to access the Paradox Editor: You can select Paradox/Editor from the Main menu, select Utilities/Editor from the System menu, press [Alt]-[E] from any mode, or

Scripts and PAL Tools

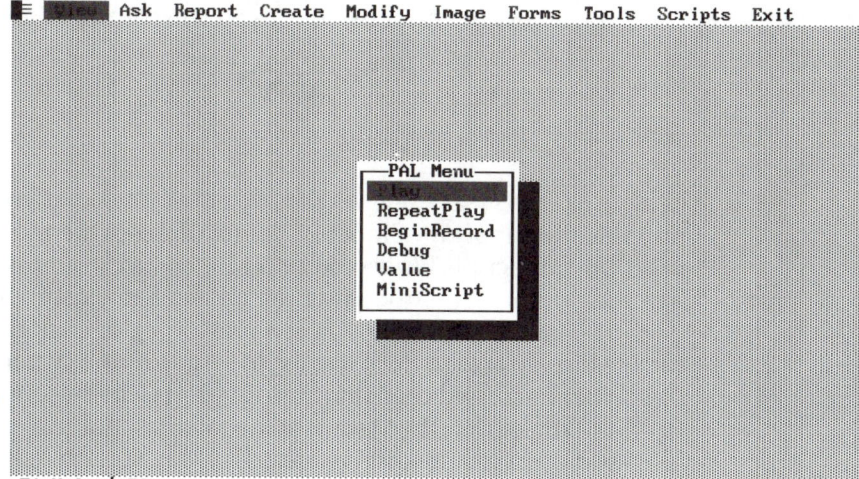

Figure 2-3.
PAL menu

the standard way to access the Paradox Editor is through the Scripts menu. You can also access it from the PAL Debugger, as described later in this chapter.

NOTE: If you have installed an alternative editor, you can still access the Paradox Editor using [Alt]-[E] or by selecting Utilities/Editor from the System menu. Using Scripts/Editor will access the alternative editor. You install an alternative editor using the PAL selection from the Custom Configuration Program.

Table 2-2.
PAL Menu Selections

Menu Selection	Description
Play	Plays a script
RepeatPlay	Plays a script a specified number of times
BeginRecord	Begins recording a script (keyboard macro)
Debug	Loads a script and enters the PAL Debugger
Value	Displays the results of a PAL expression
MiniScript	Executes a one-line script

Once you access the Paradox Editor you will see the following menu:

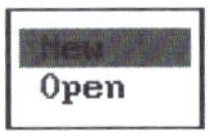

Choose New to create a new script. When you select it you are prompted to supply a valid script name. Choose Open to make changes to an existing script. When you select it Paradox prompts you for the name of an existing script. Enter the name of an existing script (without the extension), or you can press [Enter], or click the mouse in the file display area to display a list of scripts in the current directory. (If you have accessed the Editor using [Alt]-[E] or by selecting Utilities/Editor from the System menu, all files, not just script files, will be displayed in the file display area. This way you can edit or view any ASCII file using the Paradox Editor, not just scripts. When using [Alt]-[E] or Utilities/Editor, you must enter the file extension .SC to create or edit a script.)

After you provide the name of a script, your screen will look similar to Figure 2-4. The script you are creating or editing appears in its own

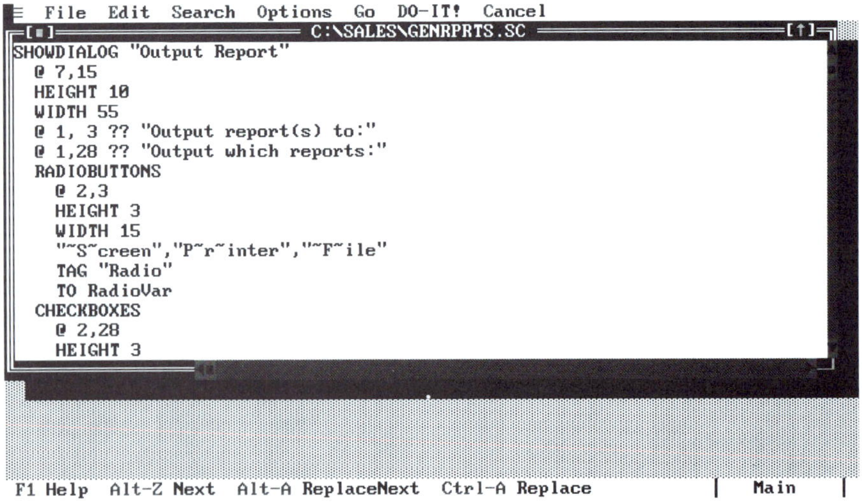

Figure 2-4. Paradox Editor showing a script being edited

Scripts and PAL Tools

window on the desktop. The Editor menu is displayed along the top line of the screen, and the Status bar is displayed along the bottom.

Because the Paradox Editor is part of Paradox, you can access all Paradox and PAL features from it. For example, you can display the PAL menu (to use the Value or MiniScript selection), and even record and play instant scripts to assist in the editing of your script. Once you become familiar with scripts using PAL commands, you can even create PAL scripts that add features to the Editor.

Using the Paradox Editor

The Paradox Editor has a variety of features to help you edit scripts. Among these are the ability to edit more than one script at a time, copy lines within a script or between scripts, and search and replace. You can access many of these features using the keyboard or a mouse, while others are available from the Editor menu.

Three main features you access using a mouse are window selection, cursor movement, and text selection. Window selection and cursor movement use the same techniques that you use for all other types of windows in Paradox. Text selection can occur only in the Editor.

You select text in order to delete it, copy it to the clipboard, or replace it with the clipboard contents. Once text has been copied to the clipboard, you can paste it into a new location in the current script window or in another Editor window. To select text, move the mouse pointer to the beginning of the text you want to select and hold down the left mouse button. Next, move the cursor to the ending position you want to select. As you move the mouse pointer the text between the beginning and ending positions is highlighted. When the text you want to select is highlighted, release the left mouse button. The selected text is ready to be deleted (by pressing [Del]), replaced (by pasting text or pressing any key), or copied to the clipboard (by pressing [Shift]-[Del], [Ctrl]-[Del], or by selecting Edit/Copy or Edit/Cut from the Editor menu).

All of the features you can access with a mouse, and more, also can be accessed using the keyboard. Each of the keys and key combinations, as well as their functions, are shown in Table 2-3.

Table 2-3. Keys and Key Combinations to Access Editor Features

Key	Description
Alt-A	Replaces highlighted text during a Search and Replace operation and then finds next Search value
Alt-F7	Prints the script in the current editor window
Alt-W	Displays the current cursor position in the active window
Alt-Z	Zooms to the next instance of a value following a Ctrl-Z
Backspace	Deletes character left of the cursor
Ctrl-A	Replaces highlighted text during a Search and Replace operation
Ctrl-F4	Makes the next editor window active
Ctrl-F5	Moves or resizes the active editor window
Ctrl-F8	Closes the current window without saving
Ctrl-G	Saves the current script, exits the Editor, and plays the script
Ctrl-←	Moves the cursor left one word
Ctrl-→	Moves the cursor right one word
Ctrl-Pg Dn	Moves the cursor to bottom of script
Ctrl-Pg Up	Moves the cursor to top of script
Ctrl-Ins	Copies highlighted text to the clipboard
Ctrl-Y	Deletes the current line
Ctrl-Z	Zooms to a value
Del	Deletes character at the cursor or highlighted text
↓	Moves the cursor to the following line
End	Moves the cursor to the end of the current line
Esc	Moves to the script from the Editor menu
F2	Saves changes and exits the Editor
F10	Activates the Editor menu
Home	Moves the cursor to the beginning of the current line
Ins	Toggles between Insert mode and Typeover mode

Scripts and PAL Tools

Key	Description
←	Moves the cursor one character left
→	Moves the cursor one character right
↑	Moves the cursor up one line
Pg Dn	Moves the cursor down one screen
Pg Up	Moves the cursor up one screen
Shift-Ctrl-←	Highlights one word to left
Shift-Ctrl-→	Highlights one word to right
Shift-Ctrl-Pg Dn	Highlights to end of script
Shift-Ctrl-Pg Up	Highlights to beginning of script
Shift-Del	Deletes highlighted text and copies it to the clipboard
Shift-↓	Highlights to next line
Shift-End	Highlights to end of line
Shift-F5	Maximizes or minimizes the current Editor window
Shift-Home	Highlights to beginning of line
Shift-Ins	Copies text in the clipboard to cursor position, replaces highlighted text with contents of the clipboard
Shift-←	Highlights one character to left
Shift-↑	Highlights one character to right
Shift-Pg Dn	Highlights one screen down
Shift-Pg Up	Highlights one screen up
Shift-→	Highlights one character to right
Shift-↑	Highlights to preceding line

Keys and Key Combinations to Access Editor Features *(continued)* **Table 2-3.**

Using the Editor Menu

While you are using the Paradox Editor, you can click on the menu bar or press F10 to activate the Editor menu. This menu contains a variety of selections that can be classified into four categories: script management, text manipulation, script navigation, and feature modification. The selections on the Editor menu are described in Table 2-4. The submenus of the Editor menu are covered in the following sections.

Menu Item	Description
File	Displays the File menu
Edit	Displays the Edit menu
Search	Displays the Search menu
Options	Displays the Options menu
Go	Saves all scripts, exits the Paradox Editor, and plays the script that was active (Ctrl-G)
Do_It!	Saves all scripts and exits the Paradox Editor (F2)
Cancel	Cancels changes to the scripts and exits the Paradox Editor (same as Ctrl-F8 when there is only one Editor window)

Table 2-4. Selections on the Editor Menu

The File Menu

Use the File menu to create new scripts, edit existing scripts, or print the script in the current window. The File menu selections and their descriptions are listed in Table 2-5.

The Edit Menu

The Edit menu displays features for text manipulation and navigation. Many of these features, including cutting, copying, and deleting text,

Menu Item	Description
New	Creates a new script
Open	Creates a new window and displays an existing script in it
Save	Saves changes made to the Editor script window
CopyToFile	Saves the current file using a new filename
InsertFile	Copies an entire existing file to the cursor location in the current script window
WriteBlock	Writes the selected text in the active Editor window to a file
Print	Prints the script in the active Editor window

Table 2-5. Selections on the File Menu

Scripts and PAL Tools

require that you first select the text, using the mouse or the keyboard. Although you can access these features and paste text, using this menu, it is nearly always faster using key combinations to achieve the same results. The remaining features on the Edit menu permit you to go quickly to a specific line in the script, display your cursor location, and see the contents of the clipboard. The Edit menu selections and their descriptions are listed in Table 2-6. If a selection has a key equivalent, this is shown at the end of the description.

The Search Menu

Use the Search menu to locate specific text in the current Editor window, or locate text and replace it with other text. The Search menu items and their descriptions are given in Table 2-7.

The Options Menu

The Options menu permits you to change the Editor settings for the current session. (You must use the Custom Configuration Program if you want to make permanent changes.) There are three Options menu settings: AutoIndent, WordWrap, and CaseSensitivity. When

Selections on the Edit Menu
Table 2-6.

Menu Item	Description
XCut	Copies the selected text to the clipboard and deletes it ([Shift]-[Del])
Copy	Copies the selected text to the clipboard ([Ctrl]-[Ins])
Paste	Pastes the contents of the clipboard to the cursor, or replaces the selected text with the contents of the clipboard ([Shift]-[Ins])
Erase	Erases the selected text ([Del])
Goto	Moves the cursor to a specified line in the active window script
Location	Displays the location of the cursor in the active window script at the bottom left corner of the active window
ShowClipboard	Opens a new window and displays the contents of the clipboard in this window

Selections on the Search Menu
Table 2-7.

Menu Item	Description
Find	Finds the first occurrence of a text string or pattern (Ctrl-Z)
Next	Finds the next occurrence of a string or pattern specified in a previous Find (Alt-Z)
Replace	Locates an occurrence of a value or pattern and replaces it with a specified value. Use this feature in combination with Alt-A, Ctrl-A, and Alt-Z to selectively replace values
ChangeToEnd	Replaces all instances of a value or pattern with a specified value, beginning from the current cursor position to the end of the script

AutoIndent is set, each new line you enter into a script, by pressing Enter, will automatically be indented to the same degree as the preceding line. Set WordWrap on if you want to have long lines automatically continue on to the next line. This feature is important when you are using the Paradox Editor to modify memo fields, but should normally be turned off when working with scripts. This is because you typically want to control any wordwrapping manually in order to preserve the readability of your scripts. The CaseSensitivity feature, when set, causes all Search menu operations, and their key combination equivalents, to match upper- and lower-case letters. If this setting is clear, the Editor will ignore the case of the search string. The Options menu selections and their descriptions are given in Table 2-8.

Selections on the Options Menu
Table 2-8.

Menu Item	Description
AutoIndent	Sets or clears the AutoIndent feature
WordWrap	Sets or clears the WordWrap feature
CaseSensitive	Sets or clears case sensitivity of Search menu selections

The Paradox 3.5 Script Editor

The Editor in Paradox 3.5 has fewer features than in Paradox 4. Not only does it not support a mouse, but it can be used to edit only one script at a time, has no clipboard, and no search capabilities. For these reasons, many Paradox 3.5 users do not use the Script Editor. Instead, they specify their own editor using the Custom Configuration Program.

The keys you use to access Editor features in Paradox 3.5 in many instances are different from those used for the Paradox 4 Editor. Paradox 3.5 keys are shown in Table 2-9.

Just as the keys are different, so are the available menus. A list of the Paradox 3.5 Script Editor menu selections, and their descriptions, is given in Table 2-10.

The PAL Debugger

You will find the PAL Debugger a valuable tool to use when you create scripts with the Editor. The word *debugger* comes from the

Keys Used in the Paradox 3.5 Script Editor
Table 2-9.

Key	Description
Alt-F7	Prints the current script
Backspace	Deletes character left of the cursor
Ctrl-End	Moves cursor to the end of the line
Ctrl-Home	Moves cursor to the beginning of the line
Ctrl-←	Moves left one-half screen
Ctrl-→	Moves right one-half screen
Ctrl-V	Displays a vertical ruler with line numbers 1 through 99 (repeats line numbers 1 through 99 if the script contains additional lines)
Ctrl-Y	Deletes all characters from the right of the cursor to the end of the line; deletes the entire line if the cursor is at the beginning of a line
Del	Deletes character at the cursor
↓	Moves cursor down one line

Key	Description
End	Moves cursor to the last line of the entire script
Enter	Inserts a new line (in Insert mode) or moves down one line (in Typeover mode)
Esc	Moves to the script from the Script Editor menu
F1	Helps with the Script Editor
F2	Saves the script and returns to the Main menu
F10	Displays the Script Editor menu
Home	Moves cursor to the first line of the entire script
Ins	Toggles between Insert and Typeover modes
←	Moves cursor left one character
Pg Dn	Moves down one-half screen
Pg Up	Moves up one-half screen
→	Moves cursor right one character
↑	Moves cursor up one line

Keys Used in the Paradox 3.5 Script Editor *(continued)*
Table 2-9.

programming term "bug," which means an error or problem with a computer program. You can use the Debugger to diagnose problems and remove errors from your scripts.

Menu Item	Description
Read	Inserts the contents of another script into the current script
Go	Saves the current script and plays it
Print	Prints the current script
Help	Accesses Paradox's help system and displays a summary of Script Editor keys
DO-IT!	Saves the current script and returns to the Main menu
Cancel	Cancels changes to the current script and returns to the Main menu

Paradox 3.5 Script Editor Menu
Table 2-10.

Scripts and PAL Tools

There are three types of errors that the Debugger can help resolve:

- **Syntax error**   Your script includes a misspelled PAL keyword or misused PAL command. For instance, if you misspell the keyword VIEW, using VIW instead, your script will stop playing when the incorrect word is encountered.

- **Run-time error**   Your script encounters an unexpected situation. An example of this is where your script instructs Paradox to view a particular table, but the table does not exist.

- **Error in logic**   Your script includes a mistake in logic. For example, instead of generating a report for the Customer table, your script generates one for the Employee table. Here, your script will not actually stop playing, but the result will not be what you intended.

Syntax errors and run-time errors result in an unexpected interruption of your script. Paradox refers to these as *script errors*. When a script error occurs, Paradox makes the Debugger available to you automatically. In contrast, errors in logic do not result in a script error, and therefore require a different debugging approach.

Script Error Debugging

When Paradox encounters a script error, the following events occur:

- Paradox stops playing the script
- The full-screen PAL canvas is dropped
- A message like the one shown in Figure 2-5 is displayed
- The Cancel-Debug menu is presented

If you select Cancel, the script is terminated and you return to interactive Paradox. The Paradox desktop remains in the same state it was in when your script terminated. For example, if two tables were present on the desktop when the error was encountered, they will still be there after you select Cancel.

Instead of selecting Cancel, you can select Debug and enter the PAL Debugger. When you select Debug, Paradox does not terminate your script as it does when you select Cancel. The script is merely held in

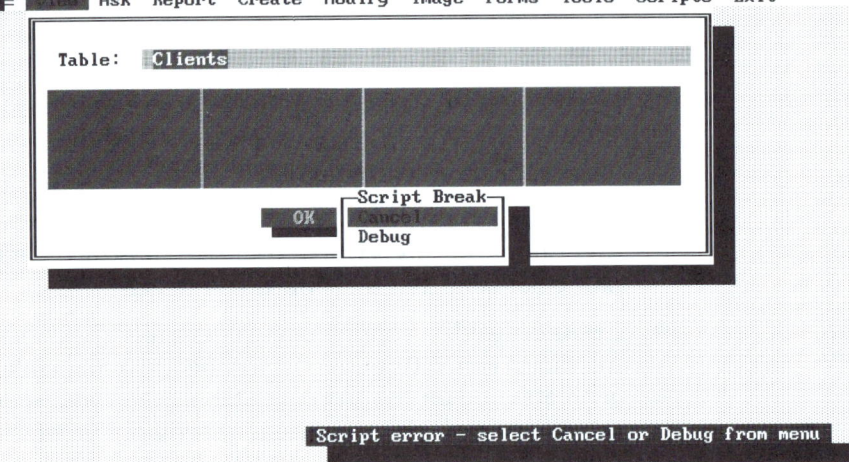

Example of a message displayed when a script error is encountered
Figure 2-5.

suspension. Even though the Debugger is active, you can still access almost any Paradox feature. This is particularly important when Paradox encounters a run-time error.

Once you enter the Debugger, a message is displayed indicating your script's problem. An example of this message is shown in Figure 2-6. Furthermore, the script instruction that Paradox was attempting to follow when the error was encountered is displayed on the bottom line of your screen. A small arrow points to this instruction, as shown in Figure 2-6.

Your options at this point depend on whether a syntax error or a run-time error occurred. If a syntax error was encountered, you can use the Debugger to determine the exact nature of the error. Then exit the Debugger. Before you try to play your script again, you will need to correct the syntax error.

When a run-time error occurs, you have an additional option. Using the available Paradox features, you can attempt to fix the problem. For example, if your script instructed Paradox to view a table that did not exist, you can create that table while the Debugger holds the script in suspension. Once the table is created, you can direct the Debugger to release the script from suspension, permitting Paradox to continue playing the script beginning with the command that failed the first time.

Scripts and PAL Tools

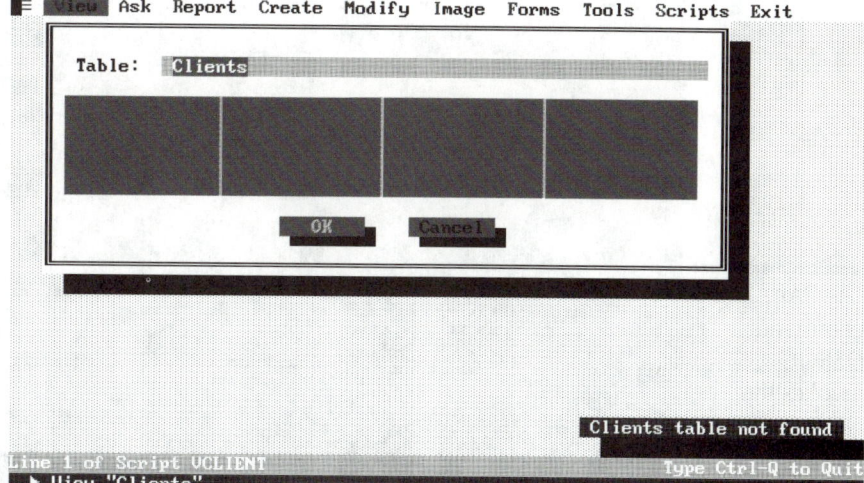

The PAL Debugger is invoked
Figure 2-6.

Debugging Errors in Logic

Errors in logic do not result in script errors (if they did, they would be called run-time errors). This makes them more difficult to correct. In some cases you can discover your error just by looking at the instructions in your script. Other times, however, you can only determine the problem by watching the script play, one command at a time. Fortunately, the Debugger provides you with the ability to do this.

There are three ways to invoke the PAL Debugger when no script error has occurred. The first is to place the PAL command DEBUG in your script at the location where you want to invoke the Debugger. The second method is to press (Ctrl)-(Break), as described earlier in this chapter, and then select Debug. Both of these methods permit you to enter the Debugger in the middle of a script. The third method is to invoke the Debugger at the very beginning of your script. Instead of playing your script, press (Alt)-(F10) and select Debug from the PAL menu.

Once the Debugger is invoked, the PAL canvas is dropped and script play temporarily suspended. Although no error message will appear, as when a script error is encountered, the current line of your script will be displayed at the bottom of your screen, as shown in Figure 2-7. Also, a small arrow will indicate which instruction has not yet been played. In Figure 2-7 you see that the instruction VIEW has not yet been

The PAL command DEBUG invokes the Debugger
Figure 2-7.

played. The command immediately prior to the VIEW command, DEBUG, caused the Debugger to be invoked.

The Debugger Features

Whether the Debugger is invoked because of a script error or intentionally invoked by you, the Debugger features become available. There are two ways to access these features: from the Debugger menu or with a keypress. To access the Debugger menu, press [Alt]-[F10] while the Debugger is active. Your screen will look similar to Figure 2-8.

The Debugger features are what you use to work with your script while the Debugger is active. For example, the Step, Trace, and Next features permit you to move through your script one command at a time. Likewise, the Go, Quit, and Editor features provide you with means to leave the Debugger. Two selections on the Debugger menu are not available through Debugger keys: Value and MiniScript. These two menu selections are also available on the PAL menu and were described earlier in this chapter. Each of the Debugger menu selections, and their corresponding key combinations, are described in the following sections.

Step ([Ctrl]-[S])   Step causes the Debugger to execute the current PAL command and then stop at the next PAL command. The current

Scripts and PAL Tools

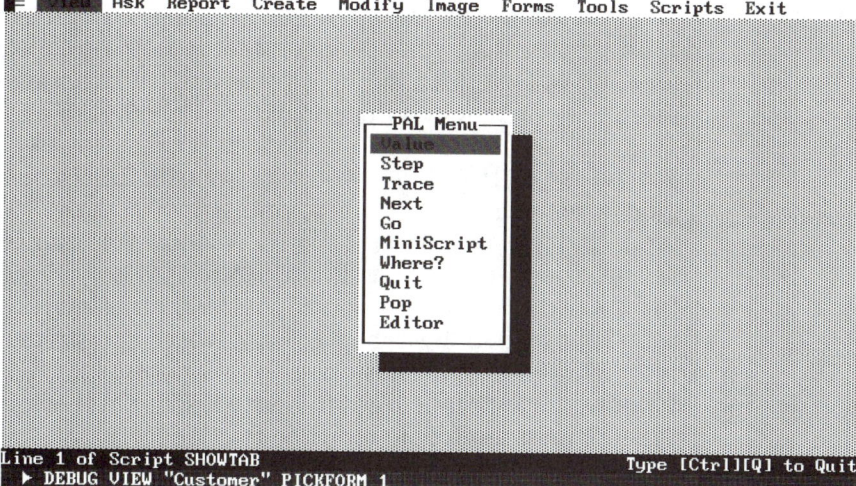

Debugger menu
Figure 2-8.

command is the PAL command the arrow points to on the bottom line of the screen. (In Paradox 3.5, Step will execute procedure calls, scripts called with the PLAY command, EXECUTE, or EXECPROC commands. In Paradox 4 these are skipped and the Debugger stops at the next command.) If the Debugger was invoked because of a syntax error, you cannot use this feature. Step is very useful when you are trying to locate errors in logic and want to view the results of each script instruction by stepping through the script one instruction at a time.

Trace (Ctrl-T)   Trace, which is not available in Paradox 3.5, is very similar to Step. The one difference is that Trace will also execute scripts or procedure calls, whereas Step will not. Therefore, Step is more valuable when you want to debug only the current script, while Trace permits you to debug all scripts or procedures encountered.

Next (Ctrl-N)   If you select Next, the Debugger ignores the current PAL command and moves to the next one. This feature is valuable when an instruction caused a run-time error and you want to skip over it and go on to the next instruction. This feature is not available if your script encountered a syntax error.

Go (Ctrl-G)   When you select Go, you exit the Debugger and your script continues to play normally, starting with the current command.

This feature is most useful after you have corrected a problem that caused a run-time error, or you no longer want to step through a script looking for errors in logic. Like the Step, Trace, and Next commands, you cannot use Go if your script entered the Debugger due to a syntax error.

*Where? (*Ctrl*-*W*)* When you select Where?, the Debugger displays a graphic representation of where your script is, relative to any other scripts that played it and interactive Paradox. For example, if the Debugger is invoked while the script Showtab is playing, select Where? to display the image shown in Figure 2-9. In this image, the script that was playing when the Debugger was invoked appears as the outermost rectangle. If this script was played by another script, then the playing script would appear beneath the current script in this image. After using Where?, press any key to return to the Debugger.

NOTE: The Debugger in Paradox 3.5 places the current script as the innermost script. If it was played by another script, that script appears outside the current script. This placement is exactly the opposite of the one used in Paradox 4.

*Quit (*Ctrl*-*Q*)* Select Quit to immediately terminate the script, exit the Debugger, and return to interactive Paradox.

Graphic representation of current script position
Figure 2-9.

Pop (Ctrl-P)   Pop is useful when you are debugging a script that was played by another script. When you select Pop, the Debugger returns to the calling script, the one that played the script you are debugging. The Debugger remains active and displays the next statement in the calling script. Pop will exit the Debugger and terminate your script if the script you are debugging was not played by another script.

Editor (Ctrl-E)   When you select Editor, the Debugger terminates execution of the script and enters the Paradox Editor in Paradox 4 (the Script Editor in Paradox 3.5). Before the Debugger can load the Editor, it cancels all operations in Paradox and clears all windows from the desktop. For example, if you select Editor while your script is editing a table, the Debugger will cancel all changes made to the table, return to the Main mode, and clear the table from the desktop before entering the Editor. When the Editor is loaded, Paradox moves your cursor to the line in the script that was current when you selected Editor.

The Editor feature is extremely useful. With it, you can make immediate changes to your scripts when you identify a syntax error or an error in logic. Moving your cursor to the line in your script that was current greatly simplifies your job of correcting the script. If you have specified an alternative editor using the Custom Configuration Program, Paradox will load your alternative editor in place of the Paradox Editor when you select Editor.

Other Script Tools

There are several other features you can use while working with PAL scripts. These are the Rename, Copy, and Delete tools located in the Tools menu.

When you select any of these from the Tools menu, you will see a menu of the various Paradox objects you can rename, copy, or delete. As you can see in the Delete menu shown in Figure 2-10, one of the objects in this list is Script. You can use Delete to erase a script when you no longer need it. Rename allows you to change the name of a script. You use Copy to make a duplicate of your script.

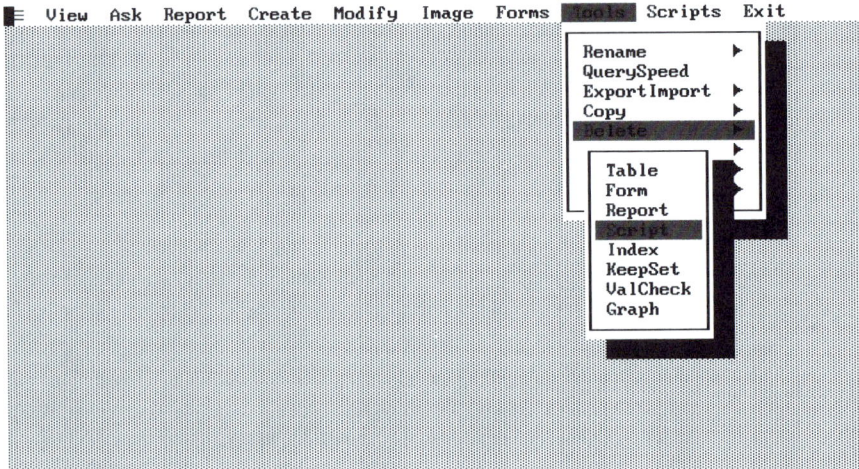

Delete menu
Figure 2-10.

Quick Review

- A script is a PAL program that contains instructions to Paradox. When you play a script, Paradox follows the instructions in the script.

- Through the Scripts menu you access basic creation and play features for scripts and the Paradox Editor (the Script Editor in Paradox 3.5). The Scripts menu is available only from the Paradox Main menu.

- The PAL menu also gives you access to basic script creation and play features, as well as the PAL Debugger and two useful features called Value and MiniScript.

- The Editor is used to write and modify scripts.

- The PAL Debugger is a useful tool for correcting problems in scripts you have written.

- With the Rename, Copy, and Delete selections from the Paradox Tools menu you can rename, copy, and delete scripts.

CHAPTER

3 CREATING SCRIPTS WITHOUT PROGRAMMING

One characteristic of Paradox that makes it so exceptional is its ability to write PAL scripts for you. Recorded scripts, instant scripts, and saved queries are all created by Paradox. Besides saving you time and effort, these scripts can improve the accuracy of your work.

In this chapter you will have your first hands-on experience with creating and playing scripts. These first examples use concepts introduced in the preceding two chapters. All the remaining chapters in this book will provide similar exercises. The tables used in these exercises are described in Appendix D. If you have not yet created these tables, you should do so now.

What Are Recorded Scripts?

Recorded scripts are recordings of part of your interactive Paradox session. That is, once you begin to record a script, Paradox "watches" the keyboard as you type. Each time you make a selection from a menu, respond to a prompt, or enter data into a table or query form, Paradox makes a note of it by placing a corresponding command into a script. Later, you can play the recorded script, causing Paradox to repeat your original selections and keystrokes.

Figure 3-1 shows an example of a recorded script. This script is displayed using the Paradox Editor—you wouldn't normally see it. The script queries the Invoice table for all of the current day's invoices, copies an existing report to the Answer table, and sends this report to the printer. By using a recorded script like this one, you can automate many of your routine tasks.

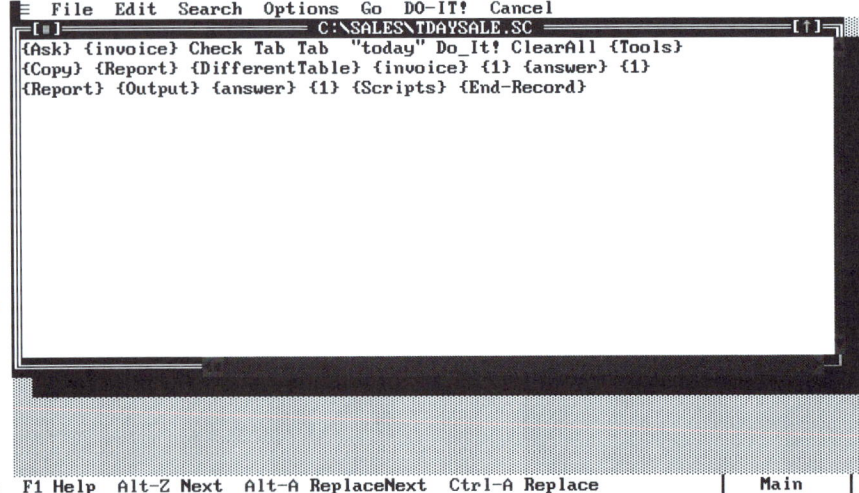

A recorded script viewed using the Paradox Editor
Figure 3-1.

Using Recorded Scripts

Recorded scripts are particularly useful for tasks you perform on an occasional basis—daily, weekly, monthly, and so forth. The following is a list of potential uses for recorded scripts:

◆ If you use directories for different Paradox projects, create a separate recorded script to move you to each of these directories. When you need to move to one of these directories, play the associated script.

◆ If you regularly edit a table with a specific form, create a recorded script that puts the appropriate table onto the workspace, enters the Edit mode, presses [F10] (Menu), selects Image/PickForm (selects Image from the Edit menu followed by PickForm from the Image menu), and chooses the appropriate form. Later, you can instantly begin editing your table with the desired form by playing the script.

◆ If you regularly create the same query for the same table and print or view the resulting report, you can save this task as a recorded script. You can even print out the report of the Answer table as part of your recorded script. Generating this report then becomes as simple as playing a script.

◆ While working on several different reports, you may want to apply a similar format to a large number of numeric fields. For example, you may want to format each of your numeric fields so it displays nine digits and two decimal places, uses commas, and encloses negative values in parentheses. To do this, you record a script when you format the first field, and then use the recorded script to format the remaining ones.

◆ If you copy your tables every week to floppy disks as a backup procedure, record this task the next time you perform it. Thereafter, you can perform your backup procedure simply by playing your recorded script.

◆ If you produce a graph on a regular basis, you can record the process of creating it. For example, your recorded script can view a table and perform a crosstab to produce a table whose contents are appropriate for graphing. Your script can even include loading the desired graph settings and can then print the graph to a specified graphics printer.

One common feature of the preceding tasks is that each requires multiple steps. This has two important consequences. The first is that each step takes time. For example, the simple task of viewing a table requires you to press [F10] (Menu) to display the Main menu, select View, then enter the name of the table you want to view. When this task is stored as part of a recorded script, the table name is entered much faster than the fastest typist could do.

The second consideration is that when you perform these tasks without the aid of a recorded script, each keystroke represents another opportunity for you to make a mistake. Once you have recorded the correct steps into a script, however, a mistake can never be made. The exact sequence of steps is permanently recorded. In summary, you can repeat any task both faster and more accurately by using a recorded script.

Creating a Recorded Script

There are two ways to create a recorded script. One is to select BeginRecord from the Scripts menu. The other is to make the same selection from the PAL menu. The second method is more versatile since you can display the PAL menu from anywhere in Paradox, unlike the Scripts menu, which must be selected from the Main menu. In the following example, you will use both of these menus: the Scripts menu to begin the recording and the PAL menu to end it.

The following script will place a table on the desktop, choose a form to display it in, enter the Edit mode, and insert a new record. A script like this can be used to instantly add new data to a table without repeating the individual menu selections. Start from the Main menu. Your desktop should be clear of all table images. If it is not, press [F8] (ClearImage) or [Alt]-[F8] (ClearAll). Now follow these steps:

1. Select Scripts to display the Scripts menu.
2. Select BeginRecord.

   Paradox prompts you for the name of the script you will record.
3. Type **Getform**, then press [Enter].

   Paradox displays a message that it is recording the script called Getform. Your cursor is now in the Main menu.
4. Select View.

Creating Scripts Without Programming

Paradox will prompt you for the name of the table to view.

5. Enter **Customer** to view the Customer table.

   Paradox displays the Customer table on the desktop.

6. Press [F10] (Menu).
7. Select Image to display the Image menu.
8. Select PickForm.

   Paradox will now ask you to select a form.

9. Select F, the standard form.
10. Press [F9] (Edit) to enter the Edit mode.
11. Press [Ins] to insert a new record into the Customer table.

    This completes the actions you want to include in your recorded script. You should now end recording your script. Because you are in Edit mode (from which the Scripts menu is unavailable), you should end recording the script by using the PAL menu.

12. Press [Alt]-[F10] (PAL menu) and select End-Record to complete the recording of the script.

    Paradox displays a message indicating that you have ended recording Getform.

You are finished. If you were actually editing the Customer table, you would add one or more records at this point. However, since the purpose of this exercise is to demonstrate recorded scripts, rather than table editing, you should now press [F2] (Do-It!) to return to the Main mode and press [F8] (ClearImage) to remove the Customer table from the desktop.

Playing a Recorded Script

You can play a recorded script just as easily as you recorded it. You do this by selecting Play from either the Scripts menu or the PAL menu. Paradox will prompt you for the name you gave your script. When Paradox plays this recorded script, it reads the commands in it, repeating all your original keypresses.

Follow these steps to play the script you just recorded. Before doing so, however, be sure you are in the Main mode and that there are no other tables on the desktop.

1. Select Scripts to display the Scripts menu.
2. Select Play.

   Paradox will prompt you for the script you want to play.
3. Type **Getform** and press [Enter].

For a moment, Paradox will appear to be frozen, as if in suspended animation. Then the standard form for the Customer table will appear, and Paradox will be in the Edit mode. It has completed playing the script. You can now enter a new record in the Customer table, if you desire. Instead of adding a record, however, press [F2] (Do-It!) to end the Edit mode and then press [F8] (ClearImage) to clear the desktop.

Remember that when you play a script, Paradox hides the screen. What you see instead is the full-screen PAL canvas, which displays a frozen picture of the screen as it appeared immediately before you played your script. Once the script has been played (which happens very quickly), the canvas is dropped and your screen is restored. Consequently, it is impossible to watch your script play under normal playing conditions. However, you can watch each step being performed by using the PAL Debugger. Using the Debugger, you can step through each command in the script individually, and control when each step is performed.

In addition, when the Debugger is being used, the PAL canvas is not displayed. This permits you to see the effect your script has on Paradox as each step of your script is played.

Stepping Through a Script

The following example makes use of the Debugger so that you can see your script perform its magic. Again, make sure that your desktop is clear of any tables and that you are in Main mode before you begin. Here is the script that will be displayed in the PAL Debugger:

```
{View} {Customer}
Menu {Image} {PickForm} {F} EditKey Ins
```

To display the script in the PAL Debugger,

1. Press [Alt]-[F10] to display the PAL menu.

Creating Scripts Without Programming

2. Select Debug.

   Paradox prompts you to enter the name of a script to load before entering the PAL Debugger:

   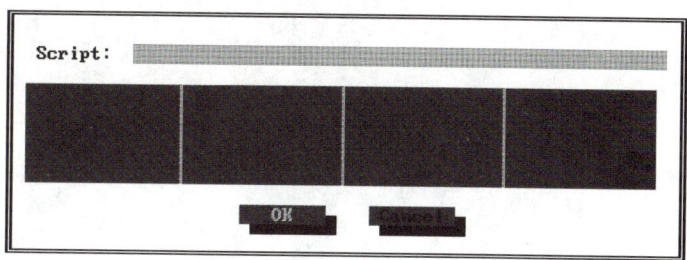

3. Type **Getform** and press [Enter].

   When you press [Enter], the PAL Debugger is loaded, and your screen will look like Figure 3-2. Notice that the first line of the recorded script appears on the bottom line of the screen and the small arrow is pointing to the first command, {View}.

   At this point, you can step through the recorded script, one command at a time, and watch Paradox perform each step in the script.

4. Press [Ctrl]-[S].

   Paradox processes the first command, {View}, and as a result displays the table prompt. Notice that the small arrow on the bottom line of the screen now points to the next command, {Customer}, as shown in Figure 3-3.

5. Press [Ctrl]-[S] again to make Paradox select the Customer table to view.

6. Press [Ctrl]-[S] six more times and note the results of each command as it is processed.

Once the last command in your script has been processed, the Debugger will terminate and control will return to Paradox. As in the preceding example, you will be in Edit mode, ready to enter a new record in the Customer table. Press [F2] (Do-It!) to return to the Main menu and [F8] (ClearImage) to remove the Customer table from the desktop.

PAL for Paradox 4 Made Easy

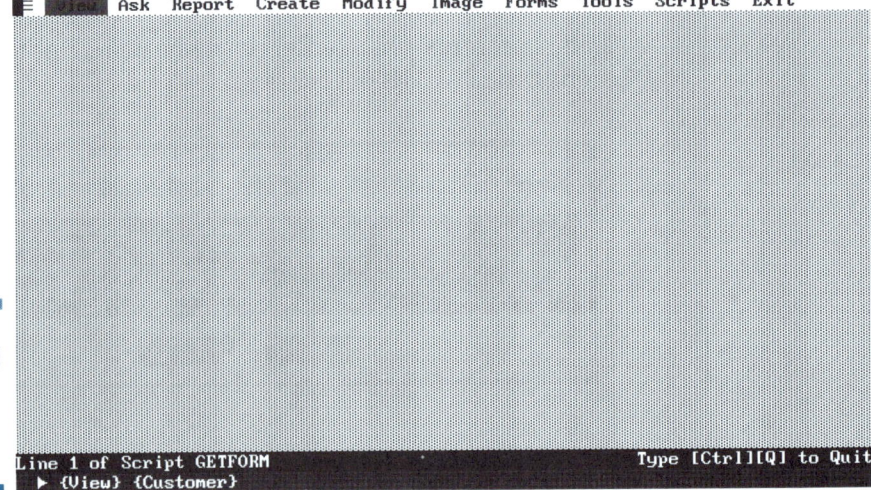

The Getform script displayed by the PAL Debugger
Figure 3-2.

What Paradox Records

While you are recording a script, Paradox keeps track of what you are doing. Paradox converts each of your actions into PAL commands. There are four types of PAL commands that make up a recorded script:

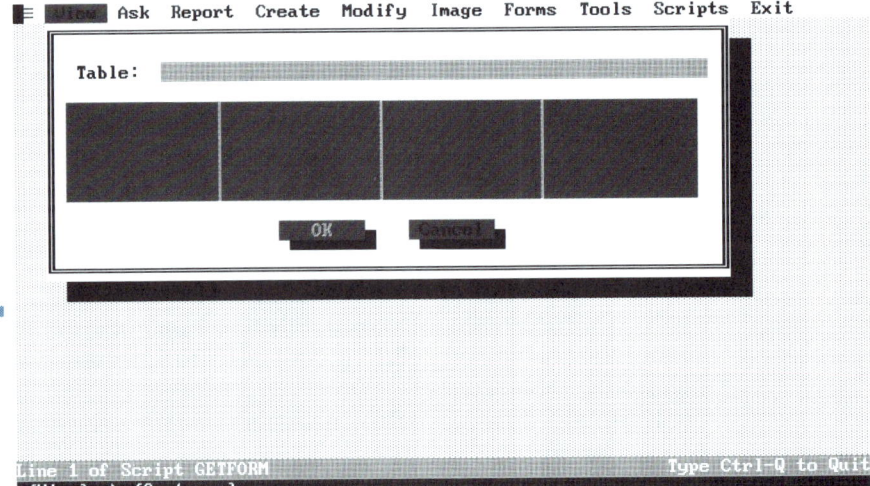

The arrow indicates the current instruction
Figure 3-3.

Creating Scripts Without Programming

Braced menu selections
Special key commands
Quoted strings
Window commands

Braced menu selections are used to record Paradox menus such as View or Ask from the Main menu. They are also used to record responses to prompts. Prompt responses are those entries you type in response to a prompt from Paradox. For example, when you select View from the Main menu, Paradox prompts you to enter a table name. Similarly, when you are entering a calculated field into a form or report, Paradox prompts you for the expression.

Special key commands are PAL commands that mimic the press of a function key. While recording your script, each time you press a function key, such as [F2] (Do-It!), or a control-key sequence, such as [Ctrl]-[F5] (FieldView), Paradox notes this by placing the appropriate special key command in your script. Examples of special key commands are DO_IT! (presses [F2]), EditKey (presses [F9]), and FieldView (presses [Ctrl]-[F]).

NOTE: The special key command for DO_IT! uses an underscore rather than a dash.

Quoted strings are any other characters typed in from your keyboard. For instance, when you enter a value into a field in a table, Paradox records the exact entry as a quoted string.

Window commands are placed in a recorded script each time you move or resize a window. There are two commands in particular that Paradox uses: WINDOW MOVE and WINDOW RESIZE. One feature of both of these commands is that they require a window handle, or label, for the command to work. A window handle is a unique value that Paradox assigns to each window that it opens. In order to provide the required window handle in the window commands in a recorded script, Paradox uses the PAL function GETWINDOW(). This assures that the window resizing and movement will occur correctly each time. You will learn more about window handles and the GETWINDOW() function in Chapters 8 and 10.

NOTE: There are no windows, and consequently, no window commands in Paradox 3.5. For this reason, the example script in the next section will generate a script error if played in Paradox 3.5.

Another Recorded Script

The following recorded script adds data to a table.

```
{View} {Customer} Window Resize GetWindow() To 11, 78
Window Move GetWindow() To 1, 0 CoEditKey Ins Right
"H121"  ENTER "Company H" ENTER
Do_It! ClearImage
```

The first word in the recorded script, {View}, instructs Paradox to select View from the Main menu. Paradox menu selections, such as View, are enclosed in curly braces in scripts. The second command, {Customer}, is the response to the prompt asking for the name of the table to view. It is also enclosed in curly braces. Like menu selections, all recorded responses to prompts are enclosed in curly braces.

The third word in this script, WINDOW, is a window command. The command WINDOW does not exist by itself, however. It requires several pieces of information to instruct Paradox what to do with the window. In this instance, the entire command is

   WINDOW RESIZE GETWINDOW() To 11, 78

This command instructs Paradox to resize the window containing the Customer table so that it is 11 characters high and 78 characters wide. The fourth command in this script is yet another window command.

Creating Scripts Without Programming

This one instructs Paradox to move the Customer table window so that its upper left corner is positioned in the second row and first column of the desktop (Paradox numbers the rows and columns of the desktop starting with row 0, column 0).

The fifth command in this script is COEDITKEY. This key simulates pressing [Alt]-[F9] on your keyboard. Every function key or key combination in Paradox has a corresponding special key command. Whenever you press a function key or special key while you are recording a script, Paradox places the special key command into the script. The recorded script in the example contains five other special key commands. These commands, and their corresponding keys, are INS (the [Ins] key), RIGHT (the [→] key), ENTER (the [Enter] key), Do-It! ([F2]), and CLEARIMAGE ([F8]).

In addition to menu selections, window commands, and special key commands, recorded scripts can contain quoted strings. Quoted strings are used to record the exact characters you type on the keyboard when you record a script; they are always enclosed in double quotation marks. In this example, "H121" is a quoted string. "H121" was recorded when H121 was entered into the Company Code field in the Customer table.

When a recorded script is played, quoted strings are entered one character at a time, as though you were pressing the corresponding key on your keyboard. For example, if you were to play this script, the "H121" command would instruct Paradox to press an H, followed by a 1, a 2, and a 1. The quotation marks themselves are not entered.

Now that you know what the parts of a recorded script are, you can see that they are easy to interpret. For example, the preceding script selects View from the Main menu and then enters the table name Customer. The size and position of the Customer table window is changed, and then [Alt]-[F9] (CoEdit) is pressed to place the Customer table in CoEdit mode. Next the [Ins] key is pressed, followed by the [→] key and then the keys H, 1, 2, and 1. The [Enter] key is pressed (moving the cursor one field to the right) and then Company H is entered. The [Enter] key is pressed once more. The [F2] (Do-It!) key is pressed, which ends the Edit mode. Finally, [F8] (ClearImage) is pressed to clear the Customer table from the desktop.

What Are Instant Scripts?

An instant script is a special type of recorded script. The difference lies in how each is used. Since you can have as many recorded scripts as you like, they are appropriate for saving many of your routine tasks, each in a separate recorded script. In contrast, you can have only one instant script at a time. However, since they are so easy to create and play, they are perfectly suited for capturing keystrokes "on the fly" and playing them back immediately.

Instant scripts can be reused as often as you like. In some cases, you will want to repeat a series of commands only twice, and other times you may want to repeat the same commands dozens of times. Either way, instant scripts are so easy to record you should make use of them anytime you need to repeat a particular sequence of steps.

Using Instant Scripts

What makes an instant script special is how you record and play it. To record an instant script, press the key combination [Alt]-[F3] (Instant Script Record). To end the recording, press this key combination again. To play an instant script, simply press [Alt]-[F4] (Instant Script Play). Paradox will immediately play the commands in your instant script.

Creating an Instant Script

The following example will demonstrate the ease with which you can improve your use of Paradox with instant scripts. Begin by designing a new report for the Customer table, as follows:

1. Press [F10] (Menu) to display the Main menu.
2. Select Report.
3. Select Design.

   Paradox will prompt you for the name of the table you want to design the report for.
4. Type **Customer**.

   Paradox will prompt you for a report number.
5. Select 5.

Creating Scripts Without Programming

6. Press [Enter] when Paradox asks for a description of the report. (You are leaving the description blank here.)
7. Select Tabular since you are designing a tabular report.

At this point, you should be viewing a report that looks like the one in Figure 3-4.

Before beginning your instant script, move the cursor to the column in the table band where "Customer Code" appears (as indicated in Figure 3-4).

This will be the first of several columns you will delete. You will now capture the steps for deleting a column in an instant script using these steps:

1. Press [Alt]-[F3] (Instant Script Record) to begin recording your instant script.

   Notice the message that is displayed briefly in the lower right-hand corner of the screen. Paradox is now recording all of your keystrokes.

2. Press [F10] (Menu) to display the Report menu.
3. Select TableBand from the Report menu.
4. Select Erase from the TableBand menu.

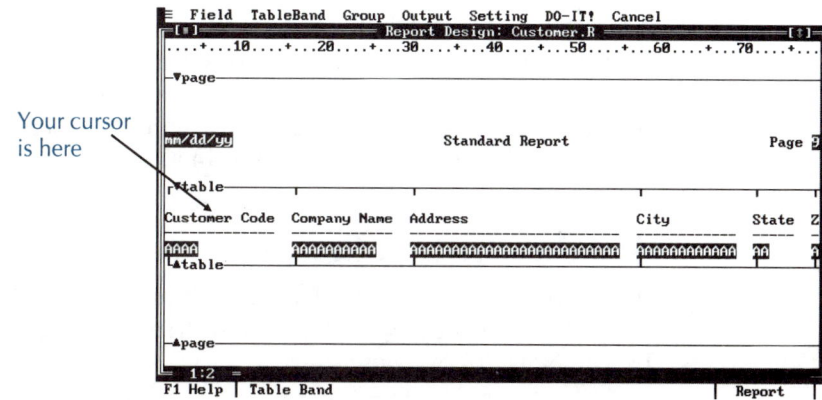

A tabular report for the Customer table
Figure 3-4.

Paradox prompts you to move the cursor to the field you want to erase. However, in this instance, you do not need to move the cursor since you already placed the cursor in the column you want to delete (the Customer Code column).

5. Press [Enter] to delete the column where the cursor is located.

   You have completed the steps to delete a column.

6. Stop the recording of your instant script now by pressing [Alt]-[F3].

The instant script you have just recorded should look exactly like this:

```
Menu {TableBand} {Erase} Enter
```

Notice that these commands are indistinguishable from the commands you would have recorded had you used a recorded script. The big difference is the ease with which it is recorded—and played.

Playing an Instant Script

Play the instant script you just created and see what happens. If you have followed this example, the cursor will now be located in the Company Name column in the report table band. Without moving the cursor, press [Alt]-[F4] (Instant Script Play). What you see next is that the Company Name column simply disappears. What you did not see was Paradox repeating the keystrokes stored in the instant script. This is because the PAL canvas is displayed while your instant script is playing. Once the script is finished playing, the screen returns to normal.

In this example, only menu selections were recorded. However, like recorded scripts, instant scripts can also be used for recording any type of keystroke. For example, you can use an instant script to quickly enter the same value repeatedly into fields in a table.

Another Instant Script

If you are still in the report generator from the last example, you must first exit by pressing [F10] (Menu), and then selecting Cancel, followed by Yes. Now, follow these steps:

1. From the Main menu, press [F10] (Menu).

Creating Scripts Without Programming

2. Select View.
3. Type **Invoice** to display the Invoice table.
4. Press [F9] (Edit) to enter the Edit mode.
5. With the cursor in the first record of the Invoice table, move the cursor to the Date field.
6. Press [Alt]-[F3] (Instant Script Record) to begin recording an instant script.
7. Press [Ctrl]-[Backspace] to erase the contents of the Date field, and then press the [Spacebar] three times to enter today's date.
8. Press [↓] to move to the next record.
9. Press [Alt]-[F3] (Instant Script Record) to end recording the instant script.

The instant script that you recorded looks like this:

```
CtrlBackspace  "   " Down
```

Playing the Second Instant Script Example

Use the following steps to play this instant script:

1. Press [Alt]-[F4] (Instant Script Play).

   Notice again that when you play the instant script, Paradox momentarily freezes. Then, as if by magic, the current date appears in the second Date field and the cursor moves down one record.

2. To return to the Main menu without saving these changes, press [F10] (Menu), and select Cancel, followed by Yes.
3. Press [F8] (ClearImage) to remove the Invoice table from the desktop.

CAUTION: If you are using Paradox 3.5, care should be taken to avoid pressing [Alt]-[F4] (Instant Script Play) while you are recording an instant script. If you press [Alt]-[F4], each time your script reaches the place where you pressed [Alt]-[F4], it will begin playing itself over again. If this should happen, press [Ctrl]-[Break] to terminate the playback of your script.

Limitations of Recorded and Instant Scripts

Recorded and instant scripts simply repeat your keystrokes. When you play one of these scripts, each command is played back exactly the same way each time. This almost always produces the results you want. Occasionally, however, a recorded or instant script does not work correctly when it is played back. This is usually because a script contains *exact* instructions. That is, unlike you, the script cannot adapt to changes in the Paradox environment. A recorded or instant script will not be able to tell if you play it from a different Paradox mode or menu than you recorded it from. Likewise, a script will not play correctly if it tries to access some feature or object that is no longer available.

For example, consider the following recorded script:

```
{Report} {Design} {Customer} {1} { } {Tabular}
```

This script was recorded during the process of designing a new tabular report number 1 for the Customer table. Report was selected, followed by Design. The name of the Customer table was entered, report number 1 was selected, no report description was entered (which is why the empty curly braces appear), and finally Tabular was selected as the report style. Can this script be played back successfully?

The answer is *no*.

Consider what happens when you try to design a report that already exists: Paradox displays a menu with the options Cancel and Replace. Thus, if you play the instant script again to create a new report, the same thing will happen. That is, Paradox will display the options Cancel and Replace since the report already exists. However, your instant script is not prepared for this event. The first four commands in the instant script will work correctly, but when Paradox displays the Cancel-Replace menu, your instant script contains the instruction to select nothing ({ }). This is not an available menu selection—only Cancel or Replace are acceptable selections. The result is that a run-time script error will occur.

A similar problem may occur if you use a recorded or instant script from a Paradox mode different from the mode it was originally recorded in. If your script attempts to make a menu selection, for

Creating Scripts Without Programming

example, and the current mode does not contain such a selection, your script will not succeed and a script error will result.

This leads to two general rules for creating successful recorded and instant scripts:

✦ Use recorded and instant scripts only for operations that behave in a consistent manner when performed repeatedly.

✦ Always play a recorded or instant script in the same mode used to record it.

What Are Saved Queries?

Queries are one of the more powerful features of Paradox. They permit you to link two or more tables and to perform calculations on data in your tables. With queries, you can explore and analyze the data you have stored in Paradox tables. Building a query, however, can be a time-consuming process. If you need to use the same query more than once, you can save yourself a lot of effort by saving it. You can then easily use this query again at a later time. When you save a query for future use, the query is called a *saved query*. Figure 3-5 shows an example of a saved query.

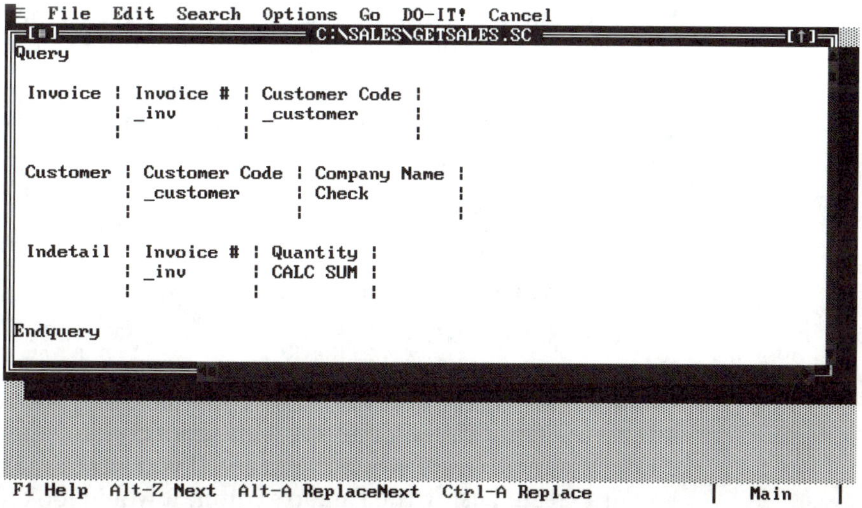

```
  File    Edit   Search   Options   Go   DO-IT!   Cancel
┌[■]─────────────────────── C:\SALES\GETSALES.SC ──────────────────[↑]┐
│Query                                                                 │
│                                                                      │
│   Invoice │ Invoice # │ Customer Code │                              │
│           │ _inv      │ _customer     │                              │
│           │           │               │                              │
│                                                                      │
│   Customer │ Customer Code │ Company Name │                         │
│            │ _customer     │ Check        │                         │
│            │               │              │                         │
│                                                                      │
│   Indetail │ Invoice # │ Quantity │                                 │
│            │ _inv      │ CALC SUM │                                 │
│            │           │          │                                 │
│                                                                      │
│Endquery                                                              │
└──────────────────────────────────────────────────────────────────────┘
 F1 Help  Alt-Z Next  Alt-A ReplaceNext  Ctrl-A Replace       │  Main  │
```

A saved query involving three tables
Figure 3-5.

Creating a Saved Query

Any query you can place on the Paradox desktop can be saved. This is done by using the QuerySave feature from the Scripts menu. After you construct a query, press [F10] (Menu) and select Scripts/QuerySave. Paradox prompts you for a name for the query and then creates a script containing the PAL commands that will re-create the query when it is played.

In the following example you will save a query of the Customer table. This query will count the number of all customers from each city. Before you begin, use [F8] (ClearImage) to remove any tables or query images that are on your desktop. Now follow these steps:

1. Press [F10] (Menu).
2. Select Ask from the Main menu.
3. Enter the name of the table, **Customer**.

   Paradox will display the query form for the Customer table on your workspace.

4. Press [Tab] twice to move the cursor to the Company Name field of the query image.
5. Press [F6] (CheckMark).
6. Press [Tab] twice more to move the cursor to the City field.
7. Type **CALC COUNT ALL**.

   Your query has now been created. Your screen should look like Figure 3-6. To demonstrate what the results of this query will be, press [F2] (Do-It!) to process the query.

   With the query now constructed, you are ready to save it.

8. Press [F10] (Menu).
9. Select Scripts.
10. Select QuerySave.

    Paradox will ask for the name of the query.

11. Enter **Countcst**.

Paradox inspects the query form that you have on your desktop and creates the script called Countcst. This script contains statements that allow Paradox to reconstruct the query. If you were to view the query you just created using the Paradox Editor, it would look like Figure 3-7.

Creating Scripts Without Programming

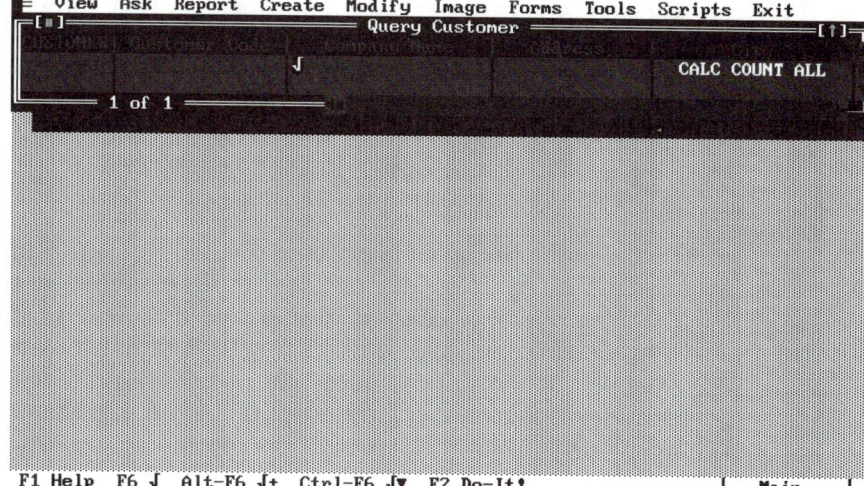

Figure 3-6.
A query on the desktop

All saved queries begin with the PAL command QUERY, and end with the keyword ENDQUERY. Between QUERY and ENDQUERY, Paradox places a table-like structure that defines the query. It specifies which tables are involved in the query as well as which fields.

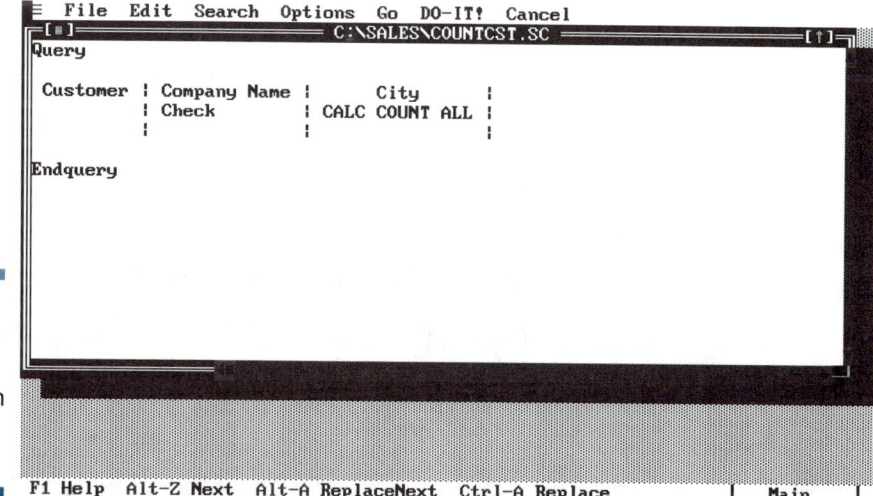

Figure 3-7.
The script created by saving the query shown in Figure 3-6

The table and fields are shown in columns, similar to those on a query form. As you can see in Figure 3-7, the first column always contains the name of the table being queried. The remaining columns contain the names of the fields within the queried table. Notice, however, that not all fields in the table are displayed in the query. Only those fields that contain a checkmark or text (such as the CALC keyword in the example) are displayed in the saved query.

Furthermore, the saved query does not use the same symbols that are used in a query image. For instance, in the example query the checkmark you placed in the Company Name field is defined using the word *Check* in the saved query. Likewise, if you had used one or more example elements in this query, they would be preceded by an underscore character (_) in the saved query rather than being displayed in reverse video as they are in a query form.

Playing a Saved Query

Because saved queries are scripts, you can play them the same way you play any other script. When you play a script containing a saved query, Paradox reconstructs the query on the desktop and displays the query form just as you originally constructed it. You can then process the query by pressing (F2) (Do-It!). The results of your query are placed in the Answer table, exactly as it happens when you process any query you create in Paradox. Playing a script that contains a saved query causes Paradox merely to display the saved query. It does not process the query until you tell it to do so.

Make sure Paradox is in Main mode. Then follow these steps:

1. Press (F10) (Menu).
2. Select Scripts to display the Scripts menu.
3. Select Play.
4. Enter the name of the saved query, **Countcst**.

Paradox will then read your saved query and reconstruct the original query on your desktop. At this point, your desktop will look like Figure 3-8. Notice that this query form is the exact same form as was originally created in Figure 3-6, before you saved the query in a script.

Just as with recorded scripts, you can create and save as many saved queries as you need. For example, you may want to save one query that calculates weekly sales totals for each employee and another query that calculates monthly sales totals by employee.

Processing a Saved Query

Once the query is displayed on the desktop, you can process it just as you would process any query you construct normally. To process the query, simply press [F2] (Do-It!).

The results of your query are placed in a temporary table called Answer, which becomes the current image on the desktop. If you want to keep the results of your query, be sure to rename the Answer table with a name of your choice using Tools/Rename. Keep in mind that your query results will be lost if you perform another query, change directories, or exit Paradox at the end of your current session without first renaming the Answer table.

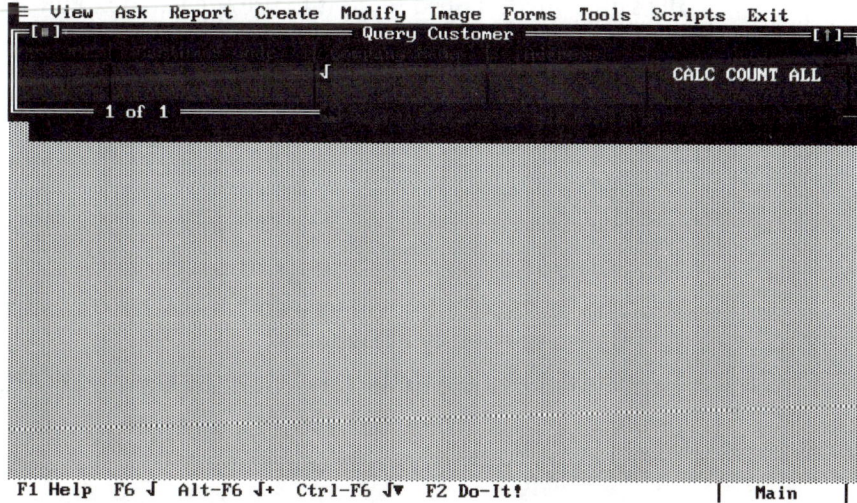

A query constructed by playing a saved query
Figure 3-8.

Instead of immediately processing a query once you play a saved query script, you can modify the displayed query before you process it. For example:

- You can make changes to any of the conditions, examples, checks, or other elements of the query. Changing the query means that you can add, remove, or modify any of the elements on the query form.
- You can link to additional tables by displaying query forms for other tables and including examples to link them together.

TIP: Saved queries can also be useful when you are interrupted in the process of constructing a query. If the query is complicated, you may want to save what you have created so far and come back to it later. To do so, use the QuerySave selection from the Scripts menu. When you are ready to work on your query again, play the script containing the saved query. You can then pick up where you left off.

Automating a Saved Query

You can easily make a saved query process automatically when you play the script. All you need to do is to use the Paradox Editor to add an additional PAL command, DO_IT!, to the saved query script. Do this by following these steps from the Main menu:

1. Select Scripts to display the Scripts menu.
2. Select Editor.
3. Select Open.
4. Enter the name of the script, **Countcst**.

    The Paradox Editor will load and display the Countcst script, as shown previously in Figure 3-7.

5. Move the cursor to the line below the keyword ENDQUERY.
6. Type the PAL command **DO_IT!**, as shown in Figure 3-9.
7. Press F2 (Do-It!) to save your script.

The DO_IT! command causes Paradox to press F2 (Do-It!) for you. When you play this saved query, Paradox constructs the saved query on

Creating Scripts Without Programming

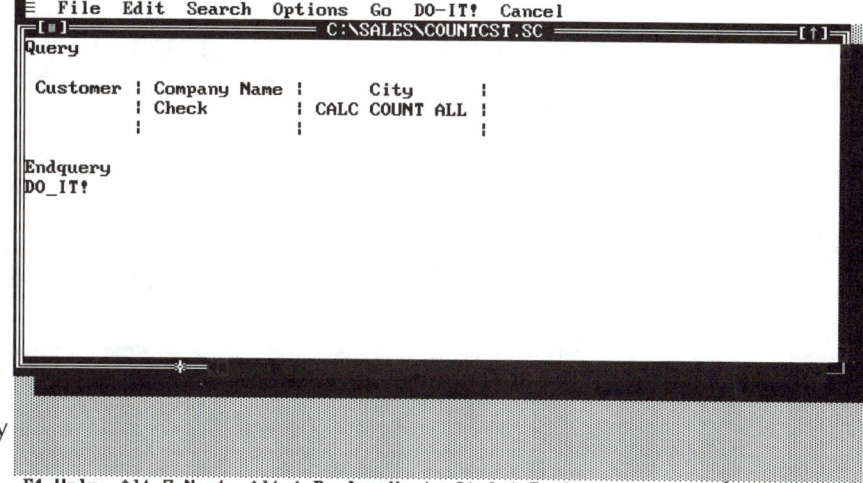

DO_IT! added to a saved query
Figure 3-9.

the desktop, then follows the next statement containing the DO_IT! command and automatically processes the query.

You should now play the Countcst script. When you do, your screen will seem frozen for a moment and then suddenly the query and the Answer table will both appear, as shown in Figure 3-10. Since the

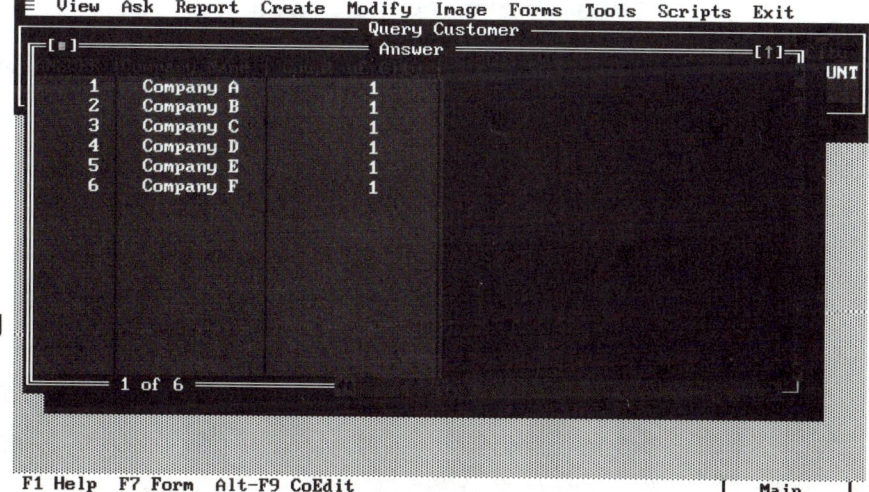

A query constructed and processed by playing a saved query
Figure 3-10.

DO_IT! statement was part of your script, the full-screen PAL canvas was displayed while the query was being processed. Only after the query was processed was the full-screen PAL canvas lowered, revealing both the query and the Answer table.

NOTE: The PAL command DO_IT! uses an underscore character between DO and IT!. Its appearance differs from the F2 key name Do-It!, which uses a hyphen between Do and It!. Paradox is insensitive to case, however, so the capitalization of command names does not matter.

Quick Review

- ◆ Recorded scripts are useful for automating tasks you perform in Paradox occasionally.
- ◆ Instant scripts are best for immediately repeating a task.
- ◆ You may have only one instant script at a time.
- ◆ QuerySave creates a script from the query on the desktop.
- ◆ You can add DO_IT! to a saved query to have it process automatically when it is played.

CHAPTER

4

EXPRESSIONS

PAL scripts consist of commands and expressions. The commands instruct Paradox to display a table, print a message on the screen, repeat a process, enter data into a table, print a report, and so on. Expressions direct this control. Expressions tell Paradox which table to display, what message to print, how many times to repeat a process, what data to enter in a table, and what report to generate.

When Paradox plays your script, it converts each expression to a value in a process called *evaluation*. This value is then used to direct the action of a PAL command.

In this chapter you will learn how to construct PAL expressions. A lot of material is covered here, and if you have not programmed a computer before, much of it will be new to you. This is simply groundwork, however. Later chapters continue to discuss expressions in conjunction with the PAL commands and functions that require them. Therefore, you will see examples of expressions in action again and again. If expressions are new to you, however, you may want to reread parts of this chapter once you have become more familiar with the PAL commands that use them.

Expression Data Types

Every field in a Paradox table has a particular data type—either alphanumeric, memo numeric, short numeric, currency, date, or binary. Similarly, every PAL expression also has a data type: alphanumeric, numeric, date, or logical. The following describes each of the data types:

Alphanumeric expressions evaluate to text.
Numeric expressions evaluate to numbers.
Date expressions evaluate to calendar dates.
Logical expressions evaluate to one of two values, True or False.

An expression's type determines where it can be used. For instance, the PAL command VIEW must be followed by an alphanumeric expression. If you follow VIEW with an expression of any other type, a script error will result. This is a fundamental programming concept that will become familiar as you work your way through this book.

The Elements of Expressions

There are six kinds of elements used to form expressions: constants, variables, arrays, field specifiers, functions, and operators. Each of the first five can be used as an expression by itself. The sixth element, operators, is used to modify an expression or to combine two or more expressions. The results of these modifications or combinations are also expressions.

Expressions

The following are examples of PAL expressions:

Expression	Element Type
"Customer"	Constant
TableName	Variable
TableNames[1]	Array
[Tables –> Table Name]	Field specifier
TABLE( )	Function
"Cust" + "omer"	Two constants with an operator (+)

Constants

Constants are literal representations of a specific value. For instance, the constant "Customer" evaluates to the word *Customer*. You use constants in a script whenever you need to refer to an exact value. For example, at a particular point in a script, if you always want to display the Customer table, you would follow the VIEW command with the constant "Customer".

Constants are the most straightforward of expressions. Unlike many other expressions, you can see a constant's value simply by looking at it. How a constant is represented depends on its data type, however.

Using Alphanumeric Constants

Alphanumeric constants are enclosed in quotation marks. You use alphanumeric constants to refer to any series of letters and numbers. In fact, any character you can produce from your keyboard can be part of an alphanumeric constant. The following are examples of alphanumeric constants:

```
"Customer"
"Mr. Pickerson"
"2000"
"Two thousand"
"True"
"7/6/92"
```

Consider this list. Because each of these values is enclosed in quotation marks, they are all alphanumeric constants. The values within the quotation marks merely refer to letters and numbers; they cannot be interpreted in any other way. For example, the value "2000" is not equivalent to the number 2000 (two thousand). Likewise, the constant "7/6/92" is not a date. If you use "2000" where Paradox expects a number, or "7/6/92" where Paradox expects a date, a script error will occur.

Let's try using the Value selection from the PAL menu to see how constants are evaluated.

1. Press (Alt)-(F10) (PAL menu) to display the PAL menu.
2. Select Value and Paradox will prompt you to enter an expression.
3. Type **"Customer"** and press (Enter).

Paradox will display the word *Customer* in the lower right corner of your screen, as shown in Figure 4-1. When the value is displayed, the quotation marks are not present. This is because the value of the expression "Customer" is Customer.

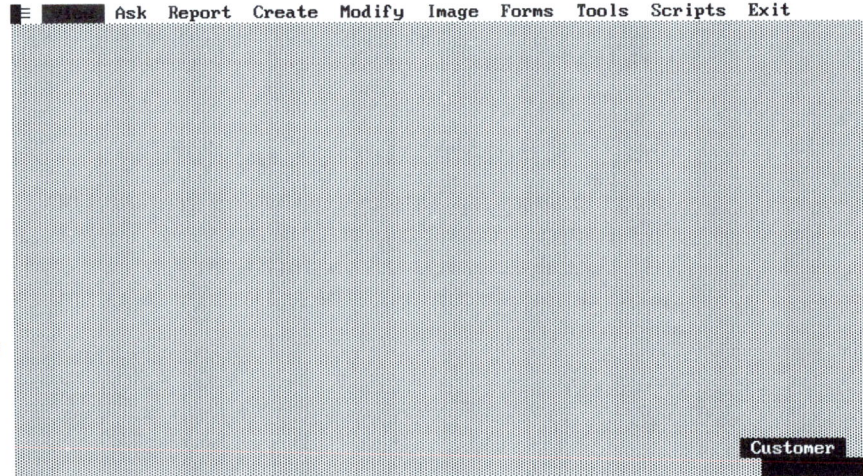

Figure 4-1. Value of the expression "Customer"

Expressions

The Backslash Character

You use the backslash when your alphanumeric constant must include a character (such as a quotation mark) that would otherwise be interpreted by Paradox to mean something else. When Paradox encounters the backslash character (\) in an alphanumeric constant, it ignores the backslash itself, and interprets the character that follows literally. For example, consider the name *Rocky "The Italian Stallion" Balboa*. If you try to use "Rocky "The Italian Stallion" Balboa" as a constant in a script, Paradox will see the quotation mark preceding the word *The* and interpret it as the end of the alphanumeric constant, which would result in a script error. Thus, in order to include a quotation mark as part of the constant, you must precede it with a backslash. The constant "Rocky \"The Italian Stallion\" Balboa" would be evaluated accurately as

```
Rocky "The Italian Stallion" Balboa
```

Using Numeric Constants

Numeric constants stand for numbers. They are represented by the numbers themselves. The following are all numeric constants:

```
1
2.0
3000.0231
.093
-4.5
-.093
```

To indicate a negative number, put a minus sign before it, for example, –400. You cannot, however, use whole number separators in numeric constants. For instance, the value 1,230.00 is an invalid numeric constant (commas are not permitted).

NOTE: If your Paradox configuration uses international notation, commas are used as decimal separators and the whole number separator, period, is not allowed.

Using Date Constants

Date constants are represented using one of the three following formats:

```
mm/dd/yyyy
dd-Mon-yyyy
dd.mm.yyyy
```

When the year is in the 1900s, you can omit the first two digits of the year (just as you can when entering dates in Paradox). Date constants can represent dates between 1/1/100 and 12/31/9999. The following are examples of date constants:

```
11/5/59
7/4/1776
8-Sep-1993
17.3.1992
```

Using Logical Constants

Logical expressions represent only one of two values, True or False. Therefore, there are only two logical constants: True and False. Capitalization does not matter. The following are all logical constants:

```
True
TRUE
False
FaLsE
```

Variables

A *variable* is a label that represents a value. When you use a variable in an expression, Paradox uses the value of the variable. The name *variable* is appropriate because, unlike constants, the value represented by the label is not fixed. The advantage of variables is that you can use the same expression in a command to achieve different results, depending on the value of the variable. This adds flexibility to your scripts.

A variable can have only one value at any given moment, and it is this value that Paradox uses. Take, for example, a variable called TabName. It is possible for this variable to have the value Customer at certain points in a script and Employee at others. If the script contains the

Expressions

command VIEW TabName, either the Customer table or the Employee table will be displayed on the desktop, depending on the value of TabName at the time the command is played.

As with constants, each variable has a data type. Unlike constants, however, you cannot determine the data type of a variable simply by looking at it. You must know the value that the variable represents to know its data type. For instance, if the variable TabName has the value Customer, then its type is alphanumeric.

NOTE: In most situations, Paradox stores the contents of variables in memory. In Paradox 4, however, when a variable is assigned an alphanumeric value greater than 255 characters in length, all characters beyond that are stored on disk. These memo-sized variables can contain as much as 64 megabytes of data.

Assigning Values to Variables

Variables get their value through a process called *assignment*. You assign a value to a variable using the PAL command = (the equal sign). When a variable name appears on the left-hand side of an equal sign, and an expression appears on the right-hand side, the variable is assigned the value of the expression. For instance, the statement

```
TabName = "Customer"
```

assigns the value Customer to TabName.

Once a value is assigned to a variable, that variable retains the value until another value is assigned to the variable, you release the variable using the PAL command RELEASE, or your Paradox session ends.

Use the following steps to assign a value to the variable TabName:

1. Press [Alt]-[F10] to display the PAL menu.
2. Select MiniScript.
3. Type **TabName = "Customer"** and press [Enter].

    Paradox then processes the script and assigns the value Customer to TabName.

Now, follow these steps to see that the value has been assigned to TabName:

1. Press [Alt]-[F10].
2. Select Value.
3. Type **TabName** and press [Enter].

Paradox will display the value of TabName, Customer, in the lower right corner of your screen, as shown in Figure 4-2.

You can use a variable anywhere an expression is required. However, you must first assign a value to the variable. If you attempt to use a variable before you assign a value to it, a script error results. You can demonstrate this yourself by following these steps:

1. Press [Alt]-[F10] to display the PAL menu.
2. Select Value.
3. Type **NewTab** and press [Enter].

   Paradox will attempt to evaluate the expression, but will find that the variable NewTab has not been assigned a value. At this point you will see the Cancel-Debug menu.

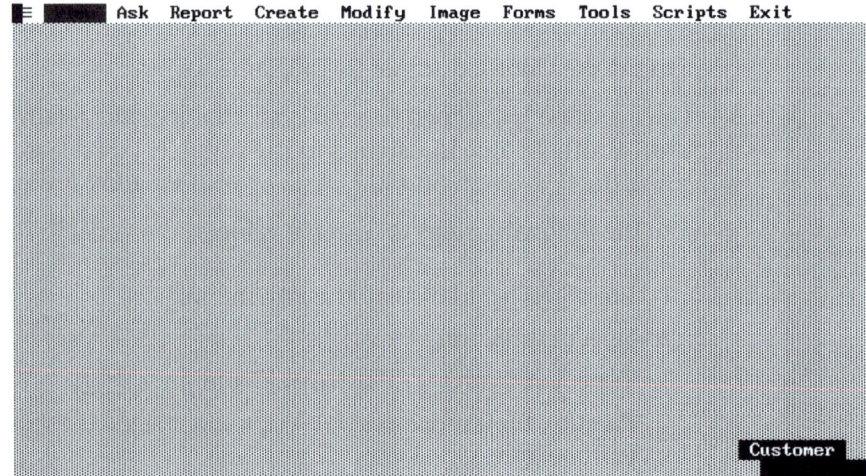

Value of the variable TabName
Figure 4-2.

Expressions

4. Select Debug.

   The Debugger displays the message "Run error: Variable NEWTAB has not been assigned a value," as shown in Figure 4-3.

5. Press [Ctrl]-[Q] to exit the Debugger.

Remember that the value you assign to a variable defines its data type. When you entered the MiniScript **TabName = "Customer"**, TabName was assigned an alphanumeric value. If you play another assignment statement, you can assign a value of a different type to TabName. For example, if you enter the MiniScript

```
TabName = 5.25
```

TabName will become a numeric expression, since it contains a numeric value. The following are all examples of variable assignments:

Assignment	Data Type of the Variable
TabName = "Customer"	Alphanumeric
Counter = 43	Numeric
ConstitutionDate = 7/4/1776	Date
LogicalValue = False	Logical
NewTab = TabName	Same as variable TabName

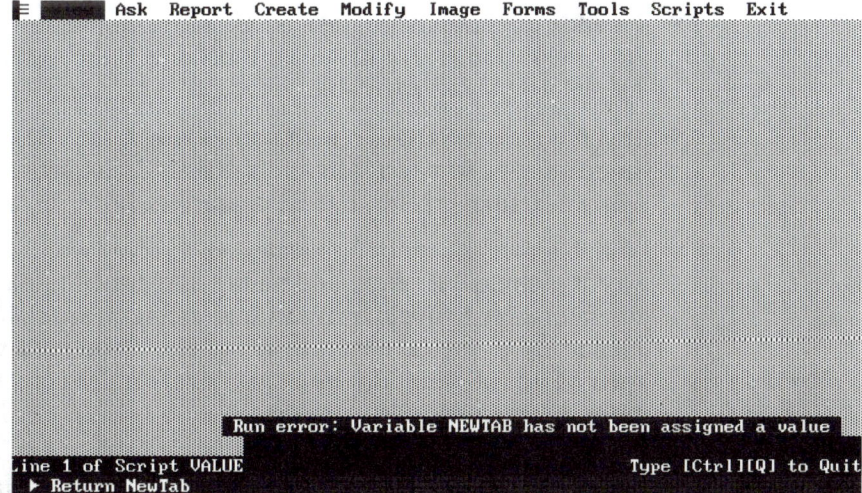

Debugger message when an undefined variable is used
Figure 4-3.

NOTE: Certain PAL commands also result in the assignment of a value to a variable. For example, if you use the SHOWMENU command to display a menu on the canvas, Paradox assigns the value representing the menu item selected by the user to a variable. Your script can then use the value in this variable to direct other PAL commands. Many of these commands are described later in this book. Most are described in Chapter 9.

Choosing Variable Names

The names used for variables are arbitrary, although there are some restrictions. For example, you cannot use a name that is already reserved by PAL. If you try to use a variable named View in a script, Paradox will automatically assume that you are referring to the PAL command VIEW. This will nearly always result in a script error.

The following are the rules for naming variables:

✦ Variable names must begin with a letter, but they can contain letters and numbers and the characters _ (underscore), . (period), ! (exclamation mark), and $ (dollar sign).

✦ Variable names can not include blank spaces.

✦ Paradox does not distinguish between upper- and lowercase letters in variable names. For instance, TabName, TABNAME, and tabname all refer to the same variable.

✦ If you have two variables with names longer than 31 characters, there must be some variation in the first 31 characters of the names. Variable names greater than 31 characters, however, are unusual.

✦ Variable names cannot duplicate PAL reserved words. PAL reserved words include PAL command names, PAL function names, and PAL operators. Try to avoid using an underscore in a variable name. This character has special meaning in a query. If you use a variable in a query, and the variable name includes an underscore, the query will not produce the results you want.

The following are examples of valid and invalid variable names:

Expressions

Variable Name	Valid?	Reason
TabName	Yes	
1TabName	No	Must start with a letter
Tab Name	No	No spaces allowed
Tab_Name	Maybe	Valid, but underscore will create a problem if variable is used in a query
View	No	VIEW is a PAL reserved word
tabname	Yes	
TabName.a	Yes	
tabname$	Yes	
$tabname	No	Must start with a letter

Arrays

Arrays are special types of variables. Instead of storing a single value, as a variable does, an array can store many different values. That is, an array can store any number of alphanumeric values, dates, numbers, and logical values using the same array name. You might think of an array as a row of variables, and each of these variables is called an *array element*. While all values in the same array have the same array name, each value has a different array element.

There are two types of arrays in Paradox 4, fixed arrays and dynamic arrays. (Paradox 3.5 only supports fixed arrays.) *Fixed arrays* can hold a fixed number of values while *dynamic arrays* can hold any number of values. The array elements in a fixed array are numbered, starting with 1, and go as high as the maximum number of values the array can hold. This number is called a *subscript*. For example, if a fixed array can hold a maximum of 100 values, the first array subscript is 1 and the last array subscript is 100. Dynamic arrays, on the other hand, are not numbered. Instead, each element of a dynamic array is labeled with alphanumeric expressions, called its *index*. Each index is unique in the dynamic array.

Arrays are named using the same conventions as variables, with one exception. Anytime you use an array in an expression, you must also indicate which element you are referring to. The array element is indicated by a subscript (fixed array) or index (dynamic array) enclosed in square brackets following the array name. For example, the first subscript in a fixed array called Counter is Counter[1], the second element is Counter[2], the third is Counter[3], and so on.

Paradox 4 makes use of dynamic arrays to store complex information about events and objects.

While array elements in a fixed array are ordered, beginning with 1 and continuing sequentially through the maximum number of elements, this is not true of dynamic arrays. The first index in a dynamic array called KeyBoardState may be "CTRL," the second may be "ALT," and so on. In a dynamic array, any array index might be the first, depending on the order in which the values were assigned to the dynamic array. In general, the first index is the last one created, the second is the second to last index created, and the last index in a dynamic array is the first one created. In most cases, however, the actual order of the indexes in a dynamic array is inconsequential.

Because arrays let you refer to more than one value using the same array name, they are useful for working with a series of values, one at a time. Dynamic arrays have an even greater role, however. They are used extensively to store information about complex events and objects. For example, each action associated with a mouse event has a number of specific characteristics, including whether the right or the left mouse button was pressed, whether the press was a single or a double click, the row-column location of the mouse pointer when the button was pressed, and so on. This information can be stored in a dynamic array, permitting your scripts to evaluate the entire action, and take the appropriate steps based on the relevant information.

Declaring an Array

In most cases, you must declare an array before you can use it. By *declaring* an array, you are informing Paradox that you want to use the same name to refer to an array of values. You declare a fixed array using the PAL command ARRAY, followed by the array name and the number of elements it can hold, enclosed in square brackets. For example, if you want to store a series of 100 numbers in an array called HoldNumbers, you must first use the following statement in your script:

```
ARRAY HoldNumbers[100]
```

In this statement, the number enclosed in the square brackets is the highest subscript you will use. (Fixed array subscripts cannot be larger than 15,000.)

Expressions

Dynamic arrays are declared in much the same way, only the command DYNARRAY is used instead of ARRAY. Furthermore, since dynamic arrays do not have a finite size, you do not specify the number of elements when you declare them. (There is no inherent size limit to dynamic arrays; this is determined by the amount of memory your computer has.) Therefore, to declare a dynamic array called HoldColors, use the following statement:

```
DYNARRAY HoldColors[]
```

Once you declare an array, you can use the array in any expression. The only difference between using an array and a variable is that you must specify which array element you are referring to when you use an array. Therefore, if HoldNumbers is a fixed array, the following assignment statement is invalid:

```
CurrentValue = HoldNumbers
```

For this statement to be valid, you must use a subscript to define which array element you are referring to. The following statement is valid:

```
CurrentValue = HoldNumbers[1]
```

Each element in an array may have a different data type. The following statements create a fixed array that contains elements of different data types.

```
ARRAY Holdem[4]
Holdem[1] = "Customer"
Holdem[2] = 5.25
Holdem[3] = 9/1/92
Holdem[4] = True
```

As with variables, the data type of any array element changes as soon as you assign an expression of a different data type to that array element. Therefore, it is perfectly acceptable to use both of the following commands in one script:

```
Holdem[1] = "Customer"
Holdem[1] = 5.25
```

Although dynamic array indexes are always uppercase alphanumeric expressions, you can use alphanumeric expressions of any case, or even numeric, logical, or date expressions, when referencing an element of a dynamic array. Paradox automatically converts alphanumeric indexes to uppercase, and date, numeric, and logical expressions to their alphanumeric equivalents. For example, consider the following commands:

```
DYNARRAY HoldValues[]
HoldValues["NOFRAME"] = True
HoldValues[1/1/93] = False
HoldValues[True] = 2
HoldValues[3] = "Excellent"
```

These commands are all valid and will have the same effect as the following statements:

```
DYNARRAY HoldValues[]
HoldValues["NoFrame"] = True
HoldValues["1/01/93"] = False
HoldValues["TRUE"] = 2
HoldValues["3"] = "Excellent"
```

In one particular instance, it is not necessary to declare an array before using it. This is when you use a PAL command that creates an array implicitly. For example, when you use the COPYTOARRAY or REPORTTABLES command, Paradox both declares a fixed array and assigns values to it. Likewise, certain PAL commands, including GETATTRIBUTES, GETEVENT, and SYSINFO, each declare and assign values to a dynamic array.

Field Specifiers

In Paradox, you store most of your data in tables. You can use this data in any PAL expression. In order to do so, however, you must use a *field specifier* to reference the table and field containing the value you want to use. Both the table name and field name must be enclosed in square brackets, and they have to be separated by a dash and greater-than sign (->), like this:

```
[tablename -> fieldname]
```

Expressions

For example, to refer to a value stored in the Company Name field of the Customer table, you would use

```
[Customer -> Company Name]
```

If you have ever used calculated fields in reports or forms, you have already used a field specifier. However, there is one major difference between using field specifiers in reports and forms and using field specifiers in a script: In order to use a field specifier in a script, the table must be on the desktop.

Although most interactive Paradox users are not aware of it, your cursor points to all tables on the desktop, even though it may be visible in only one. This feature makes it possible to refer to two or more tables at once in a single expression.

The following assignment statement makes use of this feature:

```
AmountDue = [Sales -> Total Sale] + [Tax -> Total Tax]
```

In this expression, values from two different tables, Sales and Tax, are added together and then assigned to the variable AmountDue.

Before you can successfully use statements like this, you need to be familiar with three table-related concepts: current table, current record, and current field.

The Current Table

If you have one table on the desktop, that table is your *current table*. When there is more than one table on the desktop, the current table is the one where the cursor appears. Generally, if there are no tables displayed on the desktop, you do not have a current table.

There is one situation in which you do have a current table even though the cursor is not visible in it. That is when the cursor appears in a menu (the Main menu, for instance). When this situation exists, the current table is the one the cursor returns to when it leaves the menu and returns to the desktop.

The Current Record

Every table that is displayed on the desktop has a *current record*. For example, if there are three tables on the desktop, each of them has a current record, even though only one of the tables can be the current table. For the current table, the current record is the one the cursor appears in (or will return to if the cursor is in a menu). When there is more than one table on the desktop, a table's current record is the record the cursor lands on when you use F3 (UpImage) or F4 (DownImage) to move the cursor to that table. Use the following exercise to see how this works:

1. Select View from the Main menu.
2. Type **Customer** and press Enter.

   Paradox displays the Customer table on the workspace with the cursor in the first record.
3. Press F10 (Menu).
4. Select View.
5. Type **Employee** and press Enter.

   Paradox now displays the Employee table below the Customer table. The cursor now appears in the first record of the Employee table.
6. Press ↓ twice so that the cursor is located in the third record of the Employee table.

   Your desktop will look like Figure 4-4. Notice the message at the bottom of the window that indicates the cursor is in the third record of Employee. The current record of Employee is now the third record.
7. Press F3 (UpImage) to make the Customer table current.

   Notice that the cursor moved to the first record of Customer.
8. Press F4 (DownImage).

   The cursor returns to the third record of Employee.

This exercise demonstrates that both tables, Customer and Employee, have a current record, even though only one of them can be the current table at any given time. In Customer the current record is the first record, in Employee it is the third.

Expressions

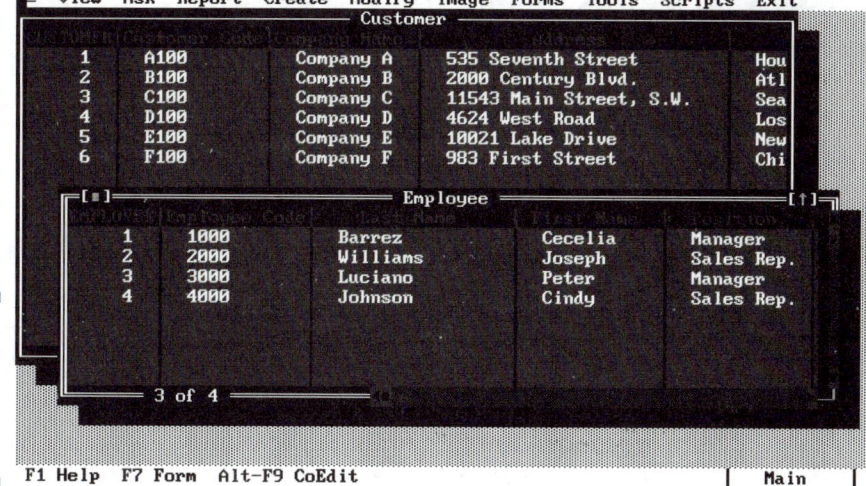

Third record of Employee table is the current record
Figure 4-4.

NOTE: When a table is first placed on the desktop, its current record is its first record, except when the table is empty. Empty tables do not have a current record.

The Current Field

Just as each table on the desktop has a current record, each table also has a *current field*. In the preceding example, when you moved the cursor between the two tables, the cursor not only landed on the same record each time it arrived on the table, but also on the same field. Demonstrate this by repeating steps 7 and 8 of the preceding exercise. If you use the ← or → key to change the current field of either table, and then repeat steps 7 and 8, you will see that the cursor returns to the field in each table that it last occupied.

Using Field Specifiers

The following exercise demonstrates the use of a field specifier. Begin with both the Customer and Employee tables displayed on your desktop. If you followed the preceding two exercises, the tables are already there. If you did not, follow steps 1 through 5 of the exercise in the section "The Current Record."

1. Press [Alt]-[F10] (PAL menu).
2. Select Value.
3. Type **[Customer -> Company Name]** and press [Enter].

Paradox displays the contents of the Company Name field for the Customer table in the lower right corner of the screen. The exact value corresponds with the current record of the Customer table. This is shown in Figure 4-5.

Now try this exercise:

1. Press [Alt]-[F10].
2. Select Value.
3. Type **[Employee -> Last Name]** and press [Enter].

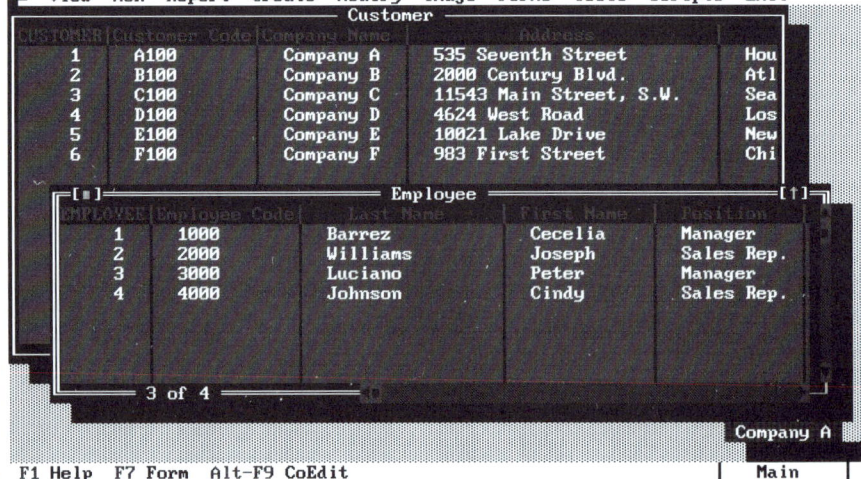

Value of the expression [Customer -> Company Name]
Figure 4-5.

Expressions

Paradox displays the value from the Last Name field of the Employee table, as shown in Figure 4-6. Again, this value corresponds to the value located in the current record of the Employee table. This demonstration shows that you can use a field specifier to refer to a table and field other than the current table and the current field. However, the field specifier always refers to the current record of the referred table.

You can omit the field name in your field specifier statement when you want to refer to the current field. For example, this statement

```
[Customer ->]
```

refers to the current field and current record of the Customer table. Likewise, this statement

```
[Employee ->]
```

refers to the current field and current record of the Employee table. Note that when you only specify the table name, it must be followed by the -> characters.

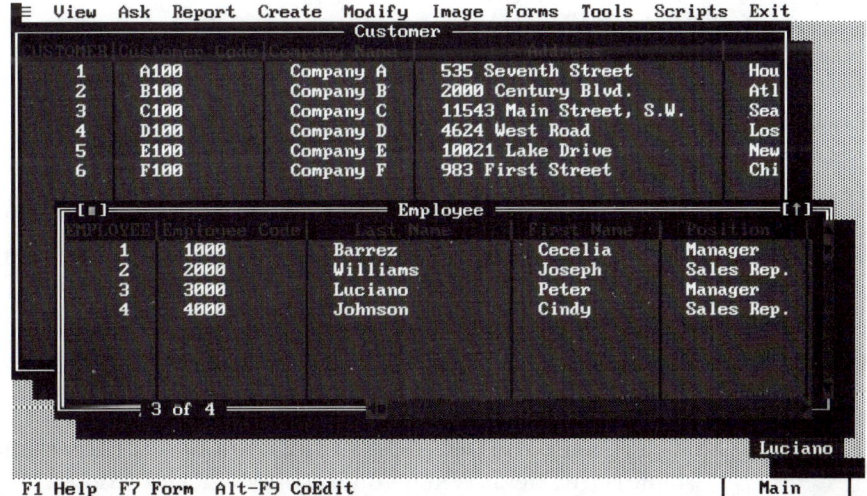

Value of the expression [Last Name]
Figure 4-6.

You can see this yourself with the following exercise:

1. If the Employee table is not current, press F4 (DownImage) to make it current.
2. If First Name is not the current field of Employee, press → or ← until it is the current field.
3. Press Alt-F10 to display the PAL menu.
4. Select Value.
5. Type **[Employee ->]** and press Enter.

   Paradox displays the value in the current field and current record of the Employee table on your screen.

If you want to refer to a specific field in the current record of the current table, you only need to specify the field name within the brackets. For instance, if the Employee table is current, the field specifier [First Name] refers to the First Name field of Employee.

TIP: When defining only the field name, you do not need to use the -> as you do when defining only the table name. When defining only the field name, both [First Name] and [-> First Name] would produce the same result.

Make sure the Employee table is current, and then try this exercise:

1. Press Alt-F10.
2. Select Value.
3. Enter **[Last Name]** and press Enter.

   Paradox displays the contents of the Last Name field for the current record of the current table (Employee). This is shown in Figure 4-6.

You can also use the field specifier without explicitly naming either the table or the field. When you use only brackets, you are referring to the current field in the current record of the current table. To see this, try the following steps:

Expressions

1. Press [Alt]-[F10].
2. Select Value.
3. Enter [ ] and press [Enter].

   Paradox displays the contents of the current field of the current record of the current table.

Examples of acceptable variations of field specifiers are shown in Table 4-1. In general, your scripts will be easier to understand and maintain if you explicitly name both the field and table in your field specifiers. However, you may encounter situations where you cannot define the table and field name in advance. In these cases, you can use a version of field specifier that defaults to the current table, current field, or both.

PAL Functions

PAL *functions* are predefined calculations that Paradox can perform for you. These functions can be used anytime an expression is required. Like all expressions, a function has a value. This value is the result of the calculation performed by Paradox.

Field Specifier	Refers To
[]	Current table, current record, current field
[#]	Record number of current table, current record
[field]	Specified field of current table, current record
[table –>]	Current record, current field of specified table
[table –> field]	Specified table, specified field of current table
[table (Q) –>]	The query image of specified table, current record, current field
[table (Q) –> field]	Current field, current record of the query image of specified table
[table (*n*) –>]	Current field, current record of the *n*th image of the specified table
[table(*n*) –> field]	*n*th image of the specified table, specified field, current record

Field Specifiers
Table 4-1.

PAL functions provide you with an invaluable source of information you can use in your scripts. They can tell you what time it is, the current date, the result of a trigonometric function (such as the cosine of an angle), the result of a financial calculation (such as the present value of a series of equal payments), and basic information about your Paradox environment (what is the current mode, is there a table on the desktop, is the current record locked, is the printer ready, and so forth). Paradox 4 provides you with over 150 different PAL functions.

PAL functions are reserved PAL keywords that are followed by opening and closing parentheses. For example, TIME( ) is a function. It returns the current time, according to your computer's internal clock.

Functions return a single value that evaluates to one of the four expression data types. The TIME( ) function, for instance, returns an alphanumeric expression. When Paradox encounters a function, it determines the value of the function at that very moment. For example, when Paradox plays the function TIME( ), it pauses briefly while it determines the current time, based on your computer's internal clock.

Using Functions

You can use a function anytime an expression is required. This exercise will demonstrate the value returned by a function:

1. Press [Alt]-[F10].
2. Select Value.
3. Type **TIME( )** and press [Enter].

   Paradox will display the current time in the lower right corner of your screen, as shown in Figure 4-7.

Some functions need information to base the calculation on. One such function is UPPER( ), which converts an alphanumeric expression to uppercase letters. In order to use this function, you must provide it with the expression you want converted, and this expression must appear between the parentheses that follow the function. For example, UPPER("Customer") evaluates to CUSTOMER. The expression you provide the function is called its *argument*. Thus the argument of the UPPER( ) function in this example is "Customer".

Expressions

Value of the expression TIME( )
Figure 4-7.

Some functions require two or more arguments. These arguments must also appear between the parentheses and must be separated by commas. One such function is ROUND( ). This function, which rounds a number to a specified number of decimal places, requires two arguments. The first argument is the number you want rounded, and the second is the number of decimal places to round the number to. For example, ROUND(1.2345, 2) evaluates to 1.23.

A complete list of PAL functions is shown in Table 4-2, categorized by the kind of information the functions return. These categories can be defined as follows:

✦ **Alphanumeric manipulation** These functions permit you to modify alphanumeric expressions. This category includes functions that return only a segment of an alphanumeric expression, those that search for one or more characters in an alphanumeric expression, and those that convert expressions of other data types to alphanumeric expressions.

✦ **Date and time** These functions provide you with the current date and time. This category also includes functions that return information concerning past and future dates, such as what day of the week a particular date falls on.

- **Financial** There are four financial functions. These provide you with present value, net present value, future value, and amortized mortgage payment calculations.

- **General information** These functions return basic information about tables, variables, arrays, your computing environment, and the Paradox configuration. Among these are functions that tell you if a variable has been assigned a value, the size of an array, if a table exists, if a table is empty, and the data type of an expression. Also available are functions that return the amount of available disk space, whether a file exists, and whether blank values will be treated as zeros in a report.

- **Mathematical** All basic mathematical and trigonometric functions are available. These include square root, absolute value, sine and cosine, and random number functions.

- **Statistical** These functions return basic, descriptive statistics such as average, frequency, minimum, maximum, standard deviation, and variance.

- **Desktop and canvas information** These functions provide you with a wealth of information concerning Paradox objects both on the desktop and the canvases. You can find out how many tables are on the desktop, the name of the current table, the handle of the active window, the contents of the field the cursor is in, the image type of the current image, how many pages are in the current form, whether a table is in form view or not, the row or column location of the cursor on the canvas, and so forth.

Operators

Operators are used to modify or combine expressions. The result of this combination or modification is itself an expression. For example, the expression 2 + 4 is a combination of two numeric constants using the + operator. This expression evaluates to the numeric value 6.

The type of operator you use depends on the data type of the expressions being combined. For example, the NOT operator can only be used with logical expressions. Other operators, such as the + operator, function differently depending on the data types of the expressions they are used with. For instance, the + operator between

Expressions

Alphanumeric Manipulation	Financial (*continued*)
ASC( )	FV( )
CHR( )	PMT( )
FILL( )	PV( )
FORMAT( )	
IIF( )*	**General Information**
LEN( )	ARRAYSIZE( )
LOWER( )	CHARWAITING( )
MATCH( )	DIRECTORY( )
SEARCH( )	DIREXISTS( )
SEARCHFROM( )*	DRIVESPACE( )
SPACES( )	DRIVESTATUS( )
STRVAL( )	DYNARRAYSIZE( )*
SUBSTR( )	ERRORCODE( )
UPPER( )	ERRORMESSAGE( )
	ERRORUSER( )
Date and Time	FAMILYRIGHTS( )
BLANKDATE( )	FIELDRIGHTS( )
DATEVAL( )	FILESIZE( )
DAY( )	FILEVERSION( )*
DOW( )	GRAPHTYPE( )
MONTH( )	ISASSIGNED( )
MOY( )	ISBLANKZERO( )
TICKS( )*	ISEMPTY( )
TIME( )	ISENCRYPTED( )
TODAY( )	ISFILE( )
USDATE( )*	ISMASTER( )*
YEAR( )	ISRUNTIME( )
	ISSHARED( )
Financial	ISTABLE( )
CNPV( )	ISVALID( )

Table 4-2. PAL Functions by Type (* indicates function is not available in Paradox 3.5)

PAL Functions by Type (*indicates function is not available in Paradox 3.5) (continued)
Table 4-2.

General Information (continued)	Mathematical (continued)
MEMLEFT( )	NUMVAL( )
MONITOR( )	PI( )
NETTYPE( )	POW( )
PRINTERSTATUS( )	RAND( )
PRIVDIR( )	ROUND( )
QUERYORDER( )	SIN( )
RETRYPERIOD( )	SQRT( )
RMEMLEFT( )	TAN( )
SDIR( )	
SORTORDER( )	**Statistical**
SYSCOLOR( )	CAVERAGE( )
SYSMODE( )	CCOUNT( )
TABLERIGHTS( )	CMAX( )
TYPE( )	CMIN( )
USERNAME( )	CSTD( )
VERSION( )	CSUM( )
	CVAR( )
Mathematical	IMAGECAVERAGE( )
ABS( )	IMAGECCOUNT( )
ACOS( )	IMAGECMAX( )
ASIN( )	IMAGECMIN( )
ATAN( )	IMAGECSUM( )
ATAN2( )	MAX( )
BLANKNUM( )	MIN( )
COS( )	
EXP( )	**Desktop and Canvas Information**
INT( )	ATFIRST( )
LN( )	ATLAST( )
LOG( )	BANDINFO( )
MOD( )	BOT( )

Expressions

Table 4-2. PAL Functions by Type (*indicates function is not available in Paradox 3.5) *(continued)*

Desktop and Canvas Information *(continued)*	Desktop and Canvas Information *(continued)*
CHECKMARKSTATUS( )	ISLINKLOCKED( )
COL( )	ISMULTIFORM( )
COLNO( )	ISMULTIREPORT( )
CONTROLVALUE( )*	ISWINDOW( )*
CURCORCHAR( )	LINKTYPE( )
CURSORLINE( )	LOCKSTATUS( )
EOT( )	MENUCHOICE( )
FIELD( )	MENUPROMPT( )*
FIELDINFO( )	NFIELDS( )
FIELDNO( )	NIMAGERECORDS( )
FIELDSTR( )	NIMAGES( )
FIELDTYPE( )	NKEYFIELDS( )
FORM( )	NPAGES( )
FORMTYPE( )	NRECORDS( )
GETCANVAS( )*	NROWS( )
GETCHAR( )	PAGENO( )
GETWINDOW( )*	PAGEWIDTH( )
HELPMODE( )	RECNO( )
IMAGENO( )	RECORDSTATUS( )
IMAGETYPE( )	ROW( )
ISBLANK( )	ROWNO( )
ISFIELDVIEW( )	TABLE( )
ISFORMVIEW( )	WINDOW( )
ISINSERTMODE( )	WINDOWAT( )*

two numeric expressions performs addition. However, you can also place the + operator between two alphanumeric expressions to combine them into a single alphanumeric value—this is called *concatenation*.

Using the Alphanumeric Operator

Only one operator is valid with alphanumeric expressions: the concatenation operator. It is represented by a +. When the + character is used between two alphanumeric expressions, the result is itself an alphanumeric expression. The following are examples of concatenation:

```
"Presi"+"dent"
[Employee -> First name]+" "+[Employee -> Last Name]
"Dear " + [Employee -> First name]+":"
Directory()+TABLE()+".DB"
"The time is "+TIME()
"Invoice has " +STRVAL(NRECORDS("Invoice"))+" records"
```

Using Numeric Operators

Numeric operators perform arithmetic with numbers. The result of such an operation is itself a numeric expression. Arithmetic expressions are evaluated from left to right. For example, in the expression 2 + 4 – 3, 2 and 4 are added first, then 3 is subtracted from the sum. Certain numeric operators are processed before others, however. For example, in the expression 2 + 4 * 3, 4 and 3 are multiplied first, before being added to 2. This occurs because division (/) and multiplication (*) are performed before addition (+) and subtraction (–).

You can, however, use the (and) operators to change the order of arithmetic processing. When parentheses are used in a numeric expression, expressions enclosed in parentheses are processed first. For example, the expression 8 – 3 * 2 results in the number 2 because 3 * 2 is processed first, and the result is then subtracted from 8. However, if you use the expression (8 – 3) * 2, the expression evaluates to 10 because 8 – 3 is calculated before the multiplication is performed.

The following are valid numeric expressions:

Expression	Value
2 + 2	4
(2 + 2)	4
2 + 2 / 3	2.67
(2 + 2) / 3	1.33

Expressions

Using Date Operators

There are two date operators, + and –, and there are two uses for them. The first is to calculate a date some number of days before or after a given date. You do this by following a date expression with the number of days you want to add or subtract. Use a + to add and a – to subtract these days. The result is a date expression. The following are examples of this type of calculation:

Expression	Result
1/1/93 + 20	1/21/93
9/5/92 – 30	8/06/92

The second use of the date operators is to calculate the number of days between two date expressions. This type of expression can only make use of the – operator. When two date expressions are separated by a – operator, the result is a numeric expression representing the number of days between the two dates. The following examples demonstrate this:

Expression	Result
9/5/92 – 8/6/92	30
8/6/92 – 9/5/92	–30
1/1/94 – TODAY( )	Days from beginning of 1994

REMEMBER: TODAY( ) is a function that returns today's date, according to your computer's internal clock.

Using Logical Operators

Logical operators are used to create logical expressions that are used by many PAL commands. The WHILE-ENDWHILE command, for example, is controlled by a logical expression. As long as the expression evaluates to True, Paradox will repeat a specific series of PAL commands.

There are two classes of logical operators: comparison operators and keyword operators.

Comparison Operators

Comparison operators permit you to compare two expressions. Although the expressions can be of any type (alphanumeric, numeric, date, or logical), the result of the comparison is *always* a logical expression. The logical comparison operators are shown in the following table:

Comparison Operator	Description
=	Equal to
<>	Not equal to
<	Less than
<=	Less than or equal to
>	Greater than
>=	Greater than or equal to

The following are examples of expressions that use comparison operators:

Logical Expression	Result
2 = 3	False
2 <> 3	True
2 < 3	True
2 <= 3	True
2 > 3	False
2 >= 3	False

These operators are not restricted only to numeric expressions, however. Any two expressions can be compared as long as both of them are of the same data type. Consider the following expressions:

Expressions

Expression	Result
"Customer" = CustName	True if value of CustName is Customer
[–> Last Name] = Cust	True if value of Cust is the same as in specified field
Choice = "Add"	True if value of Choice is Add
TODAY( ) <> Last.Date	True if value of Last.Date is not today's date
True <> False	True

Keyword Operators

There are three keyword operators in PAL: NOT, AND, and OR. Keyword operators are always used in conjunction with one or more logical expressions. The resulting expression is also a logical expression. The following are examples of expressions using these keyword operators:

Expression	Result
NOT False	True
True AND False	False
True OR False	True

You can use NOT before any logical expression. The resulting value is the opposite of the value of the expression. For example, if an expression evaluates to True, preceding it with NOT will return False.

AND is used to combine two logical expressions. When AND is used, the resulting value is True if and only if both of the logical expressions being compared by the AND evaluate to True. If one or both of the expressions is False, the resulting expression will also be False.

Like AND, OR is also used to combine two expressions. When OR is used, the resulting expression is True if either one or both of the expressions evaluate to True. The expression will evaluate to False only if both expressions are False.

The Order of Logical Operations

Like expressions involving numeric operators, expressions using logical operators are evaluated from left to right. Furthermore, some operators are processed before others. In logical expressions, all comparison operators are evaluated before any of the keyword operators. When the keyword operators are processed, NOT will be processed before AND, which in turn is processed before OR.

If you want Paradox to process your logical expressions in any other order, you must use parentheses to group operations. As with numeric operations, any expressions within parentheses are evaluated first.

The following are examples of logical expressions and their values:

Expression	Value
NOT True	False
NOT True AND False	False
NOT (True AND False)	True
True OR False	True
((2 = 3) OR (2 <> 3))	True
NOT ISTABLE("Invoice")	False if Invoice table exists
True = False	False

Expressions

Quick Review

- Expressions comprise the information that directs commands.
- Each expression evaluates to a value.
- The value of an expression is one of four types: alphanumeric, numeric, date, or logical.
- Constants are expressions that stand for a fixed value.
- Variables are labels that can change value.
- Fixed arrays are a group of variables that use the same name. The individual values are stored in array elements, which are numbered beginning with 1.
- Dynamic arrays are similar to fixed arrays, but their elements are identified by alphanumeric expressions instead of numbers.
- Functions are PAL keywords that perform special, predefined calculations. There are seven categories of PAL functions. These are

  Alphanumeric manipulation
  Date and time
  Financial
  General information
  Mathematical
  Statistical
  Desktop and canvas information

- Some functions require one or more arguments. These arguments are used in the calculation performed by the function.
- Operators are used to combine or modify expressions.
- Comparison operators are used to compare two expressions. The result of this comparison is a logical expression.
- Keyword operators are used to modify a logical expression or to combine two logical expressions.

CHAPTER

5 COMMANDS

This chapter begins by describing the various forms of PAL commands. It then introduces the concept of command syntax and presents a special notation that is used in this book to define how to use PAL commands. Finally, you will learn how to use PAL commands effectively in your scripts.

Controlling Paradox

There are two distinct ways to control Paradox in a script. The first way uses PAL commands. PAL commands use PAL keywords, which are treated specially by Paradox. These words are called *reserved words* since you may not use them for any other purpose. There are roughly 160 different PAL commands.

The second way to control Paradox is through the use of keypress interactions. Instead of using keywords, this method uses a notation to denote selections from menus or keypresses from the keyboard.

In all likelihood, your PAL scripts will contain both of these types of commands. In many cases, you can achieve the same effect using either. Which you choose depends on a number of issues, including

- *Ease of programming* In many cases, keypress interactions require two or more commands to achieve the effect of a single PAL command.

- *Readability of your script* PAL commands are more similar to natural language than are keypress interactions. Consequently, a script that makes use of PAL commands tends to be easier to read and interpret than one created using keypress interactions.

- *Availability of features* Some features are only available with PAL commands. Others are only available through the use of keypress interactions.

Using Keypress Interactions

Keypress interactions are commands that make selections from menus and press keys on the keyboard. There are two types of keypress interactions: braced menu selections and quoted strings.

You may recall braced menu selections and quoted strings from Chapter 3. In that chapter you learned how to record your exact keystrokes in scripts and play them back at a later time. In those scripts, most of your actions are recorded as braced menu selections and quoted strings.

Braced Menu Selections

Braced menu selections make selections from Paradox menus. They can be used only if the appropriate menu (containing that menu selection)

Commands

is displayed and active. To create a braced menu selection, enclose the menu selection you want in curly braces. For example, use {View} to select View from the Paradox Main menu.

TIP: Paradox menus make use of combinations of upper- and lowercase letters. Fortunately, when you use braced menu selections you do not need to match the case of the menu selection exactly. For example, both {VIEW} and {view} will result in the selection of View from the Main menu.

The following exercise demonstrates the use of braced menu selections. To follow this example, you must start from the Paradox Main menu.

1. Select Scripts to display the Scripts menu.
2. Select Editor.
3. Select New.
4. Type **Chngdir** and then press [Enter]. The Paradox Editor will appear.
5. Enter the following braced menu selections in the Editor screen:
   {Tools} {More} {Directory}
   Your screen should look like Figure 5-1.
6. Now save this script by pressing [F2] (Do-It!).

The script you created is now saved to disk as CHNGDIR.SC. This script contains the commands to select Tools/More/Directory. Demonstrate this by playing the script.

7. Press [Ctrl]-[G] (Go).

The script will play. When the PAL canvas is dropped, Paradox will prompt you for the directory you want to change to. This is shown in Figure 5-2. However, your current directory will be displayed, not the one shown in Figure 5-2.

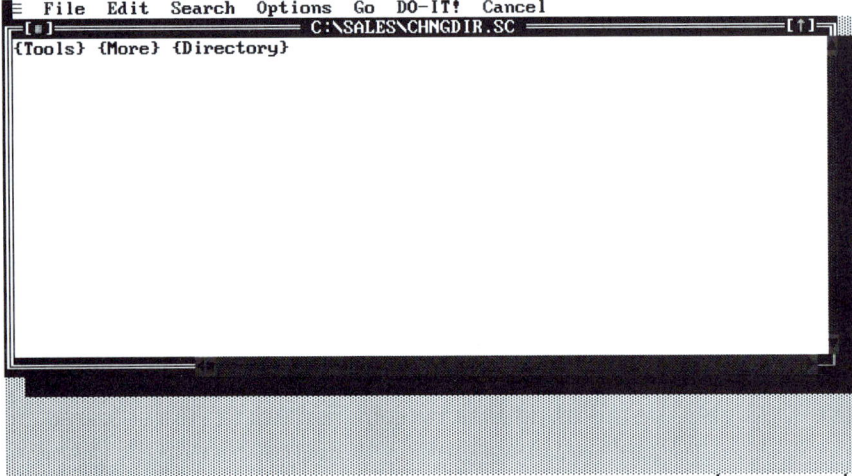

Chngdir script in the Paradox Editor
Figure 5-1.

SHORTCUT: Normally you would play this script by selecting Scripts/Play and entering the name Chngdir at the prompt. However, since you just used the Paradox Editor to write the script, there is a trick you can use to play it. When you press Ctrl-G (Go), Paradox instantly plays the most recently edited script. Try playing the Chngdir script using this trick.

Quoted Strings

Quoted strings are used to press specific keys on your keyboard. They can only be used if keyboard input is appropriate. For example, you can use a quoted string when the cursor is in a field in a table when the table is in Edit mode, but not in Main mode. To create a quoted string, enclose all characters you want typed within quotation marks. For example, to enter the word *Customer* in response to a prompt, use **"Customer"**

The following exercise demonstrates how to respond to a prompt using quoted strings:

1. Select Scripts from the Paradox Main menu.

Commands

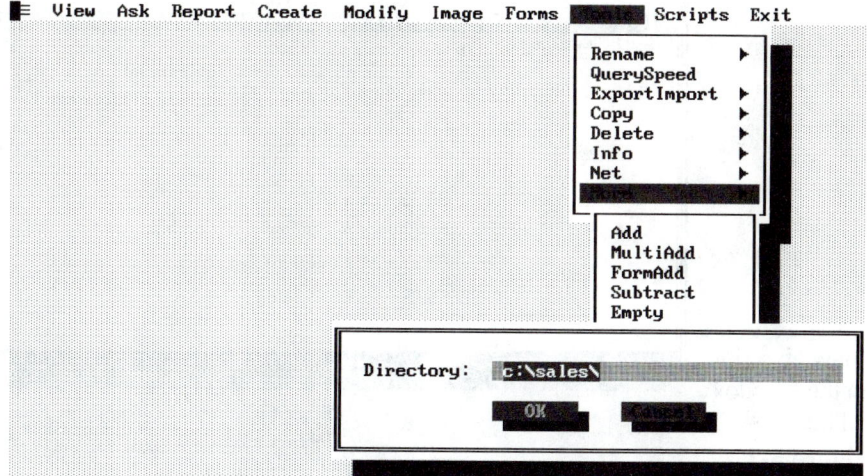

Screen after Chngdir is played
Figure 5-2.

2. Select Editor.
3. Select New.
4. Enter the script name **Viewtab**
5. Enter the following keypress interactions in the Editor screen:
   {View} "Customer"

   When you are done, your screen should look like Figure 5-3.
6. Press [F2] (Do-It!) to save your script.

   Now play your script to observe its effects.
7. Press [Ctrl]-[G] (Go).

   Once the script has been played, the word *Customer* should appear at the prompt for a table to view, as shown in Figure 5-4. This word was entered by your script, one character at a time, after the prompt for the table was displayed as a result of the {View} menu selection.
8. Press [F10] (Menu) to return to the Main menu.

Because the PAL canvas was displayed as soon as you pressed [Ctrl]-[G] (Go), you were not able to see Paradox pressing the keys in the quoted

Viewtab script in the Paradox Editor
Figure 5-3.

string. The following exercise will permit you to view the keys being entered, one by one:

1. Select Scripts.
2. Select ShowPlay.
3. Type **Viewtab** and press Enter.
4. Select Slow to show the script playing slowly.

Paradox will now play your script slowly, and the PAL canvas will not be displayed. Note that the table name Customer does not suddenly appear at the prompt, but rather is typed one character at a time. This is the nature of quoted strings.

NOTE: If you want to use this sample script to actually view the table, add the special key command ENTER after the quoted string. For example, you would type **{View} "Customer" ENTER**. ENTER presses the Enter key, resulting in the display of the Customer table.

Commands

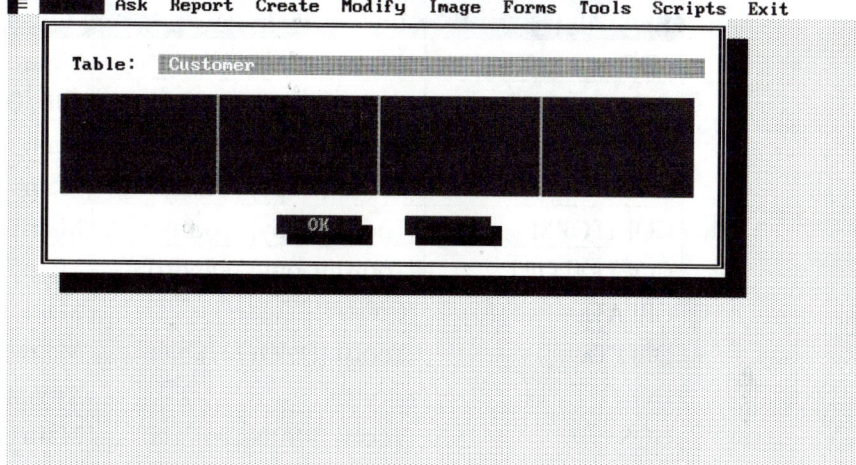

Screen after Viewtab is played
Figure 5-4.

Using PAL Commands

PAL commands are special keywords that control Paradox. When Paradox plays a PAL command in a script, it performs an action specified by the command. There are three general categories of PAL commands.

- Abbreviated menu commands
- Special key commands
- Programming commands

Each of these is described in the following sections.

Abbreviated Menu Commands

Abbreviated menu commands are PAL keywords that cause a script to make selections from Paradox menus. For instance, VIEW is an abbreviated menu command that instructs Paradox to display a table on the workspace. When you use the command VIEW, you must also specify which table to view. For example, VIEW "Customer" causes Paradox to display the Customer table on the desktop. A list of all abbreviated menu commands is given in Table 5-1.

Command	Menu Selections	Mode
ADD	{Tools} {More} {Add}	Main
CANCELEDIT	{Cancel}	Edit, DataEntry
COEDIT	{Modify} {CoEdit}	Main
COPY	{Tools} {Copy} {Table}	Main
COPYFORM	{Tools} {Copy} {Form}	Main
COPYREPORT	{Tools} {Copy} {Report}	Main
CREATE	{Create}	Main
DELETE	{Tools} {Delete} {Table}	Main
DO_IT!	{Do-It!}	Any mode
DOS	{Tools} {More} {ToDOS}	Main
EDIT	{Modify} {Edit}	Main
EDITOR FIND	{Search} {Find}	Script or File Editor
EDITOR FINDNEXT	{Search} {Next}	Script or File Editor
EDITOR NEW	{File} {Open}	
EDITOR OPEN	{File} {InsertFile}	Script or File Editor
EDITOR READ	{Search} {Replace}	Script or File Editor
EDITOR REPLACE	{File} {WriteBlock}	
EDITOR WRITE	{File} {New}	Script or File Editor
EMPTY	{Tools} {More} {Empty}	Main
EXIT	{Exit} {Yes}	Main
HELP	{Help}	Any
INDEX	{Modify} {Index}	Main
LOCK	{Tools} {Net} {Lock} or {Tools} {Net} {PreventLock}	Main
MOVETO	{Image} {Zoom}	Main, Edit, CoEdit or DataEntry
	{Image} {Move}	Main, Edit, CoEdit or DataEntry
PICKFORM	{Image} {Pickform}	Main, Edit, CoEdit or DataEntry

Abbreviated Menu Commands and Their Braced Menu Selection Equivalents
Table 5-1.

Commands

Command	Menu Selections	Mode
PROTECT	{Tools} {More} {Protect} {Password} {Table}	Main
RENAME	{Tools} {Rename} {Table}	Main
REPORT	{Report} {Output} {Printer}	Main
SETDIR	{Tools} {More} {Directory}	Main
SETPRIVDIR	{Tools} {Net} {SetPrivate}	Main
SETUSERNAME	{Tools} {Net} {UserName}	Main
SORT	{Modify} {Sort}	Main
SUBTRACT	{Tools} {More} {Subtract}	Main
UNDO	{Undo}	Edit, CoEdit, or DataEntry
UNLOCK	{Tools} {Net} {Lock} or {Tools} {Net} {PreventLock}	Main
UNPASSWORD	{Tools} {More} {Protect} {ClearPasswords}	Main
VIEW	{View}	
ZOOM	{Image} {Zoom} {Value}	Main, Edit, CoEdit, or DataEntry

Abbreviated Menu Commands and Their Braced Menu Selection Equivalents (*continued*)
Table 5-1.

Abbreviated menu commands consist of a single keyword. However, these commands usually cause Paradox to make two or more menu selections. An example is the command COPY, which makes a copy of a Paradox table. This command results in no less than five selections from Paradox menus.

Most abbreviated menu commands require one or more expressions in order to work. For example, to use COPY, you must also specify the table you want to copy and the name of the new table. Thus, to copy the Customer table and name the copy Tempcust, use the following command:

```
COPY "Customer" "Tempcust"
```

To see how this command works, follow this example, starting from the Main menu:

1. Select Scripts to display the Scripts menu.
2. Select Editor.
3. Select New.
4. Type **Copytab** and press Enter.
5. In the Editor window, type the command **COPY "Customer" "Tempcust"**
6. Press F2 (Do-It!) to save your script.

   Now use the ShowPlay feature in Paradox to display what happens when the script plays.
7. Select Scripts to display the Scripts menu.
8. Select ShowPlay.
9. Type **Copytab** and press Enter.
10. Select Slow to play the script slowly.

As you see on your screen, the COPY command causes Paradox to make the necessary menu selections to copy the Customer table to a new table called Tempcust.

Advantages of Abbreviated Menu Commands

The simple command COPY "Customer" "Tempcust" has the same effect as the following braced menu selections: {Tools} {Copy} {Table} {Customer} {Tempcust}. In addition to being easier to write, however, the COPY command is easier to read and interpret in your script.

Abbreviated menu commands are also more flexible than their braced menu selection counterparts. Remember that braced menu selections simply repeat menu selections—they cannot adapt to changes in Paradox. For example, the braced menu selections {Tools} {Copy} {Table} {Customer} {Tempcust} will not work if the Tempcust table already exists. The COPY command will, however.

You can see this with a simple exercise. Use ShowPlay again to play the Copytab script one more time (by following steps 7 though 10 in the preceding example). When you watch this script play, notice that the menu selections made by Paradox are different from the first time you played the script. Instead of ending after entering the table name Tempcust, the script selected Replace from the next menu. In other words, the COPY command was able to adjust to the fact that Tempcust already existed.

In contrast, if you wanted to use braced menu selections, you would need two different sets—one to use if the table existed already:

{Tools} {Copy} {Table} {Customer} {Tempcust} {Replace}

and one to use when the table did not exist:

{Tools} {Copy} {Table} {Customer} {Tempcust}

NOTE: Abbreviated menu commands will be successful in a script only if Paradox is in the appropriate mode at the time the script executes. Since abbreviated menu commands cause selections from menus, the current Paradox mode must offer the menu selections made by the abbreviated menu commands. For instance, the COPY command must be played while Paradox is in the Main mode. This is because only the Main mode provides the Tools menu selection, which is used by the COPY command. If Paradox encounters the COPY command while in any other mode, a run-time error occurs.

Special Key Commands

Special key commands are reserved keywords that, when used in a script, mimic the pressing of function keys and key combinations. An example of a special key command is DO_IT!. When encountered in a script, the DO_IT! command causes Paradox to press [F2] (Do-It!). Other examples of special key commands include EDITKEY ([F9]), ROTATE ([Ctrl]-[R]), FIELDVIEW ([Ctrl]-[F]), and MENU ([F10]). In fact, every Paradox function key, key combination, and navigational key has its own special key command, as shown in Table 5-2.

Recall that special key commands are also parts of recorded and instant scripts. This is because Paradox translates those keypresses into special key commands when recording your scripts. However, special key commands are different from keypress interactions since they use reserved PAL keywords.

Key	Special Key Command
Alt-A	REPLACENEXT*
Alt-C	TOGGLEPALETTE
Alt-D	DELETEWORD*
Alt-F2	SHOWSQL
Alt-F3	INSTANTRECORD
Alt-F4	INSTANTPLAY
Alt-F5	FIELDVIEW
Alt-F6	CHECKPLUS
Alt-F7	INSTANTREPORT
Alt-F8	CLEARALL
Alt-F9	COEDITKEY
Alt-F10	PALMENU
Alt-K	KEYLOOKUP
Alt-L	LOCKKEY
Alt-O	DOSBIG
Alt-R	REFRESH
Alt-S	ORDERTABLE*
Alt-Spacebar	ALTSPACE*
Alt-X	CROSSTABKEY
Alt-W	WHEREAMI*
Alt-Z	ZOOMNEXT
Backspace	BACKSPACE
Ctrl-A	REPLACE*
Ctrl-Backspace	CTRLBACKSPACE
Ctrl-Break	CTRLBREAK
Ctrl-D	DITTO
Ctrl-E	MINIEDIT*
Ctrl-End	CTRLEND
Ctrl-F	FIELDVIEW
Ctrl-F4	WINNEXT*

Function Keys and Key Combinations with Their Special Key Command Equivalents (* not available in Paradox 3.5) **Table 5-2.**

Commands

Key	Special Key Command
Ctrl-F5	WINRESIZE*
Ctrl-F6	CHECKDESCENDING
Ctrl-F7	GRAPHKEY
Ctrl-F8	WINCLOSE*
Ctrl-F10	TOQPRO
Ctrl-G	GOKEY
Ctrl-Home	CTRLHOME
Ctrl-Ins	CLIPCOPY*
Ctrl-L	RESYNCKEY
Ctrl-←	CTRLLEFT
Ctrl-O	DOS
Ctrl-Pg Dn	CTRLPGDN
Ctrl-Pg Up	CTRLPGUP
Ctrl-R	ROTATE
Ctrl-→	CTRLRIGHT
Ctrl-U	UNDO
Ctrl-V	VERTRULER
Ctrl-Y	DELETELINE
Ctrl-Z	ZOOM
Del	DEL
End	END
Enter	ENTER
Esc	ESC
F1	HELP
F2	DO_IT!
F3	UPIMAGE
F4	DOWNIMAGE
F5	EXAMPLE
F6	CHECK
F7	FORMKEY

Function Keys and Key Combinations with Their Special Key Command Equivalents (* not available in Paradox 3.5) (*continued*)
Table 5-2.

Table 5-2.
Function Keys and Key Combinations with Their Special Key Command Equivalents (* not available in Paradox 3.5) (*continued*)

Key	Special Key Command
F8	CLEARIMAGE
F9	EDITKEY
F10	MENU
Home	HOME
Ins	INS
←	LEFT
Pg Dn	PGDN
Pg Up	PGUP
→	RIGHT
Shift-Del	CLIPCUT*
Shift-F5	WINMAX*
Shift-F6	GROUPBY
Shift-Ins	CLIPPASTE*
Shift-Tab	REVERSETAB
Tab	TAB
↑ / ↓	UP / DOWN

The next exercise will demonstrate the effects of special key commands.

1. Select Scripts from the Main menu.
2. Select Editor.
3. Select New.
4. Type **Presskey** and press Enter.
5. Enter the following script into the Editor screen:

```
VIEW "Customer"
EDITKEY
DOWN
ROTATE
ROTATE
FIELDVIEW
LEFT
HOME
END
```

Commands

```
ENTER
DO_IT!
```

When you are done, your screen should look like Figure 5-5.

6. Press [F2] (Do-It!) to save the script.
7. Select Scripts again from the Main menu.
8. Select ShowPlay.
9. Type **Presskey** and press [Enter].
10. Select Slow.

Paradox will now play the script Presskey without displaying the PAL canvas. This permits you to see the result of each keypress. Except for the abbreviated menu command VIEW "Customer", every command in the script is a special key command. As you watch, Paradox will enter each keypress, just as if you were doing so yourself at the keyboard.

Programming Commands

The remaining PAL commands are *programming commands*. What distinguishes these commands from abbreviated menu commands and special key commands is that they have no equivalents in interactive

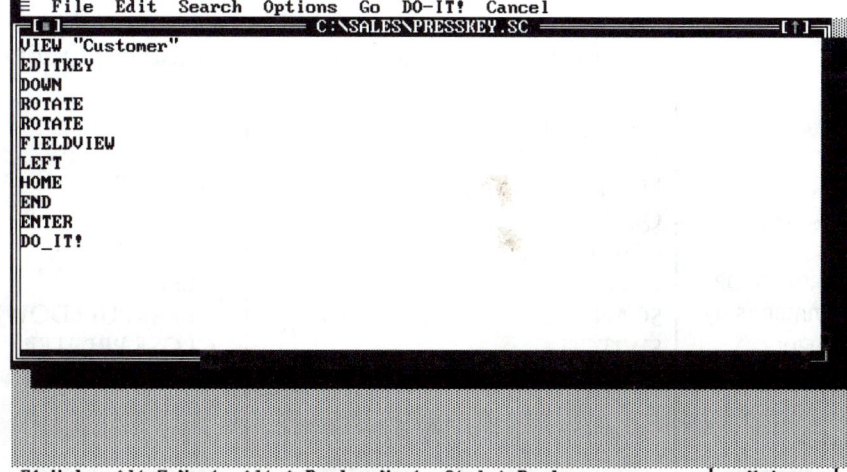

Presskey script in the Paradox Editor
Figure 5-5.

Paradox. Consider the PAL command CLEAR. This command erases the image on the full-screen PAL canvas. There is no key you can press or menu selection you can make in interactive Paradox that will produce this same result. Another example is the command SLEEP. This command causes Paradox to suspend processing of a script for a specified period of time (measured in milliseconds). This can only be done using the SLEEP command.

The following exercise uses both the CLEAR and SLEEP commands.

1. Press [Alt]-[F10] (PAL menu).
2. Select MiniScript.
3. Type the command **CLEAR SLEEP 5000** and press [Enter].

Paradox then plays the script, clearing the PAL canvas and waiting for five seconds (5000 milliseconds) before returning to interactive Paradox.

Without programming commands, PAL would be nothing more than an interesting macro language. With these commands, however, PAL is a sophisticated programming language with capabilities similar to those found in other computer languages such as BASIC, FORTRAN, and Pascal.

PAL programming commands provide you with a number of important capabilities. These can be generally grouped into seven categories. The commands are shown in Table 5-3.

PAL Programming Commands by Category (* not available in Paradox 3.5)
Table 5-3.

Control Structure Commands	Input/Output Commands
FOR	?
FOREACH*	??
IF	@
LOOP	ACCEPT
QUIT	BEEP
QUITLOOP	CANVAS
RETURN	CLEAR
SCAN	CLEARPULLDOWN*
SWITCH	CLOSE PRINTER
WHILE	CURSOR
	ECHO

Commands

Input/Output Commands (cont'd)
FILEWRITE*
FRAME*
GETMENUSELECTION*
KEYPRESS
MENUDISABLE*
MENUENABLE*
MESSAGE
MOUSE CLICK*
MOUSE DOUBLECLICK*
MOUSE DRAG*
NEWDIALOGSPEC*
NEWWAITSPEC*
OPEN PRINTER
PAINTCANVAS
PRINT
PRINTER
PROMPT
REFRESHCONTROL*
REFRESHDIALOG*
REPAINTDIALOG*
RESYNCCONTROL*
RESYNCDIALOG*
SELECTCONTROL*
SETAUTOSAVE*
SETBW
SETCANVAS*
SETCOLORS*
SETMARGIN
SETPRINTER
SHOWARRAY
SHOWDIALOG*
SHOWFILES
SHOWMENU
SHOWPOPUP*
SHOWPULLDOWN*
SHOWTABLES
SOUND*
STYLE
TEXT
WAIT
WINDOW ECHO*

Multiuser Commands
LOCKRECORD
PRIVTABLES
SETBATCH*
SETRESTARTCOUNT
SETRETRYPERIOD
UNLOCKRECORD

Procedure and Procedure Library Commands
CONVERTLIB*
CREATELIB
EXECPROC
INFOLIB
PROC
READLIB
RELEASE
SETSWAP
WRITELIB

System Control Commands
ACCEPTDIALOG*
CALCDEBUG
CANCELDIALOG*
DEBUG
EDITLOG
EXECUTE
PASSWORD
PLAY
POSTRECORD*
RESET
RUN
SAVETABLES
SETKEY

Table 5-4. PAL Programming Commands by Category (* not available in Paradox 3.5) (*continued*)

System Control Commands (cont'd)
SETKEYBOARDSTATE*
SETMAXSIZE
SETUIMODE*
SLEEP

Desktop Manipulation Commands
=
APPENDARRAY*
COPYFROMARRAY
EDITOR GOTO*
EDITOR INSERT*
EDITOR SELECT*
EXECEVENT*
FIRSTSHOW
IMAGERIGHTS
LOCATE
LOCATE INDEXORDER*
MOUSE HIDE*
MOUSE SHOW*
MOVETO
QUERY
REPLACEFIELDS*
REQUIREDCHECK
SCROLLPRESS*
SELECT
SETNEGCOLOR
SETQUERYORDER
SETRECORDPOSITION
SHIFTPRESS
SKIP
SYNCCURSOR
TYPEIN

WINDOW CLOSE*
WINDOW CREATE*
WINDOW MAXIMIZE*
WINDOW MOVE*
WINDOW RESIZE*
WINDOW SCROLL*
WINDOW SELECT*
WINDOW SETATTRIBUTES*
WINDOW SETCOLORS*

Variable and Array Manipulation Commands
=
ARRAY
COPYTOARRAY
DYNARRAY*
EDITOR EXTRACT*
EDITOR INFO*
ERRORINFO*
FILEREAD*
FORMTABLES
GETCOLORS*
GETEVENT*
GETKEYBOARDSTATE*
LOCALIZEEVENT*
RELEASE
REPORTTABLES
SAVEVARS
SYSINFO*
WINDOW GETATTRIBUTES*
WINDOW GETCOLORS*
WINDOW HANDLE*
WINDOW LIST*

Table 5-5. PAL Programming Commands by Category (* not available in Paradox 3.5) (*continued*)

- **Control structure commands** These commands control the flow of your scripts. They add flexibility to your scripts, permitting you to create "smart" scripts—scripts that can adjust to changing or unpredictable events.

- **Input/output commands** These commands can receive input from the keyboard, paint colors and text onto the PAL canvases, and even output data to your printer or a DOS file. In short, these commands permit your scripts to interact with the user.

- **Multiuser commands** Multiuser commands permit you to specifically control certain elements of Paradox's multiuser capabilities. These commands are invaluable when you are creating an application that will be used by more than one user at a time on a local area network (LAN).

- **Procedure and procedure library commands** These commands permit you to transform ordinary scripts into compact PAL procedures.

- **System control commands** These commands permit your scripts to act upon the Paradox environment, invoking the Debugger, executing DOS commands, and even playing other scripts.

- **Desktop manipulation commands** These commands provide you with the tools necessary to use tables and queries within your scripts. As in interactive Paradox, tables and queries play a large role in any database application.

- **Variable and array manipulation commands** These commands define, create, and release your variables and arrays.

Many commands from each of these categories are discussed in the following chapters of this book. However, before you are introduced to them, you need to know more about constructing commands in general. The remainder of this chapter shows you how.

Command Syntax

The requirements for constructing a particular PAL command are called its *syntax*. The syntax of a command defines which keywords and expressions are required and which are optional. If you use the wrong syntax with a command, a script error results.

In most cases, PAL commands are more than a single word. Many of them also require additional information in the form of an expression. The VIEW command is one such command. The keyword VIEW by itself would cause a script error—a syntax error, to be precise. When you use the VIEW command, you must also provide an alphanumeric expression that evaluates to the name of a table—for example, VIEW "Customer".

Sometimes PAL commands also require more than one keyword. An example of this is the SCAN command. This command is a control structure that is used to execute any number of PAL commands, once for each record in a table. Anytime you use SCAN in a script, it must be followed by a corresponding ENDSCAN keyword. Failure to do so will also result in a syntax error.

Required keywords and expressions are not the only elements of PAL commands. Many PAL commands permit you to specify one or more optional keywords or expressions, the command CLEAR, for example. When CLEAR is used by itself, the entire PAL canvas is erased. However, you can use CLEAR with the optional keyword EOL to clear only to the end of the line, starting from the current cursor position on the canvas. This command looks like this:

```
CLEAR EOL
```

How can you know whether a PAL command requires expressions or other keywords, or what they are? The answer can be found in the syntax of the command. Each command described in this book is shown with its syntax. For the syntax of commands not described, refer to the *PAL Reference* (or the *PAL User's Guide* for version 3.5).

Understanding Syntax Notation

To use a command properly, you must know its syntax. Fortunately, there is a notation for presenting the syntax of commands. The notation as presented here closely follows that used in the *PAL User's Guide*. It is as follows:

- ◆ Keywords appear in uppercase letters.
- ◆ Expressions use an initial capital letter and other capitals as necessary to enhance readability.

- Square brackets enclose keywords or expressions that are optional.
- Curly braces enclose a list of alternatives, only one of which can be used. The different alternatives are separated by a vertical bar (|).
- An ellipsis (. . .) denotes a list of zero, one, or more elements.

The syntax of many PAL commands is fairly straightforward. For instance, this is the syntax of the COPY command:

```
COPY SourceTable DestinationTable
```

COPY's syntax requires that the COPY keyword be followed by two expressions: the name of the table being copied and the name that will be used for the copy.

Now consider a slightly more complicated command, CLEAR:

```
CLEAR [{EOL | EOS}]
```

This command has one required keyword, CLEAR. The square brackets indicate that what is enclosed is optional. However, within the square brackets is a set of curly braces that contains a list of alternative keywords. This means that you can use either the EOL keyword or the EOS keyword with the CLEAR command, but not both.

A command whose syntax makes use of all of these symbols is the PAL command WAIT:

```
WAIT {WORKSPACE | TABLE | RECORD | FIELD}
   [PROMPT Prompt]
   [MESSAGE Message]
   UNTIL KeyCode1 ...[, KeyCodeN]
```

Although the syntax of WAIT is one of the most complicated, it isn't difficult to interpret if you take it one piece at a time. For example:

- Three keywords are required. These are WAIT, UNTIL, and one of the three enclosed in the curly braces, either TABLE, RECORD, or FIELD.
- One expression is required following the UNTIL keyword.

- If two or more expressions follow the UNTIL keyword, they must be separated by commas.
- The PROMPT keyword, followed by an expression, is optional.
- The MESSAGE keyword and its expression are optional.

Examples of three different, though syntactically correct, uses of the WAIT command are shown in Figure 5-6. Throughout the remainder of this book, when a command is presented, its syntax will be given using the notation presented here.

TIP: Although all PAL commands in this book are printed in uppercase letters, you are not required to use uppercase. In a script, CLEAR will have the same effect as Clear, clear, or cLeAr.

Using Commands in Scripts

Writing a script with PAL commands is not much different than writing a letter. You write a letter by putting down the appropriate words in a

Figure 5-6. Three valid uses of the WAIT command

```
E  File  Edit  Search  Options  Go  DO-IT!  Cancel
                              C:\sales\wait.sc
EDIT "Customer"   ;Place the customer table on the desktop

;This WAIT permits the user to move throughout the table.  F2 continues.

WAIT TABLE
  PROMPT "Move cursor using "+CHR(24)+" and "+CHR(25)+".  Press F2 when done."
  MESSAGE "Viewing the Customer table."
  UNTIL "F2", "ESC"

;This WAIT permits the user to view the current record.  F2 or ESC continues.

WAIT RECORD
  PROMPT "Edit this record.  Press F2 when done."
  UNTIL "F2", "ESC"

;This WAIT keeps the user on a single field.  ESC continues.

WAIT FIELD
  PROMPT "Esc to exit."
  MESSAGE "You are stuck on this field."
  UNTIL "ESC"

F1 Help  Alt-Z Next  Alt-A ReplaceNext  Ctrl-A Replace           Script
```

specific order. You select the words and their order depending on the meaning you want to convey. Similarly, you add PAL commands to your script in the order that produces the results that you desire.

As in letter writing, script writing has both restrictions and options, principally in the following three areas:

Arranging PAL commands
Using blank spaces
Using comments

Arranging Commands

There are two rules for arranging PAL commands in your scripts:

- A command must include all of its required keywords and expressions. In other words, you must use the correct syntax when writing a PAL command.

- One PAL command must be completed before you can use the next one. In other words, if a command has two or more elements (keywords or expressions), all of these elements must appear before the next PAL command in the script.

Consider the following correct example:

```
WAIT TABLE
   PROMPT "Press [F2] when done entering this record"
   UNTIL "F2"
CLEAR
```

In this example, the CLEAR command does not appear until after the last element of the WAIT command. The next example is incorrect:

```
WAIT TABLE
   PROMPT "Press [F2] when done entering this record"
   CLEAR
   UNTIL "F2"
```

Here, the CLEAR command appears before the WAIT command is complete. If you used this script segment in one of your scripts, a syntax error would result.

The category of PAL programming commands called *control structures* is the one exception to the second rule. By their very nature, control structures are only meaningful when they have other PAL commands embedded in them. The acceptable placement of these embedded commands is specified by the syntax of each control structure.

For example, consider the PAL command IF:

```
IF LogicalExpression
   THEN
        one or more PAL commands
ENDIF
```

In this command, the IF, THEN, and ENDIF commands are required, as is an expression that must evaluate to True or False. If the expression evaluates to True, any commands that appear after the keyword THEN will be played. These commands can be of any type and may even include another IF command.

Using Blank Spaces

With few exceptions, Paradox does not care how you enter PAL commands into your scripts, as long as one blank space appears between each. Since the Paradox Editor allows up to 255 characters on each line of a script, it is possible to place many PAL commands on a single line. (Be aware, however, that Paradox only reads the first 175 characters on a line.)

NOTE: The Script Editor in Paradox 3.5 permits you to include a maximum of 132 characters per line.

The judicious use of blank space can greatly improve the appearance and readability of your scripts. An example of a script that makes extensive use of white space is shown in Figure 5-7. The script begins each command and keyword on a new line, making it easy to follow.

There are three situations in which blank spaces are permissible in scripts:

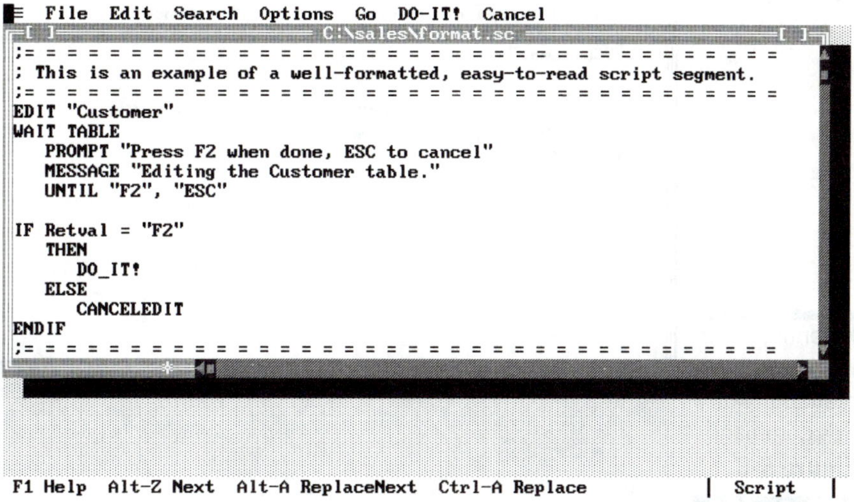

Commands

A well-formatted, easy-to-read script
Figure 5-7.

At the beginning of a line (also called *indenting*)
Between elements in a single PAL command
To produce entirely blank lines

Indenting PAL Commands

Indenting is especially useful when PAL commands with many elements occupy more than one line in your script. In those cases, it is good to indent all lines after the first. In the script shown in Figure 5-8, each of the optional keywords and expressions in the WAIT command appears on a new line and has been indented by the same amount. This indentation forms a conceptual grouping of the commands, emphasizing that they are part of a single unit even though they appear on separate lines. The results are more readable than if the indentation was not used.

How scripts are indented is often a matter of preference. For example, some like to indent the UNTIL in the WAIT command like this:

```
WAIT TABLE
   PROMPT "Press [F2] when done."
   UNTIL "F2"
```

Others might indent like this:

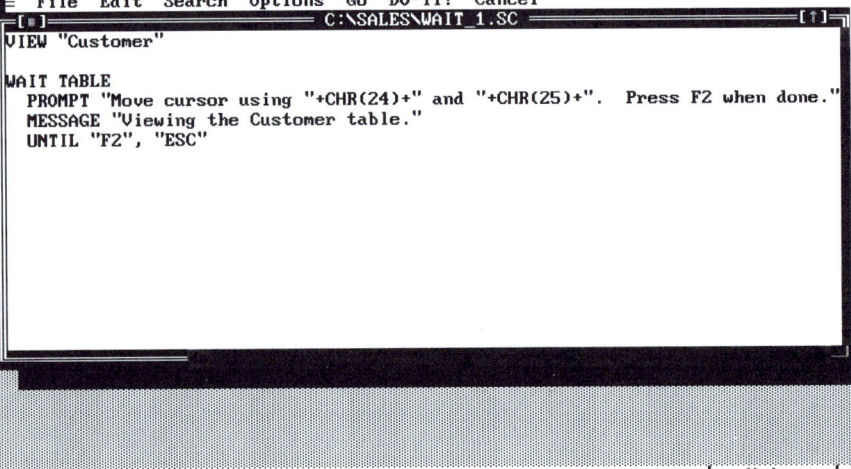

Indenting improves the readability of this command
Figure 5-8.

```
WAIT TABLE
    PROMPT "Press [F2] when done."
UNTIL "F2"
```

You should adopt the style that you feel most comfortable with.

Spacing Within a Line

Sometimes it is helpful to add space within a line. For instance, consider the commands

```
CurrentCust = [Customer -> Company Name]
CustCity    = [Customer -> City]
Zip         = [Customer -> Zip]
```

versus

```
CurrentCust=[Customer -> Company Name]
CustCity=[Customer -> City]
Zip=[Customer -> Zip]
```

The spaces in the first example serve no purpose other than to make the assignment statements easier to read. In general, if the use of spaces within a line makes your script more readable, use them.

There is one situation where you cannot add spaces within a line. This is when the space would break up a keyword or variable name. Take, for example, the PAL special key command DO_IT!. The following is an incorrect use of space:

```
DO _IT!
```

Paradox cannot recognize this as the PAL command DO_IT!. Instead, Paradox would interpret DO to be a variable name, which would result in a syntax error if a variable was not expected. The _IT! would definitely result in a syntax error since no variable can begin with an underscore.

Blank Lines in Scripts

Since Paradox ignores blanks, blank lines are perfectly acceptable in your scripts. Blank lines are particularly desirable when placed between conceptually separate parts of your script. This use will make your scripts easier to read and modify.

Using Comments in Your Scripts

A *comment* is text in your script that Paradox ignores when it plays your script. Comments begin with a semicolon (;). When Paradox sees the semicolon, it knows that anything from the right of the semicolon to the end of the line is part of a comment. To create a comment that is longer than one line, place a semicolon at the beginning of each line of your comment. The use of comments is shown in Figure 5-9.

The following exercise demonstrates how Paradox treats comments. It makes use of the PAL command BEEP, which produces a short beeping sound.

1. Press [Alt]-[F10] (PAL menu).
2. Select MiniScript.
3. Type **BEEP SLEEP 1000 BEEP** and press [Enter].

   Paradox should beep twice. (The SLEEP 1000 command serves to separate the beeps by one second; otherwise they may run together and be difficult to distinguish.)
4. Press [Alt]-[F10] again.

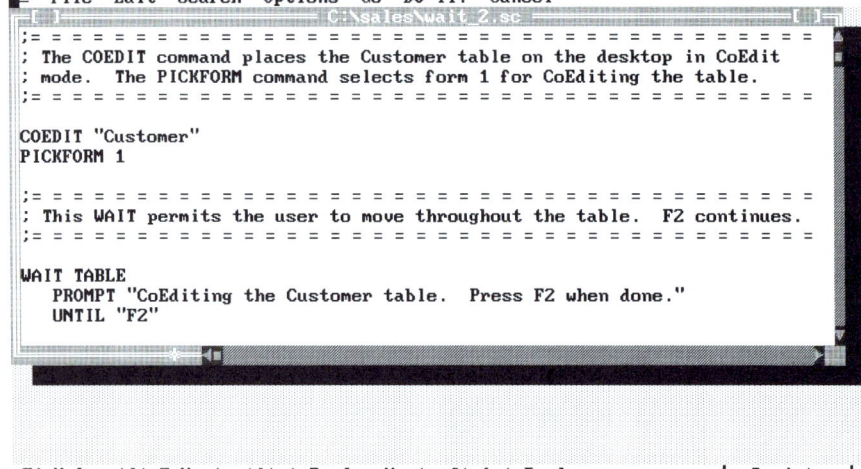

Script with multiline comments
Figure 5-9.

5. Select MiniScript.
6. This time type **BEEP ; SLEEP 1000 BEEP** and press Enter.

   Notice that this time, Paradox only beeps once. When Paradox played the miniscript, the first BEEP command instructed Paradox to produce a beep. The next command, ; (the semicolon), instructed Paradox to ignore the remaining text.

You can use comments for several useful functions in your scripts:

Documenting your script
Adding a header in your script
Debugging errors in logic

Documentation

You can document a script by adding comments that describe what the script does. Although these descriptions do not have to be eloquent, they should be informative. Comments are invaluable if you later need to change your script. They are even more important if someone else must read or modify your script.

Commands

Even when the documentation is only for yourself, its importance cannot be overemphasized. While you are writing your script, you may come up with a clever way of performing some task. Unless you document the script, you may find yourself in the uncomfortable position of trying to change the script later, but being unable to remember how it works. Although this may sound unlikely to you, it has already happened to almost everyone who has failed to document a script.

The segment of script shown in Figure 5-10 contains a complicated assignment statement. Without the documentation, you may have to spend a long time trying to figure out what the expression produced. With the documentation, however, you can more easily understand the task it performs.

Script Headers

Another common use of comments is to add a header to your script. A *header* typically contains your name, the date you created the script, the date or dates you modified it, and a general description of what it does. Headers are particularly important when other people will be working with the script. However, even when you are the only one to use it, a header can serve as a valuable reminder. An example of a script header is shown in Figure 5-11.

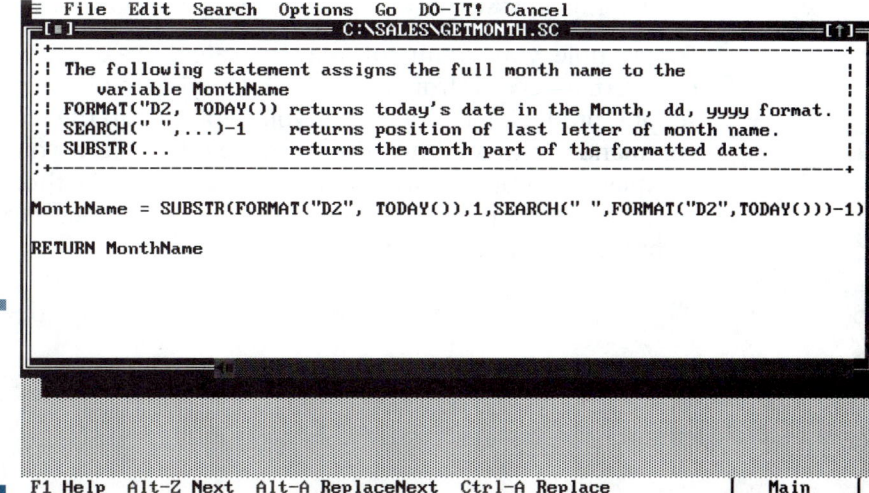

Comments describe this complicated assignment
Figure 5-10.

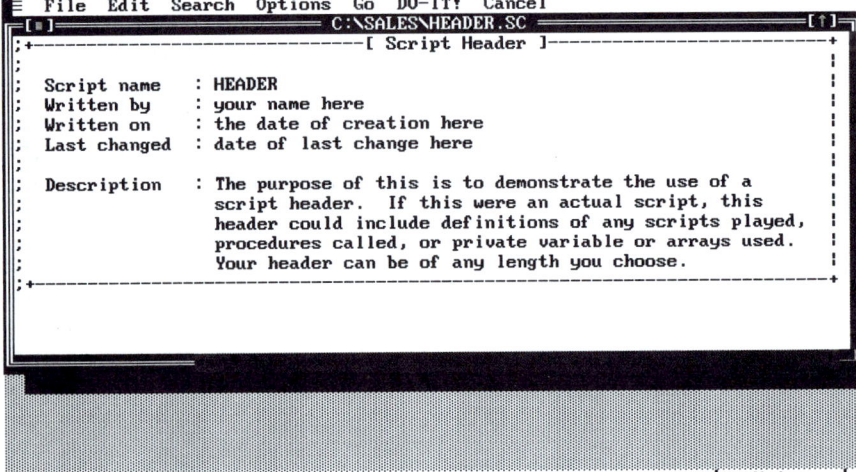

Example of a script header
Figure 5-11.

A Debugging Tool

Comments in scripts can serve as a valuable aid in debugging errors in logic in your scripts. This is because your comments define what you think your script should do. Unfortunately, this is not always the same as what the script actually does. By comparing your comments to the behavior of your script, you can more easily locate and solve problems.

For example, your comments may indicate that a query will extract only certain records from a table. While trying to discover why the script is producing faulty results, you step through the script one command at a time. When the script plays the query, you notice that the query did not produce the results you wanted. Without the comments in your script as a reminder, you might not recall which records the query was supposed to produce.

Quick Review

- Paradox is controlled by keypress interactions and PAL commands.

- Keypress interactions are created using curly braces to enclose menu selections and responses to prompts. Quoted strings are used to define typed entries.

- PAL commands are reserved keywords. There are three types of commands: abbreviated menu commands, special key commands, and programming commands.

- Abbreviated menu commands make selections from Paradox menus. They are more flexible and easier to interpret than braced menu selections.

- Special key commands are reserved words that mimic the effects of function keys and key combinations.

- Programming commands provide features that are unavailable in interactive Paradox. These can be divided into the following seven categories:

    Control structures
    Input/output commands
    Multiuser commands
    Procedure and procedure library commands
    System control commands
    Desktop manipulation commands
    Variable and array manipulation commands

- You have flexibility in constructing PAL commands. However, with the exception of control structures, one PAL command must be completed before the next one begins.

- Blank spaces are acceptable and even desirable in scripts.

- The generous use of comments makes your scripts easy to understand and modify.

CHAPTER

6 SYSTEM CONTROL COMMANDS

This chapter introduces you to six PAL commands you will use often. Although none of these commands is required by Paradox, you will likely find that the features of one or more of them greatly improve your scripts. Of particular benefit are the RETURN and QUIT commands, which display a message on the screen when your script is finished playing.

Two other commands, DEBUG and SETKEY, are less common in typical scripts, but nonetheless have a very important place in your PAL repertoire. The DEBUG command permits you to invoke the Debugger from within a script. This command is useful when you are writing a script. SETKEY is the command you use to add new features to your interactive Paradox session.

The remaining two commands discussed here, PLAY and SLEEP, are also useful. However, as you become a more sophisticated PAL user, you will learn alternative ways to achieve the effects of these commands.

The RETURN Command

Normally, when the last command in a script is played, control returns to Paradox. The RETURN command has the same effect, even if RETURN is not the last command in a script. When Paradox encounters a RETURN in a script, the script immediately stops playing and control returns to Paradox.

The syntax of the RETURN command is

```
RETURN [Expression]
```

One of the really useful features of the RETURN command is that you can follow it with an optional expression. When you do so, the value of the expression is displayed at the lower right corner of your screen once the PAL canvas is dropped. This value is displayed until you press any key. Using this feature, the RETURN command can present an informative message, indicating that the script is finished playing. In certain situations, this message may be the only indication that the script is finished playing, since the full-screen PAL canvas hides the actual operation of the script.

RETURN Exercise

To try out the RETURN command, follow these steps:

1. Press [Alt]-[F10] (PAL menu) and select MiniScript.
2. Type **RETURN "This is a return message"** and press [Enter].

Paradox displays the message in the lower right corner of your screen, as shown in Figure 6-1.

System Control Commands

Effect of the RETURN command
Figure 6-1.

The SLEEP Command

The SLEEP command is used to suspend Paradox for a specified period of time, defined in milliseconds. When the time expires, play of the script continues normally. For example, the command

```
SLEEP 1000
```

causes Paradox to pause for 1000 milliseconds, or exactly 1 second. The command

```
SLEEP 250
```

on the other hand, causes Paradox to pause for 250 milliseconds, which is equal to one-quarter of a second.

The syntax of the SLEEP command is

```
SLEEP [Milliseconds]
```

The SLEEP command is particularly useful when events created within your script would otherwise pass too quickly. You may recall the miniscript in Chapter 5, which was used to make Paradox beep twice. Between the two beeps, the SLEEP 1000 statement was used. Without it, the two beeps would be nearly indistinguishable from a longer single beep. Using the SLEEP command, however, a short pause was placed between the two beeps, making them distinct.

The DEBUG Command

The DEBUG command invokes the PAL Debugger from within a script. The PAL Debugger, which is described in detail in Chapter 2, is a useful tool for debugging and inspecting scripts. Its single most important feature is that it allows you to suspend script play momentarily while you inspect the Paradox desktop, objects, and variable values. The syntax is

    DEBUG

The DEBUG command can be placed anywhere in a PAL script. You may want to make it the first command in a script you are debugging, or place it in the middle of your script, somewhere close to where you suspect the problem with your script lies.

When Paradox encounters the DEBUG command, it immediately invokes the Debugger, displaying the current line of the script at the bottom of your screen, and showing an arrow pointing to the current command. You can then control the Debugger by pressing a control key combination or by pressing [Alt]-[F10] and making a selection from the Debugger menu. The most common commands you would perform here would be [Ctrl]-[S] (Step) or [Ctrl]-[T] (Trace) to continue through the script one command at a time.

DEBUG Exercise

Perform this exercise from the Main menu. Note that this exercise also uses the SLEEP and RETURN commands described in the preceding sections.

1. Select Scripts/Editor/New.
2. Type **Twobeeps** and press [Enter].
3. Enter the following text into the Editor window:

    DEBUG
    BEEP

System Control Commands

```
SLEEP 1000
BEEP
RETURN "Twobeeps has been played."
```

4. Play this script by selecting Go from the Editor menu.

   Paradox will begin to play the script. However, the first command, DEBUG, will invoke the PAL Debugger. At this point, your screen should look like Figure 6-2. (In Paradox 3.5 the arrow will point to the command following the DEBUG command instead.)

5. Press Ctrl-S five times (four times in Paradox 3.5) to play each of the four remaining commands.

   The first time you press Ctrl-S, Paradox advances to the BEEP command. The second and third times result in a beep followed by a one-second pause. When you press Ctrl-S the last time, the script terminates and the message "Twobeeps has been played" is displayed.

The PLAY Command

PLAY is a programming command that permits you to play one script from inside another. When PLAY is used, it must be followed by an

The DEBUG command in a script invokes the Debugger
Figure 6-2.

alphanumeric expression that evaluates to the name of a script. For example, if you use the command

```
PLAY "Getdate"
```

in a script, Paradox plays the script named Getdate. Since no directory was included in the script name, the Getdate script must reside in the current directory.

The syntax of the PLAY command is

```
PLAY ScriptName
```

The PLAY command is particularly useful when you are writing database applications in PAL. In these instances, your application will often consist of a series of scripts, each one responsible for a particular feature of the application. To access these different features, one script plays another.

You can use PLAY to play scripts even when they are located in a directory other than the current one. To do so, you must also specify the directory where the script is located. There is a trick to doing this, however. You may remember from Chapter 4, that the backslash character is given special status by Paradox. Specifically, a backslash denotes that the character that follows it should be taken literally. This affects how you specify the directory name since the backslash appears in the DOS path. To be sure the backslash is read, you simply use two backslashes in a row. The first one tells Paradox to interpret the next character literally, as a backslash character. Therefore, to play a script named Getdate stored in the C:\PALTOOLS directory, use the following command:

```
PLAY "C:\\PALTOOLS\\Getdate"
```

PLAY Exercise

In this exercise you will create a script that plays the one you created in the preceding exercise. First, however, you need to remove the DEBUG statement from Twobeeps. Begin this exercise from the Main menu.

1. Select Scripts/Editor/Open.

System Control Commands

2. Type **Twobeeps** and press Enter.
3. Delete the DEBUG statement.

    Do this by moving your cursor to the word *DEBUG* and pressing Ctrl-Y. (In Paradox 3.5 you must move your cursor to the first character of the DEBUG line before pressing Ctrl-Y.)

4. Press F2 (Do-It!) to save this change to the Twobeeps script.

    You are now ready to create a new script that will play Twobeeps.

5. Select Scripts/Editor/New.
6. Type **Playit** and press Enter.
7. Enter the following script:

    ```
    PLAY "Twobeeps"
    RETURN "Playit has been played."
    ```

8. Press F2 (Do-It!) to save this script.

You should now play the script Playit by pressing Ctrl-G (GoKey). Remember that Go only plays the last script you edited using the Paradox Editor. Since Playit was the last script edited, you can instantly play it using Ctrl-G.

When you play Playit, Paradox will beep once, pause for one second, beep a second time, and then the message "Playit has been played." will appear on your screen, as in Figure 6-3. When you play Playit, the first command it encounters is PLAY "Twobeeps". At this point, control is passed to the script Twobeeps, which plays until the RETURN command is encountered. Then, control reverts to Playit, beginning with the statement that follows the PLAY command. This command, RETURN, prints the message to your screen and terminates the script.

Notice that you did not see the message "Twobeeps has been played.", even though the RETURN command in Twobeeps included this expression. This demonstrates an important feature of the RETURN command. When RETURN is encountered, it always terminates the current script. If an optional expression is provided, it is only displayed if the RETURN command returns control to Paradox. If control is returned to a calling script, the expression is not displayed. Instead, the expression is assigned to a system variable named Retval.

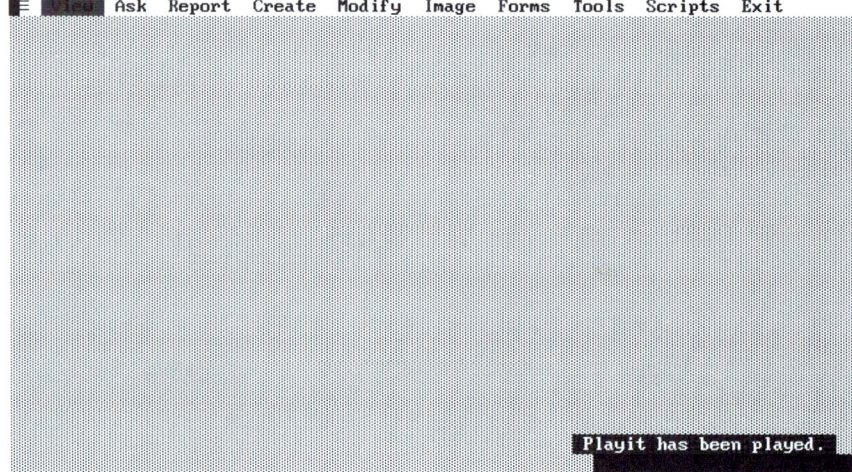

A RETURN message from the Playit script
Figure 6-3.

NOTE: The value of the expression that follows the RETURN command is always assigned to the system variable Retval, even when the RETURN also results in the expression being displayed on the desktop. This characteristic of the RETURN command is extremely valuable, since it provides your scripts with a mechanism to pass information between them. You will learn more about the system variable Retval in later chapters.

The QUIT Command

The PAL commands QUIT and RETURN are very similar. When Paradox encounters QUIT in a script, the script terminates and an optional expression is displayed on the screen. In contrast with the RETURN command, however, QUIT terminates all script play. That is, it always returns to interactive Paradox whether or not the script it appeared in was played by another script. Similarly, when the optional expression is used with the QUIT command, it is always displayed on the screen.

The syntax of the QUIT command is

System Control Commands

```
QUIT [Expression]
```

QUIT Exercise

In this exercise, you will modify the Twobeeps script, replacing the RETURN command with the QUIT command. You will then play the Playit script, which plays Twobeeps. Begin this exercise from the Main menu.

1. Select Scripts/Editor/Open.
2. Type **Twobeeps** and press Enter.
3. Move to the last line of Twobeeps and replace the RETURN keyword with QUIT. Do not change the expression that follows. When done, your screen should look like Figure 6-4.
4. Press F2 to save Twobeeps.

   You now want to play the script Playit.

5. Select Scripts/Play.
6. Type **Playit** and press Enter.

Paradox will play the script Playit, which will in turn play the script Twobeeps. While Twobeeps is playing, Paradox will beep once, pause

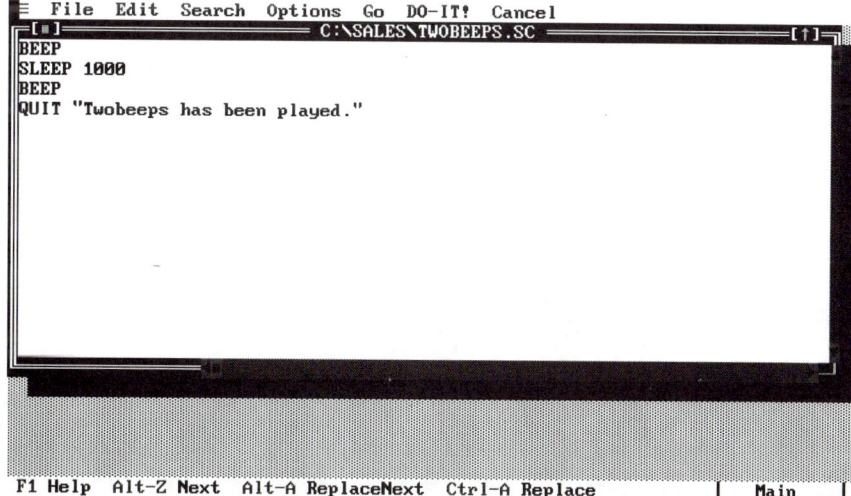

Twobeeps script
Figure 6-4.

for a second, and then beep again. When Paradox plays the QUIT command, all script play will terminate and the expression "Twobeeps has been played." will be displayed on your screen, as shown in Figure 6-5. You can tell that Paradox did not return to the Playit script because the expression "Playit has been played." was not displayed.

The SETKEY Command

Like the PLAY command, SETKEY is used to play a script. Its use, however, is very special. The SETKEY command permits you to assign one or more commands to any key, or key combination, on your keyboard. Commands played this way are called *key macros*.

Key macros permit you to define new features for Paradox. For instance, you can use one SETKEY command to assign the command RETURN TIME( ) to the key combination [Alt]-[T]. For the remainder of your Paradox session, pressing [Alt]-[T] will display the current time, the value returned by the TIME( ) function. Likewise, if you write a script that allows you to copy entire records in a table, you can assign this script to another key, [Ctrl]-[C] for example, by using the PLAY command in the key macro.

The syntax of the SETKEY command is

```
SETKEY { keyname | ASCII code} [one or more commands]
```

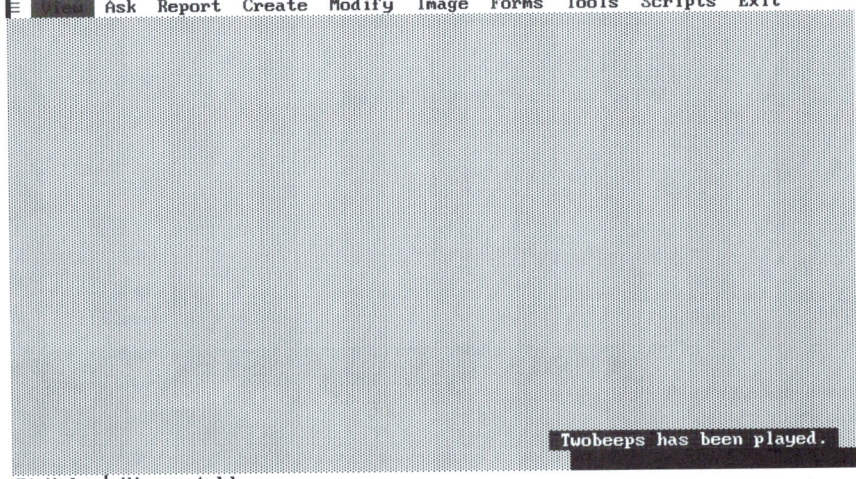

Message displayed with the QUIT command
Figure 6-5.

System Control Commands

Once you have used the SETKEY command during a Paradox session, any press of the key or key combination will instantly play the assigned commands. This assignment will last for the remainder of your Paradox session or until you issue a new SETKEY command for that key or key combination. If you omit the optional commands from the SETKEY statement, you remove the key macro from the key, returning it to its original function.

NOTE: The SETKEY definition is not honored during script play. For example, if you reassign the [F2] key with a SETKEY command (which is a very bad idea, by the way), including the command DO_IT! or KEYPRESS "F2" in your script will result in the true [F2] function, not the one assigned using SETKEY. Once script play ends, the SETKEY definitions are again honored.

When you use the SETKEY command, it must be followed by either a key name or an ASCII code. The key name or ASCII code defines the key or key combination to which you are assigning the commands. Examples of key names are "A," "3," "F5," and "F25." These correspond to the keys [A], [3], [F5], and [Ctrl]-[F5]. Instead of using the key name, you can use the corresponding extended ASCII code. The ASCII codes 65, 51, -63, and -98 also correspond to [A], [3], [F5], and [Ctrl]-[F5]. Furthermore, "Example" and "Fieldview" also can be used for [F5] and [Ctrl]-[F5], respectively.

Not all keys have key names, but they do all have ASCII codes. Appendix A contains a list of all ASCII codes and their corresponding key name(s), where available.

SETKEY Exercise

Begin this exercise from the Main menu.

1. Press [Alt]-[F10] to display the PAL menu.
2. Select MiniScript.
3. Type **SETKEY -20 RETURN TIME( )** and press [Enter].

Paradox plays the miniscript, which assigns the command RETURN TIME( ) to the `Alt`-`T` key combination on your keyboard. (`Alt`-`T` is represented by the extended ASCII code -20. There is no key name for this key combination.) When you press `Alt`-`T`, this short script is played. Press `Alt`-`T` now to see the results.

Although you can use more than one command following the key code, you are limited to a maximum of 175 characters. (Note that this maximum is different than the line length in the Paradox Editor, which permits 255 characters in Paradox 4 and 132 in version 3.5.) If you want to assign a longer segment of script to a key or key combination, you can use the PLAY command in your SETKEY statement. For instance, the command

```
SETKEY 16 PLAY "Playit"
```

will play the script Playit when you press `Ctrl`-`P`. Try this yourself using a miniscript, as in the preceding exercise. Now when you press `Ctrl`-`P`, you should hear two beeps.

NOTE: The SETKEY command is one of the most important commands for improving your productivity in Paradox. With a little PAL programming, you can create scripts that customize and expand your Paradox environment substantially. In fact, most PAL users include one or more SETKEY statements in their INIT script. Since the INIT script is played each time you start Paradox, these key macro definitions are initialized at the outset of each Paradox session.

System Control Commands

Quick Review

- The RETURN command terminates the current script. RETURN can include an optional expression, which will be displayed on your screen if control is being returned to Paradox.

- The SLEEP command causes Paradox to pause for a specified period of time.

- DEBUG is used to invoke the PAL Debugger from within a script. You will use this feature frequently to help you discover errors in your scripts.

- The PLAY command permits you to play a script from within a script.

- QUIT is used to immediately terminate all script play and return to interactive Paradox. When you include an optional expression, it will be displayed on your screen once the script has terminated.

- SETKEY is used to assign one or more commands to a key or key combination. Use the SETKEY command to add new features to your normal Paradox session.

CHAPTER

7
CONTROL STRUCTURES

In this chapter you will learn to use the PAL commands that control the playing of commands within your scripts. In essence, these commands add intelligence to your scripts. They are necessary if your scripts need to adapt to varying conditions. These commands are referred to as control structures. *Except in the simplest cases, one or more of these commands will be involved in every script you write.*

Control structures never appear by themselves in your

scripts. Rather, they are used to direct other commands in order to achieve the desired effects. The examples in this chapter have been kept relatively simple so that you can see how control structures work with commands you are already familiar with. Later chapters will demonstrate each of these commands used in more realistic ways.

Control Within Scripts

One of the advantages of writing a script, as opposed to using a recorded one, is that a script you write can control itself. That is, it can determine characteristics of the Paradox environment and alter which commands it plays, if necessary. For example, before attempting to print a report for a table, your script can first verify that the table exists. If the table does not exist, the script will not try to report it. Without this flexibility, the script would terminate with a script error.

Of course, this control does not appear in your script automatically. You must build it in when you write your script, by using a control structure. When you add the control structure to your script, you also define the feature or features of the Paradox environment the script should test for, as well as what actions should be taken under the various conditions.

There are two types of control structures. The first type consists of those that evaluate a logical expression (called a *condition*) and then play one or more PAL commands, depending on the result. These are called *branching commands*. Like the fork in a road, branching commands permit a script to go in one of several different directions. The second type is used to play one or more PAL commands repeatedly. The number of times the commands are played depends on conditions you specify when you write the script. This type of command is called a *looping command,* with the "loop" being the repetition controlled by these commands.

Branching Control Structures

Branching control structures are used to optionally play one or more PAL commands. They are played only if certain conditions are met. When you write your script, you define the conditions under which the commands will be played.

Control Structures

Two PAL commands provide you with branching: IF and SWITCH. Which one you choose depends on your needs. Specifically, if you need simple branching—playing one of two sets of commands based on a single condition—the IF command will suffice. However, when the number of conditions your script must consider is greater than two, the SWITCH control structure is the most useful.

Using the IF Command

The syntax of the IF statement is as follows:

```
IF Condition
   THEN one or more PAL commands
  [ELSE one or more PAL commands]
ENDIF
```

The IF statement is used to evaluate Condition, which must be a logical expression. If the condition evaluates to True, then any PAL commands that follow the keyword THEN are played. Once all the commands following the THEN keyword are played, script play resumes with the first command that follows the ENDIF keyword. If the condition evaluates to False, and the ELSE keyword is not used, the commands following the THEN statement are skipped and the script immediately resumes with the first command that follows the ENDIF keyword.

When the optional keyword ELSE is included in the IF statement, the one or more commands that follow the ELSE keyword are played only if the condition evaluates to False. Once these commands have been played, the script continues with the first command following ENDIF. An example of the IF command is shown in Figure 7-1.

The IF command is particularly important whenever your script includes statements that will fail under certain circumstances. By using the IF command and the appropriate logical expression, you can determine whether your script will be successful before attempting to perform the task. If the conditions are such that the commands will be successful, the IF statement will direct Paradox to play the commands. Otherwise, the IF statement can steer Paradox around the commands that cannot work.

Consider the following example. During the play of your script, a table called Holddata may have been created to temporarily hold the results

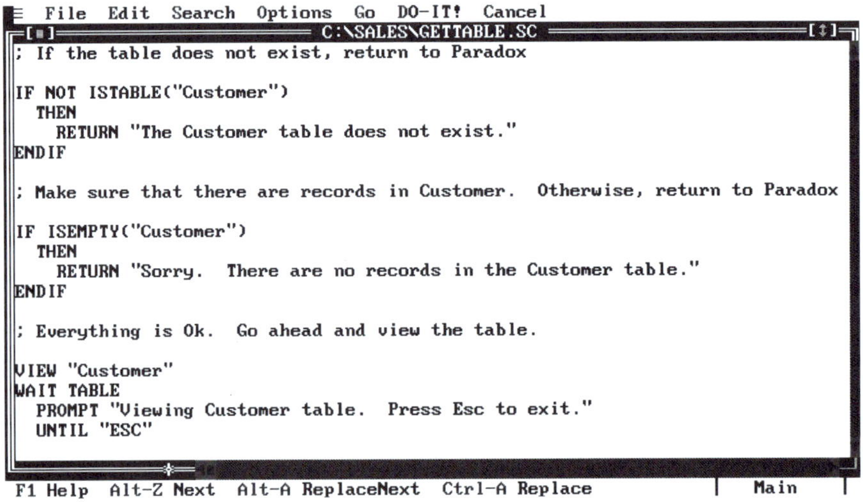

```
  File  Edit  Search  Options  Go  DO-IT!  Cancel
[■]═══════════════════ C:\SALES\GETTABLE.SC ═══════════════════[↕]
; If the table does not exist, return to Paradox

IF NOT ISTABLE("Customer")
  THEN
    RETURN "The Customer table does not exist."
ENDIF

; Make sure that there are records in Customer.  Otherwise, return to Paradox

IF ISEMPTY("Customer")
  THEN
    RETURN "Sorry.  There are no records in the Customer table."
ENDIF

; Everything is Ok.  Go ahead and view the table.

VIEW "Customer"
WAIT TABLE
  PROMPT "Viewing Customer table.  Press Esc to exit."
  UNTIL "ESC"

F1 Help  Alt-Z Next  Alt-A ReplaceNext  Ctrl-A Replace            Main
```

IF command in a script
Figure 7-1.

of a query. At the end of the script, you want your script to delete this table, if it exists. However, the Holddata table is not necessarily created every time you run the script. This situation could create a problem because the PAL command used to delete a table, DELETE, will cause a run-time error if you attempt to delete a table that does not exist.

In this situation you can use the IF statement and the PAL function ISTABLE( ). ISTABLE( ) lets you ask Paradox whether a particular table exists. If the table exists, ISTABLE( ) returns the value True; otherwise it returns the value False. Consider the following command:

```
IF ISTABLE("Holddata")
  THEN
     DELETE "Holddata"
ENDIF
```

When this segment of script is run, the command DELETE "Holddata" will be played only if the table Holddata exists. Through the IF command, your script acts intelligently, only performing the task when it will be successful.

IF Exercise

In this exercise you will write a script that determines what day of the week it is, and displays one of two messages based on this information. This exercise makes use of two PAL functions. The first is the TODAY( ) function, which returns the current date, based on your computer's internal clock. The second is the DOW( ) function, which returns the three-letter abbreviation of the day that a specified date falls on. The DOW( ) function requires one argument, a date. In order to evaluate what day of the week it is, you will use the TODAY( ) function as the argument of the DOW( ) function. Begin this exercise from the Main mode.

1. Select Scripts/Editor/New.
2. Type **Whatday** and press Enter.
3. In the Editor window, enter the following commands:

```
IF DOW(TODAY()) = "Fri"
  THEN
    RETURN "TGIF!"
  ELSE
    RETURN "Today is "+DOW(TODAY())
ENDIF
```

Now, play this script by selecting Go from the Editor menu. When the script plays, the expression DOW(TODAY()) is compared with the value "Fri". This comparison results in a logical value of True if today is Friday, and False if today is any other day. If the condition evaluates to True, the alphanumeric expression "TGIF!" is displayed on your screen. If the condition evaluates to False, an alternative message displays the day.

Using the SWITCH Command

The SWITCH statement is similar to the IF statement. SWITCH, however, is a more flexible command. While the IF command evaluates only one condition, the SWITCH command can evaluate many.

The syntax of SWITCH is

```
SWITCH
  [CASE Condition: one or more PAL commands]
```

```
    . . .
    [CASE Condition: one or more PAL commands]
    [OTHERWISE: one or more PAL commands]
ENDSWITCH
```

SWITCH and ENDSWITCH are the only required keywords in the SWITCH command. However, in all cases you will use at least one, and nearly always more than one, CASE keyword. After each CASE keyword is a condition and one or more commands, which are separated from the condition by a colon.

When Paradox encounters a SWITCH statement, it begins evaluating the expressions following each CASE keyword in the order they appear. If an expression is found that evaluates to True, the commands associated with that CASE statement are played. Once a True expression has been found, and its associated commands played, script play resumes with the first command following the ENDSWITCH keyword. In other words, commands associated with only one CASE keyword are played.

If none of the expressions evaluates to True, and the optional OTHERWISE keyword is not used, then script play continues with the first command following the ENDSWITCH keyword. If the OTHERWISE keyword is used, the commands associated with it will only be played if none of the CASE expressions evaluates to True. An example of a use of SWITCH is shown in Figure 7-2.

A SWITCH command is almost always preferable to two or more IF statements. Consider the following examples:

Example 1

```
IF SYSMODE()="Script"
   THEN
      MESSAGE "You are in the Script Editor."
ENDIF
IF SYSMODE()="Edit"
   THEN
      MESSAGE "You are in Edit mode."
ENDIF
IF SYSMODE()="CoEdit"
   THEN
```

Control Structures

```
   File  Edit  Search  Options  Go  DO-IT!  Cancel
┌─[■]────────────────── C:\SALES\GETMENU.SC ──────────────────[↕]─┐
│SHOWMENU                                                          │
│  "Add"    :"Add a new record to the Customer table.",            │
│  "View"   :"View the Customer table.",                           │
│  "Report" :"Print the Customer report.",                         │
│  "Exit"   :"Exit to Paradox."                                    │
│  TO Choice                                                       │
│                                                                  │
│SWITCH                                                            │
│  CASE Choice = "Add":                                            │
│    PLAY "AddRecs"                                                │
│                                                                  │
│  CASE Choice = "View":                                           │
│    PLAY "ViewRecs"                                               │
│                                                                  │
│  CASE Choice = "Report":                                         │
│    PLAY "Reportit"                                               │
│                                                                  │
│  OTHERWISE:                                                      │
│    RETURN                                                        │
│                                                                  │
│ENDSWITCH                                                         │
└──────────────────────────────────────────────────────────────────┘
 F1 Help  Alt-Z Next  Alt-A ReplaceNext  Ctrl-A Replace    Main
```

Example of SWITCH in a script
Figure 7-2.

```
         MESSAGE "You are in CoEdit mode."
ENDIF
```

Example 2

```
SWITCH
   CASE SYSMODE()="Script":
      MESSAGE "You are in the Script Editor."
   CASE SYSMODE()="Edit":
      MESSAGE "You are in Edit mode."
   CASE SYSMODE()="CoEdit":
      MESSAGE "You are in CoEdit mode."
ENDSWITCH
```

In Example 1, even if SYSMODE returns "Script", Paradox must still process the next two IF statements. However, in Example 2, only the first CASE statement would be evaluated if SYSMODE returns "Script". The next two CASE statements would be skipped. Using SWITCH in these situations results in shorter, more readable, and faster playing scripts.

Looping Commands

There are four looping commands in PAL: FOR, FOREACH, WHILE, and SCAN. Unlike branching commands, that play one of several possible series of commands, looping commands play a single series. Also, in most cases, the looping command plays this series more than once. How many times the series is actually played depends on how the looping command is used.

Repetition is one of the tasks that computers perform very well. Looping provides the control for this repetition. This is an important capability because, although you may know that your script must perform a certain task more than once, you may not know in advance exactly how many times the task must be performed. For example, suppose you have a short script that you want to play once for each record in a table. Using a looping command, you can write the script once, and let the looping command take control of playing it once per record.

Using the FOR Command

The FOR command is used to repeat a series of instructions a predefined number of times. For example, if you wanted to repeat a particular sequence five times, FOR would be the appropriate command.

The syntax of the FOR command is

```
FOR Value
   [FROM BeginningValue]
   [TO EndingValue]
   [STEP StepValue]
   [one or more commands]
ENDFOR
```

The FOR command has two required keywords, FOR and ENDFOR, and one required expression. This expression may either be numeric or of the type date. The most common uses of the FOR command also include two optional keywords, FROM and TO. In fact, the use of these keywords is so common that you will almost never see a FOR command without them. The FROM keyword defines the beginning value of the variable, and TO defines its ending value. For example, in this statement,

Control Structures

```
FOR Counter FROM 1 TO 10
   BEEP
ENDFOR
```

the beginning value of the variable Counter is 1. Each time the FOR command loops, the variable Counter is increased by 1. Therefore, the first time BEEP is played, Counter is equal to 1, the second time it is equal to 2, and so forth.

FOR will continue to loop as long as the variable, in this case Counter, is not larger than the value following TO (10 in this example). Thus, this FOR loop will repeat ten times. After looping ten times, the variable Counter will increase to 11, which is larger than the 10 defined by the TO variable. At this point, Paradox will no longer process the commands within the FOR-ENDFOR statement, and will continue with the first command following ENDFOR.

By default, the variable will increment by 1 each time the FOR command loops. However, you can use the optional keyword STEP to use an increment different from 1. For example,

```
FOR Pitch
   FROM 100
   TO 1000
   STEP 100
      SOUND Pitch 20
ENDFOR
```

will also repeat only ten times. In this example script, the Paradox 4 command SOUND is combined with the FOR loop to create a special noise. SOUND requires two expressions, the first one must be a number that specifies a pitch (in cycles per second) and the second specifies a duration (in milliseconds). During the first loop, the variable, Pitch, is equal to 100. As a result, the command SOUND produces a 100-cycles-per-second tone that lasts for 20 milliseconds on the first loop. During the second loop Pitch is equal to 200, and SOUND produces a higher pitched tone. Once the tenth loop has been completed, Pitch is equal to 1100 (1000 + 100). Once Pitch has incremented to more than 1000, Paradox will terminate the loop.

The FOR command is particularly useful when you need to refer to a sequence of numbers, one at a time, since it increments the value of the variable automatically. Consider the following statement:

```
ARRAY HoldNumbers[20]
FOR Pointer FROM 1 TO 20
  HoldNumbers[Pointer] = 0
ENDFOR
```

The first statement, ARRAY, is used to define the array HoldNumbers. The FOR statement systematically refers to each element of this array, and places a 0 in that element. The first time through, the variable Pointer has the value of 1. Therefore, the assignment statement HoldNumbers[Pointer] refers to the first element of HoldNumbers. On the second loop, the second element of HoldNumbers is assigned the value 0. When the FOR loop is completed, all elements of the array have been assigned the value 0. Thus the preceding example has the same effect as the following 20 statements:

```
HoldNumbers[1]=0
HoldNumbers[2]=0
HoldNumbers[3]=0
HoldNumbers[4]=0
HoldNumbers[5]=0
HoldNumbers[6]=0
HoldNumbers[7]=0
HoldNumbers[8]=0
HoldNumbers[9]=0
HoldNumbers[10]=0
HoldNumbers[11]=0
HoldNumbers[12]=0
HoldNumbers[13]=0
HoldNumbers[14]=0
HoldNumbers[15]=0
HoldNumbers[16]=0
HoldNumbers[17]=0
HoldNumbers[18]=0
HoldNumbers[19]=0
HoldNumbers[20]=0
```

FOR Exercise

The purpose of this exercise is to demonstrate that the variable used in the FOR command increments automatically.

Control Structures

1. From the Main menu, select Scripts/Editor/New.
2. Type the name **Printnum** and press [Enter].
3. Enter the following commands into the Editor window:

   ```
   CLEAR
   FOR Counter
       FROM 1 TO 20
       ? Counter
   ENDFOR
   SLEEP 5000
   RETURN Counter
   ```

   In this script, the FOR command will loop 20 times, each time increasing the variable Counter by 1. The ? is used to print a value on the PAL canvas. Because the variable Counter follows the ?, the value of Counter will be printed.

   The SLEEP 5000 command is added so that the PAL canvas will continue to be displayed for five seconds after the last loop of the FOR command. This enables you to see the effects of this script. Finally, the RETURN statement will display the value of Counter. This will demonstrate that Counter has incremented to one more than the TO value, in this case, 21.

4. Save this script by pressing [F2] (Do-It!).
5. Play the script by pressing [Ctrl]-[G] (Go).

   Once you play the script, your screen should look like Figure 7-3 for five seconds. The value of Counter was printed 20 times, each time one greater than the previous value.

Using the FOREACH Command

FOREACH is a looping command used exclusively for processing dynamic arrays. It permits you to execute one or more PAL commands for each element in a dynamic array. Furthermore, FOREACH provides you with the only means available for accessing the indexes associated with dynamic array elements.

FOREACH has the following syntax:

```
FOREACH Element IN DynamicArrayName
 one or more PAL commands
ENDFOREACH
```

When Paradox encounters the FOREACH command, it assigns the value of the first index of the dynamic array to the variable listed after the FOREACH command. (You might recall that this first element is associated with the last element created for the dynamic array.) When Paradox reaches the ENDFOREACH command, it evaluates whether there are still elements remaining in the dynamic array. If there are, Paradox assigns the value of the next index to the variable and processes the PAL commands again. Once Paradox loops once for each element in the dynamic array, the loop is exited, and Paradox continues processing the script beginning with the first command that follows the ENDFOREACH keyword.

NOTE: Dynamic arrays and the FOREACH command are not available in Paradox 3.5.

PAL canvas after playing the script Printnum
Figure 7-3.

FOREACH Exercise

In this exercise you will use the FOREACH command to display the indices and contents of a dynamic array created using the WINDOW GETATTRIBUTES command. Begin this exercise from the Main menu.

1. Select Scripts/Editor/New.
2. Type **Sysatts** and press Enter.
3. In the Paradox Editor window, enter the following commands:

```
SYSINFO TO SystemArray
FOREACH Element IN SystemArray
   ? Element, "   ",SystemArray[Element]
ENDFOREACH
MESSAGE "Press any key to continue"
a = GETCHAR()
```

4. Play the script by selecting Go from the Editor menu.

The first command in this script is SYSINFO, which creates a dynamic array that holds information about your current system. The second command, FOREACH, initiates a loop that will process each element in the array, one at a time. The ? command is used within the FOREACH loop to print information to the screen. In this case, three expressions are printed. The first one is the value of the variable Element, which corresponds to an index of the dynamic array, SystemArray. The second value is an alphanumeric constant, which consists merely of several blank spaces. This constant is used to visually separate the first and third expressions. The third expression is the contents of the dynamic array. Notice that the variable, Element, the index, is used to reference the value in the array, SystemArray.

Following the ENDFOREACH command are two more statements. The first one, MESSAGE, displays the expression "Press any key to continue" on the screen. The second command, a=GETCHAR(), waits for you to press any key before ending the script. You can use this same technique with any dynamic array to display its contents.

Using the WHILE Command

The WHILE loop is like a combination of the FOR loop and the IF statement. It is like FOR in that it repeats a series of one or more PAL commands. It is like IF because it is controlled by a logical expression, or condition.

The syntax of the WHILE command is

```
WHILE Condition
   one or more PAL commands
ENDWHILE
```

The WHILE command has no optional keywords or expressions, and each WHILE command must end with the keyword ENDWHILE. When Paradox processes a WHILE, it evaluates the condition. If the condition evaluates to True, the commands between the WHILE and ENDWHILE keywords are played. When the ENDWHILE command is reached, Paradox loops back to the WHILE command and again evaluates the expression. When the condition evaluates to False, Paradox continues with the first command that follows the ENDWHILE keyword.

Consider the following statement:

```
WHILE NIMAGES() > 0
   CLEARIMAGE
ENDWHILE
```

The condition in this statement is NIMAGES( )>0. NIMAGES( ) is a PAL function that returns a number indicating how many images (tables, forms, or queries) are on the desktop. Used this way, with the WHILE command, as long as there is at least one image on the desktop, NIMAGES( )>0 will evaluate to True, resulting in the CLEARIMAGE key being pressed. Once the last image has been removed from the desktop by the CLEARIMAGE key, the expression NIMAGES( )>0 will evaluate to False, and Paradox will skip to the first statement after ENDWHILE. If there are no images on the desktop to begin with, the expression will evaluate to False the first time, and Paradox will never play the CLEARIMAGE command.

The WHILE command is one of the most useful in PAL. It is especially useful in receiving input from a user. In later chapters, you will see

Control Structures

many examples in which the WHILE command provides the essential control over the flow of scripts.

The SCAN Command

The SCAN statement is a loop specifically designed for working with tables. Therefore, a table must be on the desktop before the SCAN command can be used. The syntax of the SCAN command is

```
SCAN
   [FOR Condition]
   one or more PAL commands
ENDSCAN
```

When Paradox first plays the SCAN command, it moves the cursor to the first record in the table. Paradox then plays each of the commands within the SCAN-ENDSCAN loop. When the ENDSCAN keyword is encountered, Paradox moves down one record in the table and plays the commands again. Paradox will continue to play the commands between SCAN and ENDSCAN until every record in the table has been processed.

The SCAN command can optionally use the FOR keyword and a condition. When the FOR command is used, Paradox will only play the commands between SCAN and ENDSCAN when the condition evaluates to True. If you want to follow the SCAN keyword with a FOR loop, you must precede the FOR keyword with a colon to signify that it is not the optional keyword FOR.

Consider the following statement:

```
VIEW "Customer"
SCAN
   ? [Company Name]
ENDSCAN
SLEEP 2000
```

The first command, VIEW, places the Customer table on the desktop and makes it the current table. Next, SCAN moves through each of the records individually. For each record, the customer's company name is printed on the PAL canvas. When the last company name has been printed, Paradox continues to the next command, SLEEP 2000, which will cause the canvas to continue to be displayed for two seconds. Note that this is similar to the exercise for the FOR command, with the exception that data from a table, rather than from a variable, is displayed.

NOTE: A colon is not used in the SCAN command in Paradox 3.5.

Controlling Loops

There are two special PAL commands designed specifically for use within looping control structures: LOOP and QUITLOOP. When Paradox encounters one of these commands within a loop, it deviates from the normal processing of the loop.

When Paradox encounters the LOOP command, the remaining commands within the loop are ignored and Paradox immediately returns to the top of the loop. When LOOP is used with the FOR command, it causes the variable to be incremented by 1 (or by the value specified in a STEP statement). In a FOREACH loop, LOOP causes Paradox to immediately return to the FOREACH command and increment to the next dynamic array element. If LOOP is used with the SCAN statement, Paradox moves the cursor down to the next record in the table.

The effect of QUITLOOP is to immediately terminate a loop. When QUITLOOP is encountered, no further commands within the loop are played and Paradox skips to the command that immediately follows the loop.

In some cases, you may want not only to terminate a loop, but to immediately stop playing the script within which the loop exists. This is done using either RETURN or QUIT. These commands were discussed in the preceding chapter.

Nesting Control Structures

It is not uncommon to use one control structure within another. This is called *nesting*. For example, you may nest an IF statement within a

Control Structures

SCAN loop to evaluate one or more expressions. If the expression evaluates to True, you may then play the QUITLOOP command. For example:

```
VIEW "Customer"
SCAN
   IF [Company Name] = "Company C"
      THEN
         QUITLOOP
   ENDIF
ENDSCAN
```

There is an important rule to follow when nesting control structures. This is that when one control structure appears within another, the second control structure must begin and end within the one it is nested in. Consider the preceding example, in which the IF statement is nested within the SCAN statement. For this nesting to work, the ENDIF command must appear before the ENDSCAN command. If you fail to provide an ENDIF statement in your script, or you place the ENDIF command outside the ENDSCAN command, a syntax error will occur.

Failure to properly nest control structures is one of the most common sources of script errors. You can avoid this problem by making it a habit to indent every time you nest a control structure.

Quick Review

- Control structures are used to control the playing of other commands.
- There are two types of control structure commands: branching commands and looping commands.
- Branching commands are controlled by conditions. Conditions are expressions that evaluate to either True or False.
- IF and SWITCH are both PAL branching commands.
- Looping commands are used to repeat one or more commands.
- FOR, FOREACH, WHILE, and SCAN are PAL looping commands.
- When you use a looping command, you can use the PAL keyword LOOP to immediately return to the top of the loop. The QUITLOOP command, in contrast, immediately terminates a loop.
- Nesting refers to enclosing one control structure within another.
- A nested control structure must lie entirely within the control structure in which it is nested.

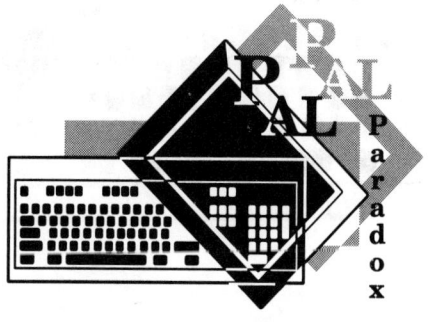

CHAPTER

8 DISPLAYING INFORMATION TO THE USER

It is often necessary for your script to interact with the person using it. For example, your script may need to ask the user for the name of a customer in your Customer table. In return, your script must be able to accept the name entered by the user. This example highlights the two sides of computer interaction, output and input. The output *in this case is what your script displays to the user. The* input *is what the user provides the script.*

Paradox provides you with a rich selection of features for controlling what is displayed and how users can enter information. This chapter, and the two that follow, introduce you to the commands and techniques you use to manage and control this important interaction. In this chapter, you will learn the distinction between the full-screen PAL canvas and canvas windows, and how to control these from within a script. In Chapter 9, you will learn the commands and techniques for receiving information from the user. In both of these chapters, the PAL commands that explicitly control these interactions are discussed without resorting to tables. Of course, most databases rely on a user's interaction with a table to control input and output. Table-related input/output topics are covered in Chapter 10.

The Desktop, Canvases, and Windows

In most cases, you want to have complete control over what a user sees when your script is running. Canvases provide you with this control. On the one hand, the canvas covers the desktop, hiding the workings of your script from the user. This offers you two significant advantages. First, Paradox runs very quickly when the canvas hides what's going on. If Paradox had to display all changes occurring on the desktop, processing would be slowed down, since writing to the screen is a time-consuming process. Secondly, many of the things your script does on the desktop may either be of no interest to the user, distracting, or even secret.

On the other hand, canvases permit you to control what is displayed to the user. For example, while your script is working with several tables on the desktop, you can be displaying a message on the canvas informing the user that the process is proceeding as expected. Instead of seeing a flurry of activity, such as the cursor moving rapidly between tables, the user sees the reassuring message.

In Paradox 3.5 there is only one canvas, and in the terminology of Paradox 3.5, this canvas covers the workspace. In Paradox 4, the full-screen canvas provides this same characteristic, covering the entire desktop. In Paradox 4, unlike 3.5, you can have more than one canvas. In addition to the full-screen canvas, there is one canvas for each open window. Like the full-screen canvas, these canvases permit you to optionally hide, display, or modify what appears in their respective

Displaying Information to the User

windows. This provides you with an enormous amount of control over what the user sees when your script is running.

All canvases, however, are not created equal. That is, they exist in layers. When two or more canvases overlap, the ones at the higher layer obscure those in lower layers. Each canvas occurs in one of three layers. From lowest to highest, these layers are called the desktop layer, the echo layer, and the application layer. Understanding the relationship between the layers, and how canvases interact at each layer, is essential to mastering what the user sees.

Desktop Layer

The lowest layer in the canvas hierarchy is called the *desktop layer*. By default, there are two elements in this layer, the menu bar and the status line. In addition, any Paradox object displayed on the desktop also exists in this layer, each in its own window. Examples of these objects are tables, forms, reports, queries, and so on. Each window has its own canvas, which you can control, independent of other windows in the desktop layer.

Canvases permit you to control what is displayed to the user.

You can also create windows in the desktop layer that do not contain a Paradox object. These windows are fittingly called *canvas windows*, since their sole purpose is to display information on that window's canvas. You will learn how to create and control canvas windows later in this chapter.

The windows in the desktop layer also exist within a hierarchy. The first window you place on the desktop is at the bottom of this layer. As you add new objects to the desktop, they are placed on top of the windows already there. The active window is always at the top of this layer, and obscures any windows it overlaps. Later in this chapter you will learn how to create windows and use the PAL commands WINNEXT and WINDOW SELECT to change the order of windows in the desktop layer.

Echo Layer

The *echo layer* does not contain a window. Instead, it contains a single canvas, called the *full-screen*, or default, *canvas*. When you begin playing a script, the full-screen canvas is raised and a snapshot of the desktop is displayed on it. Any time the canvas is raised, all objects in the desktop layer are hidden (although their image is captured on the full-screen canvas). This is why Paradox appears to freeze when a script is running. Although all kinds of activity may be occurring on the desktop layer, all you see is the echo layer and its captured image of the desktop.

The echo layer is given its name because you use the PAL command ECHO to drop and raise this canvas, permitting you to reveal and hide the desktop from within your script. If you want, you can drop the echo layer, revealing all activity on the desktop. Alternatively, you can drop and then immediately raise the echo layer, updating the snapshot captured on this canvas.

Application Layer

The *application layer* is the highest layer. Anything that appears in the application layer will always hide anything beneath it in any lower layer, whether the full-screen canvas is raised or not. The elements that appear in the application layer are those that you would not want to hide, ever. These include screen messages, displayed menus, and dialog boxes. Also included in the application layer are special canvas windows you can create called *floating windows*. Floating windows are described in this chapter. Menus and dialog boxes are covered in Chapter 9.

Controlling Canvas Display

Think of a *canvas* as a grid of rows and columns. How many rows and columns a canvas contains depends on a number of things. For a canvas that appears in a window, the number of rows and columns depends on the size of the window. The full-screen canvas, in most cases, contains 25 rows and 80 columns. (This can be different if you have selected an alternative video mode from the System menu. For example, most users can display up to 50 rows and 80 columns on a VGA monitor, if they want.)

Whether you are working with the full-screen canvas, or canvas window, the commands you use to control the canvas contents are the same. Therefore, the exercises in this section will discuss these commands using the full-screen canvas for demonstration. Later in this chapter you will learn how to create canvas windows, as well as how to use the commands that apply specifically to canvas windows.

Displaying Information to the User   173

There are three ways you can manipulate the PAL canvas. The first is by controlling the cursor's row and column position on the canvas. The second is by erasing or displaying text on the canvas, and the third way is by controlling the color and other attributes of any displayed text.

Controlling the Cursor

If you want your script to display information on the PAL canvas, you must exercise control over the row and column position of the cursor. This is because the location of the cursor is the location on the canvas where any text you print will be displayed. In other words, if you want to display a message in the middle of a canvas, you must first move your cursor there.

When a script begins, and the full-screen canvas is displayed, the cursor is automatically placed in the top row and first column of the PAL canvas. This position is the top left corner of your screen. You can see this yourself with the following exercise:

1. Press [Alt]-[F10] (PAL menu).
2. Select MiniScript.
3. Type **SLEEP 5000** and press [Enter].

This command instructs Paradox to pause for five seconds, during which time the full-screen PAL canvas is displayed. Notice the cursor blinking in the upper left corner of the canvas. The rows of the PAL canvas are numbered beginning with row 0 and the columns beginning with column 0. Therefore, the default position of the cursor on the PAL canvas is row 0, column 0.

TIP: The numbering of rows and columns on the canvas can be confusing since it differs from the screen's numbering system. It is easy, however, if you remember that the row number on the canvas is one less than the row number on your screen. For example, the first row on your screen is row 0 on the full-screen PAL canvas. This also works with column numbers. The first column on your screen is column 0 on the canvas.

The @ Command

The command to move your cursor to a particular location on the PAL canvas is the @ (at) command. When you use @, it must be followed by the row number and column number corresponding to the position on the canvas where you want to move the cursor. The row and column numbers must be integers (0, 1, 2, and so forth) and must be separated by a comma.

The syntax of the @ command is

```
@ RowNumber,ColumnNumber
```

The following exercise will move the cursor to the second row and third column on the canvas.

1. Press [Alt]-[F10] (PAL menu).
2. Select MiniScript.
3. Type **@ 2,3 SLEEP 5000** and press [Enter].

When this script plays, Paradox first moves the cursor to the second row and third column of the full-screen PAL canvas. This position corresponds to the third row and fourth column of your screen. (Remember, the rows and columns in the PAL canvas are numbered beginning with 0, not 1.) Next, the SLEEP 5000 statement causes Paradox to suspend script play for five seconds. During this time, the cursor appears at the position it was moved to on the canvas.

You can use the @ command as many times as you need to within your script. In many situations, you will precede any command that displays information on your screen with the @ command, in order to control where the information is displayed. Once you move the cursor to a location on the PAL canvas, it remains there until you move it again, or you issue one of the commands that displays text on the PAL canvas.

Clearing the Canvas

By default, the PAL canvas displays a picture of the Paradox desktop while your script is playing. This is not always desirable. For example, when your script is part of an application, you do not want a frozen picture of the Paradox desktop displayed. Instead, you want to create

Displaying Information to the User

your own picture, or interface, to present to the user. Consequently, one of the first commands used in a script is often one that removes the current picture from the PAL canvas.

The CLEAR Command

The CLEAR command contains a single required keyword, CLEAR. The syntax is

```
CLEAR [ { EOL   EOS } ]
```

When Paradox encounters the CLEAR command in a script, it erases all characters from the PAL canvas. The optional EOL and EOS keywords are useful when you want to clear only a portion of the canvas. When you use CLEAR EOL, Paradox clears the characters from the current position of the cursor to the end of the line the cursor is on. For example, if your cursor is at row 10 and column 12 of the full-screen canvas, CLEAR EOL will erase the characters on row 12 from column 11 through 79 (assuming that the canvas has 80 columns). Similarly, CLEAR EOS clears the canvas from the current position of the cursor to the end of the canvas. In other words, everything from the current cursor position to the bottom right corner of the canvas is erased. However, the most common use of CLEAR is by itself, without either of the optional keywords. The following example demonstrates the use of CLEAR:

1. Press [Alt]-[F10] (PAL menu).
2. Select MiniScript.
3. Type **CLEAR SLEEP 5000** and press [Enter].

This script clears all text from the PAL canvas and causes a five-second pause. Notice that the cursor still appears on the desktop at position 0,0 on the canvas (the default position). When the script is through playing, the canvas is dropped, and the Paradox desktop reappears. This exercise also serves to demonstrate that the menu bar and the status line exist below the echo layer, since the CLEAR command erases them from the full-screen canvas.

Clearing the canvas does not affect the position of your cursor. The following exercise demonstrates this:

1. Press [Alt]-[F10] (PAL menu).
2. Select MiniScript.
3. Type **@ 12,39 CLEAR SLEEP 5000** and press [Enter].

When you play this script, Paradox first moves the cursor to about the center of the PAL canvas. Next, the CLEAR statement clears the canvas of all text, and the SLEEP statement holds this image for five seconds. During this time, you will notice that the cursor remains in the center of the canvas.

Printing Text on the Canvas

Paradox provides you with a number of ways to display information to the user on the PAL canvas. This is a necessary and important part of many scripts. The following are examples of when this is necessary:

- When a process being performed by your script is taking a long time, the script can periodically display a message indicating that the process is continuing smoothly. This information is reassuring to the user, confirming that the process is working.

- When an unexpected situation is encountered, your script can display an informative error message so the user can take the appropriate action.

- Your application can offer online help. When the user requests this help, your script displays appropriate information on the screen.

- A message can be displayed prompting the user for input.

PAL provides you with a series of commands whose sole purpose is to print information on the PAL canvas. These commands are the focus of this section. Although there are several other commands that also display information, such as SHOWDIALOG, their display is a side effect of the command, not its main purpose. Consequently, those commands will be discussed elsewhere in this book.

The ? and ?? Commands

The ? and ?? commands are used to display a list of one or more expressions on the canvas. These expressions may be of any type:

Displaying Information to the User

alphanumeric, numeric, date, or logical. Most commonly, the type is alphanumeric.

The syntaxes of the ? and ?? commands are

```
?  Expression1 ...[,ExpressionN]
?? Expression1 ...[,ExpressionN]
```

The ?? command is used to print the expression list at the position of the cursor. For example, if the cursor is at row 5 and column 10, the leftmost character of the first expression will appear at that location. Once the expressions have been displayed, the cursor will appear one column to the right of the last character in the last expression. This is demonstrated in the following exercise:

1. Press [Alt]-[F10] (PAL menu).
2. Select MiniScript.
3. Type **CLEAR @ 5,10 ?? "Display this" SLEEP 5000** and press [Enter].

Playing this script will clear your canvas and cause the message "Display this" to appear on the fifth row, tenth column of the full-screen canvas. Note also that during the five-second sleep, the cursor is positioned immediately after the *s* in "this."

The ? character, in contrast, always displays the expression list beginning at column 0 on the canvas on the row following the cursor position. This command provides less flexibility in placement—always displaying the expression in column 0—but is appropriate in certain situations.

To see the effect of ?, repeat the preceding exercise. This time, however, use the ? command in place of ??. You will see the expression printed at row 6 and column 0. As with the ?? command, the cursor position is immediately after the *s* in "this."

The information displayed on the canvas using the ? and ?? commands remains displayed until either the script ends (at which time the canvas is removed), another CLEAR command is displayed, a new snapshot of what lies beneath the canvas is captured, or a new expression is displayed at the same location.

The MESSAGE Command

When the MESSAGE command appears in your script, it must be followed by one or more expressions.

The syntax of the MESSAGE command is

```
MESSAGE Expression1 ...[,ExpressionN]
```

If you display two or more expressions with a single MESSAGE command, they must be separated by commas. The expression(s) in the MESSAGE command can be of any type—alphanumeric, numeric, date, or logical—up to a combined total of 255 characters. Furthermore, each expression may be of a different type. Try the following exercise:

1. Press [Alt]-[F10] (PAL menu).
2. Select MiniScript.
3. Type **CLEAR MESSAGE "The time is ",TIME( ) SLEEP 5000** and press [Enter].

When Paradox plays this script, it clears the canvas and then displays the message at the lower right corner of the screen, as shown in Figure 8-1. This message has two expressions: the first is an alphanumeric constant and the second is a PAL function that returns the current time, according to your computer's clock. This message will appear using the same color combinations defined in your Paradox configuration for Paradox error messages.

The display of expressions using MESSAGE is very similar to the standard messages Paradox displays while you are using it interactively. This is advantageous; it permits your scripts to have a look that is similar to interactive Paradox. Another advantage of MESSAGE is that it does not affect the cursor position on the canvas, which makes MESSAGE a useful companion to the ? and ?? commands.

Like those displayed with the ? and ?? commands, messages displayed by MESSAGE remain on the canvas until script play terminates, another MESSAGE command is played, the canvas is cleared, or other text is printed to the location of the message. The message can be removed intentionally by including another MESSAGE command followed by an empty alphanumeric string, like this:

Displaying Information to the User

```
MESSAGE ""
```

NOTE: In Paradox 3.5, the message displayed using the MESSAGE command is removed when the user presses any key or your script issues a command that results in a cursor movement on the workspace. In some cases, this can result in the message being displayed so briefly as to be unreadable. In these cases, the ? or ?? command is preferable. Furthermore, the command MESSAGE "" will display an empty message window (using the system message colors), instead of erasing the previous message.

The TEXT Command

Sometimes, you do not need the flexibility of the ?, ??, and MESSAGE commands. Those commands permit you to display any type of expression, even those that include variables, arrays, or functions. Sometimes, you might want merely to display a block of text that does

The current time is displayed using MESSAGE
Figure 8-1.

not change. Although you could do this with a ? or ?? command, there is an easier way—the TEXT command.

The syntax of the TEXT command is

```
TEXT
 one or more lines of text
ENDTEXT
```

When Paradox plays a TEXT command, everything between the keywords TEXT and ENDTEXT is printed, beginning at the current cursor position. Any lines of text after the first one begin in column 0 of the canvas. After the text between the TEXT and ENDTEXT keywords has been displayed, the cursor is located in column 0, one row below the last line of text.

Within the TEXT command, everything is taken literally. No PAL commands or comments will be recognized between the two keywords, TEXT and ENDTEXT. Likewise, blank spaces are preserved—even leading blanks. This means that all indentation of text within TEXT-ENDTEXT statements will appear in the displayed text.

The following exercise demonstrates the effects of TEXT-ENDTEXT:

1. From the Main menu select Scripts/Editor/New.
2. Type **Textdemo** and press (Enter).
3. Enter the following lines into the Editor screen:

   ```
   @ 5,0
   TEXT
   This is the first line of text.


   The preceding two lines of text are blank.
      This line is indented three spaces.
   This is the last line of text.
   ENDTEXT
   SLEEP 5000
   ```

4. Select Go from the Editor menu.

Paradox plays the script and displays the text on your screen for five seconds. Your screen should look like that in Figure 8-2. You will notice

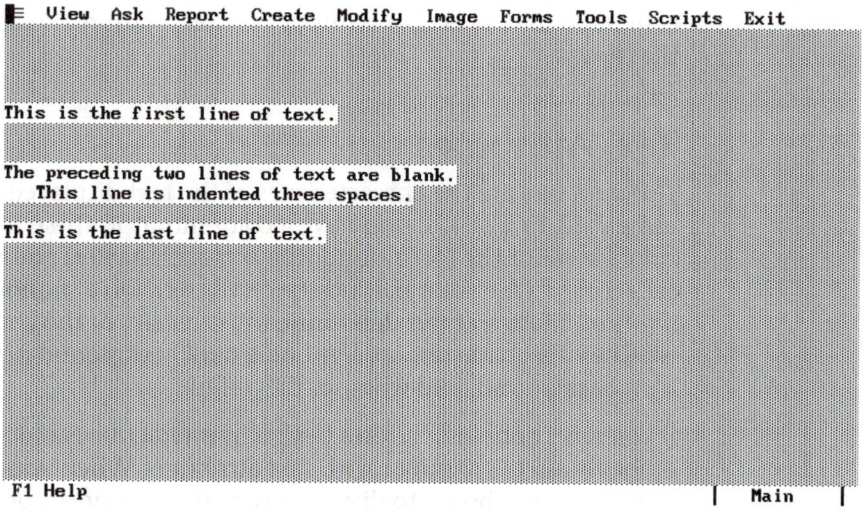

Displaying Information to the User

```
  View  Ask  Report  Create  Modify  Image  Forms  Tools  Scripts  Exit


This is the first line of text.

The preceding two lines of text are blank.
   This line is indented three spaces.

This is the last line of text.




F1 Help                                                        | Main |
```

Figure 8-2. Text displayed using the TEXT command

on your screen that the cursor is located in the first column below the last line of text.

The TEXT-ENDTEXT statement is particularly useful when you want to display a fixed screen of information. For instance, the TEXT command is often used to display a screen of help information. TEXT is also used to display a splash screen for an application. (A *splash screen* is typically the picture or logo presented at application startup.)

It is usually necessary to position the cursor before using a TEXT command, as you did in the preceding exercise. For example, if the cursor is not in column 0 of the canvas, the first line of text will be indented. Therefore, at a minimum you should probably position the cursor in column 0 before using TEXT-ENDTEXT. Another potential problem arises if there is not enough room below the cursor for the text in your TEXT command. In these cases, the overflow lines will wrap around to the top of the canvas.

Be sure that any indentation you use between TEXT and ENDTEXT will be acceptable when displayed on the canvas. Although indenting improves the readability of your scripts between the TEXT and ENDTEXT commands, all characters are taken literally, including leading blank spaces. Therefore, you cannot indent the text of the TEXT command in your scripts without this indentation also appearing on the canvas.

Text Attributes

Text attributes are the characteristics of the text displayed on the canvas using ?, ??, or TEXT. If you have a color monitor, these features set the colors used for the foreground (the actual character) and the background (the color behind the character). On a monochrome monitor, these features determine the intensity of the characters, whether the characters are light on a dark background or dark on a light background, and whether they blink.

If you have done much form design in interactive Paradox, you are probably already familiar with text attributes. When you work with a form, you can choose to display any of the text, areas, or borders in the form with specific text attributes. In PAL, two commands are used to achieve these same effects on the canvas: STYLE and PAINTCANVAS.

The STYLE Command

The STYLE command is used to define the default display characteristics for text. Once you use the STYLE command in a script, all text displayed on the canvas using ?, ??, and TEXT will use that setting until another STYLE command is used or all script play terminates.

There are two versions of the STYLE command:

```
STYLE [BLINK] [INTENSE] [REVERSE]
```

and

```
STYLE [ATTRIBUTE number]
```

The first version is intended for use with monochrome monitors. In this version there is one required keyword and three optional keywords. You can use two or even all three optional keywords in a single command, as long as they are separated by commas. The BLINK keyword causes subsequent text to blink on and off. The INTENSE keyword displays text in high intensity, that is, brighter than normal. REVERSE displays dark text on a light background.

Displaying Information to the User

You can use this form of the STYLE command with color monitors as well; however, the effects are not exactly the same as on monochrome monitors. For example, the INTENSE option does not produce high-intensity text. Instead the text is displayed in an alternate color. When you have a color monitor, the second version of the STYLE command gives you greater control.

The second version of STYLE enables you to define the colors of the foreground and the background. You do this by following the optional keyword ATTRIBUTE with a number between 0 and 255, called the *attribute number*. The attribute number is calculated by adding the number corresponding to the desired foreground color to the number associated with the desired background color. Furthermore, if you want to produce blinking text, you add the number 128 to the sum of the foreground and background colors. The 8 possible background colors and their associated numbers, along with the 16 foreground colors with their associated numbers, are shown in Table 8-1.

For example, assume that you want to display white text on a blue background. Table 8-1 shows that white text is designated by the number 15 and that a blue background is defined by 16. Therefore, the attribute number to use is 16 + 15, or 31. Try this yourself in the following example:

1. Press [Alt]-[F10] (PAL menu).
2. Select MiniScript.
3. Type **STYLE ATTRIBUTE 31 @ 10,12 ?? "White on blue" SLEEP 5000** and press [Enter].

Paradox will display the text "White on blue" at position 10,12 on the PAL canvas. The background of this text is blue and the text itself is white. On your screen, it appears as though the text is displayed in a blue box.

The PAINTCANVAS Command

Unlike the STYLE command, which is used to set the attributes for text that is yet to appear, the PAINTCANVAS command defines the attributes for characters already placed on the canvas. This command has a number of optional keywords, but they are not relevant to the discussion at hand. In the syntax given below, these have been omitted

Background Color	Number
Black	0
Blue	16
Green	32
Cyan	48
Red	64
Magenta	80
Brown	96
Light gray	112
Foreground Color	**Number**
Black	0
Blue	1
Green	2
Cyan	3
Red	4
Magenta	5
Brown	6
Light gray	7
Dark gray	8
Light blue	9
Light green	10
Light cyan	11
Light red	12
Light magenta	13
Yellow	14
White	15

Background and Foreground Color Attribute Numbers **Table 8-1.**

for ease of discussion. The complete syntax for this command can be found in the *PAL Reference* (or the *PAL User's Guide* for version 3.5).

```
PAINTCANVAS ATTRIBUTE Number {Row1, Col1, Row2, Col2 | ALL}
```

Displaying Information to the User

In this usage, the PAINTCANVAS command is used with one keyword, ATTRIBUTE, which is followed by an attribute number. This attribute number is calculated by adding the desired foreground color to the desired background color (Table 8-1). If you want to apply color to less than the entire canvas, enter the row and column position that defines the upper left corner, followed by the row and column position that defines the lower right corner of this region you want to color, separated by commas. To paint the entire canvas, use the ALL keyword instead of defining the rows and columns.

NOTE: The ALL keyword is not available in the 3.5 version of the PAINTCANVAS command. You *must* specify the row and column positions for the upper left and lower right corners of the region you want to color.

When you use PAINTCANVAS, the color you apply remains until script play terminates, another PAINTCANVAS command changes the color, a CLEAR statement is played, a new snapshot is captured on the canvas, or text is displayed in the area using a different attribute.

In many cases, you use PAINTCANVAS in conjunction with a STYLE ATTRIBUTE command to define the text colors. This is because the PAINTCANVAS command only influences existing colors, while the STYLE command influences text that is added. Thus, if you use PAINTCANVAS without also using STYLE ATTRIBUTE, any text printed into the colored region will be displayed using the current style attributes rather than those produced by PAINTCANVAS.

You can see this use of the PAINTCANVAS command with the following exercise:

1. Select Scripts/Editor/New.
2. Type **Paintbox** and press Enter.
3. Enter the following commands in the Editor window:

   ```
   CLEAR
   STYLE ATTRIBUTE 31
   PAINTCANVAS ATTRIBUTE 7 6, 12, 16, 72
   PAINTCANVAS ATTRIBUTE 31 5,10,15,70
   ```

```
@ 10,22 ?? "This text appears in the box"
SLEEP 10000
```

4. Select Go from the Editor menu.

Paradox will paint a blue box and display the text "This text appears in the box" in the middle. This box also has a drop shadow, which is produced by the first of the two PAINTCANVAS commands. The shadow effect is created because the first PAINTCANVAS command displays a dark gray on black box which is offset from the blue box by one row and two columns.

Echoing the Full-Screen Canvas

There are times when you want to drop a canvas. This serves two purposes. The first is to provide the user a look at what lies beneath the canvas. For example, if you never drop the full-screen canvas, the user will not see what is happening on the desktop. (This may or may not be desirable.) The second reason to drop the canvas is to capture a snapshot of what lies beneath onto the canvas.

Dropping and raising the canvas is accomplished with the PAL command ECHO. ECHO has the following syntax:

```
ECHO {NORMAL | FAST | SLOW | OFF }
```

If you use the ECHO command with the keywords NORMAL, FAST, or SLOW, Paradox drops the canvas and displays the contents beneath. Any images that were on the canvas prior to its being dropped are lost. When you use ECHO NORMAL, the goings on beneath the canvas are displayed at normal speed, which is to say that Paradox continues as fast as it can, given the fact that it must update the screen constantly. (Even under the best situations, ECHO NORMAL slows down Paradox considerably compared to ECHO OFF.) ECHO FAST and ECHO SLOW also drop the canvas, but display changes at a much slower pace. (Obviously, ECHO FAST displays changes faster than ECHO SLOW.)

To raise the canvas again, use ECHO OFF. When you use ECHO OFF, the current image of the desktop is captured on the canvas. If you want to capture a snapshot of the current desktop on the canvas, without

Displaying Information to the User

having to show actual changes occurring, use the following commands in your script.

```
ECHO NORMAL
ECHO OFF
```

 **NOTE:** The ECHO command is the only canvas command covered in this chapter that does not also apply to a window canvas. It controls the full-screen canvas only. To control the echoing of window objects to the window canvas, use the WINDOW SETATTRIBUTES command (described later in this chapter) or the WINDOW ECHO command. The echo of a window that contains a Paradox object (table, form, and so forth) can also be controlled by the WAIT command, described in Chapter 10.

Canvas Windows

In addition to the full-screen canvas, each window has a canvas of its own. When a canvas is current you can use any of the commands described so far in this chapter to modify its contents.

The canvases associated with windows provide you with two primary benefits. First, they provide you with areas in which to display information without affecting the full-screen canvas. Second, they permit you to selectively display information on the desktop. In other words, when there are two or more Paradox objects on the desktop, you can control the canvases of each window separately, and can raise, drop, and modify these canvases as needed.

In this section, and those that follow, you will learn to create and manipulate canvas windows. Canvas windows are windows that do not contain a Paradox object. If you want to use canvas windows, you must create them explicitly. In contrast, any time you place a Paradox object on the desktop, Paradox creates a window for it. There is essentially no difference between these types of windows, however. Once a window exists, you can perform all of the same manipulations on it, regardless of how it was created. Therefore, any window manipulation topics covered here also apply to windows that contain Paradox objects.

NOTE: There are no windows, and consequently no canvas windows, in Paradox 3.5. None of the remaining material in this chapter applies to Paradox 3.5.

NOTE: All canvas commands that specify a row and column position do so relative to that canvas. While this is obvious with regards to the full-screen canvas, it is sometimes tricky when it comes to window canvases. For example, using the command @ 1,1 will move the cursor to the second row, second column of the current canvas. If this canvas is a window canvas, the actual position of the cursor as it appears on your monitor depends on the location of the window. Within the window itself, however, the cursor will be positioned at the second row, second column.

Creating a Canvas Window

You create a canvas window using the WINDOW CREATE command. When Paradox encounters this command in a script, it immediately creates a window. The following is the syntax of this command:

```
WINDOW CREATE
   [FLOATING]
   [@ row, col]
   [HEIGHT rows]
   [WIDTH columns]
   [ATTRIBUTES DynamicArrayName]
   TO WindowHandle
```

There are four required components to this command, three keywords and a variable name. You must use the keywords WINDOW CREATE TO followed by a variable name. This variable is used to hold the window's handle. The *handle* is an integer that Paradox assigns to a window when it is created. Every window has a handle, and every handle is unique. Furthermore, Paradox will not reuse a window handle within a Paradox session, even if a window is subsequently closed.

Displaying Information to the User

Window handles provide you with a means of referring to a particular window. As you will see, many of PAL's window-specific commands require you to specify which window you want to perform an operation on. You indicate this by using the window handle.

In addition to the required components, there are five optional elements of the WINDOW CREATE command. If you use the optional keyword FLOATING, the window is created in the application layer, appearing above the full-screen canvas. Omitting this keyword creates the window in the desktop layer, which may or may not be hidden by the full-screen canvas.

The next optional keyword is the @ command, which you follow with numbers that define the row and column location for the upper left corner of the window. If you do not tell Paradox where to place the window, it will place the window approximately in the center of the screen.

Using the optional keywords HEIGHT and WIDTH, you can specify the height of the window in rows, and the width of the window in columns. And finally, using the optional keyword ATTRIBUTES, you can define the characteristics of the window based on the contents of a dynamic array. The use of dynamic arrays to get and assign window attributes is discussed later in this chapter.

The following exercise demonstrates the creation of a canvas window. Perform this exercise from the Main menu.

1. Select Scripts/Editor/New.
2. Type **Makewin1** and press Enter.
3. Enter the following script into the Editor:

```
WINDOW CREATE TO Win1
RETURN Win1
```

4. Select Go from the Editor menu.

    When you play this script, Paradox creates the window on the desktop using the default size and placement. The return command will display the value of the window handle. Your screen looks similar to that shown in Figure 8-3; however, the value of the window handle will likely be different. Notice that the window is still displayed on your screen even though the script is complete. Since the window is an actual object placed on the desktop, it will remain after the script is through. While the window is on the desktop you can treat it like any other window. You can resize it, move it, and even maximize it if you want. To remove the window, you must close it.

5. Close the window by pressing [Ctrl]-[F8] (WinClose).

   Paradox removes the window from the desktop.

Getting Window Attributes

All windows have attributes. These attributes include the row and column position of the window's upper left corner, the height and width of the window, and its title. Paradox provides you with a command that assigns the window attributes to a dynamic array. This command is WINDOW GETATTRIBUTES. Following is the syntax of the WINDOW GETATTRIBUTES command:

```
WINDOW GETATTRIBUTES WindowHandle TO DynamicArrayName
```

The following exercise demonstrates a use of this command. Begin this exercise from the Main menu:

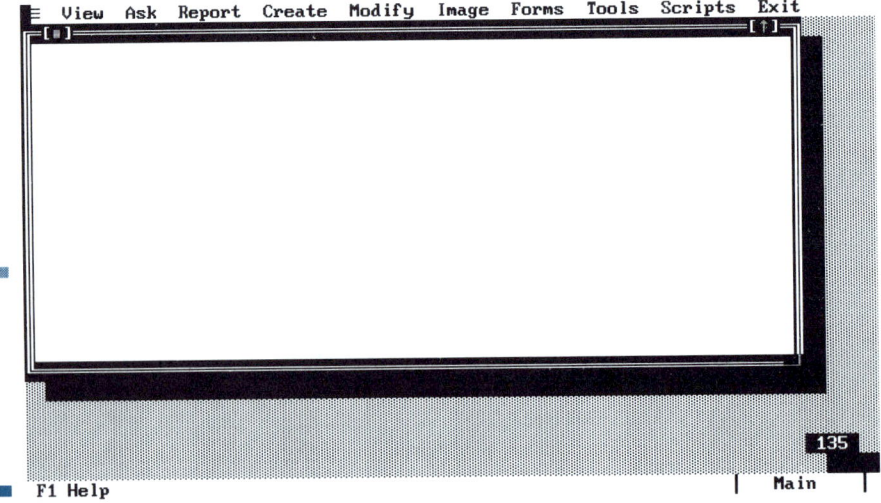

A canvas window is displayed and its handle is returned

Figure 8-3.

Displaying Information to the User

1. Select Scripts/Editor/New.
2. Type **Makewin2** and press Enter.
3. Type the following script.

```
WINDOW CREATE @ 1,0
  HEIGHT 24
  WIDTH 70
  TO Win1
WINDOW GETATTRIBUTES Win1 TO WinAttributes
FOREACH Element in WinAttributes
  ? Element, "=",WinAttributes[Element]
ENDFOREACH
```

4. Select Go from the Editor menu to play this script.

   This script creates a window that is 24 rows high and 70 characters wide. The WINDOW GETATTRIBUTES command creates a dynamic array called WinAttributes that holds the attributes of the newly created window. The FOREACH loop processes each one of the elements in WinAttributes, and the ? command prints the element index, the equal sign, and the contents of the WinAttributes array to the canvas. When this script is through running, the canvas window remains, and the contents of the WinAttributes array are displayed in it.

> **NOTE:** This demonstrates one of the exceptional values of a canvas window: it is the only canvas that persists after the script returns to interactive Paradox. All other canvases, including the global desktop, canvases associated with Paradox object windows, and floating window canvases, are lost when all script play terminates.

5. When you are through inspecting the window attributes, close the canvas window by pressing Ctrl-F8 (WinClose).

You can use the WINDOW GETATTRIBUTES command with any window, not only canvas windows. The dynamic array elements created using this command are described in Table 8-2.

Index	Description
SCROLLROW	Records or rows scrolled off the top of the window
SCROLLCOL	Fields or columns scrolled to the left of the window
MARGIN	OFF if no margin is set; otherwise, the number of characters defined for the window canvas using the SETMARGIN command
STYLE	Color attribute of the window canvas
CANVASHEIGHT	Height of the window in rows
CANVASWIDTH	Width of the window in rows
CANVAS	True if the window's canvas is on; otherwise, False
ECHO	True if the contents of the window are being echoed onto the window canvas
MAXIMIZED	True if the window is maximized
HASSHADOW	True if the window has a drop shadow
CANRESIZE	True if the window can be resized by the user
CANMAXIMIZE	True if the window can be maximized by the user
CANMOVE	True if the window can be moved by the user
CANCLOSE	True if the window can be closed by the user
FLOATING	True if the window is a floating window
HASFRAME	True if the window has a frame
HEIGHT	Total height of the window, including frame
WIDTH	Total width of the window, including frame
ORIGINROW	Row of the upper left window corner
ORIGINCOL	Column of the upper left window corner
TITLE	Title of the window

Window Attributes **Table 8-2.**

Setting Window Attributes

There are two ways to set the attributes of a window. When you create a window, you can use the ATTRIBUTES command and supply the name of a dynamic array containing the attributes you want to apply to the window. You can define as many or as few of the elements of this

Displaying Information to the User

dynamic array as you want. In other words, even though there are 20 different window attributes, the dynamic array you use to assign attributes to a window may have fewer than 20 elements. For example, the following script will create a canvas window with no frame and no shadow. All other attributes will be default window attributes. The canvas created by this script is shown in Figure 8-4.

```
DYNARRAY ApplyAttributes[]
ApplyAttributes["HASSHADOW"] = False
ApplyAttributes["HASFRAME"] = False
WINDOW CREATE
   ATTRIBUTES ApplyAttributes
   TO MyWindow
```

NOTE: If you actually use this script, you will need to press Ctrl-F8 (WinClose) to remove the canvas from your desktop.

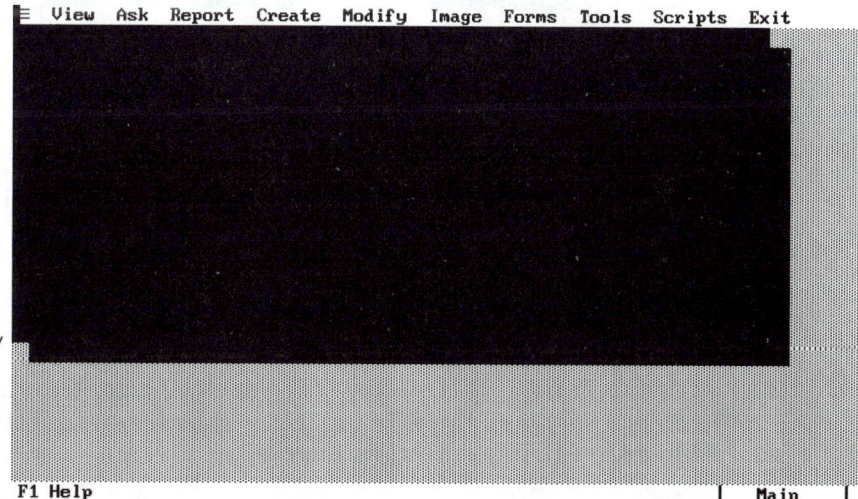

Canvas window with customized attributes
Figure 8-4.

This application of attributes to a window only works when you are creating a window. It cannot be used if the window is already created. To apply attributes to a window that already exists, use the WINDOW SETATTRIBUTES command. This command has the following syntax:

```
WINDOW SETATTRIBUTES WindowHandle FROM DynamicArrayName
```

The following script produces the same effect as the preceding one:

```
DYNARRAY ApplyAttributes[]
ApplyAttributes["HASSHADOW"] = False
ApplyAttributes["HASFRAME"] = False
WINDOW CREATE TO MyWindow
WINDOW SETATTRIBUTES MyWindow FROM ApplyAttributes
```

The benefit of the WINDOW SETATTRIBUTES command is that it permits you to apply changes to a window during the course of your script, as well as apply your own attributes to a window created by Paradox when you view a table, or other Paradox object.

NOTE: If you want to get or change colors of individual elements in a window, without changing all of the Paradox color settings, use WINDOW GETCOLORS and WINDOW SETCOLORS. These commands are described in the *PAL Reference* (or the *PAL User's Guide* for version 3.5).

Closing Windows

When you are through using a canvas window, you should close it. There are two commands you can use to close a window. The first is the special key command WINCLOSE, which simulates pressing Ctrl-F8. This command is only appropriate if the window you want to close has the CANCLOSE attribute set to True. Alternatively, you can use the WINDOW CLOSE command to close a window regardless of the CANCLOSE attribute. Both of these commands require that the window you want to close is the current window. Furthermore, if the window you are closing contains a Paradox object, such as a table, the object will be removed from the desktop when the window is closed.

Selecting the Current Canvas

Each window has a canvas, and you can control each canvas using the same set of commands that apply to the full-screen canvas. However, before you can use these commands on a window, that window must be made the current canvas.

When a script first begins, the current canvas is the full-screen canvas, which is why it is also referred to as the *default canvas*. However, as soon as you create a canvas window, the window associated with that canvas becomes the current canvas. This is why the ? command printed the dynamic array attributes to the canvas window instead of the full-screen canvas in an earlier exercise (the exercise associated with the earlier section, "Getting Window Attributes").

In general, it is a good idea to specifically define the current canvas prior to outputting information to the screen. You define the current canvas using the SETCANVAS command.

The syntax of the SETCANVAS command is

```
SETCANVAS {DEFAULT | WindowHandle}
```

If you want to make sure that any subsequent canvas commands apply to the full-screen canvas, precede them with the SETCANVAS DEFAULT command. To select any other canvas, use SETCANVAS followed by the handle of the window the canvas is associated with.

The Current Canvas and the Active Window

The current canvas is not the same as the active window. The active window is the window that appears with a double border. In contrast, the current canvas is the canvas that Paradox will print to if you use commands such as ?, ??, and TEXT-ENDTEXT. This distinction is easiest to grasp when you consider the relationship between the full-screen canvas and windows on the desktop. Imagine that your script displays a table on the desktop, moves to the first record in that table, and then issues the command:

```
? "The current field has the value ",[]
```

This information is displayed to the current canvas. Note, however, that since the cursor is on the table, the window that holds this table is the active window.

If your script ever needs to locate the active window and the current canvas, you can use the functions GETCANVAS() and GETWINDOW(), respectively. GETCANVAS() returns the handle of the window that is assigned the current canvas, while GETWINDOW() returns the handle of the active window. (If GETCANVAS() returns the value 0, the full-screenl canvas is the current canvas.) The following exercise demonstrates the use of these two functions, as well as several of the other commands covered in this chapter.

1. Select Scripts/Editor/New.
2. Type **Makewin3** and press [Enter].
3. Type the following script:

```
ALTSPACE {Desktop} {Empty}
WINDOW CREATE @ 1,1 HEIGHT 15 WIDTH 40 TO Win1
WINDOW CREATE @ 1,50 HEIGHT 10 WIDTH 20 TO Win2
SETCANVAS Win1
? "The value of the variable Win1 is ",Win1
? "The value of the variable Win2 is ",Win2
? "The current canvas handle is ",GETCANVAS()
? "The active window handle is ",GETWINDOW()
? "This is the current canvas"
? "The other window is the active window"
MESSAGE "The full-screen canvas is raised"
SLEEP 5000 ECHO NORMAL
MESSAGE "The full-screen canvas is dropped"
SLEEP 10000 ECHO OFF
SETCANVAS DEFAULT CLEAR
MESSAGE "The full-screen canvas is raised and cleared."
SLEEP 5000
WINDOW CREATE FLOATING TO WIN3
? "This is a floating canvas"
? "It appears above the full-screen canvas"
SLEEP 5000 RETURN "Done"
```

4. Select Go from the Editor menu.
5. When the script is done playing, press [Ctrl]-[F8] twice to remove the canvas windows.

Displaying Information to the User

Quick Review

- There are three layers to Paradox: the desktop layer, the echo layer, and the application layer. The menu bar and status line reside on the desktop layer. Any Paradox object window and all canvas windows, with the exception of floating canvas windows, also reside in the desktop layer. The echo layer consists of the full-screen PAL canvas. The application layer is where your application menus, dialog boxes, and floating canvas windows exist.

- You use the @ command to move a cursor on a canvas.

- The CLEAR command erases some or all of a canvas.

- You use the ?, ??, MESSAGE, and TEXT commands to write to canvases.

- Use the STYLE and PAINTCANVAS commands to apply and define color for canvases.

- The ECHO command turns the full-screen canvas on and off. The WINDOW ECHO command does this for canvases associated with windows.

- Use WINDOW CREATE to make a canvas window.

- All windows have attributes, which you can inspect and modify using WINDOW GETATTRIBUTES and WINDOW SETATTRIBUTES, respectively.

- You select the current canvas using the SETCANVAS command. The WINDOW CREATE command also changes the current canvas.

- The current canvas is not necessarily the same as the active window.

- You can close the current window using WINCLOSE or WINDOW CLOSE.

CHAPTER

GETTING INPUT FROM THE USER

In many cases, you display information on the canvas in order to receive other information back—usually information essential to the operation of your script. When the information is entered by the user, you will typically use a control structure to evaluate it and choose an appropriate course of action.

Examples of information your scripts might receive from the user include the following:

- Your script displays a menu of possible choices. The user selects one of the choices.
- The choice the user makes from a menu is to query a table based on a date range. This range must be entered by the user. Your script asks the user for the dates to use in the query, and the user enters them.
- The user makes a menu selection that will result in the loss of some data. Although this is an acceptable menu selection, your program asks for confirmation of the selection from the user before continuing, just in case the original selection was a mistake.
- An error has occurred and your script displays an error message. Since it is essential that the user read the error message, your script displays the message and instructs the user to acknowledge by pressing (Enter). The script waits and does not continue until the key is pressed.

There are four ways of getting information from the user:

- Displaying a menu and waiting for the user to make a selection
- Getting user-typed input from the keyboard
- Displaying a dialog box and permitting the user to fill it out
- Displaying a table and permitting the user to enter data into it

This last method is described in the next chapter. The remaining three are described in the following sections.

Using Menus

Menus are one way to provide users several options, only one of which may be selected. There are six PAL commands that permit you to display a menu. Five of these show options to the user and then wait for a response. These commands are SHOWMENU, SHOWARRAY, SHOWTABLES, SHOWFILES, and SHOWPOPUP. Each of these commands creates a vertical menu that appears above the PAL canvas. Each line in this menu displays one of the menu items. A prompt for the menu appears in the status bar. An example of a menu created with the SHOWMENU command is shown here:

Getting Input from the User

```
Add
Edit
View
Query
Sort
Report
Leave
```

The sixth menu command, SHOWPULLDOWN, creates a menu, but does not wait for user input. Instead, the menu is displayed and then Paradox continues on to the PAL commands that follow. Menus created using this command tend to be more complicated, yet permit you to create more flexible applications.

NOTE: Only four of these menus are supported in Paradox 3.5: SHOWMENU, SHOWARRAY, SHOWFILES, and SHOWTABLES. Instead of producing a vertical menu, these menus are of the ring-style menu consistent with Paradox 3.5 menus. If you are running Paradox 4 in the compatibility mode, all menu commands will produce ring-style menus as well.

There are several advantages to these menu commands. The first is that Paradox itself takes responsibility for the user's navigation through the menu. When the user presses the ↓ key, for example, Paradox moves the highlighting to the next menu selection. None of this needs to be explicitly programmed by you.

Another advantage is that these menus behave exactly like any other Paradox menu. That is, if each menu selection begins with a unique letter, the user can instantly select the desired item by typing the first letter. Users familiar with the interactive Paradox menus will have no difficulty using the ones created by your script.

NOTE: When the syntax is given for the menu commands in this chapter, an optional keyword sequence is not included. This sequence, UNTIL Key1 ...[,KeyN] KEYTO KeyVar, is useful in only limited situations, and is therefore omitted for ease of discussion. The complete syntax for these commands is given in the *PAL Reference* (or the *PAL User's Guide* for version 3.5).

The SHOWMENU Command

SHOWMENU is the simplest of the menu commands. It has two required keywords, SHOWMENU and TO. You must also follow the TO keyword with the name of a variable. Between the SHOWMENU and TO keywords, you enter a list of menu selections and their prompts. A colon separates the selections from the prompts. If more than one combination of selections and prompts is used, they must be separated by commas. The syntax is as follows:

```
SHOWMENU
   Item 1: prompt 1
...
  [,item N: prompt N]
  [DEFAULT MenuItem]
  TO variable
```

The DEFAULT command permits you to define one of the menu selections as a default. This is the selection that will be highlighted when the menu is displayed. If no default is defined, the first menu selection will be highlighted when the menu is displayed.

When Paradox plays the SHOWMENU command, it displays the menu and waits for the user to make a selection. When the user makes a selection, the actual text of that menu selection is assigned to the variable listed after the TO command, and script play resumes with the first command that follows. In the following exercise you will create a short menu:

1. Select Scripts/Editor/New.
2. Type **Menu1** and press (Enter).
3. Enter the following script into the Editor screen:

   ```
   SHOWMENU
     "One":"This is the first selection",
     "Two":"This is the second selection"
     TO Choice
   RETURN Choice
   ```

Getting Input from the User

4. Select Go from the Editor menu.

   Paradox will display the menu shown here:

   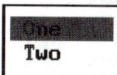

   Use the arrow keys to highlight the selection Two, and press (Enter). Paradox will then continue and play the command RETURN, which you supplied with the expression Choice. Since Choice is the variable you named after the TO keyword, the value of Choice, Two, will be displayed at the lower right corner of your screen.

Anytime a menu is displayed, the user has one additional choice that is not shown in the menu, the (Esc) key. If (Esc) is pressed, Paradox assigns the key name Esc to the variable listed after the keyword TO. Demonstrate this yourself by playing the Menu1 script once again. Since Menu1 was the last script you edited, press (Ctrl)-(G) (Go) to play it again. This time, instead of choosing one of the selections from the menu, press (Esc) to leave the menu. You will see "Esc" displayed in the lower right corner of your screen.

Immediately following a menu command your script should test the value assigned to the variable. Since this variable has a number of possible values, the SWITCH control structure is usually the branching control structure of choice. Within this control structure, you should test the value of the variable for each of the possible menu selections, as well as for the value Esc (make sure you test for this exact capitalization). This use of the SHOWMENU command followed by a SWITCH command is shown in Figure 9-1. Based on the value of the variable Choice, one of four scripts is played. In order for the script shown in Figure 9-1 to work properly, the four scripts (AddRecs.sc, EditRecs.sc, RepMenu.sc, and UtilMenu.sc) must exist.

NOTE: When you press (Esc) in response to a menu, Paradox also assigns the value False to the system variable Retval. It is just as valid to test Retval for False as it is to test the variable listed after the TO keyword for the value Esc.

```
  File  Edit  Search  Options  Go  DO-IT!  Cancel
[■]========================= C:\SALES\DEMOSWCH.SC =========================[↕]
WHILE True        ;This WHILE will loop until Exit is selected or Esc pressed.
  SHOWMENU
    "Add"      :"Add a new customer to the customer table.",
    "Change"   :"Change one or more records in the customer table.",
    "Reports"  :"Display the reports menu.",
    "Utilities":"Display the utilities menu.",
    "Exit"     :"Return to Paradox."
  TO Choice
  SWITCH
    CASE Choice = "Exit" OR Choice = "Esc":
      RETURN "Thank you for using this program."   ;==========================
    CASE Choice = "Add":                           ; After any of these
      PLAY "AddRecs"                               ; scripts is played, this
    CASE Choice = "Change":                        ; script will resume
      PLAY "EditRecs"                              ; playing and the ENDWHILE
    CASE Choice = "Reports":                       ; command will loop back
      PLAY "RepMenu"                               ; to WHILE, resulting in
    CASE Choice = "Utilities":                     ; the menu being displayed
      PLAY "UtilMenu"                              ; again. The only way to
  ENDSWITCH                                        ; exit this loop is to
ENDWHILE                                           ; select Exit or press Esc.
  F1 Help   Alt-Z Next   Alt-A ReplaceNext   Ctrl-A Replace        |   Main   |
```

Typical use of the SHOWMENU command
Figure 9-1.

Creating Hot Keys for Menus

By default, the first character in a menu is the *hot key*. When the menu is displayed, this character is displayed in a color different from the remainder of the menu item. In Paradox 4, you should not have two or more menu items use the same hot key. If you do, pressing the hot key will result in the selection of the first menu item that uses the hot key—the other menu items will be ignored.

Instead of permitting Paradox to use the first letter as the hot key, you can select your own hot key using the tilde character (~). To do this, place the tilde character before and after the letter you want to make the hot key. When Paradox displays the menu, it will not include the tildes, but will assign the enclosed letter as the hot key. Be aware, however, that the tildes *will* appear in the value assigned to the variable following the TO keyword when one of these menu items is selected.

The use of the tilde character to define a different hot key is demonstrated in the following script:

```
SHOWMENU
  "One":"This is the first selection",
  "Two":"This is the second selection",
```

Getting Input from the User

```
"T~h~ree":"This is the third selection"
  TO Choice
RETURN Choice
```

NOTE: Hot keys are not supported in Paradox 3.5 menus. When two or more menu items begin with the same first letter, pressing this letter will create a menu consisting only of those items. You can continue pressing letters until you have uniquely identified one of the menu items. Using tildes in Paradox 3.5 does not affect this behavior, but displays the tildes as part of the menu items.

The SHOWARRAY Command

The SHOWARRAY command is nearly identical to the SHOWMENU command. One difference is that instead of using a list of the menu items and their prompts, two fixed arrays are used. The first array contains the menu selections. The first menu selection is stored in the first element of the array, the second in the second, and so forth. The second array contains the prompts. Each element in the array of prompts corresponds to its counterpart in the array of menu selections.

The syntax of the SHOWARRAY command is

```
SHOWARRAY
  ItemArray
  PromptArray
  [DEFAULT item]
  TO variable
```

SHOWARRAY is useful in those scripts where you make heavy use of fixed arrays to hold information. In most scripts, however, it is more convenient to use SHOWMENU than SHOWARRAY. An example of a script employing SHOWARRAY is shown in Figure 9-2.

NOTE: Another difference between SHOWARRAY and SHOWMENU is that SHOWARRAY creates a dialog box instead of a simple menu. (SHOWTABLES and SHOWFILES also create dialog boxes.) These dialog boxes can be positioned by the user, they contain OK and Cancel pushbuttons, and they give an attractive look to your application. There are no dialog boxes in versions prior to 4.0.

The SHOWTABLES and SHOWFILES Commands

SHOWTABLES and SHOWFILES are two commands that permit you to easily display a menu of existing tables or files. When you use these commands, you do not define each of the menu selections, as you do with SHOWMENU and SHOWARRAY. Instead, Paradox constructs these menu selections based on the files it finds in a directory.

The syntax of SHOWTABLES is

```
SHOWTABLES
  DOSPath
  PromptExpression
  TO Variable
```

The syntax of SHOWFILES is

```
SHOWFILES
  [NOEXT]
  DOSPath
  PromptExpression
  TO Variable
```

```
≡  File   Edit   Search   Options   Go   DO-IT!   Cancel
┌─[■]─────────────────── C:\SALES\SHOWARRY.SC ───────────────────[↕]─┐
│ ARRAY MenuArray[5]                          ;You must first declare the│
│ ARRAY PromptArray[5]                        ;fixed arrays              │
│                                                                        │
│ MenuArray[1] = "Add"                        ;Next, you assign the menu items│
│ MenuArray[2] = "Change"                     ;and their corresponding prompts│
│ MenuArray[3] = "Reports"                    ;to these arrays.         │
│ MenuArray[4] = "Utilities"                                              │
│ MenuArray[5] = "Exit"                                                   │
│ PromptArray[1] = "Add a new customer to the customer table."            │
│ PromptArray[2] = "Change one or more records in the customer table."    │
│ PromptArray[3] = "Display the reports menu."                            │
│ PromptArray[4] = "Display the utilities menu."                          │
│ PromptArray[5] = "Return to Paradox."                                   │
│                                                                        │
│ SHOWARRAY                                   ;SHOWARRAY displays a menu using│
│   MenuArray PromptArray                     ;the first array elements as menu│
│   TO Choice                                 ;items and the second array│
│   IF Choice = "Exit" OR Choice = "Esc"      ;elements as prompts.     │
│     THEN                                                               │
│       RETURN "Thank you for using this program."                       │
│   ENDIF                                                                │
└────────────────────────────────────────────────────────────────────────┘
  F1 Help   Alt-Z Next   Alt-A ReplaceNext   Ctrl-A Replace         Main
```

Example of the SHOWARRAY command
Figure 9-2.

Getting Input from the User

The syntax of these two commands is nearly identical. Consider SHOWTABLES first, which requires the keywords SHOWTABLES and TO. SHOWTABLES must be followed by a valid DOS path that defines the location of the table you want to display on your menu. You can default to the current directory by using two pairs of quotation marks with nothing between them (" ").

A prompt is also required. This prompt is a message that will be displayed in the status bar. It should instruct the user to select one of the displayed tables. The following command will display all tables on the current directory:

```
SHOWTABLES
  ""
  "Please select a table"
  TO TabName
```

When Paradox plays this command, it displays a menu of table names from the current directory and waits for the user to select one. The table name the user selects is assigned to the variable named after the TO keyword. There is one exception, however. If no tables are found on the directory, the menu is not displayed. Paradox assigns the value None to the variable and continues playing the script with the next command.

NOTE: In Paradox 3.5, and compatibility mode of Paradox 4, SHOWTABLES and SHOWFILES display the tables and files, respectively, on the second line of the menu. The prompt appears on the top line. This is different from the SHOWMENU and SHOWARRAY commands, which display the menu selections on the top line and the prompts on the second.

SHOWFILES works almost exactly the same as SHOWTABLES, with two exceptions. The first is that the SHOWFILES command offers the optional keyword NOEXT. If you use NOEXT, the file extensions are not displayed in the menu, only the filenames. The second difference is that you can use DOS wildcards in the DOS path to display only selected files within the directory. For example, to display a menu of only the scripts (files that use the .SC extension) on the current directory, suppressing the extension, you would use the following command:

```
SHOWFILES
  NOEXT
  "*.SC"
  "Please select a script"
  TO ScriptName
```

REMEMBER: If you define a full path for the directory, such as C:\PDOX40, you must use double backslashes (for example, C:\\PDOX40).

The SHOWPOPUP Command

The SHOWPOPUP command permits you to display a pop-up menu, which is more flexible than any of the previously covered menus. SHOWPOPUP produces a menu similar to that produced by the SHOWMENU command, with the following additions:

- ✦ A pop-up menu can be displayed at any location on the screen.
- ✦ A pop-up menu has a title.
- ✦ A pop-up menu supports submenus.
- ✦ A pop-up menu can contain one or more separators. A *separator* is a line in the menu that visually separates the menu items.
- ✦ Instead of assigning the selected menu item to the TO variable, SHOWPOPUP permits you to define the value that is assigned to this variable. This value, called a *tag,* is not displayed to the user.

Following is the syntax of the SHOWPOPUP command:

```
SHOWPOPUP Title
  {@ RowNumber, ColumnNumber | CENTERED }
  menu
  ENDMENU
  TO Var
```

The syntax of the menu is as follows:

Getting Input from the User

```
Selection : Description : [DISABLE] Tag1
  [SUBMENU
     menu
  ENDSUBMENU]
[,SEPARATOR ]
...
[, Selection : Description : [DISABLE] TagN
  [SUBMENU
     menu
  ENDSUBMENU]]
```

The menu consists of a list of one or more menu items, item descriptions, and item tags. If the menu consists of more than one item, they must be separated by commas. One or more of the selections may be followed by the keyword SUBMENU followed by a menu and the keyword ENDSUBMENU. If a menu selection has a submenu, and it is not the last menu item, the comma appears after the ENDSUBMENU keyword, and not after the tag (when a menu item has a submenu, the tag is optional). Any menu item can have a submenu, even one that appears in a submenu.

Pop-up menus support submenus.

The last menu item does not have a comma after it, or, if it has a submenu, there is no comma following the ENDSUBMENU keyword for this last item. Instead, it is followed by the ENDMENU keyword, then the required keyword TO, followed by a variable name.

When Paradox plays the SHOWPOPUP command, it constructs the menu at the row and column location specified after the @ keyword (this is the location of the upper left corner of the menu), or in the middle of the screen if the keyword CENTERED is used. Paradox waits until the user either selects an item from the pop-up menu, or presses [Esc] before continuing. When the user makes a selection from the menu, the value of the tag is assigned to the variable listed after the TO keyword. The tag is any alphanumeric expression, although it is an alphanumeric constant in most cases.

If a menu item is preceded by the keyword SEPARATOR, a line appears above that menu item in the pop-up menu. This feature permits you to group conceptually related menu selections by separating them from other items in the menu.

If a tag is preceded by the optional keyword DISABLE, the corresponding menu item is displayed in a different color from the other menu items, and cannot be selected by the user. You can use this feature to display the same complete menu each time a menu is displayed in your application, disabling those you do not want the user to select.

The SHOWPOPUP command is the first you have encountered in which tags are used. You can think of tags as labels that identify the menu items in the menu. In this respect, tags are similar to handles you use to identify windows on the Paradox desktop.

The following script is an example of a use of the SHOWPOPUP command. You might consider typing this script into the Editor and playing it to demonstrate the use of the various SHOWPOPUP concepts. Figure 9-3 contains the image this script will produce if you select Exit from this pop-up menu.

```
SHOWPOPUP "Popup Demonstration" @10,10
  "View":"View a table":"Viewtab"
    SUBMENU
      "Customer":"View the customer table":"Viewcust",
      "Employee":"View the employee table":"Viewemp"
    ENDSUBMENU,
  "Edit":"Edit a table":"Edittab"
    SUBMENU
      "Customer":"Edit the customer table":"Editcust",
      "Employee":"Edit the employee table":"Editemp"
    ENDSUBMENU,
  SEPARATOR,
  "Query":"Construct a query":DISABLE "Querytables",
  "E~x~it":"Exit this popup menu":"Exit?"
    SUBMENU
      "Cancel":"Do not exit this popup":"CancelExit",
      "Ok":"Exit this popup":"OkExit"
    ENDSUBMENU
  ENDMENU
  TO Choice
RETURN Choice
```

The SHOWPULLDOWN Command

All of the menu commands described up to this point cause Paradox to stop playing the script until the user makes a selection from the menu or presses the [Esc] key. The SHOWPULLDOWN command, which is very similar to the SHOWPOPUP command in many respects, does not

Getting Input from the User

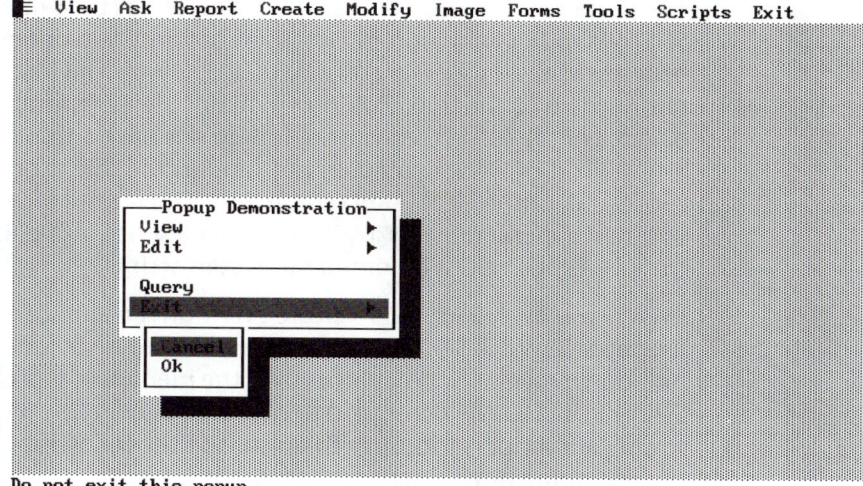

Pop-up menu with a submenu
Figure 9-3.

have this same effect. Instead, when Paradox encounters the SHOWPULLDOWN command, it builds the menu and then continues on to the PAL commands that follow. While the menu is displayed, the user is free to interact with objects other than the menu. For example, if a table is on the desktop, and you have permitted the user to edit this table, the user can freely work with the table while the menu is displayed. Users can select from the displayed menu any time they want. This is similar to how Paradox behaves in the Interactive mode. There is always a menu available, regardless of what the user is doing on the desktop.

If the user makes a selection from a displayed pull-down menu, Paradox generates an event that is similar in many respects to a keypress or a mouse interaction. Whether your script detects this interaction depends on how you programmed your script. Programming in this way is called *event-driven programming*. In other words, your script waits for events to happen, such as a user interaction with a pull-down menu, and then decides whether or not to act on that event.

The following is the syntax of the SHOWPULLDOWN command:

```
SHOWPULLDOWN
   menu
ENDMENU
```

The syntax of the menu part of this command is the same as for the SHOWPOPUP command. In fact, there are only two differences between SHOWPOPUP and SHOWPULLDOWN. The first is in the look of these two commands. Pull-down menus always appear in the menu bar area of the full-screen canvas and do not have a title. Therefore, the SHOWPULLDOWN menu does not support the title expression, the @ command, or the CENTERED command. The second difference is that a pull-down menu remains available until all script play ends, or you use the CLEARPULLDOWN command in your script.

Even if you do not intend to create event-driven applications, you can use the SHOWPULLDOWN menu command to your benefit. Since a pull-down menu always appears over the menu bar, you can use the SHOWPULLDOWN command to obscure the contents of the menu bar while your script is running. To do so, add the following command at the beginning of your script:

```
SHOWPULLDOWN ENDMENU
```

When Paradox encounters this command it will create a pull-down menu with no selections on it. This blank menu is displayed in place of the Paradox menu.

NOTE: You can also control the status bar display. To replace the contents of the status bar with your own message, use the keyword PROMPT followed by the text of your prompt. To restore the status bar contents, use PROMPT without an accompanying expression.

Although the SHOWPULLDOWN command is best suited for event-driven programming, it is possible to create scripts that use a pull-down menu in a manner similar to the way you use other menu commands. This is possible with the PAL command GETMENUSELECTION. The relevant parts of this command's syntax are

```
GETMENUSELECTION TO Choice
```

When Paradox encounters the GETMENUSELECTION command, it waits until the user selects one of the items from the displayed pull-down menu. The tag of the selected item is assigned to the variable following the TO keyword and Retval is set to True. If the user presses

Getting Input from the User

[Esc] to exit the pull-down menu without making a selection, the TO variable is set to Esc and Retval is set to False. Unlike the other menu commands, the pull-down menu is not automatically removed after the user's response. If you want to remove this menu, you need to use the CLEARPULLDOWN command to explicitly remove it.

The following sample script demonstrates this use of a pull-down menu.

```
SHOWPULLDOWN
   "View":"Display the View table menu":"Viewtab"
     SUBMENU
        "Customer":"View the customer table":"Viewcust",
        "Employee":"View the employee table":"Viewemp"
     ENDSUBMENU,
   "Edit":"Display the Edit table menu":"Edittab"
     SUBMENU
        "Customer":"Edit the customer table":"Editcust",
        "Employee":"Edit the employee table":"Editemp"
     ENDSUBMENU,
   SEPARATOR,
   "Query":"Construct a query":DISABLE "Querytables",
   "E~x~it":"Exit this pull-down menu":"Exit?"
     SUBMENU
        "Cancel":"Do not exit this pull-down":"CancelExit",
        "Ok":"Exit this pull-down":"OkExit"
     ENDSUBMENU
ENDMENU

GETMENUSELECTION TO Choice
CLEARPULLDOWN
RETURN Choice
```

To create event-driven programs using pull-down menus, you use a SHOWPULLDOWN command with either a GETEVENT command or a special version of the WAIT command. These commands are described in Chapter 13.

NOTE: Paradox 3.5 does not support the SHOWPULLDOWN command.

Getting Keyboard Input

Menu commands are not enough to satisfy all of your user input needs. There are times when you cannot anticipate all of the possible values a user would want to enter. If you need to get only a single value, or a single character from the keyboard, you can use the ACCEPT command or the GETCHAR function. Both of these keywords accept input directly from the keyboard and are described in this section. If you need to get more than one piece of information, or you want greater control over the way you enter this information, you will usually use a table or a dialog box instead. Using tables for data entry is described in the next chapter. Dialog boxes are covered later in this chapter.

The ACCEPT Command

The ACCEPT statement permits you to receive typed input from the user. Like the menu commands, this input is assigned to a variable, which you then use in your script. The syntax of the ACCEPT statement is

```
ACCEPT DataType
   [PICTURE Picture]
   [MIN MinimumValue]
   [MAX MaximumValue]
   [LOOKUP TableName]
   [REQUIRED]
   [DEFAULT DefaultValue]
   TO variable
```

The ACCEPT command has two required keywords, ACCEPT and TO. An expression that holds a data type definition must follow the ACCEPT statement. Most of the time this will be an alphanumeric constant of the form A20, N, or S. These data types use the same notation that you use when you define the data type for a field in a table. ACCEPT also requires that a variable follow the TO keyword. The input by the user will be assigned to this variable.

There are six optional keywords in the ACCEPT command. If you are familiar with field Valchecks in interactive Paradox, you will recognize these immediately. The PICTURE command permits you to define a picture specification for data entry. MIN and MAX let you define the minimum and maximum values for the data. LOOKUP permits you to define a lookup table. This feature is identical to the TableLookup Valcheck,

Getting Input from the User

with the exception that HelpAndFill is not available. The REQUIRED keyword specifies that the user may not press [Enter] without entering a value. Finally, the DEFAULT keyword permits you to define a default value.

When you use ACCEPT, Paradox waits for the user to enter a value. If you use one or more of the optional keywords with the ACCEPT command, Paradox will only permit a value to be entered if it meets the requirements of the keyword. If a user enters a value that is not acceptable, based on the data type or the optional keywords, an error message is displayed automatically by Paradox, the value is not accepted, and Paradox continues to wait for the user to supply correct input.

When the ACCEPT statement is played, Paradox activates a window at the position of the cursor. The window, which is displayed using the current text attributes, will erase any characters formerly occupying the space where the window is displayed. When the user responds to an ACCEPT command, the characters entered appear in this window.

The size of the window is defined by the data type. For example, if you use the statement

```
ACCEPT "A10" TO InputValue
```

Paradox will activate a window ten characters wide. You can see this in the following example.

1. Press [Alt]-[F10] (PAL menu).
2. Select MiniScript.
3. Type **ACCEPT "A10" TO InputValue** and press [Enter].

    Paradox opens a window ten characters wide at the position of the cursor. Since the default cursor position is row 0, column 0 of the PAL canvas, the window opens up over the first characters of the Main menu. Your screen will look like Figure 9-4. (Notice that the ten-character window erased the first two menu selections, System and View, of the Main menu.)

    Now type some data into the window. Do not press [Enter]. As you type, the characters you enter appear in this window. Now press [Backspace] a few times; the characters are erased. Paradox waits until you press [Enter] or [Esc] before it continues.

4. Continue by pressing [Enter].

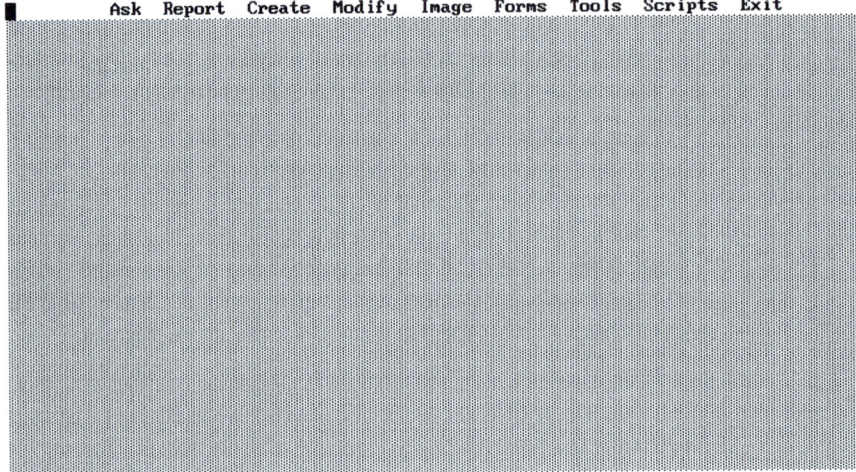

Figure 9-4. Screen appearance after playing ACCEPT "A10" TO InputValue

Adding a Prompt

One important element missing from the preceding exercise was a prompt informing the user what to do. Whenever you use an ACCEPT statement to receive information from the user, you should first prompt the user for input. This prompt can be as short or as long as necessary, and can be created using any of the commands that display text onto the canvas. At a minimum, however, it should inform the user that some type of input is expected.

The following exercise demonstrates the use of a simple prompt:

1. Select Scripts/Editor/New from the Main menu.
2. Type the script name **Accept1** and press (Enter).
3. Enter the following script into the Editor screen:

   ```
   CLEAR
   @ 10,12
   ?? "Please enter your response: "
   ACCEPT "A10" TO InputValue
   RETURN InputValue
   ```

4. Press (F10) (Menu) and select Go.

Getting Input from the User

When Paradox plays your script, the screen is cleared and then the prompt appears.

5. Type any response and then press (Enter).

   Once you press (Enter), Paradox accepts your response and assigns it to the variable you named after the TO keyword, InputValue in this case. The last command is RETURN, with the optional expression InputValue. Paradox terminates script play and displays this expression on the desktop.

Making the ACCEPT Window Visible

The window activated by the ACCEPT statement is displayed using the current text attribute settings. This makes it essentially invisible if the rest of the canvas is also displayed using these settings. However, creative use of the STYLE command can easily make the window visible. To do this, use the STYLE REVERSE or STYLE ATTRIBUTE command immediately before the ACCEPT statement in your script. Then, when you use ACCEPT, the window will appear in the foreground and background colors defined by the STYLE statement. In the statement immediately following the ACCEPT statement, you use the STYLE command by itself. This resets the text attributes to the default. Try the following exercise:

1. Select Scripts/Editor/New from the Main menu.
2. Type **Accept2** and press (Enter).
3. Enter the following script into the Editor screen:

   ```
   @ 10,12
   ?? "Please enter a value in the window: "
   STYLE REVERSE
   ACCEPT "A10" TO InputValue
   STYLE
   RETURN InputValue
   ```

4. Press (F10) (Menu) and select Go.

   Paradox clears the screen and displays your prompt. The STYLE REVERSE command then changes the text attributes so that when the ACCEPT statement is played, a window appears after the prompt.

5. Type any response and press (Enter).

The Variable Retval and ACCEPT

After each ACCEPT statement, Paradox assigns one of two values to the system variable Retval, True or False. (A *system variable* is a variable that is used internally by Paradox.) Paradox sets Retval to True if the user presses [Enter] in response to the ACCEPT command. Likewise, if the user presses [Esc], Paradox sets Retval to False.

In writing scripts, you should usually assume that a user who presses [Esc] wants to cancel whatever he or she is doing. Therefore, the command following the ACCEPT statement in your script should test the value of Retval. If Retval is False, your script should terminate, or at least cancel the current process. (If you have used the STYLE REVERSE-STYLE trick to display the ACCEPT window, your test of Retval should follow the second STYLE command.)

You should test the value of Retval after every ACCEPT statement. Because Retval will always evaluate to a logical expression after an ACCEPT, you can use one of the branching control structures to test Retval. The following is an example of this usage:

```
CLEAR
@ 10,12 ?? "Please enter a value: "
STYLE REVERSE
ACCEPT "A20" TO InputValue
STYLE
IF NOT Retval    ;NOT Retval equals True if ESC was pressed.
  THEN
     RETURN "You pressed ESC. Operation canceled."
ENDIF
 ;commands to play if ENTER was pressed.
```

The GETCHAR() Function

The GETCHAR() function returns the ASCII code associated with a character entered from the keyboard. You use it in an assignment statement, most often assigning the ASCII code to a variable. For instance, the command

```
a = GETCHAR()
```

assigns the ASCII value of a single keystroke to the variable *a*.

Getting Input from the User

When Paradox plays the GETCHAR() function, it waits until a key is pressed. When a key is pressed, the ASCII value for that pressed key is immediately returned. Therefore, with the ACCEPT command, the user does not need to press [Enter] in order to input a value. A complete list of ASCII codes is shown in Appendix A.

You can see the processing of the GETCHAR() function in the following exercise.

1. Press [Alt]-[F10] (PAL menu).
2. Select MiniScript.
3. Type **TheValue=GETCHAR() RETURN TheValue** and press [Enter].

   Once you press [Enter], Paradox does not assign a value to the variable TheValue until you press a key. When you do press a key, the GETCHAR() function returns the ASCII code for that key, and it is assigned to the variable. Next, the RETURN command terminates the script and displays the value of the variable. Demonstrate this now by typing a **1**. Paradox displays the value 49, the ASCII code for 1, in the lower right corner of the screen.

Using GETCHAR() to Pause Your Script

Since the GETCHAR() command pauses script play until the user presses any key, you can use it to pause a script for an indefinite period of time before resuming play. Use GETCHAR() in situations like the following:

- ◆ An unacceptable condition was detected by your script, which in turn displays an error message. This error message needs to remain displayed until the user acknowledges he or she has read it. If the user has left to get a cup of coffee, the message should still be displayed when the user returns and reads it.

- ◆ If your script offers online help, this help should be displayed as long as the user needs it. Your script should not clear the Help screen until the user wishes to proceed.

- ◆ You may write a utility script that displays information on the screen. Instead of using the SLEEP command to display the information for a set period of time, you may want the information displayed until it is no longer needed.

♦ You can use the canvas writing commands to paint your own custom menu on the full-screen canvas. You can associate a single character with each menu item and instruct the user to press the desired character. Your script can include the GETCHAR() function to accept this character, evaluate it, and then perform the selected menu operation.

In all cases where GETCHAR() is used to pause a script, your script should also display a message telling the user that a keypress is expected. The use of GETCHAR() in conjunction with a message is demonstrated in the next exercise. In this exercise, you will create a handy script that you can use to display all the nonblinking STYLE ATTRIBUTE colors on your monitor. This script is useful when you need to decide on an appropriate foreground and background color combination for use with the STYLE, PAINTCANVAS, or SETCOLORS command. Since you will want to inspect this information for a variable length of time, the GETCHAR() function is used here to pause until you are ready to continue.

1. Select Scripts/Editor/New.
2. Type **Colors** and press [Enter].
3. Enter the following commands:

    ```
    CLEAR
    FOR BackGround FROM 0 TO 7
      FOR ForeGround FROM 0 TO 15
        STYLE ATTRIBUTE BackGround*16+ForeGround
        @ BackGround+8,ForeGround*5
        ?? FORMAT("W5,AR",STRVAL(BackGround*16+ForeGround))
      ENDFOR
    ENDFOR
    MESSAGE "Press any key to continue."
    a=GETCHAR()
    RETURN "Thank you for using Colors."
    ```

4. Select Go from the Editor menu.

    When you are done viewing the screen, press any key; the script will terminate. A commented version of this script is shown in Figure 9-5.

Getting Input from the User

```
≡ File  Edit  Search  Options  Go  DO-IT!  Cancel
┌─[■]──────────────── C:\sales\colors.sc ────────────────[↕]─┐
│CLEAR                                                        │
│FOR BackGround FROM 0 TO 7                                   │
│  FOR ForeGround FROM 0 TO 15                                │
│    ;===========================================================
│    ;Multiply BackGround by 16 to calculate the background color and add the
│    ;product to the foreground color number to calculate the attribute number.
│    ;===========================================================
│    STYLE ATTRIBUTE BackGround * 16 + ForeGround             │
│    @ BackGround + 8,ForeGround * 5                          │
│    ;===========================================================
│    ;The FORMAT function is used to format the attribute number to five char-
│    ;acters wide and to align it right.  The STRVAL function is used to con-
│    ;vert the numeric expression defining the attribute number to an alpha-
│    ;numeric expression, since FORMAT only works with alphanumeric strings.
│    ;===========================================================
│    ?? FORMAT("W5,AR",STRVAL(BackGround * 16 + ForeGround))  │
│  ENDFOR                                                     │
│ENDFOR                                                       │
│MESSAGE "Press any key to continue."   ;The message tells the user what
│a = GETCHAR()                          ;is expected, and GETCHAR() waits
│RETURN "Thank you for using Colors"    ;until the user presses a key.
└─[◄]─────────────────────────────────────────────[ Script ]──┘
 F1 Help  Alt-Z Next  Alt-A ReplaceNext  Ctrl-A Replace
```

Colors script with comments
Figure 9-5.

The Keyboard Buffer

The *keyboard buffer* is the part of your computer's memory where it stores keypresses that have not yet been processed. When your script is ready to process these keystrokes, they are read from the keyboard buffer. This is why you can sometimes "type ahead" while using your computer. That is, you can type faster than your computer can process your keystrokes. However, if you get too far ahead, your keyboard buffer fills up and can no longer accept any keystrokes. When this happens, normally your computer simply beeps at you.

The only time that GETCHAR() will not wait for a keypress is when one or more keystrokes are already waiting to be processed in the keyboard buffer. For example, if you press a key while your script is printing a message on the canvas, the computer will hold that keypress. If a GETCHAR() function follows immediately after this message has been displayed, it will read the keypress from the keyboard buffer and continue without pausing.

Thus, the fact that your computer can store keystrokes in the keyboard buffer has important implications for how you use the GETCHAR() function. If you are using it to force a pause in a script, you must first make sure there are no keystrokes waiting in the keyboard buffer. Fortunately, there is a special function, CHARWAITING(), that does this. CHARWAITING() returns the value True if there are one or more keystrokes in the keyboard buffer, and False if there are none.

When you need to ensure that a GETCHAR() function will wait until a key is pressed, use the following segment in your script to first empty the keyboard buffer:

```
WHILE CHARWAITING()
   ;As long as there is at least one
   ;keystroke in the keyboard buffer,
   ;read a character.
   a=GETCHAR()
ENDWHILE
;The keyboard buffer is now empty.
;Use GETCHAR to wait until a key is pressed.
a = GETCHAR()
```

Dialog Boxes

The ACCEPT command and GETCHAR() function are fine when you need to get a single value from the user. They can be difficult to use, however, when you need the user to input more than one piece of information. Consider the following situation. Your application provides the user with the ability to create a report for a selected range of dates. To provide the greatest amount of flexibility, your application asks the user to input a beginning date and an ending date for the report range. One way to receive the two dates from the user is to use two consecutive ACCEPT statements, but this is not entirely flexible. For example, if the user enters the first date incorrectly and presses [Enter], continuing to the next ACCEPT statement before realizing the mistake, there is no way for the user to go back to the first date to correct it without pressing [Esc] and starting over.

There are two ways you can get more than one piece of information while providing the user the flexibility to move between the values being accepted. The first is to use a table or a form. This technique is described in the following chapter. The second is to use a *dialog box*.

Getting Input from the User

NOTE: Dialog boxes are not available in Paradox 3.5.

Dialog boxes, like forms, can include more than one field, or input area, where the user can enter information. Unlike forms, however, dialog boxes provide your applications with a wide range of ways of accepting data. These include scrollable pick lists, check boxes, radio buttons, ACCEPT windows, pushbuttons, and slider bars. The extraordinary flexibility of these objects makes dialog box input superior to form input in many situations.

Accepting information is not the only use of dialog boxes. They also make effective devices for displaying any kind of message where acknowledgment from the user is needed. These include error messages, help screens, login password prompts, and copyright screens.

Creating a Dialog Box

You build a dialog box using the PAL command SHOWDIALOG. The syntax is as follows:

```
SHOWDIALOG  DialogTitle
  [PROC DialogProcedureName EventList]
  @ RowNumber, ColumnNumber
  HEIGHT NumberOfRows
  WIDTH NumberOfColumns
  [zero, one, or more canvas elements]
  [one or more control elements]
ENDDIALOG
```

When Paradox encounters the SHOWDIALOG command, it constructs a special, floating canvas. This canvas will contain any canvas elements you define for the dialog box, as well as all control elements you specify. Paradox then waits until the user either accepts or cancels the dialog box. If the user accepts the dialog box, Paradox assigns the value True to the system variable Retval. Retval is set to False if the dialog box is canceled. While the dialog box is active, the user cannot interact with any other windows or menus on the desktop.

A dialog box can make use of a dialog procedure. A *dialog procedure* is a special type of script you write that permits you to create highly interactive dialog boxes, or merely add additional flexibility. You can use dialog boxes successfully without using dialog procedures. Therefore, dialog procedures will not be covered in this chapter. You can read about them in Chapter 13.

There are two types of elements that can be displayed in a dialog box, canvas elements and control elements. *Canvas elements* are noninteractive images that can be displayed on the dialog box. Examples of these are text, colors, and borders. *Control elements*, on the other hand, are interactive. The user uses the control elements to enter values, initiate processes, select data, or navigate the dialog box.

There are seven commands you can use to create canvas elements in a dialog box. They are STYLE, @, ?, ??, CLEAR, FRAME, and PAINTCANVAS. The use of these commands is the same for dialog boxes as they are for any other type of canvas. For this reason, the syntax of these commands is not repeated here.

There are 11 types of control elements. The following table contains a list of all 11 types and a description of each one.

Element	Action
ACCEPT	Enter a value from the keyboard
CHECKBOXES	Select one or more items from a list of one or more nonexclusive alternatives
LABEL	Move the cursor to a defined control element
PICKARRAY	Select a fixed array's contents from a pick list
PICKDYNARRAY	Select a dynamic array's contents from a pick list
PICKDYNARRAYINDEX	Select a dynamic array's element from a pick list
PICKFILE	Select a file from a specified directory from a pick list
PICKTABLE	Select a table from a specified directory from a pick list

Getting Input from the User

Element	Action
PUSHBUTTON	Accept or cancel a dialog box; initiate a process, assign a value
RADIOBUTTONS	Select one item from a list of exclusive alternatives
SLIDER	Assign a value by moving a horizontal or vertical slider bar

In the discussion, only the PUSHBUTTON, PICKTABLE, RADIOBUTTONS, and CHECKBOX control elements are covered in detail. The syntax of the remaining control elements is listed here:

```
[ACCEPT
  @ RowNumber, ColumnNumber
  WIDTH NumberOfColumns
  DataTypeExpression
  [LOOKUP LookupTableName]
  [MAX MaximumValue]
  [MIN MinimumValue]
  [PICTURE PictureExpression]
  [REQUIRED]
  TAG ElementTag
  TO VarName]
[LABEL
  @ RowNumber, ColumnNumber
  LabelText
  FOR ElementTag]
[PICKARRAY
  @ RowNumber, ColumnNumber
  HEIGHT NumberOfRows
  WIDTH NumberOfColumns
  [COLUMNS NumberOfDisplayColumns]
  FixedArrayName
  TAG ElementTag
  TO VarName]
[PICKDYNARRAY
  @ RowNumber, ColumnNumber
  HEIGHT NumberOfRows
  WIDTH NumberOfColumns
  [COLUMNS NumberOfDisplayColumns]
  DynamicArrayName
```

```
      TAG ElementTag
      TO VarName]
[PICKDYNARRAYINDEX
   @ RowNumber, ColumnNumber
   HEIGHT NumberOfRows
   WIDTH NumberOfColumns
   [COLUMNS NumberOfDisplayColumns]
   DynamicArrayName
   TAG ElementTag
   TO VarName]
[PICKFILE
   @ RowNumber, ColumnNumber
   HEIGHT NumberOfRows
   WIDTH NumberOfColumns
   [COLUMNS NumberOfDisplayColumns]
   DOSPath
   [NOEXT]
   TAG ElementTag
   TO VarName]
[SLIDER
   @ RowNumber, ColumnNumber
   { HORIZONTAL | VERTICAL }
   LENGTH NumberOfCharacters
   MIN LowestValue
   MAX HighestValue
   ARROWSTEP ArrowClickIncrement
   PAGESTEP SliderClickIncrement
   TAG ElementTag
   TO VarName]
```

Planning a Dialog Box

Even the simplest dialog box requires planning. At the very minimum, you must decide where to place each canvas and control element. You must also define a unique tag for each control element you place. These tags, like the tags used for pull-down menu selections and the handles used for windows, uniquely identify each control element. Finally, each control element must be assigned a variable. These variables serve two purposes. They define the initial value for each control element when the dialog box is opened, and they hold the value assigned to the control element by the user when the dialog box is accepted.

Getting Input from the User

NOTE: You are not required to assign initial values to control element variables. You only need to assign an initial value to a variable when you want the corresponding control element to be initialized with a default value. Any control element associated with an unassigned variable will have no value when the dialog box is first displayed.

The remainder of this chapter provides you with exposure to building dialog boxes. The examples used are small and manageable. In each case, the number of elements is kept to a minimum. This is done only for demonstration purposes. The dialog boxes you create may contain many more control elements, using many different combinations of the available control element types. As will become obvious, scripts that define dialog boxes grow in size proportionally to the number of control elements.

Because of the length of dialog box scripts, there are no exercises for the remainder of this chapter. However, you might consider entering one or more of the example dialog box scripts, and experimenting with their behavior.

Creating a Pushbutton

A *pushbutton* is a button-like control element that the user can click on, or Tab their cursor to and press Enter, to activate. Almost every dialog box contains at least one pushbutton. This is the button that either accepts or cancels the dialog box. Other pushbuttons can be added that assign a value to a variable, or even initiate a process.

The syntax of the pushbutton control element is

```
PUSHBUTTON
  @ RowNumber, ColumnNumber
  WIDTH NumberOfColumns
  ButtonLabel
  [OK | CANCEL ]
  [DEFAULT]
  VALUE [Expression | Procedure]
```

```
TAG ElementTag
TO VarName
```

To create a pushbutton element, you use the keyword PUSHBUTTON followed by the row and column location on the dialog box where the pushbutton will appear, and the width of the button, in characters. The final required component of a pushbutton element is the *button label*, which is an alphanumeric expression that is displayed inside the button. The size of the label must be at least two characters shorter than the defined width of the button. If you want to have a hot key for the button, enclose one of the characters in the button label between tilde characters (~). The user can then select the button, even when the cursor is on another control element, by pressing the [Alt] key followed by the hot key character.

If the button you are defining is used to permit the user to either accept or cancel the dialog box, it must be followed by an optional keyword, OK or CANCEL. If you define your pushbutton as an OK button, the dialog box is accepted if the user pushes the button. Likewise, the dialog box is canceled if a pushbutton defined as a Cancel dialog button is pushed. For all other pushbuttons, omit this keyword.

NOTE: Most dialog boxes have at least one OK or Cancel button, and often both types, but rarely more than one of each.

If you want a pushbutton to be a default pushbutton, use the optional keyword DEFAULT. When a pushbutton is a *default pushbutton*, that button is automatically pushed if the user presses [Enter] while in the dialog box. While you need not have any default pushbuttons on your dialog box, you cannot have more than one.

The required keyword VALUE must be followed by either an alphanumeric expression or the name of a defined procedure that returns an expression, also called a *user-defined function*. (Procedures like these are discussed in Chapter 12.) When the pushbutton is pressed, the expression is assigned to the pushbutton variable if the dialog box is accepted. The last two components of the pushbutton control element are the keyword TAG, followed by an expression, and the keyword TO, followed by the name of the pushbutton variable. As described earlier, the tag is a unique identifier of the control element. The pushbutton

Getting Input from the User

variable is assigned the value of the pushbutton (the value of the expression that follows the keyword Value) if the pushbutton is selected by the user.

Consider the following script:

```
SHOWDIALOG "Pushbutton Demonstration"
  @ 5,20
  HEIGHT 10
  WIDTH 40
  @ 3,5  ?? "This text is a canvas element"
  PUSHBUTTON
     @ 6,7 WIDTH 10
     "~O~k"
     OK
     DEFAULT
     VALUE True
     TAG "Okbutton"
     TO Button1
  PUSHBUTTON
     @ 6,21 WIDTH 10
     "~C~ancel"
     CANCEL
     VALUE False
     TAG "Cancelbutton"
     TO Button2
ENDDIALOG
```

This script segment produces the dialog box shown in Figure 9-6. It contains one canvas element (the text) and two pushbutton control elements. Notice that the row and column locations of the canvas and control elements are positioned in the dialog box relative to the dialog box, and not the full-screen canvas.

NOTE: Although Cancel pushbuttons must use the TO keyword followed by the name of a variable, this variable is never assigned a value. This is because accepting a Cancel button cancels the dialog box, in which case no control element variables are assigned values. Therefore, you must evaluate the system variable Retval to determine if a dialog box was accepted, and not the variables assigned by OK and Cancel pushbuttons.

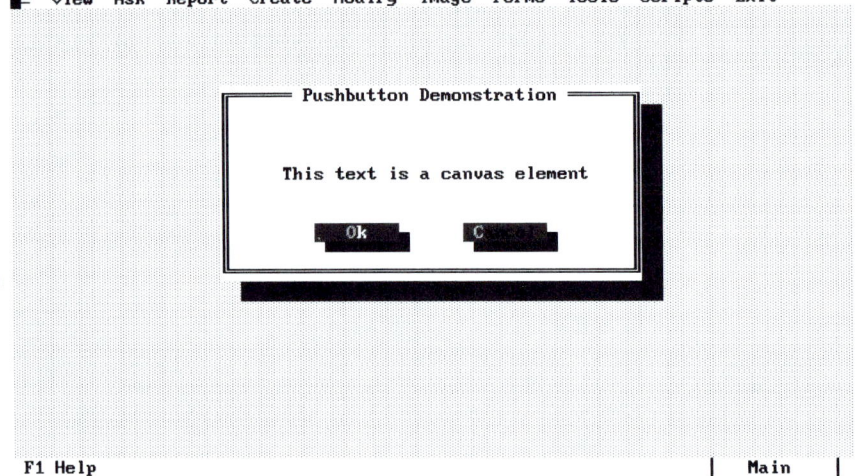

Dialog box with one canvas element and two control elements
Figure 9-6.

Creating a Pick List

Use the PICKTABLE control element to display a pick list of tables. Pick lists are also created using the PICKARRAY, PICKDYNARRAY, PICKDYNARRAYINDEX, and PICKFILE control elements.

The syntax of the PICKTABLE control element is

```
PICKTABLE
   @ RowNumber, ColumnNumber
   HEIGHT NumberOfRows
   WIDTH NumberOfColumns
   [COLUMNS NumberOfDisplayColumns]
   DOSPath
   TAG ElementTag
   TO VarName
```

The pick list will appear beginning at the row and column position specified after the @ command. This pick list will be NumberOfRows tall and NumberOfColumns wide in the dialog box. If you omit the optional keyword COLUMNS, the pick list will consist of one column of selections to pick from. If you want to create a multicolumn pick list, indicate the number of columns following the COLUMNS keyword.

Getting Input from the User

The next component of the PICKTABLE command is the DOS path where the tables you want to display are stored. (Remember to use double backslashes in DOS paths.) If the tables you want displayed in the pick list are in the current directory, use the PAL function DIRECTORY() or specify a null expression (""). The DOS path must be followed by the required keyword TAG and a tag for the control element. The final element of the PICKTABLE control element is the required keyword TO, which must be followed by a variable name. This variable will hold the name of the table the user selects from the pick list.

The following script demonstrates one use of the PICKTABLE control element. The dialog box that results from this script is shown in Figure 9-7.

```
SHOWDIALOG "Select a table to view"
  @ 5,20
  HEIGHT 10
  WIDTH 40
  PICKTABLE
    @ 1, 5
    HEIGHT 4
    WIDTH 28
    COLUMNS 2
    DIRECTORY()
    TAG "Tablelist"
    TO TabName
  PUSHBUTTON
    @ 6,7 WIDTH 10
    "~O~k"
    OK
    DEFAULT
    VALUE True
    TAG "Okbutton"
    TO Button1
  PUSHBUTTON
    @ 6,21 WIDTH 10
    "~C~ancel"
    CANCEL
    VALUE False
    TAG "Cancelbutton"
    TO Button2
ENDDIALOG
```

```
IF Retval AND ISASSIGNED(TabName)
   THEN
      VIEW TabName
ENDIF
```

Creating Radio Buttons and Check Boxes

Radio buttons and check boxes permit your dialog box to display two types of graphically based selection tools. *Radio buttons* are used to display two or more mutually exclusive choices. When the user selects one of the choices, a radio button appears selected in front of the choice. If the user then selects one of the alternative choices from the same bank of radio buttons, the previously selected choice is deselected before the new one is selected. Users select the radio button they want by clicking it with a mouse, or by using the cursor keys to highlight the desired button.

Check boxes are used to display one or more choices, which each toggle independently. All, none, or any combination of the check boxes can be selected. To select or deselect a check box, the user clicks the check box with the mouse or moves the cursor to the check box and presses

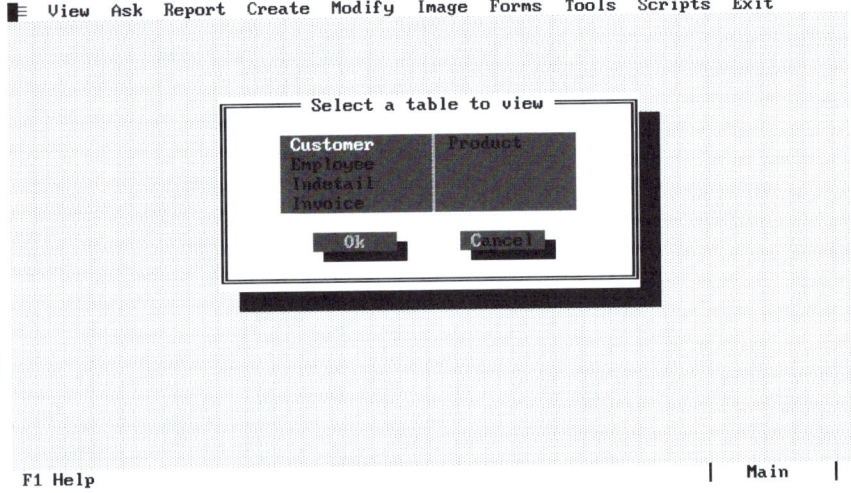

Dialog box with a two-column pick list
Figure 9-7.

Getting Input from the User

the [Spacebar]. Selecting or deselecting any of the boxes has no influence on any of the other check boxes in the same check box bank.

The syntax of the RADIOBUTTONS command is

```
RADIOBUTTONS
   @ RowNumber, ColumnNumber
   HEIGHT NumberOfRows
   WIDTH NumberOfColumns
   ButtonName1 ...[,ButtonNameN]
   TAG ElementTag
   TO VarName
```

The syntax of the CHECKBOX control element is

```
CHECKBOX
   @ RowNumber, ColumnNumber
   HEIGHT NumberOfRows
   WIDTH NumberOfColumns
   TAG ElementTag
   BoxName1 TO Var1
...
   [,BoxNameN TO VarN]
```

Both commands begin with the keyword that identifies the type of control element to be placed (RADIOBUTTONS or CHECKBOX). These keywords are then followed by the upper right corner location of the bank that the control elements will be drawn in. Furthermore, the HEIGHT and WIDTH keywords define the horizontal and vertical size of the area that the buttons or boxes will appear in. The width of the bank must be wide enough to support the buttons or check boxes, and the labels. The height must be a number at least equal to the number of buttons or boxes.

When defining radio buttons, you next provide a comma-separated list of the labels for the radio buttons. These labels are followed by the tag specification and the radio button variable definition.

To create check box elements, follow the WIDTH keyword with the width of the bank of check boxes, which in turn is followed by the TAG keyword and the tag for the check box element. Following the tag is a list of one or more check box labels, each followed by the keyword TO and the name of the variable associated with that check box. If you are defining two or more check boxes in the control element, you must separate the check box labels with commas.

Once the dialog box is accepted, the radio button variable is assigned a value based on the sequential position of the selected button's label in the button label list. For example, if the first radio button is selected, the radio button variable is assigned the value 1, if the second button is selected the variable is assigned the value 2, and so on. If none of the buttons is selected, the radio variable is set to 0. In contrast, check box variables are assigned the value True if the corresponding check box is selected, and False if it is not.

The following script demonstrates the use of radio buttons and check boxes.

```
SHOWDIALOG "Output Report"
  @ 7,15
  HEIGHT 10
  WIDTH 55
  @ 1, 3 ?? "Output report(s) to:"
  @ 1,28 ?? "Output which reports:"
  RADIOBUTTONS
    @ 2,3
    HEIGHT 3
    WIDTH 15
    "~S~creen","P~r~inter","~F~ile"
    TAG "Radio"
    TO RadioVar
  CHECKBOXES
    @ 2,28
    HEIGHT 3
    WIDTH 20
    TAG "Checks"
    "~W~eekly Report" TO Check1,
    "~B~udget Report" TO Check2,
    "~T~ime sheets" TO Check3
  PUSHBUTTON
    @ 6,14 WIDTH 10
    "~O~utput"
    OK
    DEFAULT
```

Getting Input from the User

```
        VALUE True
        TAG "Okbutton"
        TO Button1
    PUSHBUTTON
        @ 6,25 WIDTH 10
        "~C~ancel"
        CANCEL
        VALUE False
        TAG "Cancelbutton"
        TO Button2
ENDDIALOG
```

The dialog box created by this script is shown in Figure 9-8.

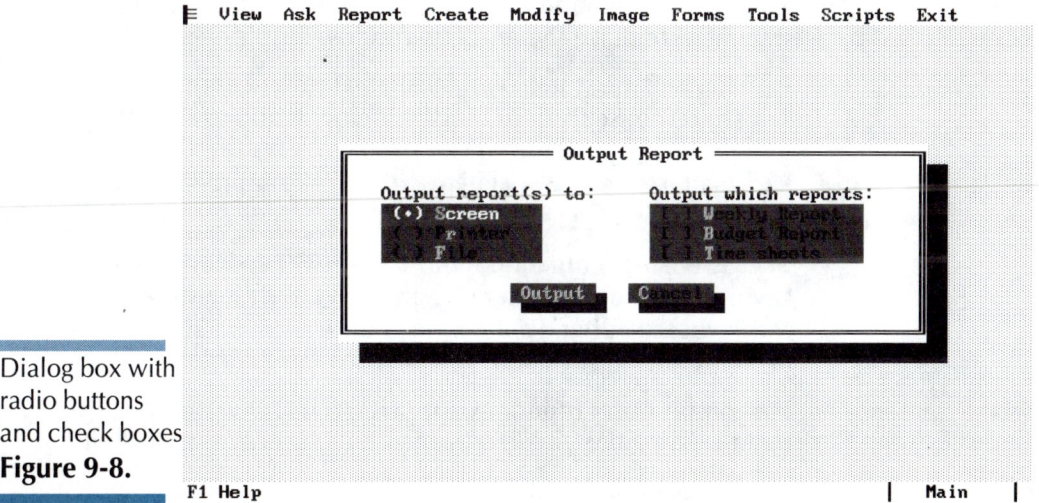

Dialog box with radio buttons and check boxes
Figure 9-8.

Quick Review

- PAL provides you with six menu commands: SHOWMENU, SHOWARRAY, SHOWTABLES, SHOWFILES, SHOWPOPUP, and SHOWPULLDOWN. When you use one of the first five, Paradox waits until the user selects from the menu, or presses [Esc], before continuing on to the remaining commands in the script. When you use SHOWPULLDOWN, Paradox does not wait for the user's input before continuing to the remaining script commands.

- You can use the GETMENUSELECTION command to make a SHOWPULLDOWN menu behave like the other menu commands.

- When you want to get simple input directly from the keyboard, you can use ACCEPT or GETCHAR().

- The STYLE command can be used before and after the ACCEPT statement to make the ACCEPT window visible.

- Paradox sets the system variable Retval to True if the user presses [Enter] in response to an ACCEPT statement, and to False if the user presses [Esc]. Your program should always test the value of Retval after an ACCEPT statement and take appropriate action if the user presses [Esc].

- The GETCHAR() function returns the ASCII code for a single keypress, without the user pressing [Enter]. If no keystrokes are in the keyboard buffer, Paradox waits until the next key is pressed before returning a value.

- For complex user input, use the SHOWDIALOG command to build a dialog box.

- Dialog boxes can display canvas elements and control elements.

- There are 11 different control elements. Among these are pick lists, pushbuttons, ACCEPT windows, slider bars, radio buttons, and check boxes.

CHAPTER

10

VIEWING AND EDITING TABLES

Tables are the central feature of any database. They hold the data that is the essence of your database. Many of your scripts will need to work with Paradox tables. For example, you may need to permit a user to add new data to a table from within one of your scripts. At a minimum, you will want to permit the user to view some or all of the data stored in the database.

This chapter presents the basics of table management using PAL scripts. It starts with a discussion of how to bring a table onto the desktop, select a form for it, and clear it from the desktop when you are through. Next, you will learn how to drop the canvas and display the table to the user. The final table viewing consideration covers how to output or view a table using a report.

Next, you will see how your script can permit the user to edit a table while maintaining control over what the user can and cannot do to it. The chapter concludes with a look at some advanced table-editing topics. In these final sections, you will learn important tricks you can use in your own scripts to manage and control the editing of tables.

NOTE: Windows, window handles, and window attributes are essential features of scripts that manage tables in Paradox 4. As you know, there are no windows in Paradox 3.5. Much of the material in this chapter is also relevant to Paradox 3.5 users, but discussions pertaining to windows do not apply.

Desktop Management

Whenever you use a table, it must first be placed on the desktop. Although this can be done manually by selecting from menus in interactive Paradox before playing your script, this approach is never practical. Instead, your script must take responsibility for placing the table on the desktop, selecting the forms to use (if desired), and removing the table when it is no longer needed. In other words, your scripts must manage the desktop.

Placing a Table on the Desktop

In earlier chapters you were repeatedly exposed to the command that displays a table on the desktop, VIEW. The syntax of this command is

```
VIEW TableName
```

VIEW has one required keyword, VIEW, and a single required expression that must evaluate to the name of a table. When Paradox plays the VIEW command, it displays the table named in the expression. If you need to work with two or more tables on the desktop at once, you must use VIEW once for each table. You can see this in the following exercise:

Viewing and Editing Tables

1. Press [Alt]-[F10] (PAL menu).
2. Select MiniScript.
3. Type **VIEW "Customer"** and press [Enter].

Paradox plays the VIEW command and places the named table, in this case Customer, on the desktop. Your screen should now look like that shown in Figure 10-1.

The table placed on the desktop appears in a window. This window, like all others, is assigned a handle when it is created. Unless you know that you will not be using any window commands that require a handle, it is a good practice to get the handle of the window as soon as it is created. To do this, follow the VIEW command with an assignment statement. On the left side of the assignment command (=) is the variable that holds the window handle, and the function GETWINDOW( ) is on the right. Since the VIEW command makes the newly created window the active window, GETWINDOW( ) returns its handle. From this point on, you can refer to the window holding the table using the window handle.

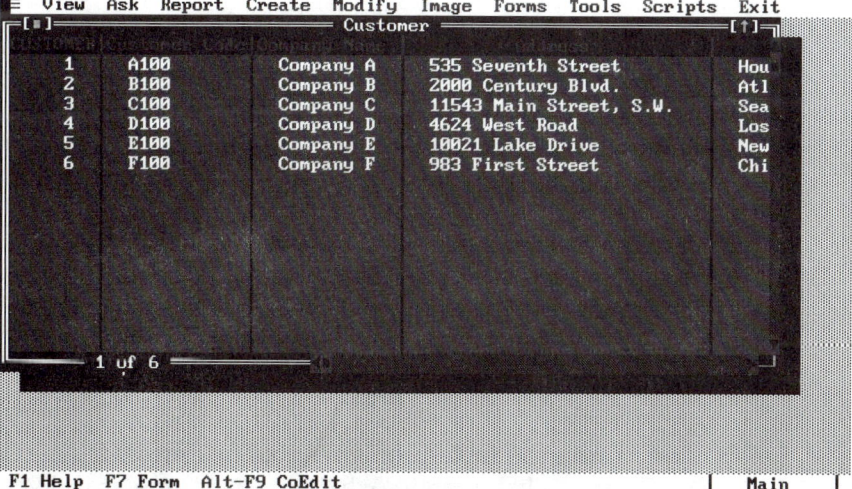

The VIEW "Customer" script displays the Customer table
Figure 10-1.

For example, the following script views a table and immediately gets its handle:

```
VIEW "Customer"
CustHandle = GETWINDOW()
```

NOTE: If you fail to get a window's handle, but later find that you need it, you can use the WINDOW LIST command to generate a fixed array of window handles currently assigned to windows on the desktop. The first element of this array contains the handle for the active window, and the second element holds the handle for the preceding window—the one that was most recently the active window. In most cases, however, it is more efficient to get the handle of each window as it is created.

Picking a Form

When a table is placed on the desktop, it is initially displayed in *table view*. That is, the table appears as a series of columns (fields) and rows (records). Normally, however, you will want to display the table in *form view*, using one of the forms you have designed for the table. This is done using the abbreviated menu command PICKFORM. Its syntax is

```
PICKFORM FormNumber
```

When Paradox encounters the PICKFORM command in a script, it opens a new window and displays the selected form in it. (In Paradox 3.5, the table view is converted to form view: both views do not appear simultaneously, as they do in Paradox 4.) For example, the command PICKFORM 1 creates a new window and displays the current table in form view within it. If you are picking forms 1 through 14, you can represent the form either as an alphanumeric expression ("1") or a numeric expression (1). When you pick form F, however, you must use an alphanumeric expression ("F").

Forms provide you with a number of important advantages over tables, especially in applications.

- ◆ Forms can include only selected fields from a table. This is especially important when you want a user to add data to most of,

Viewing and Editing Tables 243

but not all, the fields in a table. For example, the script itself may assign a unique value to a key field. Therefore, this field would not be displayed on the form.

◆ Forms permit you to display literal text on the screen. You can use this feature to include instructions to users, informing them how to fill out the form.

◆ When you use a single-record form, only one record can be viewed at a time. This is ideal in data entry situations, where viewing more than one record would be distracting. It's also useful when your data is confidential, and you want to control exactly which records the user sees.

◆ Because color and borders can be placed on a form, forms can provide your application with an attractive look.

◆ Forms can display the results of calculations—even those using variables and certain PAL functions. You cannot do this in table view.

◆ Different forms can be used for different situations. For instance, you might design one form for entering new records. This form could display a description to the user describing how to enter the data. A second form might be used for editing records. On this form, only those fields that can be edited would be displayed. A third form might be used for viewing data. This could be a multirecord form.

◆ When you store your data in two or more related tables, you can view and enter your data using a multitable form. Multitable forms, especially ones that use linked-embedded tables, reduce data entry errors and give you a more complete picture of your data.

The following example displays a table on the desktop and selects a form for it. In this exercise, and all remaining exercises that make use of PICKFORM, form 1 for the Customer table will be used. If you did not create a form 1, use Tools/Copy/Form to copy form F to form 1 before you continue.

1. Press [Alt]-[F10] (PAL menu).

2. Select MiniScript.
3. Type **VIEW "Customer" PICKFORM 1** and press Enter.

After a moment's pause, form 1 of the Customer table will appear on the screen. The first record of the Customer table will appear in the form, as shown in Figure 10-2. (Your screen may differ if you designed a different form, used PICKFORM F, or if your Customer data is different.)

Because Paradox 4 places the form in a new window, this window has a handle different from the one that is assigned to the table view window. If you suspect that you will need to refer to the table and form view windows individually, you should get the handle of the form window as soon as you have picked the form (picking the form makes the form window the active window). This is demonstrated in the following script:

```
VIEW "Customer"
CustTable = GETWINDOW()
MESSAGE CustTable
SLEEP 2000
PICKFORM 1
CustForm = GETWINDOW()
MESSAGE CustForm
SLEEP 2000
```

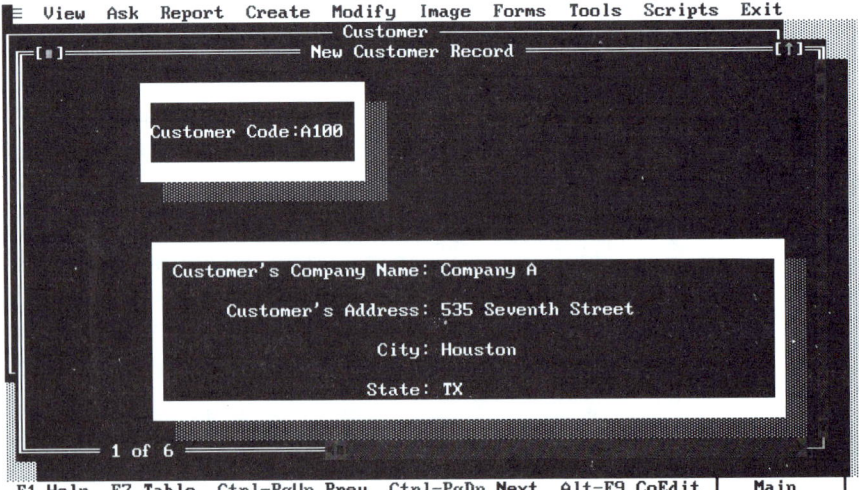

PICKFORM displays a table in form view
Figure 10-2.

Changing Between Table View and Form View

Sometimes you will want to switch from form view to table view within your script. If you are not sure whether your table is in form view or table view, you can use the ISFORMVIEW( ) function before using PICKFORM. For example, when your script moves back and forth between two tables on the desktop, you may not know if the current table is in form view or table view. This is because Paradox always switches to table view when it moves to another table on the desktop (unless the table is an embedded table on a multitable form).

The ISFORMVIEW( ) function returns the value True if the current table is in form view and False if it is not. In order to use this function, a table must be on the desktop; otherwise, a script error will occur.

If you want to place a table in form view, using form 1, and you are not sure if the table is in form view already, use the following lines in your script:

```
IF NOT ISFORMVIEW()
  THEN
    PICKFORM 1
ENDIF
```

If you want to change a table in form view to table view, use the special key command FORMKEY. This command simulates the pressing of [F7] (FormKey). If you are not sure whether the table is already in table view, use the following in your script:

```
IF ISFORMVIEW()
  THEN
    FORMKEY
 ENDIF
```

If you grab the window handles as the table and form view windows are created, you can also move between these two views using the WINDOW SELECT command. The following script uses the window handles to change from form view to table view (assuming that CustTable is the variable that holds the handle of the table view of the window, and CustForm is the variable that holds the form window handle):

```
IF NOT GETWINDOW() = CustTable
  THEN
    WINDOW SELECT CustTable
ENDIF
```

Setting Attributes of Object Windows

When your script brings tables onto the desktop, but never drops the full-screen canvas to display them, you really don't care how the tables look. However, if you give your users a look at the desktop, either using the ECHO or the WAIT command, you will probably want to control how the tables appear and how their windows behave. (WAIT is discussed in detail later in this chapter.)

In Paradox 4, all tables, forms, and query images appear within windows. These windows, created by Paradox when you issued the relevant command (VIEW, for instance), are created using *default window display attributes*. These include their location on the desktop, the presence of a frame, the height and width, and so on. These default settings may not be appropriate for your needs. For example, when you view a form, you may want the user to see all of the form. By default, however, Paradox displays less than the entire form (since the form window includes a border and shadow, and usually places that over less than the entire desktop). This may hide those parts of the form that cannot fit entirely into the window or permit any windows behind the form to be visible.

To control the attributes of windows, use the WINDOW SETATTRIBUTES command, as discussed in Chapter 8. The following example displays a table on the desktop using form view. The display attributes of this form are controlled, however. This is done by declaring a dynamic array and creating a window attribute element for it. Using the WINDOW SETATTRIBUTES command, these attributes are assigned to the form window. You will use this technique often, which is one of the more convincing arguments for getting a window's handle when the window is created.

```
VIEW "Customer"
CustomerTable = GETWINDOW()
PICKFORM 1
CustomerForm = GETWINDOW()
DYNARRAY BetterForm[]
```

Viewing and Editing Tables

```
BetterForm["HASSHADOW"] = False
BetterForm["HEIGHT"] = 23
BetterForm["WIDTH"] = 80
WINDOW SETATTRIBUTES CustomerForm FROM BetterForm
```

Keeping the Desktop Clear

A common problem that can easily arise with your scripts is that your desktop becomes crowded with windows or tables. This typically occurs because you do not see them on the desktop while your script is running, since the PAL canvas is displayed then. When the canvas is finally dropped, you may be surprised to find windows displayed there.

You can avoid this problem by following a simple rule of thumb. When you are done using a table, form, query, or canvas window, remove it from the canvas. If you follow this rule religiously, your canvas will always be clear of unwanted objects when your script is through playing.

Keeping unwanted windows and tables off the desktop is a good idea for several reasons. The most compelling reason is that each window on the desktop reduces the amount of memory available for your scripts. The second reason is that if you permit a user to use [Ctrl]-[F4] (WinNext) to move between windows on the desktop, the unnecessary windows will make working with the desired windows more difficult.

Clearing Tables from the Desktop

There are two commands used to remove tables from the desktop: CLEARIMAGE and CLEARALL.

The syntax of CLEARIMAGE is

```
CLEARIMAGE
```

The syntax of CLEARALL is

```
CLEARALL
```

Both these commands are special key commands. CLEARIMAGE simulates the press of [F8] (ClearImage) and CLEARALL simulates the press of [Alt]-[F8] (ClearAll). When Paradox plays CLEARIMAGE, it removes the current image (table or query) from the desktop. CLEARALL, in contrast, removes all images from the desktop simultaneously.

Two more commands you can use are WINCLOSE and WINDOW CLOSE. These close the active window, and if the active window contains a table, form, or query, that object is removed from the desktop as well. Finally, if you want to remove all windows from the desktop simultaneously, you can use the following:

```
ALTSPACE {Desktop} {Empty}
```

While CLEARIMAGE, CLEARALL, WINCLOSE, and WINDOW CLOSE can only be used when Paradox is in Main mode, selecting Desktop/Empty from the System menu can be used in any mode. Any changes that have not been saved, however, will be lost. To use the other four commands from any mode other than Main, your script must first return to Main mode.

CAUTION: Do not confuse CLEARALL and CLEARIMAGE with the CLEAR command. CLEARALL and CLEARIMAGE both remove images from the desktop. In contrast, CLEAR erases the current PAL canvas.

Desktop Movement

After you have placed one or more tables on the desktop, you often need to move within them and between them. There are two ways to do this. First, use special key commands. These provide you with all the cursor movement features you are accustomed to using in interactive Paradox. Second, use programming commands. These two methods are described next.

Special Key Commands

The special key commands listed in Table 10-1 permit you to move your cursor within a table and between tables on the desktop. These commands perform exactly as their corresponding keypresses do in interactive Paradox. For example, some keys will provide different movements, depending on whether you are in table view or form view. The DOWN key command, for instance, moves the cursor to the

Viewing and Editing Tables

following record in a table in table view, but moves to the next lower field in form view.

ASCII Code	Key Name	Keypress
CTRLEND		Last field in current record (table or form)
CTRLHOME		First field in current record (table or form)
CTRLLEFT		Left one screen of fields (table)
CTRLPGDN		Down one record (form)
CTRLPGUP		Up one record (form)
CTRLRIGHT		Right one screen of fields (table)
DOWN		Down one record (table) or down one field (form)
DOWNIMAGE		Down one image (table or form)
END		To last record in table (table or form)
HOME		First record in table (table or form)
LEFT		Left one field (table or form)
PGDN		Down one screen of records (table) or first field in next record (form)
PGUP		Up one screen of records (table) or last field in preceding record (form)
REVERSETAB		Left one field (table or form)
RIGHT		Right one field (table or form)
TAB		Right one field (table or form)
UP		Up one record (table) or up one field (form)
UPIMAGE		Up one image (table or form)
WINNEXT		Next window on the desktop (not available in Paradox 3.5)

Cursor Movement Commands
Table 10-1.

Using Programming Commands

Although special key commands can provide all your navigational needs, Paradox also provides you with a number of programming commands you can use for this purpose. You should use these programming commands in place of their special key counterparts whenever practical, since programming commands are more precise and easier to interpret.

There are two important programming commands that permit you to move your cursor between and within tables: MOVETO and LOCATE.

The MOVETO Command

The MOVETO command provides you with nearly all the cursor movement control that your scripts need. This command has five variations. Taken together, they permit you to move to a specific table, a specific field, a specific record, or a specific image number on the desktop. The syntaxes of the five versions of the command are

```
Version 1    MOVETO FieldSpecifier
Version 2    MOVETO RECORD RecordNumber
Version 3    MOVETO ImageNumber
Version 4    MOVETO TableName
Version 5    MOVETO FIELD FieldName
```

The most efficient of these commands is the first version. If you follow the MOVETO command with a field specifier, Paradox responds by moving the cursor to the named table and field. If you omit the table or field, as is permitted with field specifiers, Paradox defaults to the current table or field, whichever was omitted. You can find a table of all valid field specifiers in Chapter 4.

The second and third versions of the MOVETO command permit you to move to a specific record in a table and a specific image on the desktop, respectively. For example, if you issue the command MOVETO RECORD 2, Paradox moves the cursor to the second record in the current table. MOVETO 2 moves your cursor to the second image on the desktop.

There are superior alternatives to both of these versions of MOVETO. Consider MOVETO RECORD. Rarely will a specific record number in a table be of use to you. Instead, you typically are interested in moving to

Viewing and Editing Tables

a record that contains a specific value. The LOCATE command, described in the next section, provides this service. The case is the same with the third version of MOVETO. It is more common to move to a named table, rather than base the movement on the order of images on the desktop.

The final two versions of MOVETO, however, are very useful. Unlike the first version, which permits you to move to a particular table and field, the last two permit you to move to a particular table or a particular field, but not both. What makes versions 4 and 5 so special is that the table name and the field name are specified by expressions. In contrast, version 1 specifies the table and/or field explicitly. In other words, you can use versions 4 and 5 with constants, variables, arrays, field specifiers, or functions, which you cannot with version 1. Version 1, however, does offer the advantage of moving you to a table and field in a single command. If you must use an expression to make this movement, you have to use both versions 4 and 5 in your script.

The following exercise demonstrates the use of each version of the MOVETO command. After each command in the script a comment shows which version of the command is being used. When you enter this script, it is not necessary for you to enter the comments.

1. Select Scripts/Editor/New.
2. Type **Moving** and press [Enter].
3. Enter the following script into the Editor screen:

```
CLEARALL
VIEW "Customer"
VIEW "Employee"
MOVETO [Customer -> Company Name]   ;version 1
MOVETO RECORD 3                     ;version 2
MOVETO 2                            ;version 3
TabName = "Customer"                ;variable assignment
MOVETO TabName                      ;version 4
FieldName = "Customer Code"         ;variable assignment
MOVETO FIELD FieldName              ;version 5
MOVETO [Employee ->]                ;version 1
MOVETO "Customer"                   ;version 4
MOVETO FIELD "Address"              ;version 5
CLEARALL                            ;clear the desktop
```

4. Press [F2] to save the Moving script.
5. Select [Alt]-[F10] (PAL menu).
6. Select Debug.
7. Type **Moving** and press [Enter].

   The Debugger displays the first command in the script, CLEARALL, at the bottom of your screen. If there are any tables currently on the desktop, CLEARALL will remove them. If there are no tables on the desktop, CLEARALL will have no effect.

8. Press [Ctrl]-[S] (Step) three times to play CLEARALL and the next two commands, which display the Customer and Employee tables on the desktop.

   The remaining commands all use the MOVETO command to move your cursor between and within the tables.

9. Press [Ctrl]-[S] (Step) repeatedly until the script is complete.

   Each time you press [Ctrl]-[S] (Step), observe how Paradox responds and moves the cursor.

Since versions 1, 4, and 5 of the MOVETO command permit you to move directly to a named table and/or field, they should be used whenever possible. The result will be to make your scripts easier to interpret and maintain.

NOTE: You can also use the window handle to move to a table with the WINDOW SELECT command. If the window handle belongs to a window that contains a table, form, or query, that object becomes the current table. If the window is a canvas window, that window becomes active, but the current table does not change. Using WINDOW SELECT is a good command when you want to select the form view of a table on the desktop. However, when tables are not duplicated in windows on the desktop, the MOVETO command is the most direct.

The LOCATE Command

You use the LOCATE command to move to a specific value in a table. For example, you can use LOCATE to move to the first record in the Customer table that has the company name B100. In some respects,

Viewing and Editing Tables

LOCATE is very similar to the ZOOM feature in Paradox. However, LOCATE is always preferable to ZOOM, since Paradox sets the system variable Retval to True when LOCATE is successful. This does not happen if you use ZOOM.

There are two versions of the LOCATE command:

```
LOCATE [NEXT] [PATTERN] Value
```

and

```
LOCATE [NEXT] Value1, Value2 ... [,ValueN]
```

Use the first version of LOCATE to find a value in the current field of the current table. LOCATE requires one expression, the value you are searching for. For example, if your cursor is in the Company Name field of the Customer table, and you use the command,

```
LOCATE "B100"
```

Paradox will move the cursor to the first record of the table and search until it finds the value B100. If B100 is found, Paradox will move the cursor to the record that contains that value. If you use the optional keyword NEXT in the LOCATE command, Paradox will begin its search from the current record.

PATTERN is also an optional keyword for use with this first version of LOCATE. When you use PATTERN, Paradox permits you to use wildcard characters in the search string. These characters are

@	One character of any type
..	Zero or one or more characters of any type

For example, the command,

```
LOCATE PATTERN "S.."
```

will cause Paradox, beginning at the first record in the table, to search for the first value in the current field that begins with the letter S. Even if you do not use wildcard characters in the search string, using the PATTERN keyword results in a case-insensitive search.

The second version of the LOCATE command has two significant features. The first is that you can specify a list of values to search for. Paradox will attempt to locate a record whose first fields contain the values in the list. For example, if you use the command,

```
LOCATE "B100", "Company B"
```

Paradox will attempt to locate the record that contains B100 in the first field and Company B in the second. If you supply a list of three values, Paradox will attempt to match these against the contents of the first three fields in the table.

This process leads to the second difference. Unlike the first version of LOCATE, the field position of the cursor does not matter, since the list is always compared with the first fields in the table.

Like the first version of LOCATE, Paradox allows use of the optional keyword NEXT, which will begin the search from the current record. Otherwise, a LOCATE command always begins with the first record in the table.

LOCATE and Retval

LOCATE is preferable to ZOOM (the equivalent of Ctrl-Z) because LOCATE is one of the PAL commands that assigns a value to the Paradox system variable Retval. If Paradox finds a match in response to a LOCATE command, Retval is assigned the value True. If no match is found, Retval is assigned the value False. This does not happen with ZOOM.

Since Retval indicates whether the LOCATE was successful or not, your script should always test Retval after every LOCATE. This is demonstrated in the following exercise:

1. Select Scripts/Editor/New.
2. Type **Locateit** and press Enter.
3. Enter the following script into the Editor screen (the comment lines are optional):

Viewing and Editing Tables

```
CLEAR
CLEARALL
VIEW "Customer"
MOVETO [Customer -> Company Name]
WHILE TRUE
   @ 10,12 ?? "Enter the company name (press ESC to quit): "
   STYLE REVERSE
   ACCEPT "A10" To FindValue
   STYLE
   ;Check Retval to see if ESC was pressed.
   IF NOT Retval
     THEN
        ; ESC was pressed. Return to Paradox.
        RETURN "Thank you for using LocateIt"
   ENDIF
   ;A value was entered. Try to locate it.
   LOCATE FindValue
   ;Check Retval to see if the locate was successful.
   IF NOT Retval
     THEN
        ;Retval was False, the value was not found.
        MESSAGE FindValue, " not found"
     ELSE
        ;Retval was True, the value was found.
        MESSAGE FindValue, " Found"
   ENDIF
ENDWHILE
CLEARIMAGE
```

4. Press F10 (Menu) and select Go.

   Paradox will play the script and display the prompt "Enter the company name (Press ESC to quit):", as shown in Figure 10-3. When you enter the name of a company that appears in the Company Name field of the Customer table, the LOCATE command will find it, which sets Retval to True and causes your script to display a message indicating that the value was found. When you enter a name that is not found in that field, Retval is set to False, and a message indicating that the value was not found is displayed. This process will repeat, because of the WHILE command, until you press Esc in response to the prompt.

```
                    Enter the company name (press ESC to quit): ███████
```

LOCATE command locates a requested record
Figure 10-3.

NOTE: The LOCATE command begins at the first record in the table, searching the records in the order of the primary table key (the key field or fields), or in the order of the records in the table if the table is not keyed. If you need to locate values based on secondary indices (created either using the INDEX command or the Modify/Index or Image/OrderTable menu selections), use LOCATE INDEXORDER. The LOCATE INDEXORDER command also provides a number of advanced options when working with indices. The syntax for this command is found in the *PAL Reference* (or the *PAL User's Guide* for version 3.5).

Viewing Tables

One of the main reasons a table is displayed on the desktop from within a script is to permit the user to use it. For example, you may want to display a table and permit the user to view its contents. Unfortunately, simply placing a table on the desktop does not permit the user to view it, since the canvas appears in front of the desktop.

However, Paradox does provide you with a command for permitting the user to interact with a table on the desktop. This command is WAIT, one of the most useful commands in PAL.

Viewing and Editing Tables

The following sections cover one version of this command. There is a second version used when you want to provide extensive control over the viewing or editing session. In many cases, it is also combined with a pull-down menu. Since this version of the WAIT command is related to the larger topic of event-driven programming, it is covered in Chapter 13.

WAITing on a Table

The WAIT command can only be used if there is at least one table or query on the desktop. When Paradox encounters the WAIT command, it drops the canvas and waits until one of the keys listed after the UNTIL keyword is pressed. The syntax of the WAIT command is

```
WAIT { WORKSPACE | TABLE | RECORD | FIELD }
   [PROMPT Expression1 ... [,ExpressionN]
   [MESSAGE Message]
   UNTIL KeyCode1 ...[, KeyCodeN]
```

There are four variations of the WAIT command: WAIT WORKSPACE, WAIT TABLE, WAIT RECORD, and WAIT FIELD. Use WAIT WORKSPACE to provide the user with all privileges associated with working on the desktop. These users may move between all windows on the desktop, including query images, tables in both table and form views, and between multiple tables on a multitable form. The user is also free to move and resize windows. Canvas windows can be moved to and closed within a WAIT WORKSPACE, but windows containing objects cannot.

While in a window that contains a table, form, or query, Paradox permits the user to move freely. All standard Paradox keystrokes can be used to move within the table, including (End), (Home), (Pg Up), and (Pg Dn). Within a single record, the user can use the arrow keys to move from field to field.

NOTE: WAIT WORKSPACE is not available in Paradox 3.5.

WAIT TABLE provides all of the table movement capabilities as WAIT WORKSPACE. The user can even move or resize the table during a WAIT TABLE—unless the window attributes prohibit this. (This is also true of WAIT RECORD and WAIT FIELD.) However, the user cannot leave the current table. For instance, if there are two or more tables on the desktop, the user cannot press [F3] (UpImage), [F4] (DownImage), or [Ctrl]-[F8] (WinNext) to move to another table.

WAIT RECORD is even more restrictive than WAIT TABLE. WAIT RECORD will not permit the user to leave the current record of the current table.

WAIT FIELD is the most restrictive of all the WAIT commands. When WAIT FIELD is used, the user may not leave the current field of the current record of the current table. This is the least used of all the WAIT commands.

The WAIT command has one required keyword, UNTIL, which must be followed by at least one key code. The WAIT command holds your script in suspension, allowing only the permissible keypresses, until the user presses the key listed after the UNTIL keyword.

Consider the following script segment:

```
VIEW "Customer"
WAIT TABLE
  UNTIL "ESC"
CLEARIMAGE
```

This script begins by placing the Customer table on the desktop. Next, the WAIT command is played, which drops the canvas and permits the user to move freely within the Customer table. When the user finally presses the [Esc] key, the script continues to play with the statement that follows the WAIT command, CLEARIMAGE, in this case. Try this script in the following exercise:

1. Select Scripts/Editor/New.
2. Type **Viewtab** and press [Enter].
3. Type the following script into the Editor screen:

    ```
    CLEAR
    CLEARALL
    ```

Viewing and Editing Tables

```
VIEW "Customer"
WAIT TABLE
   UNTIL "ESC"
CLEARIMAGE
```

4. Press F2 (Do-It!) to save the script.

5. Press Ctrl-G (Go) to play the script.

   After a moment's pause, during which time Paradox is placing the Customer table on the desktop, the Customer table suddenly appears.

6. Try moving around the Customer table pressing Home, End, and so on.

   If you try to press a key that is not related to moving around the table, such as F10 or F2, you will hear Paradox beep at you.

7. When you are done exploring the keypresses permitted by the WAIT command, press the Esc key.

   Because Esc is listed following the UNTIL command, pressing it causes Paradox to exit the WAIT statement and proceed to the next command in the script, CLEARIMAGE, which results in the table being removed from the desktop.

Prompting a WAIT

Whenever you use WAIT, you should use the optional PROMPT keyword to display a prompt. The prompt you display will appear on the status line. This prompt should tell the user how to exit the WAIT as demonstrated in the following exercise:

1. Select Scripts/Editor/Open.

2. Type **Viewtab** and press Enter.

3. Edit the WAIT command so that it looks like the following:

```
CLEAR
CLEARALL
VIEW "Customer"
WAIT TABLE
   PROMPT "You are viewing the Customer table.  "+
          "Press ESC to return to Paradox."
```

```
    UNTIL "ESC"
CLEARIMAGE
```

4. Press [F2] (Do-It!) to save the change to Viewtab.
5. Play Viewtab by pressing [Ctrl]-[G] (Go).

   Again, Paradox will play the script and display the Customer table on the desktop. This time, however, the prompt will appear in the status line. This is shown in Figure 10-4.

A WAIT command also permits you to specify an optional message. This message, which appears at the lower right corner of the desktop, is displayed until the user presses a key. Its appearance matches that of the message produced by the MESSAGE command.

For example, the following script,

```
VIEW "Customer"
PICKFORM 1
WAIT TABLE
   PROMPT "Press ESC to continue"
   MESSAGE "You are viewing the Customer table"
   UNTIL "ESC"
CLEARIMAGE
```

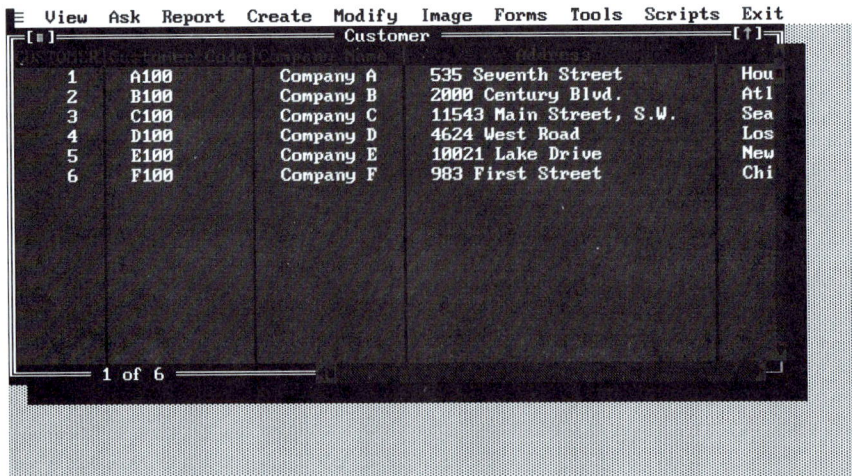

Viewtab script displays a table and a prompt
Figure 10-4.

Viewing and Editing Tables

will produce a result like that shown in Figure 10-5. Note that PICKFORM was used with WAIT in this example.

NOTE: When you use WAIT in Paradox 3.5, you can include two prompts, if separated by a comma. The first prompt is displayed on the first line of the screen, and the second prompt on the second.

Using Retval in a WAIT

WAIT is another one of the PAL commands that assigns a value to the Paradox system variable Retval. Retval is assigned the value of the key pressed to exit WAIT. In the preceding exercise, the value of Retval is always (Esc). If you performed the preceding exercise, you can test this now by following these steps:

1. Press (Alt)-(F10) (PAL menu).
2. Select Value.
3. Type **Retval** and press (Enter).

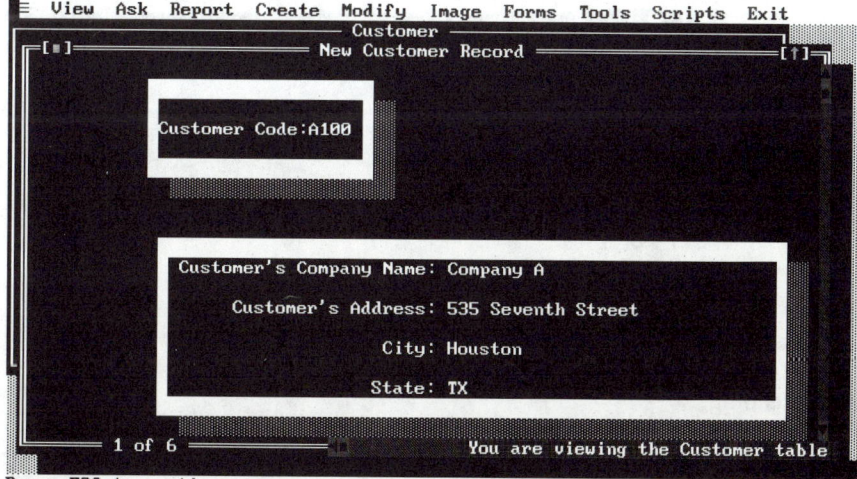

WAITing on a form
Figure 10-5.

Paradox displays the value ESC in the lower right corner of your screen, as shown in Figure 10-6.

CAUTION: The capitalization of ESC will match what you used following the UNTIL keyword in the preceding script. In other words, if your WAIT ended with UNTIL "ESC", then ESC will be displayed on your screen. If instead, you used UNTIL "esc", esc will appear. This point has important implications for how you use Retval.

The UNTIL keyword often has more than one key listed after it. At a minimum, a key that will permit the user to leave the table and continue with the script is included. But you will also list the keys whose actions you want to control. This is called *trapping*. You trap the keypress and your script decides what to do with it.

There are two keypresses that your script should always trap: Ctrl-O (DOS) and Alt-O (DOSBig). If the user presses either of these keys during a WAIT, Paradox exits to DOS. This could prove disastrous for your application, especially if the user does not know how to get back into Paradox (by typing **EXIT**). If the user begins deleting files or simply turns off the computer, Paradox tables could be damaged.

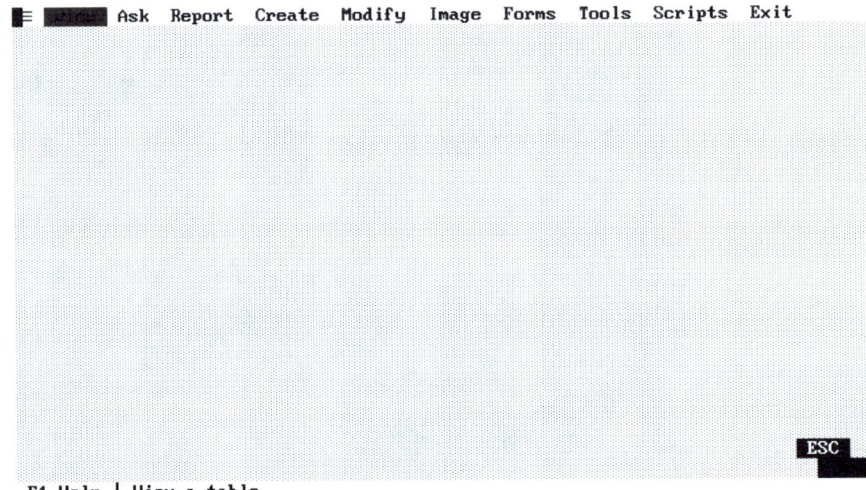

Value of Retval after escaping from a WAIT
Figure 10-6.

Using WHILE with WAIT

Paradox will stay within the WAIT command until one of the keys listed after the UNTIL keyword is pressed. However, if you are trapping one or more keypresses, you will want to return to the WAIT command when one of these keys is pressed. This is done with a WHILE loop.

Placing a WHILE loop around a WAIT is one of the fundamental techniques of processing this version of the WAIT command. The command that is used immediately following the UNTIL keyword of the WAIT command should be one of the branching control structures, either IF or SWITCH. This control structure should test the value of Retval. If Retval evaluates to the keypress that permits the user to leave the loop, your script should issue the QUITLOOP command. If it is any other key, your script should return to the WAIT command, using the LOOP command.

Consider this script:

```
VIEW "Customer"
WHILE True
  WAIT TABLE
    PROMPT "Press ESC to continue"
    UNTIL "ESC", "DOS", "DOSBig"
  SWITCH
    CASE Retval = "ESC":
      QUITLOOP
    CASE Retval = "DOS" OR Retval = "DOSBig":
      BEEP
      LOOP
  ENDSWITCH
ENDWHILE
CLEARIMAGE
```

In this segment, the condition for the WHILE loop is the logical constant True. This means that WHILE will loop until a QUITLOOP, RETURN, or QUIT command is played. The next command, WAIT TABLE, will continue to display the Customer table until one of three keys is pressed, [Esc], [Ctrl]-[O] (DOS), or [Alt]-[O] (DOSBig). When one of these keys is pressed, the SWITCH statement is used to determine which one. Within the SWITCH statement, the script compares the value of Retval with each of the possible values. If Retval evaluates to ESC (the [Esc] key is pressed), Paradox plays the QUITLOOP command.

The QUITLOOP command causes Paradox to immediately exit the WHILE loop and play the next command, CLEARIMAGE in this example. If either of the other keys is pressed, Paradox beeps and then loops back to the WHILE command, which then reenters the WAIT.

NOTE: In the preceding script, the use of the LOOP command is optional, since Paradox will automatically loop back to the WAIT statement when it reaches the ENDWHILE command. The use of LOOP, however, makes the script easier to interpret, since it makes the intention to loop unmistakable.

TIP: Rather than using a branching control structure to evaluate Retval, many PAL programmers assign the value of Retval to a second variable and then evaluate it instead. This preserves the value returned by the WAIT command. Retval, on the other hand, is assigned a value by so many PAL commands, it rarely holds the same value for long.

Reports

In addition to viewing tables and forms, you can use reports to access the data stored in Paradox tables. The advantage of reports is that they are formatted, can output on paper, and may include calculations, summary statistics, and multitable views of your data. The two most common ways to use a report are to print it and preview it. Printing is discussed first, followed by previewing. A third way to use a report, by sending it to an ASCII file, is not described, but is useful in certain types of applications.

Printing Reports

You can easily print any report from your script by using the REPORT command. The syntax is

Viewing and Editing Tables

```
REPORT TableName ReportName
```

This command has one required keyword, REPORT, and two required alphanumeric expressions. The first expression must evaluate to a table name, and the second must evaluate to one of the reports for the named table. For example, to print report number 1 for the Customer table, use the following command:

```
REPORT "Customer" "1"
```

Using the PRINTERSTATUS( ) Function

Before your script attempts to print a report, you should test to make sure the printer is ready. If it is not, your script should not send a report to it. Use the PRINTERSTATUS( ) function to determine whether the printer is ready before attempting to print a report.

When Paradox plays the function PRINTERSTATUS( ), it checks to see if the printer connected to your computer is ready to receive output. If it is, PRINTERSTATUS( ) returns the value True; if not, it returns the value False. You can use the following script segment in your own script to ensure that the printer is on before attempting to send a report to it.

```
IF NOT PRINTERSTATUS()
   THEN
      RETURN "Cannot print the report. The printer is off."
   ELSE
      REPORT "Customer" "1"
ENDIF
```

CAUTION: The value returned by PRINTERSTATUS( ) is less informative when your computer is on a local area network (LAN) and you are printing to a network printer. Depending on your network, and how it makes use of printers, PRINTERSTATUS( ) may return True even if the printer is off. You should test PRINTERSTATUS( ) with your network to learn how to best use this function. Also, PRINTERSTATUS( ) is unreliable when printing to a local printer connected to any port other than LPT1.

Previewing Reports

Paradox 4 provides a *report previewer* that you can use to view a report without having to send it to a printer. You can use this feature within your scripts to give your users the same capability. Using the report previewer prior to printing a report can save time and paper.

There are no PAL keywords to access the report previewer. You can, however, use braced menu selections to access it. To see how this works, try the following exercise:

1. Select Scripts/Editor/New.
2. Type **Viewrep** and press [Enter].
3. Enter the following script into the Editor screen:

   ```
   MESSAGE "Preparing report for preview..."   ;Display a message
   MENU {Report} {Output} {Customer} {R}
   MESSAGE ""              ;Turn the message prompt off.
   ;The next command redefines the status bar message.
   PROMPT "Press CTRL-F8, or select Cancel to return."
   {Screen}
   PROMPT              ;This command resets the status bar.
   RETURN "Done"
   ```

4. Press [F2] to return to the Main menu.
5. Press [Ctrl]-[G] (Go) to play this script.

   After a moment, the report preview appears and the message defined by the PROMPT command is displayed in the status bar. While in the report previewer, your script is suspended, and the user is free to use any report previewer features to inspect the report.

6. Exit the report previewer by pressing [F2] (Do-It!), clicking on the window close button, selecting Cancel from the displayed menu, or pressing [Ctrl]-[F8] (WinClose). Once the report preview is closed, the script continues. At this point the PROMPT command restores the status bar and the RETURN command displays the message "DONE" on the screen.

Viewing and Editing Tables

Editing Tables

Up to this point, you have seen the WAIT command used to permit a user to view a table. More common, however, is its use to permit the user to enter data into a table. Just as in interactive Paradox, you cannot add data to a table in Main mode. Instead, you must be in Edit, CoEdit, or DataEntry mode. The following section discusses the use of Edit mode. CoEdit mode is described later in this chapter, as well as in Chapter 14. DataEntry mode, another useful editing mode, is also described in Chapter 14.

Entering Edit Mode

There are two ways to enter Edit mode from a script. The first is to place a table on the desktop using the VIEW command and then use the special key command EDITKEY to mimic pressing the  (Edit) key. The second is to use the abbreviated menu command EDIT. The special key command is

```
EDITKEY
```

and the EDIT command syntax is

```
EDIT TableName
```

The EDITKEY command places Paradox into Edit mode. Use of the EDITKEY command assumes that the table you want to edit is already displayed on the desktop and is the current table. Therefore, the EDITKEY command is commonly preceded by the VIEW command.

Use the EDIT command when you want to both add a table to the desktop and enter Edit mode with a single command. The EDIT command works like a combination of VIEW and EDITKEY. Because the EDIT command opens a new window on the desktop and makes it active, you should get the handle of this new window in the statement that follows the EDIT command, if you need to use any of the window commands that require a handle.

Exiting Edit Mode

When you no longer need the desktop to be in Edit mode, you should immediately return to Main mode. You can do this with DO_IT! or CANCELEDIT. The syntaxes are

```
DO_IT!
```

and

```
CANCELEDIT
```

When DO_IT! is played, any changes made to the table are saved, and Paradox returns to Main mode. CANCELEDIT, on the other hand, mimics the selection of Cancel/Yes from the Edit menu. When CANCELEDIT is played, all changes to the table are canceled and Paradox returns to Main mode. In both cases, the table, and the window it appears in, remain on the desktop.

Editing a Table in a WAIT Command

Once in Edit mode, your script uses the WAIT command to give the user access to the table or tables they need to edit. However, unlike when the script simply displays a table to view, you should give the user two ways to exit Edit mode. The user should have a choice of saving any changes to the table or exiting without saving the changes.

The following exercise will make use of WHILE to trap for keys, as well as DO_IT! and CANCELEDIT statements to exit Edit mode.

1. Select Scripts/Editor/New.
2. Type **Edittab** and press Enter.
3. Type the following script into the Editor window:

```
CLEAR
CLEARALL
EDIT "Customer"
PICKFORM 1
WHILE True
  WAIT TABLE
    PROMPT "Press F2 to save or ESC to cancel."
```

Viewing and Editing Tables

```
        UNTIL "DO_IT!", "ESC", "DOS", "DOSBig"
     SWITCH
       CASE Retval = "DO_IT!":
         DO_IT!
         QUITLOOP
       CASE Retval = "ESC":
         CANCELEDIT
         QUITLOOP
       CASE Retval = "DOS" OR Retval = "DOSBig":
         BEEP
         LOOP
     ENDSWITCH
  ENDWHILE
  CLEARIMAGE
```

4. Press [F2] (Do-It!) to save the script.
5. Press [Ctrl]-[G] (Go) to play it.

   Paradox will display the table and wait for you to make any changes to it. Your screen will look like Figure 10-7. If you press the [Esc] key, any changes you make will be lost. Alternatively, if you press [F2] (Do-It!), the changes will be saved.

NOTE: In this example, special key names are used in the key code list, but you can use any valid key name. For instance, you can use "F2" instead of "DO_IT!". You can also use ASCII codes. For example, instead of "DO_IT!" you can use –60 (the ASCII code for [F2]). Whether you use ASCII codes or special key names, you must be consistent within your script. For example, if you use "F2" following the UNTIL keyword, you must compare Retval to the value F2, not DO_IT! or –60. Key names and their ASCII code equivalents are provided in Appendix A.

Advanced Editing Topics

You now know the basic script commands necessary to navigate the tables on the desktop as well as those that permit the user to view and edit tables. There are also other features you will probably want to build into your scripts. These topics are covered in the remaining pages of this chapter. Unlike many of the features covered earlier, explicit

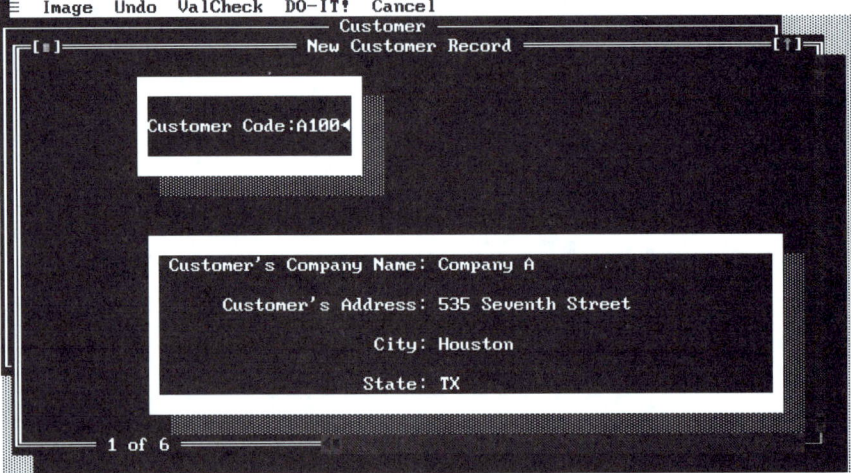

Screen after playing the Edittab script
Figure 10-7.

exercises are not provided. Instead, examples of scripts you can use to achieve certain effects are given. These scripts tend to be long. If you have the time, however, you will certainly benefit from entering these scripts and observing their effects.

Getting User Confirmation

Earlier in this chapter you learned that you can trap for unwanted keypresses, such as [Ctrl]-[O] (DOS) and [Alt]-[O] (DOSBig). During an editing session, there are additional keys you will probably want to trap for. The most common of these are the keys that can be used to delete a record and cancel the editing session. Instead of simply accepting these keypresses, however, your script should ask the user to confirm the keypress. If the user confirms that he or she indeed wants to delete the record or cancel the editing session, your script should then comply with the request.

In general, whenever the user makes a request that will result in the loss of work or data, your script should ask for confirmation before carrying out the request. Consider the following script:

Viewing and Editing Tables

```
CLEAR
CLEARALL
EDIT "Customer"
PICKFORM 1
WHILE True
  WAIT TABLE
    PROMPT "Press F2 to save or ESC to cancel."
    UNTIL "F2", "DEL", "ESC", "DOS", "DOSBig"
  SWITCH
    CASE Retval = "F2":
      DO_IT!
      QUITLOOP
    CASE Retval = "ESC":
      MESSAGE "Do you want to cancel your changes?"
      SHOWMENU
        "No" :"Do not cancel changes.",
        "Yes":"Cancel changes."
      TO Choice
      IF VERSION() > 3.5 THEN MESSAGE "" ENDIF
      IF Choice = "Yes"
        THEN
          CANCELEDIT
          QUITLOOP
        ELSE
          LOOP
      ENDIF
    CASE Retval = "DEL":
      MESSAGE "Do you want to delete this record?"
      SHOWMENU
        "No" :"Do not delete this record.",
        "Yes":"Delete this record."
      TO Choice
      IF VERSION() > 3.5 THEN MESSAGE "" ENDIF
      IF Choice = "Yes"
        THEN
          DEL
          LOOP
        ELSE
          LOOP
      ENDIF
    CASE Retval = "DOS" OR Retval = "DOSBig":
```

```
        BEEP
        LOOP
    ENDSWITCH
ENDWHILE
CLEARALL
```

In this script, if the user presses [Esc], a message asks the user to confirm that he or she wants to exit. Furthermore, a menu appears on the screen with two options: No and Yes, as shown in Figure 10-8. If the user selects Yes, the command CANCELEDIT is played and the WHILE loop is exited. If the user selects No, or simply presses the [Esc] key, the script loops back into the WAIT.

A similar series of events occurs if the user presses [Del]. However, instead of canceling the edit if the user selects Yes from the displayed menu, the script deletes the current record, using the DEL command, and then loops back to WAIT.

If you display a menu asking for confirmation, the menu should default to the selection that will not result in data loss. You can do this with SHOWMENU, either by using the optional keyword DEFAULT or by listing the nondestructive selection first, as is done in the example script.

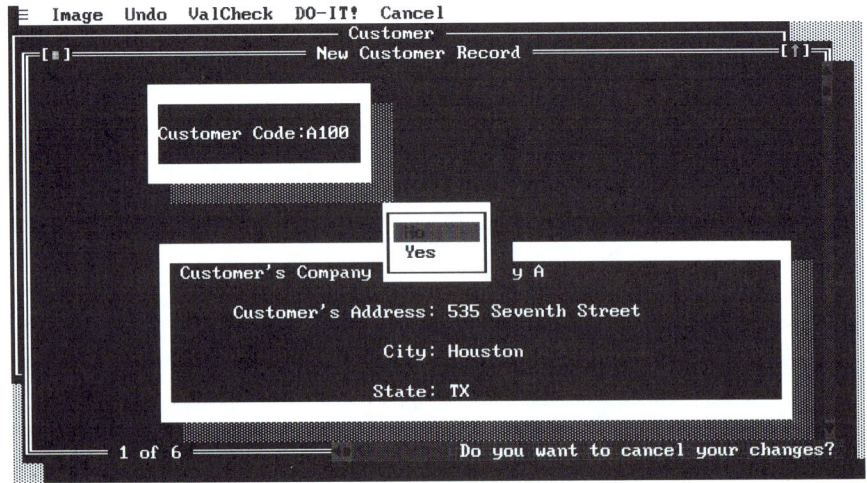

Getting confirmation of a user's request
Figure 10-8.

Viewing and Editing Tables

NOTE: VERSION( ) is a function that returns the current version number of Paradox. The preceding script includes the following commands so that the script will behave properly under either version 3.5 or 4:

```
IF VERSION() > 3.5 THEN MESSAGE "" ENDIF
```

If you are using Paradox 3.5 exclusively, you can omit the entire line. If you use only Paradox 4, you can replace the line with this command:

```
MESSAGE ""
```

Editing a Specific Record

Depending on the needs of your application, you may not want to give users unlimited access to all tables, or even to an entire table in Edit mode. In fact, a common requirement is that the user must specify which record needs editing, and then only that record is displayed. The user then completes the edit by pressing [F2] (or any other key you designate).

There are many different ways you can restrict access. The following script provides this feature by prompting the user to enter a value that identifies the record to edit. If the record is found (using the LOCATE command), the table is placed in Edit mode and a WAIT RECORD displays the requested record to the user. When the user is done editing, the record is removed from the screen and the user is prompted for the next record to edit.

```
CLEAR
CLEARALL
VIEW "Customer"
PICKFORM 1
;Enter a loop to control the ACCEPT command.
WHILE TRUE
   @ 10,12 ?? "Enter the company name (press ESC to quit): "
   STYLE REVERSE
   ACCEPT "A10" TO FindValue
   STYLE
   ;test Retval to see if the user pressed ESC.
```

```
                IF NOT Retval
                  THEN
                    CLEARIMAGE
                    RETURN
                ENDIF
                ;The user did not press ESC.
                ;Search for the entered value in the Company Name field.
                MOVETO [Customer -> Company name]
                LOCATE FindValue
                ;test Retval to see if FindValue was found.
                IF NOT Retval
                  THEN
                    ;The value was not found. Return to the ACCEPT command.
                    MESSAGE FindValue, " not found. Try again"
                    LOOP
                ENDIF
                CLEAR
                ;The value was found. The current record holds the value.
                ;Press EDITKEY to enter the Edit mode.
                EDITKEY
                ;Enter a loop to control the WAIT command.
                WHILE True
                  ;Permit the user to edit the record.
                  WAIT RECORD
                    PROMPT "Press F2 to save or ESC to cancel."
                    UNTIL "F2", "DEL", "ESC", "DOS", "DOSBig"
                  SWITCH
                    CASE Retval = "F2":
                      DO_IT!
                      QUITLOOP
                    CASE Retval = "ESC":
                      ;Require confirmation.
                      MESSAGE "Cancel changes to this record?"
                      SHOWMENU
                        "No" :"Do not cancel changes.",
                        "Yes":"Cancel changes."
                       TO Choice
                      IF VERSION() > 3.5 THEN MESSAGE "" ENDIF
                      IF Choice = "Yes"
                        THEN
                          CANCELEDIT
                          QUITLOOP
                        ELSE
                          LOOP
```

Viewing and Editing Tables

```
            ENDIF
         CASE Retval = "DEL":
            ;Require confirmation.
            MESSAGE "Delete this record?"
            SHOWMENU
               "No" :"Do not delete this record.",
               "Yes":"Delete this record."
              TO Choice
            IF VERSION() > 3.5 THEN MESSAGE "" ENDIF
            IF Choice = "Yes"
               THEN
                  ;Delete the record and return
                  ;to the ACCEPT command.
                  DEL
                  QUITLOOP
               ELSE
                  ;Return to the WAIT RECORD.
                  LOOP
            ENDIF
         CASE Retval = "DOS" OR Retval = "DOSBig":
            ;Do not permit these keypresses.
            BEEP
            LOOP
      ENDSWITCH
   ENDWHILE        ;End of the loop for the WAIT command.
   CLEAR           ;Clear the canvas before returning to ACCEPT.
ENDWHILE           ;End of the loop for the ACCEPT command.
CLEARALL           ;Remove the table from the desktop.
```

Adding New Records

It is not uncommon for an application to provide at least two different features that involve table editing. One may permit only new records to be added, while the other is used solely for editing existing records. One reason for this is that the form used for adding a new record may be different from that used to edit a record. For instance, the form used to add a record may contain fields that the user should not be able to edit at a later date. The key field or fields for a keyed table are often treated this way.

Another consideration is that you may want to check the data in one or more fields before you permit the record to be added. For example, you may want to verify that certain, necessary fields in the record have not been left blank. You may also want to compare values in two or more fields to ensure that the data is consistent. For example, in a record where a beginning date and an ending date must be entered, you should verify that the beginning date is earlier than the ending date.

Following is an example script for adding records to a table. Once Edit mode is entered, the INS command is issued, which opens a new record. The WAIT RECORD command then displays this new record to the user. When the user presses F2, fields in the record are checked to see if they are acceptable. In this script example, only one check is made, verifying that the Customer Code field has been assigned a value using the PAL function ISBLANK(). However, within the same SWITCH command, any number of data checks are possible. If any of the checks reveal that the record is not acceptable, a message should be displayed, describing the problem, and then a LOOP should return to the WAIT so that the user can make corrections.

```
CLEAR
CLEARALL
EDIT "Customer"
;Insert a new record
INS
;Use a form for entering the data
PICKFORM 1
;Initialize a variable to use with the WAIT MESSAGE.
WaitMessage = "Adding a new record."
;This loop controls the WAIT RECORD.
WHILE True
  WAIT RECORD
    PROMPT "Press F2 to save or ESC to cancel."
    MESSAGE WaitMessage
    UNTIL "F2", "ESC", "DOS", "DOSBig"
  ;Reset WaitMessage to a null value.
  WaitMessage = ""
  SWITCH
    CASE Retval = "F2":
      ;Here is the opportunity to check to see
      ;if the user filled out the record properly.
      SWITCH
        CASE ISBLANK([Customer -> Customer Code]):
          ;The Customer Code field is blank.
```

Viewing and Editing Tables

```
            BEEP
            WaitMessage = "Customer Code cannot be blank"
            MOVETO [Customer -> Customer Code]
            LOOP
            ;You can use additional CASE statements
            ;to test for any other invalid data.
        ENDSWITCH
        ;Open a new record.
        INS
        ;Move to the first field on the form.
        CTRLHOME
        ;Assign a message to the variable WaitMessage.
        WaitMessage = "Adding a new record."
        ;LOOP back to the WAIT RECORD.
        LOOP
      CASE Retval = "ESC":
        ;Confirm that the user wants to exit.
        MESSAGE "Exit without adding this record?"
        SHOWMENU
           "No" :"Return to adding this new record.",
           "Yes":"Exit without adding this new record."
           TO Choice
        ;Check if Yes was selected.
        IF Choice = "Yes"
           THEN
              ;Delete this unwanted record.
              DEL
              ;Return to the Main mode.
              DO_IT!
              ;Exit the WHILE loop.
              QUITLOOP
           ELSE
              ;Yes was not selected, return to the record.
              LOOP
        ENDIF
      CASE Retval = "DOS" OR Retval = "DOSBig":
        ;Do not process either of these keypresses.
        BEEP
        LOOP
    ENDSWITCH
  ENDWHILE
  CLEARIMAGE
```

TIP: The preceding script makes use of a valuable technique you can use with any WAIT command. Instead of using an alphanumeric constant as the expression for the optional WAIT keyword MESSAGE, you can use a variable. Before entering the WHILE loop that encloses the WAIT, this variable is initialized. That is, it is assigned the value it will display when the WAIT is first entered. Immediately following the UNTIL keyword, this variable is assigned a null value (empty quotation marks). When the expression following the MESSAGE keyword is empty, no message is displayed. Within the SWITCH control structure, this variable can be assigned a new value if you want to loop back to the WAIT, and have a specific message displayed. Notice that this happens after the CASE statement that verifies that the Customer Code is not blank.

Adding a Record to a Keyed Table

Adding a record to a keyed table offers an additional challenge. You must ensure that the new record contains a unique value in its key field(s). Using the Customer table, for example, you must ensure that each record added does not use the same Customer Code as one already in the table. If you were to add a record that duplicated the Customer Code of an existing record, the existing record would be lost when the table is saved. In almost all cases, losing data this way is unacceptable.

There are many different approaches you can take to solve this problem. Some are more complex than others. The solution provided in the following sections is one of the less complicated ones, but it is also less flexible. In this solution, you simply do not permit the user to add the record if it will replace an existing record.

The following example makes use of two new concepts: CoEdit and record locking.

CoEdit Mode

CoEdit mode is similar to Edit mode in that it permits the user to edit a table. However, unlike Edit mode, CoEdit mode will not automatically replace an existing record when you enter a new record with the same

Viewing and Editing Tables

key field value. This makes CoEdit mode particularly useful when keyed tables need to be edited. In fact, once you are comfortable with programming using CoEdit mode, you will probably use it exclusively.

As with Edit mode, there are two ways to enter CoEdit mode. One is an abbreviated menu command, COEDIT, and the other is a special key command, COEDITKEY. The syntaxes are

```
COEDIT TableName
```

and

```
COEDITKEY
```

The COEDIT command has one required expression, which must evaluate to the name of a table. When Paradox plays the COEDIT command, it brings the named table onto the desktop and enters CoEdit mode. As in Edit mode, you cannot add or remove any tables from the desktop while in CoEdit mode. In order to do so, you would have to first return to Main mode.

The COEDITKEY command mimics the press of [Alt]-[F9] (CoEdit). When Paradox plays the COEDITKEY command, it enters CoEdit mode. If you use the COEDITKEY command, you normally precede it with the VIEW command to bring the table onto the desktop.

To return to Main mode from CoEdit mode, you must use DO_IT!. You cannot use the CANCELEDIT command to exit CoEdit mode, because Paradox adds the data to a table in CoEdit mode one record at a time. You will read more about CoEdit mode in Chapter 14.

The LOCKRECORD Command

LOCKRECORD is only available when you are in CoEdit mode. When Paradox plays LOCKRECORD, it immediately attempts to add the current record to the table. If the current record contains values that duplicate the key field value(s) in an existing record, LOCKRECORD fails and the record is not added.

The syntax of the LOCKRECORD command is

```
LOCKRECORD
```

LOCKRECORD is another PAL command that assigns a value to Retval. If LOCKRECORD is successful in adding the record to your table—meaning that the key value is unique—Retval is assigned the value True. If, however, LOCKRECORD fails because the new record duplicates an existing record's key values, Retval is assigned the value False. Therefore, when you use the command LOCKRECORD, you should immediately test the value of Retval. If Retval is False, the key of the current record conflicts with an existing one and cannot be added as entered. The approach used in the following script is to delete this duplicate record and display a message to the user that the record was not added.

The following script permits the user to add records to a keyed table without the risk of replacing existing records. It is similar to the preceding script, with the exception of the CoEdit mode and the LOCKRECORD command. Therefore, the comments that were presented in the preceding script are not repeated here.

```
CLEAR
CLEARALL
;Enter the CoEdit mode.
COEDIT "Customer"
INS
PICKFORM 1
WaitMessage = "Adding a new record."
WHILE True
  WAIT RECORD
    PROMPT "Press F2 to save or ESC to cancel."
    MESSAGE WaitMessage
    UNTIL "F2", "ESC", "DOS", "DOSBig"
  WaitMessage = ""
  SWITCH
    CASE Retval = "F2":
      ;Test for invalid data before adding the record.
      SWITCH
        CASE ISBLANK([Customer -> Customer Code]):
          BEEP
          WaitMessage = "Customer Code cannot be blank."
          LOOP
          ;You can use additional CASE statements
          ;to test for any other invalid data.
      ENDSWITCH
      ;Now, verify that the record's key value is unique.
```

```
            LOCKRECORD
            IF NOT Retval
              THEN
                ;The record was not unique.
                ;Delete it.
                DEL
                MESSAGE "This record already exists."
                ;Require the user to acknowledge the message.
                SHOWMENU
                   "Ok":"Press ENTER to try again."
                   TO Choice
                IF VERSION() > 3.5 THEN MESSAGE "" ENDIF
            ENDIF
            ;Open up a new record.
            INS
            CTRLHOME
            WaitMessage = "Adding a new record."
            LOOP
         CASE Retval = "ESC":
            MESSAGE "Exit without adding this record?"
            SHOWMENU
               "No" :"Return to adding this new record.",
               "Yes":"Exit without adding this new record."
               TO Choice
            IF VERSION() > 3.5 THEN MESSAGE "" ENDIF
            IF Choice = "Yes"
              THEN
                 DEL
                 DO_IT!
                 QUITLOOP
              ELSE
                 LOOP
            ENDIF
         CASE Retval = "DOS" OR Retval = "DOSBig":
            BEEP
            LOOP
      ENDSWITCH
   ENDWHILE
   CLEARIMAGE
```

Quick Review

- VIEW places a table on the desktop.
- Use PICKFORM to select a form for the current table on the desktop.
- CLEARIMAGE and CLEARALL are used to remove one or more tables from the desktop.
- It is always a good practice to remove tables from the desktop as soon as you are through using them.
- The MOVETO and LOCATE commands permit you to move your cursor between and within tables.
- When either MOVETO or LOCATE cannot be used, you can use any of the special key commands to move your cursor between and within tables.
- The WAIT command drops the PAL canvas and provides the user with access to the desktop.
- During a WAIT, your script can maintain control over what the user is doing by trapping certain keypresses.
- When one of the keys listed after the UNTIL keyword of the WAIT statement is pressed, that key is assigned to the variable Retval, and the WAIT is exited.
- In nearly every situation, you will include a WHILE loop around the WAIT. This permits you to return to the WAIT after trapping unwanted keypresses. This WHILE must also enclose a branching control structure, either IF or SWITCH, to test the value of Retval. Depending on the value of Retval, the script should either loop back to the WHILE in order to reenter the WAIT, or use QUITLOOP to exit the WHILE loop.
- Using the EDIT or EDITKEY command, Paradox is placed in Edit mode. A WAIT can then be used to permit the user to edit the current table.
- Use CoEdit when working with keyed tables to prevent losing records with conflicting keys.

CHAPTER

11
MANIPULATING DATA

In the previous chapter you learned how to display a table and permit the user to change its contents. Sometimes, however, you want the script to make the changes instead of the user. For instance, when a user enters a new record in a keyed table, instead of the user assigning the values to the key field(s), you can have your script do it. You do this by excluding the key field or fields from the form your script displays to the user. When the user is finished entering the values into the record, your script determines a unique value for the key field and performs the assignment.

This chapter describes how to manipulate the data in a table. It is divided into two general topics: assigning values to fields one record at a time and using queries to manipulate one or more tables simultaneously.

Assignment

There are three techniques used to assign a value to a field: quoted strings, the command TYPEIN, and direct assignment. These techniques only work when a table is on the desktop and Paradox is in a mode that permits data entry (Edit, CoEdit, or DataEntry).

Using Quoted Strings

Quoted strings are the least flexible method of entering data into a table. When you enclose text within quotation marks, those values are entered into the current field as if they were typed from the keyboard. Quoted strings are limited in that they can only be used to enter literal characters—those between the quotation marks. You cannot use variables or functions in quoted strings. This is demonstrated as follows:

```
MOVETO [Company Name] "Company G"
```

The MOVETO command moves the cursor to the field Company Name, making it the current field. The quoted string that follows results in the letters *C, o, m, p,* and so on, to be typed, as if from the keyboard. The result is that the value Company G is entered into this field.

When using quoted strings be careful that the cursor is not on a Paradox menu. Quoted strings can make selections from active Paradox menus. For example, consider what would happen if you played the following script from Main mode:

```
MENU "tmd"
```

The first command, MENU, activates the Main menu. Next, the quoted string results in typing the keys *t, m,* and *d.* This would have the same

Manipulating Data

result as if you typed these keys on the keyboard when the Main menu is displayed; it selects Tools/More/Directory from the Main menu.

Using the TYPEIN Command

When Paradox encounters the TYPEIN command, it enters the value of the expression into the current field. The syntax is

```
TYPEIN Expression
```

As when quoted strings are used, the value of the expression is entered as though typed in through the keyboard, one character at a time. However, TYPEIN is far more flexible than quoted strings, since any expression can be used. For instance, if the Invoice table is on the desktop (and the desktop is in Edit, CoEdit, or DataEntry mode), the following two lines of script can be used to assign the current date to the Date field of the Invoice table:

```
MOVETO [Invoice -> Date]
TYPEIN TODAY()
```

Using Direct Assignment

There are four commands you can use to assign values directly to a field. The most common of these is the assignment command (=). The three remaining commands are more specialized, and can be used to assign two or more values to two or more fields in a single command. These are COPYFROMARRAY, APPENDARRAY, and REPLACEFIELDS.

When the = command is preceded by a field specifier, Paradox assigns the value of the expression that follows to the specified field. The syntax is as follows:

```
FieldSpecifier = Expression
```

Three features of the assignment command demonstrate why it is preferable to quoted stings and TYPEIN. First, as with the TYPEIN command, you can follow the = command with any expression. Second, the cursor does not need to be in the table or field to which you are assigning the value. For example, if you include the statement,

```
[Invoice -> Date] = TODAY()
```

in your script, the cursor does not need to be in the Date field, or even in the Invoice table, for the assignment to be successful. The only requirements are that the Invoice table be on the desktop and in a mode that permits data entry (Edit, CoEdit, or DataEntry). The third feature of the = command, is that it replaces any existing contents of the field with the value of the expression. Using quoted strings and TYPEIN adds to the contents. If you must use quoted strings or the TYPEIN command to assign a value to a field, and you cannot be certain that the field is empty, you can use the command CTRLBACKSPACE to remove existing contents from the field.

The three remaining direct assignment statements also replace the contents of fields. COPYFROMARRAY is used to copy the contents of an array to the current record. This array is usually created by using the COPYTOARRAY command, which copies the contents of the current record to an array. In most cases, you use COPYTOARRAY to duplicate one record's contents, and then move to a different record, or even a different table, and use COPYFROMARRAY.

The syntax of the COPYFROMARRAY command is

```
COPYFROMARRAY ArrayName
```

The contents of the fixed array used by COPYFROMARRAY must be compatible with the structure of the table being copied to. There are two requirements. First, this array must have one more element than there are fields in the table. Second, the contents of the second element of the array must have the same data type as the first field in the table, the third element in the array must match the second field in the table, and so on.

The APPENDARRAY command is quite similar to COPYFROMARRAY, although it can be used in CoEdit mode only. The main difference is that you use it to copy the contents of one or more arrays to a table in a single command. Also, instead of placing the values in the current record, APPENDARRAY adds the contents of the arrays as new records at the bottom of the table. This command can only be used in CoEdit mode, however.

The syntax of the APPENDARRAY command is

Manipulating Data

```
APPENDARRAY ArrayName1 ... [, ArrayNameN]
```

The final direct assignment command, REPLACEFIELDS, is used to assign the value of one or more expressions to one or more fields in the current record. Like APPENDARRAY, REPLACEFIELDS is also only available in CoEdit mode.

The syntax of the REPLACEFIELDS command is

```
REPLACEFIELDS FieldSpecifier1 Expression1 ...
             [,FieldSpecifierN ExpressionN]
```

When Paradox plays the REPLACEFIELDS command, it replaces each of the fields specified with the corresponding expressions. While any expressions can be used, the field specifiers can only be of the form [Field name]. This means that this command can be used to replace the contents of the specified fields on the current record and current table only. For example, to assign the value G100 and Company G to the Customer table fields Customer Code and Company Name, the Customer table must be current, the record that you want to assign these values to must be current, and you would use the following command:

```
REPLACEFIELDS [Customer Code]"G100",[Company Name]"Company G"
```

NOTE: APPENDARRAY and REPLACEFIELDS are not available in Paradox 3.5.

Processing at the Record Level

Changing data in a table one record at a time is called *record-level processing*. With record-level processing, you can accomplish any changes to a table that can also be performed using a Changeto query. For example, you can use a query to replace blank values in a field with zeros. You would do this by placing the query operator BLANK in the corresponding field of the query, followed by the instruction CHANGETO 0. A query that performs this manipulation on the Quantity field on the Indetail table is shown in Figure 11-1.

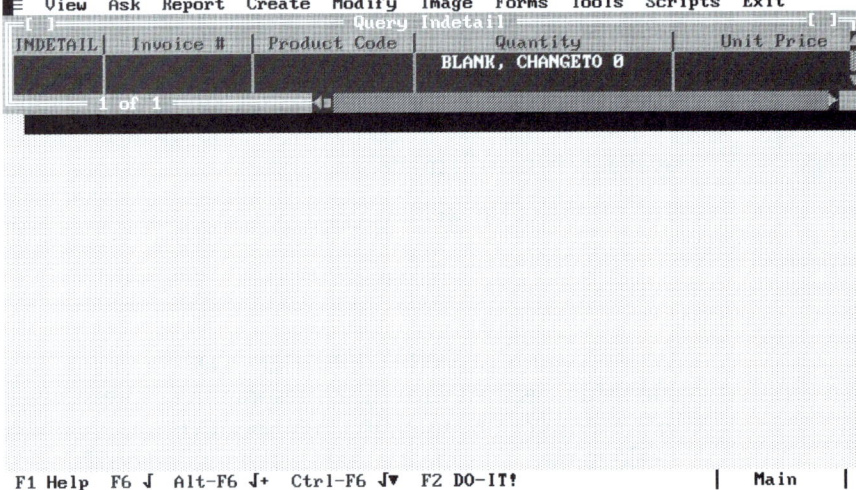

This Changeto query will convert blanks to zeros
Figure 11-1.

Instead of using a Changeto query, you can use a script to move the cursor to each record of Indetail, one at a time, and test whether the Quantity field is blank using the PAL function ISBLANK(). If a blank value is found, you can then assign the value 0 to that field. The following script performs this task.

```
EDIT "Indetail"
SCAN
   IF ISBLANK([Indetail -> Quantity])
      THEN
         [Indetail -> Quantity] = 0
   ENDIF
ENDSCAN
DO_IT!
```

In a situation like this, where you can use either a query or record-level processing, it is nearly always preferable to use a query. This is because queries are usually much faster than record-level processing. The greater the number of records in a table, the greater the advantage of queries.

There are tasks that can only be accomplished through record-level processing, however. Since functions cannot be used in queries, you must use record-level processing if you want to use functions with

Manipulating Data

tables. For example, if you are changing a value in a field to a value that includes a function, you must use record-level processing.

The following exercise demonstrates the use of record-level processing in a task that cannot be duplicated with a query. In it you will use the = command and the UPPER() function to convert the values in the Company Name field of the Customer table to uppercase letters.

1. Select View from the Main menu.
2. Type **Customer** and press [Enter].
3. Press [F9] (EditKey).
4. Press [Tab] twice to move the cursor to the Company Name field.
5. Press [Alt]-[F10] (PAL menu).
6. Select MiniScript.
7. Type the following command and then press [Enter].

   ```
   SCAN [] = UPPER([]) ENDSCAN
   ```

   This command tells Paradox to move to the first record of the current table, Customer, and play the command [ ] = UPPER([ ]) for each record, one at a time. The command [ ] = UPPER([ ]) converts the value in the current field to uppercase and then assigns this value to the current field. (Recall that [ ] refers to the current field and current record of the current table.)

8. Exit Edit mode without saving these changes by pressing [F10] (Menu) and selecting Cancel/Yes.

The SCAN command is used in this exercise. SCAN is particularly useful for record-level processing since it permits you to move easily through a table one record at a time. You simply enclose the calculation you want to perform on every record of the table between the SCAN and ENDSCAN keywords. Paradox takes care of the rest.

Other Editing Commands

Since your script is in complete control during record-level processing, it must control all editing commands. In addition to the special key commands you can normally use on a table, there are five additional commands that can be used when you are in a system mode that permits changes to the table. They are as follows:

Command	Effect
BACKSPACE	Delete one character to the left
CTRLBACKSPACE	Erase contents of current field
DEL	Delete the current record
DITTO	Repeat contents of same field in preceding record
INS	Insert a new record

Giving Feedback

Although record-level processing tends to take longer than an equivalent query, it has the advantage of permitting you to give the user feedback during the processing. *Feedback* is information displayed to the user indicating that the script is working. This feedback may be as simple as a display of the number of records processed. Feedback is especially important when there are many records to process, and/or a large number of assignments are being performed for each record.

One of the easiest ways to provide feedback during record-level processing is to display the contents of the Record Number field to the user with the MESSAGE command. Recall from Chapter 4 that the field specifier [#] returns the current record number. Simply include the following command within the SCAN, and your script will display the number of each record as it is processed.

```
MESSAGE [#]
```

This technique is demonstrated in the following exercise:

1. Select Scripts/Editor/New.
2. Type **Progress** and then press [Enter].
3. Enter the following script:

    ```
    VIEW "Indetail"
    SCAN
      SLEEP 100
    ```

Manipulating Data

```
    MESSAGE "Processing record ",[#]
ENDSCAN
CLEARIMAGE
```

4. Press [F2] (Do-It!) to save the script.
5. Play Progress by pressing [Ctrl]-[G] (Go).

While the script is scanning through the Indetail table, it will keep the user updated, displaying the number of the record the script is currently processing.

The SLEEP command is used in this example to slow down the processing of the SCAN loop. If SLEEP 100 had not been used, the script would play so fast that you may not see the message being displayed. When you use record-level processing, do not include the SLEEP command. Usually, the complexity of the calculations or the sheer number of records that need to be processed will result in the message being displayed long enough to be effective.

NOTE: Since all script play ends when this SCAN loop is finished processing the table, the contents of the last message are automatically removed from the global desktop. However, if you use a loop like this within a script that does not end immediately, you should include the command MESSAGE "" after the ENDLOOP keyword to erase the last message. This does not apply to Paradox 3.5, however, since a MESSAGE command rarely persists for long in that version.

Queries

When you need to manipulate data within a script, a query is nearly always the method of choice. This is because a query typically works faster than record-level processing and is easier to use in most cases.

There are three steps to using a query in a script:

1. Create a query form on the desktop.
2. Make changes to the displayed query form (optional).
3. Process the query, using the PAL command DO_IT!.

Although these three steps are listed in the order in which you must perform them in a query, since step 2 is optional, it is covered last in the following sections.

NOTE: In the following discussion, the term query form is used repeatedly. A *query form* is the image Paradox displays when you are constructing a query. Do not confuse a query form with a table form, which is used to present a table in form view.

Displaying a Query Form

There are two distinct ways to display a query form on your desktop. The first is to play a saved query, and the second is to use commands to construct the query from scratch. If you are creating a query that involves two or more tables, you can use both of these methods together, one to display the first set of query forms and the other to display the rest. (If you do this, you must play the saved query first. When a saved query is played, all query forms currently on the desktop are removed.) Typically, however, you will use one method or the other.

To display a query form using a saved query, either use the PAL command PLAY to play the saved query, or read the saved query into your script using the InsertFile selection from the Editor menu (the corresponding menu selection in Paradox 3.5 is Read). Either way, when Paradox encounters the QUERY command contained in the saved query, it places the specified query forms on the desktop. If any checks, conditions, examples, or keywords appear in the saved query, they are automatically entered into the query image when the QUERY statement is played. Saving queries is described in detail in Chapter 3.

Constructing a query from scratch uses the braced menu selection {Ask} from Main mode, followed by the name of the table you want to query. For example, to place the query form for the Customer table onto the desktop, use the following command:

```
{Ask} {Customer}
```

If your query involves two or more tables, use this technique once for each table you want to query. For instance, to produce a query that will involve both the Invoice table and the Indetail table, use these commands:

Manipulating Data

```
{Ask} {Invoice}
{Ask} {Indetail}
```

NOTE: Paradox brings each query form onto the desktop in its own window. Just as you do with tables and forms, you must get the handle of each window as each query form is placed on the desktop if you intend to use commands that require a window handle.

The SELECT Command

If you want to use an expression to define the table whose query form you want to display, you must use the {Ask} braced menu selection followed by the SELECT command. The syntax of the SELECT command is

```
SELECT Expression
```

When Paradox encounters the SELECT command, it enters the value of the expression at the prompt, or selects the value of the expression from a menu. (Thus, SELECT can only be used when Paradox prompts for an expression or a selection from a menu.) Following the {Ask} command with SELECT and an expression that evaluates to a table name will cause Paradox to display the query form for the specified table. For example, consider the following script:

```
TabName = "Invoice"
{Ask} SELECT TabName
```

In this script, the value "Invoice" is assigned to the variable TabName. Next, the {Ask} command chooses Ask from the Main menu, and SELECT is used to enter Invoice at the prompt for a table name. The result is that the query form for Invoice is displayed on the desktop.

Processing Queries

Once the query has been displayed and any desired modifications have been made to it, you use the PAL command DO_IT! to process the query. After the query has been processed, Paradox continues playing the script with the command that follows DO_IT!.

TIP: In Chapter 10 you learned that it is important to keep the desktop free of unnecessary tables. This is particularly true when you are working with queries. Not only are queries also images that can clutter the desktop, but an Answer table is typically placed on the desktop when a query is processed. Your script should respond by using CLEARIMAGE or CLEARALL to remove all query forms and the resulting Answer table when they are no longer needed on the desktop.

Under some circumstances a query will not be processed. Unfortunately, Paradox will continue on to the command that follows DO_IT! even though the query has failed. In some situations this causes a script error, often because your script then attempts to do something with the Answer table, which is not available because the query failed. In other situations, your script produces unexpected results, even though these might never cause a script error.

Certain queries are more likely to fail than others. For instance, those that make use of tilde variables (described later in the section, "Using Variables in Queries") will fail if the variables have not been assigned a value. Queries constructed by the user, using the WAIT command, (described later in "User-Defined Queries") are also more prone to failure. If your script includes a query that may fail in some situations, you should always follow the DO_IT! command with a test to determine whether the query succeeded or not. If the test indicates that the query failed, your script should respond by taking an appropriate action.

Did Paradox Do It?

Consider what happens in interactive Paradox when a query cannot be processed: Paradox displays a message in the lower right corner of the screen. During a script, Paradox also displays this message, although you cannot see it because the PAL canvas covers it. However, you can use the PAL function WINDOW( ) to determine if any message is present. If WINDOW( ) returns a value, the query failed. If WINDOW( ) returns a blank value, the query was processed.

Manipulating Data

CAUTION: Do not confuse the WINDOW( ) function with window commands. WINDOW( ) returns the contents of the message window. This message window has nothing to do with windows on the desktop.

The following exercise demonstrates one use of the WINDOW( ) function to determine if a script failed:

1. Select Scripts/Editor/New.
2. Type **Badquery** and press [Enter].
3. Type the following query:

   ```
   {Ask} {Customer}
   DO_IT!
   IF WINDOW() <> ""
      THEN
         RETURN WINDOW()
   ENDIF
   ```

4. Press [F10] (Menu) and select Go to play the query.

Paradox displays the query form for the Customer table on the desktop. The next command, DO_IT!, makes Paradox attempt to process the query. However, since there are no checked fields in the query, the query is not processed and no Answer table is produced. The test of WINDOW( ) shows that it does not equal " " (a blank value), meaning that a message was displayed in the message window. The IF command directs Paradox to play the RETURN command. In this script, WINDOW( ) is also used as the expression following the RETURN command so that its value is displayed on the desktop for you to see. Your screen should look like Figure 11-2.

You may want to edit this script by adding the special key command CHECK between the first and second lines of the Badquery script. If you then play the script again, you will see the Answer table appear on the desktop, since the query is successful.

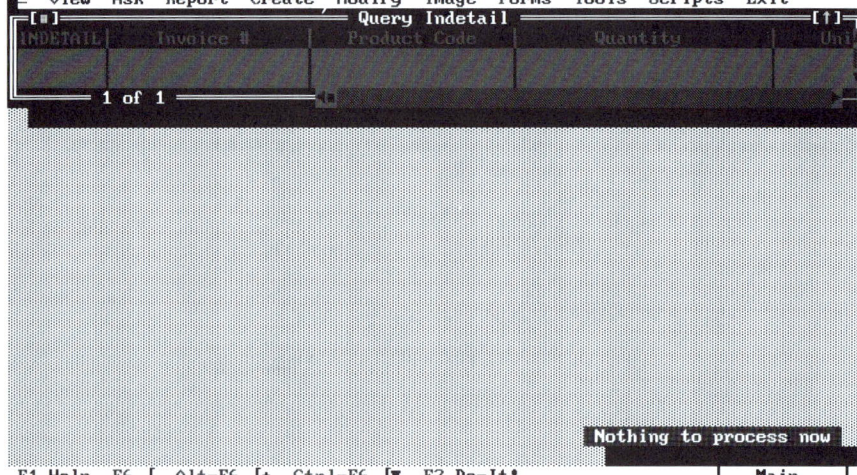

Text of the WINDOW( ) function after a failed DO_IT!
Figure 11-2.

Changing a Query Form

Whether you use a saved query or the {Ask} braced menu selection to display a query form, the query is not processed until the PAL command DO_IT! is played. This permits your script to make changes to the query form once it appears on the desktop. For example, after displaying the query for the Invoice table, your script could enter a condition in the Customer Code field to query only those records for a specific customer. Once all of the necessary changes have been made to the query form, the DO_IT! command is played.

When you construct a query on the desktop using the {Ask} braced menu selection, the displayed query image is always blank. Therefore, you must use one or more PAL commands to add the desired checks, conditions, examples, or operators to the query. This is different from a saved query, which usually includes one or more of these features. However, even with queries displayed using saved queries, you may want to add additional checks, conditions, examples, or operators to the displayed query form.

The techniques used for changing query forms are nearly identical to those used for changing tables. Since query forms are images, just like Paradox tables, any command you can use to move the cursor within

Manipulating Data

and between tables can also be used to move the cursor within and between query forms. With the exception of the following points, you can treat query forms and tables identically:

- You can make changes to a query form from the Paradox Main mode. Tables, on the other hand, can only be changed while Paradox is in Edit, CoEdit, or DataEntry mode.

- Most queries have only one record, although you can create queries up to 64 records in length (22 in Paradox 3.5). Therefore, you usually do not need to use commands such as LOCATE, SCAN, or MOVETO RECORD on query forms.

- It is possible to display both the table image and a query form for a single table on the desktop simultaneously. However, because this may cause confusion when moving or referring to an image, you should avoid this situation whenever possible. If you must do so, use window handles to move between the windows containing these two objects. Alternatively, use the MOVETO command with a field specifier that specifically refers to either the query image ([Table (Q) -> Field]), or image number ([Table (N) -> Field]).

Checking Fields in Queries

Fields in a query form are checked using the special key commands CHECK, CHECKPLUS, and CHECKDESCENDING. These commands mimic the keypresses [F6] (Check), [Alt]-[F6] (CheckPlus), and [Ctrl]-[F6] (CheckDescending). As in interactive Paradox, you must first move your cursor to a field in the query form to place a check there. For example, the following script displays the Customer table query form and places a check in the Company Name field.

```
{Ask} {Customer}
MOVETO [Customer -> Company Name]
CHECK
```

As when using Paradox interactively, you can place a check in every field of a query form by placing the check in the Table field (the leftmost field in the query form). Since the cursor is always placed in this field when a query form is first displayed, you do not need to move the cursor before placing this type of check. For example, the following query will place a check in every field in the query form for the Invoice table.

```
{Ask} {Invoice}
CHECK
```

Conditions, Calculations, and Operators

Conditions, calculations, and operators are placed in fields of a query form using the same techniques described earlier in this chapter for assigning values to a field (with the exception of COPYTOARRAY, APPENDARRAY, and REPLACEFIELDS). Two of these methods, quoted strings and the TYPEIN command, require that you first move your cursor to the field where you want to enter the condition, calculation, or operator. The PAL command =, however, can be used without first moving the cursor. The following exercise makes use of each of these three methods.

1. Select Scripts/Editor/New.
2. Type **Askinv** and press [Enter].
3. Enter the following commands in the Editor screen:

   ```
   CLEARALL
   {Ask} {Invoice}
   CHECK
   [Invoice -> Date] = "< 10/1/92"
   MOVETO [Invoice -> Customer Code]
   "A100"
   MOVETO [Invoice -> Employee Code]
   TYPEIN "1000"
   DO_IT!
   ```

4. Press [F2] (Do-It!) to save this script.
5. Press [Alt]-[F10] (PAL menu).
6. Select Debug.
7. Type **Askinv** and press [Enter].

   The Debugger will display the first command on the bottom of your screen. Press [Ctrl]-[S] (Step) repeatedly to play the script one command at a time. Observe as Paradox responds to each

Manipulating Data

command and enters the specified conditions in the query form. When you have stepped through the final command in the script, the completed query and resulting Answer table appear on the desktop, as shown in Figure 11-3.

8. Press Alt-F8 (ClearAll) to remove the images from the desktop.

As when you assign values to fields in a table, the type of assignment statement you use will depend on the needs of your script. For example, if you are assigning the value of an expression to a field in a query form, you must use either the PAL command = or the TYPEIN command, since quoted strings can only be used with literal characters. In most cases, however, the PAL command = is easier to use and results in a script that is easier to read and modify.

Creating Example Elements

In a query, example elements are used to link two or more tables or to use the values from a field in a calculation. There are two ways to create example elements in a query: using the EXAMPLE special key command, and using the underscore character.

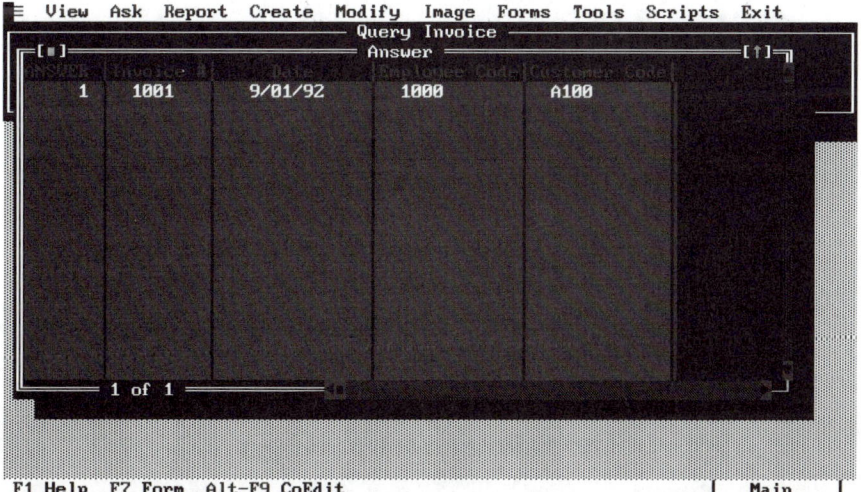

Results of a successful query
Figure 11-3.

The EXAMPLE Command

The EXAMPLE special key command mimics the press of F5 (Example). In order to use EXAMPLE, you write a script that duplicates the action of defining an example element in interactive Paradox. This involves three steps:

1. First move your cursor to the field in which you want to enter an example element.
2. Play the EXAMPLE command.
3. Immediately use an assignment command to enter the example element.

Each example element must be entered separately using this technique. The following exercise demonstrates how these example elements are used. In it, a calculation is defined for the Indetail table that multiplies the Unit price field by the Quantity field to produce a new field called Total (using the query operator AS).

1. Select Scripts/Editor/New.
2. Type **Examples** and press Enter.
3. Enter the following script in the Editor screen:

   ```
   CLEARALL
   {Ask} {Indetail}
   CHECK
   MOVETO [Quantity]
   EXAMPLE
   TYPEIN "Q"
   MOVETO [Unit Price]
   EXAMPLE
   TYPEIN "P, CALC "
   EXAMPLE "P * "
   EXAMPLE "Q AS Total"
   ```

4. Press F2 (Do-It!) to save this script.
5. Press Alt-F10 (PAL menu).
6. Select Debug.
7. Type **Examples** and press Enter.

Manipulating Data

The Debugger will display the first command on the bottom of your screen. Press Ctrl-S (Step) repeatedly to play the script one command at a time. As you step through the script, you will observe Paradox responding exactly as though you were entering the examples interactively. When you have played the final command in the script, the completed query will appear on the desktop, as shown in Figure 11-4.

8. Press Alt-F8 (ClearAll) to remove the query form from the desktop.

The Underscore Character

You can also use the underscore character to define an example element. This technique is used by Paradox to define example elements in saved queries. If you assign a value to a field, and it contains an underscore, any uninterrupted sequence of numbers and letters that follow the underscore will be defined as an example element.

The advantage to using an underscore instead of the EXAMPLE command is that it permits you to define two or more example elements in a single assignment statement. For instance, the following script produces the exact same query as the preceding script. The difference is that this script is easier to write and interpret.

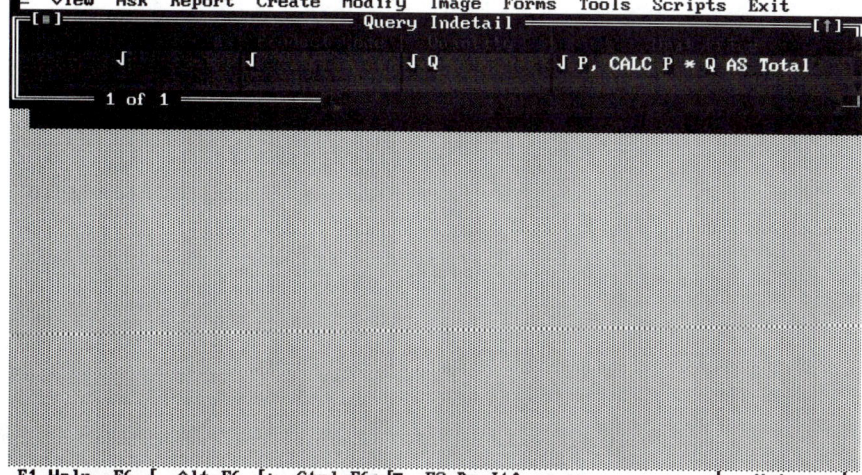

Example elements placed by a script
Figure 11-4.

```
CLEARALL
{Ask} {Indetail}
CHECK
[Quantity] = "_Q"
[Unit Price] = "_P, CALC _P * _Q AS Total"
```

Another advantage of the underscore character is apparent in this script. That is, the assignment can be made directly to a field without first moving the cursor there. This further reduces the complexity of using example elements in a script.

Using Variables in Queries

Variables can be used in queries as either conditions or expressions in calculations. For example, if a variable holds the customer code, you can use this variable in a query of the Invoice table to extract only those records associated with a particular customer.

In order to use a variable in a query, however, you must precede it with the tilde character (~). For this reason, these variables are called *tilde variables*. When Paradox encounters a tilde in a query, it assumes that a variable name follows.

The following exercise demonstrates the use of tilde variables in a saved query. Before trying this exercise you should clear all images from the desktop by pressing (Alt)-(F8) (ClearAll).

1. Select Ask from the Main menu.
2. Type **Invoice** and press (Enter).
3. With your cursor in the Table field, press (F6) (Check) to check every field in the table.
4. Press (Tab) four times to move your cursor to the Customer Code field.
5. Type **~CustCode**.
6. Press (F10) (Menu) and select Scripts/QuerySave.
7. Type **Getcust** and press (Enter).
8. Press (F8) (ClearImage) to clear the desktop.
9. Select Scripts/Editor/Open.
10. Type **Getcust** and press (Enter).

Manipulating Data

The query form you just saved, including the tilde variable, is displayed.

11. Move the cursor to the bottom of the saved query script and insert a new line after the ENDQUERY command.
12. Add the following commands:

```
CLEAR
@ 10,12 ?? "Enter the customer code (press ESC to quit): "
STYLE REVERSE
ACCEPT "A10" To CustCode
STYLE
IF NOT Retval
   THEN
      CLEARIMAGE
      RETURN
ENDIF
DO_IT!
```

Your screen should look like Figure 11-5. Press F10 (Menu) and select Go to play the script. The prompt "Enter the company code (press ESC to quit):" will appear on your screen.

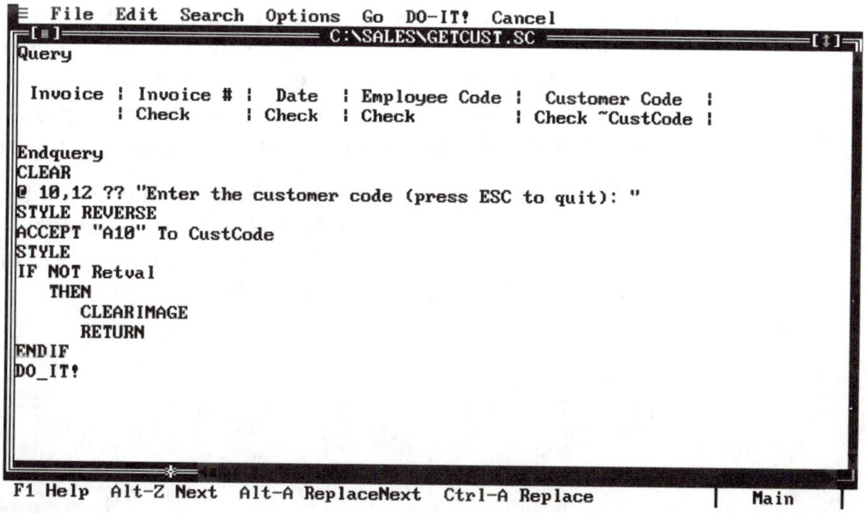

Modified Getcust saved query
Figure 11-5.

13. Type **B100** in response to the prompt and press Enter.

The ACCEPT statement will assign the value B100 to the variable CustCode, and this value is then used in the query. The last command in the script, DO_IT!, causes the query to be processed. The resulting Answer table contains all the records with the customer code of B100.

REMEMBER: When you refer to the variable CustCode in the ACCEPT statement, do not use the tilde character. Only when using a variable in a query do you precede it with a tilde.

User-Defined Queries

As with a table, you can use the WAIT command to display a query and permit the user to enter conditions, examples, and operators. However, this feature is rarely used, because the user could potentially damage the table being queried. For example, if the user entered the word DELETE in the table field of the query, one or more records could be deleted from the table. Similarly, if the user entered the keyword CHANGETO in a field, data in one or more records could be changed. In most situations, it is not acceptable to give the user this amount of flexibility.

Instead of using WAIT, it is common practice to use an ACCEPT statement or a dialog box to receive one or more values that will then be used as tilde variables in the query, or entered by the script into the query form using an assignment statement. By using one of these methods, the script maintains complete control over the query.

Consider the following script, which uses a dialog box to receive dates (Paradox 3.5 users should use two ACCEPT commands). These two dates are then used to select records from the Invoice table that are dated within the range of the two dates.

```
CLEAR
CLEARALL
SHOWDIALOG   "Enter Report Date Range"
  @ 4,20 HEIGHT 10 WIDTH 40
  ACCEPT
```

Manipulating Data

```
    @ 2,20 WIDTH 14 "D" REQUIRED
    TAG "BeginRange" TO BeginningDate
  ACCEPT
    @ 4,20 WIDTH 14 "D" REQUIRED
    TAG "EndRange" TO EndingDate
  LABEL
    @ 2, 2
    "~B~eginning date:"
    FOR "BeginRange"
  LABEL
    @ 4, 2
    "~E~nding date:"
    FOR "EndRange"
  PUSHBUTTON
    @ 6,8 WIDTH 10
    "~O~K" OK
    VALUE True
    TAG "OkButton" TO Retval
  PUSHBUTTON
    @ 6,22 WIDTH 10
    "~C~ANCEL" CANCEL
    VALUE False
    TAG "CancelButton" TO Retval
ENDDIALOG

SWITCH
  CASE NOT Retval:                   ;NOT Retval is True if the
    RETURN "Canceled"                ;dialog box was canceled
  CASE NOT (ISASSIGNED(BeginningDate) AND
            ISASSIGNED(EndingDate)):
    RETURN "Dates not specified."
  CASE BeginningDate > EndingDate:
    RETURN "Beginning date later than ending date."
  OTHERWISE:
    {Ask} {Invoice}
    CHECK
    [Date] = ">=~BeginningDate, <=~EndingDate"
    DO_IT!
    ;Check whether the query worked
    SWITCH
      CASE WINDOW() <> "":
        RETURN WINDOW()
      CASE ISEMPTY("Answer"):
        CLEARALL
```

```
        RETURN "No records in selected range."
      ENDSWITCH
ENDSWITCH
;The query was successful, continue.
```

Quick Review

- You can use a script to change the data in a table.
- When you cannot use a query to change the data in a table, you can use a SCAN loop to process one record at a time.
- When using record-level processing, it is often a good idea to give users feedback so that they know that the script is working.
- Queries should be used instead of record-level processing whenever possible.
- A query form can be displayed on the desktop by using either a saved query or the braced menu selection {Ask}.
- The WINDOW( ) function lets you test whether the query was processed.
- Once a query form is on the desktop, you can make changes to it before processing it. These changes include adding checks, conditions, examples, and query operators.
- A query is processed using the DO_IT! command.

CHAPTER

12

PROCEDURES AND PROCEDURE LIBRARIES

In this chapter you will learn how to convert your scripts to procedures. PAL procedures have a number of important advantages over scripts, so most PAL applications consist almost entirely of procedures. You will also learn how to create procedure libraries. Together, procedures and procedure libraries permit you to create better applications and utilities.

Procedures

In Paradox 4, you are already using procedures and procedure libraries without knowing it, although in a limited way. When you play a script for the first time, Paradox converts the script to a procedure before executing the commands in it. This procedure is also stored in a file that has the same name as the script, and the file extension .SC2. The process of converting a script into a procedure is called *parsing*.

When Paradox parses a script, it does so one command at a time. Paradox takes a single command and converts it into a form that can be directly executed (played). This parsed form of the command is stored in memory. Paradox then proceeds to the next command and parses it. If Paradox detects a syntax error in a script while it is being parsed, the Cancel-Debug menu is displayed. If you select Debug, Paradox loads the script and displays the command that generated the error at the bottom of your screen. When parsing is complete, the entire parsed copy of the script is stored in memory. This parsed version of a script is called a *procedure,* and when the procedure is loaded in memory, it is said to be *defined*.

If you play a script a second time, without making any changes to it, Paradox does not need to parse it again. The parsed commands already exist in the .SC2 file. Paradox loads these commands into memory, which makes the procedure defined again, and executes them. The process of loading the procedure is much faster than the original parsing process. Consequently, a script played a second time is executed much faster than the first.

If you make a change to a script, Paradox must parse the script again, and re-generate the .SC2 file before it can execute the script. Likewise, if for some reason the .SC2 file does not exist when you tell Paradox to play the script, Paradox must create this file again before continuing.

NOTE: In Paradox 3.5, the script is parsed one command at a time, the command is executed, and then the next command is parsed. Since this process occurs at run time, and must be repeated each time the script is run, a script is substantially slower than a procedure in Paradox 3.5. Furthermore, since only those commands that are actually executed are parsed, it is possible for syntax errors to exist in sections of a script that have not been played.

Procedures and Procedure Libraries

In addition to the procedure that Paradox automatically creates when you play a script, you can define a procedure explicitly using the PAL commands PROC and ENDPROC. (In Paradox 3.5, this is the only way to create a procedure.) A procedure created explicitly has a number of advantages over an .SC2 file. The following list of these advantages contains several new concepts that are discussed in detail later in this chapter.

- You can pass arguments only to explicitly defined procedures.
- You can declare private variables only in explicitly defined procedures.
- Only explicitly defined procedures can be closed procedures.
- Only explicitly defined procedures can be used as wait procedures or dialog procedures (discussed in Chapter 14).
- All your explicitly defined procedures can be stored in a single procedure library. Only one procedure can be stored in each .SC2 file.
- Explicitly defined procedures can be given names longer than eight characters in length. This permits you to create procedures with names that reflect what they do. For example, you can create a procedure that verifies that a newly entered record does not have a key conflict with an existing record. You can name this procedure DoesKeyConflict, if you like. Using informative procedure names makes your scripts easier to read and interpret.

You explicitly define a procedure by enclosing a script in the keywords PROC and ENDPROC and providing a name for the procedure. These keywords cause Paradox to parse the enclosed script and store it in memory, making it a defined procedure. Instead of executing these commands right away, however, Paradox waits until the procedure is *called* before executing the commands contained in it. You call a procedure by referring to its name from within a script.

Because of the advantages of explicitly defined procedures over scripts, the remainder of this chapter will discuss explicitly defined procedures exclusively.

Calling a Procedure

When you call a defined procedure, Paradox executes the instructions contained in it. The process of calling a procedure from a script is almost identical to the process of playing one script from another. However, instead of using the PAL command PLAY to play a script, you place the name of the procedure at the location within the script where you want it called, just as if it were a PAL command. For example, if you create a procedure called LastRecord( ), you call it by including the following command in your script:

```
LastRecord()
```

Once you define a procedure, you can call it repeatedly. Consequently, procedures are especially useful when you have a series of PAL commands that you want to use over and over. For instance, you may have two or more places in your script where you need to display a warning message on the screen and wait until the user acknowledges it. Instead of including that sequence of commands in the script repeatedly, you define them as a procedure. Then, any time you need to display the warning and pause, you call the procedure. The result is that your scripts are shorter, easier to interpret and modify, and they run much faster.

Defining a Procedure

All procedures start as scripts. You explicitly convert a script to a procedure using PROC. The syntax of this command is

```
PROC [CLOSED] ProcedureName([Expression1]...[, ExpressionN])
  [USEVARS UVarName1 ... [, UVarNameN]]
  [PRIVATE PVarName1 ... [, PVarNameN]]
  ;any script
ENDPROC
```

At a minimum, defining a procedure requires two keywords, PROC and ENDPROC, as well as a procedure name followed by a pair of parentheses. A procedure name must begin with a letter, but can include letters, numbers, and the special characters . (period),

Procedures and Procedure Libraries

_ (underscore), ! (exclamation point), and $ (dollar sign). A procedure name cannot include blank spaces or duplicate a PAL reserved word.

The PROC command also provides three optional keywords. Two of these keywords, CLOSED and USEVARS, are only used with a closed procedure. (Closed procedures are described later in this chapter.) The third keyword, PRIVATE, permits you to specify that one or more variables should be private to the procedure. Private variables are described in the following section.

When Paradox plays the PROC command, it immediately parses the commands between the PROC and ENDPROC keywords and stores this defined procedure in memory. A procedure remains defined until one of three events occurs:

- All script play ends and you return to interactive Paradox.
- You release the procedure definition from memory by using the PAL command RELEASE PROCS.
- A closed procedure is exited, at which time it is released from memory.

In the following exercise, you will create a procedure from the script called Colors that you created in Chapter 9. If you did not really create it, refer now to the section "Using GETCHAR to Pause Your Script" in Chapter 9, and create it. Then return to this exercise.

This exercise shows you how to create a defined procedure from any script, or part of a script. In this script, the entire body of the script is defined as a procedure. On the line of the script immediately following the ENDPROC command, the procedure is called. When the procedure is done executing, script play ends and the procedure is released from memory.

Begin this exercise from the Main menu:

1. Select Scripts/Edit/Open.
2. Type **Colors** and press Enter.

    The text of the Colors script appears in the Editor window, as shown in Figure 12-1.

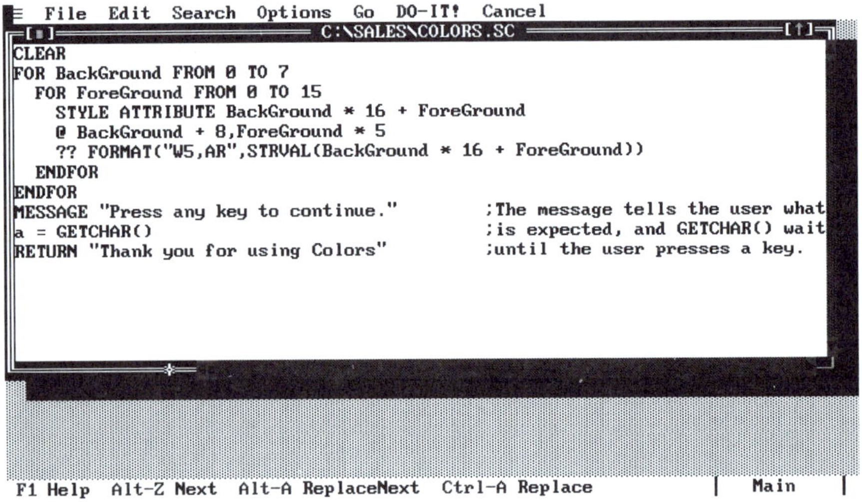
File Edit Search Options Go DO-IT! Cancel
C:\SALES\COLORS.SC
CLEAR
FOR BackGround FROM 0 TO 7
FOR ForeGround FROM 0 TO 15
STYLE ATTRIBUTE BackGround * 16 + ForeGround
@ BackGround + 8,ForeGround * 5
?? FORMAT("W5,AR",STRVAL(BackGround * 16 + ForeGround))
ENDFOR
ENDFOR
MESSAGE "Press any key to continue."
;The message tells the user what
a = GETCHAR()
;is expected, and GETCHAR() wait
RETURN "Thank you for using Colors"
;until the user presses a key.
F1 Help Alt-Z Next Alt-A ReplaceNext Ctrl-A Replace
Main

Colors script
Figure 12-1.

3. Enter a new blank line as the first line of the script.
4. Type **PROC Colors( )**

   This line begins the procedure definition that will assign the name Colors to this procedure.
5. Enter a new line after the last line in the script.
6. Enter the following two lines:

   ```
   ENDPROC
   Colors()
   ```

   Your screen should look like Figure 12-2.
7. Select Go from the Editor menu.

Paradox begins by defining the procedure Colors, parsing the commands included between PROC Colors( ) and ENDPROC. The last line of the script, Colors( ), is the name of the procedure. When Paradox encounters the name of this defined procedure, it immediately executes the parsed commands of the procedure.

When you press any key to end the display created by Colors, Paradox returns from the procedure to the script. Since the command Colors( )

Procedures and Procedure Libraries

```
  File  Edit  Search  Options  Go  DO-IT!  Cancel
                    C:\SALES\COLORS.SC
PROC Colors()
CLEAR
FOR BackGround FROM 0 TO 7
  FOR ForeGround FROM 0 TO 15
    STYLE ATTRIBUTE BackGround * 16 + ForeGround
    @ BackGround + 8,ForeGround * 5
    ?? FORMAT("W5,AR",STRVAL(BackGround * 16 + ForeGround))
  ENDFOR
ENDFOR
MESSAGE "Press any key to continue."
a = GETCHAR()
RETURN "Thank you for using Colors"
ENDPROC
Colors()
```

This script defines a procedure named Colors
Figure 12-2.

is the last command in the script, the script immediately ends, returning you to interactive Paradox and causing the Colors procedure to be released from memory.

There is another observable change in the playing of Colors as a procedure: the return message "Thank you for using Colors" is not displayed. You may recall from Chapter 6 that an expression returned by RETURN is only displayed when RETURN returns to interactive Paradox. In the procedure, RETURN returns to the Colors script, which then returns to Paradox. In fact, a procedure can never use RETURN to return to Paradox directly; it always returns to the script or procedure that called it. (The QUIT command does, however, return to Paradox, and can include an expression to display.) Although the RETURN command is very useful with procedures, as described later in this chapter, the expression following the RETURN command is never displayed on the screen.

Using Private Variables

All variables you assign values to retain those values for the remainder of your Paradox session. Since these values are available globally, these variables are referred to as *global variables*. Global variables pose a number of problems, however. Not only do they take up memory, but they can cause unwanted side effects if two or more scripts use the same variable names. It is desirable, therefore, to release global variables when you are through using them. (You do this using the RELEASE VARS command.)

If you want to use a variable, and do not want it to be globally available, you can declare it as a *private variable*. A private variable is automatically released when the procedure in which it is declared is through executing. This relieves you of the responsibility of releasing a variable explicitly when you are through with it.

NOTE: All issues and techniques discussed here concerning global and private variables apply equally to both fixed and dynamic arrays.

In addition to keeping memory free, private variables allow you to use the same variable names in different parts of your application without side effects. For example, you can always use the same variable name to refer to the value selected from a menu using the SHOWMENU command. If you declare this variable private to each procedure that displays a menu, the variable will always contain the value assigned within that particular procedure and never from another.

You define a private variable by including the PRIVATE keyword in your procedure. This keyword must be the first command that follows the procedure name, with the exception of comments and the optional keyword USERVARS. Follow the PRIVATE keyword with a comma-separated list of one or more variables you are declaring private to that procedure.

Consider the Colors procedure. It makes use of three different variables that are not needed once the procedure has been executed. Therefore, they should be declared private to the procedure. To declare them private, insert the PRIVATE command in the script following the PROC command. The resulting script looks like the following:

Procedures and Procedure Libraries

```
PROC Colors()
PRIVATE ForeGround, BackGround, a
CLEAR
FOR BackGround FROM 0 TO 7
  FOR ForeGround FROM 0 TO 15
    STYLE ATTRIBUTE BackGround * 16 + ForeGround
    @ BackGround + 8,ForeGround * 5
    ?? FORMAT("W5,AR",STRVAL(BackGround * 16 + ForeGround))
  ENDFOR
ENDFOR
MESSAGE "Press any key to continue."
a = GETCHAR()
RETURN "Thank you for using Colors"
ENDPROC
Colors()
```

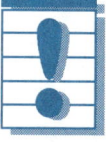

TIP: When using the PAL Debugger on a procedure, use Ctrl-W (Where?) to display the list of variables private to that procedure and their currently assigned values, as shown in Figure 12-3. If you are using Paradox 3.5, the current procedure is the last one displayed. This order is reversed in Paradox 4.

Passing Values to a Procedure

You can pass one or more values to a procedure you call by enclosing the values in the parentheses that follow the procedure name. For example, if you want to pass the name of a table to the procedure named ViewTable, use the following command in your script:

```
ViewTable("Customer")
```

Displaying private variables with Ctrl-W in the PAL Debugger
Figure 12-3.

```
Proc VIEWTABLE **Debugger**
Formals: TABNAME = "Customer"
Private: RETURNMESSAGE = "Viewing Customer"
         CHOICE
         WHICHFORM = 1

Proc MAINMENU
Private: AUTOLID = "Mylib,Utillib,Paradox"
         ERRORPROC = "CatchErrors"
         CHOICE = "View"

Script APP
```

A value passed to a procedure in this way is called an *argument*. Whether or not your procedure uses arguments is something you decide when you create the procedure. If you want your procedure to use arguments, list one or more variable names within the parentheses following the procedure name in the PROC command, one variable name for each argument. When you call the procedure, you must provide one expression for each argument.

The variable names that appear within the parentheses following the PROC command are called *formal parameters* of the procedure. When the procedure is called, the first argument is assigned to the first formal parameter, the second argument to the second formal parameter, and so on. Formal parameters of a procedure are automatically treated as private variables. Therefore, they do not retain the value of the argument they where passed when the procedure is exited, and you do not need to declare them private using the keyword PRIVATE.

NOTE: In Paradox 4, you can use fixed and dynamic arrays as arguments of a procedure. In Paradox 3.5, only variables can be used.

In the following exercise you will create a procedure that requires one argument. This procedure receives the name of a table and displays it using the WAIT command. This exercise demonstrates the flexibility that procedures can add to your scripts. Begin this exercise from the Main menu.

1. Select Scripts/Editor/New.
2. Type **Viewit** and press [Enter].
3. Enter the following script in the Editor window:

```
CLEAR
CLEARALL
;Define the procedure
PROC ViewTable(TabName)
   VIEW TabName
   WAIT TABLE
```

Procedures and Procedure Libraries

```
      PROMPT  "Press ESC when you are done viewing this table."
      UNTIL "ESC"
  CLEARIMAGE
ENDPROC

WHILE True
  SHOWTABLES ""
    "Please select a table to view or press ESC to cancel."
    TO Choice
  SWITCH
    CASE Choice = "None":
      RETURN "Sorry, there are no tables to view."
    CASE Choice = "Esc":
      RETURN "You pressed Esc."
  ENDSWITCH
  ;This is where the procedure is called.
  ;The variable choice is used as the argument
  ViewTable(Choice)
  CLEAR
ENDWHILE
```

Returning a Value

There are many situations in which you will want to have your procedure return a value. For example, you may create a procedure which performs a calculation that is not provided by one of the PAL functions. The value you want to return is the result of this calculation.

There are two ways to return a value from a procedure. One is to have your script assign a value to a variable. This technique is acceptable when the variable you assign the value to is not private to the procedure (otherwise, it would be released when the procedure terminated). The second method is to use a special feature of the PAL command RETURN.

You can follow the RETURN command with an expression. When you do, two special effects result. First, the value of this expression is assigned to the system variable Retval. Second, any procedure that returns a value can be used in an expression as if it were a function. Consider the following procedure definition:

```
PROC IsWeekDay(TheDate)
IF DOW(TheDate) = "Sat" OR DOW(TheDate) = "Sun"
```

```
   THEN
      RETURN False
   ELSE
      RETURN True
ENDIF
ENDPROC
```

Since the procedure IsWeekDay returns a logical value, it can be used in any expression where a logical value is valid. For example, the following script segment uses the procedure IsWeekDay as a logical expression:

```
IF IsWeekDay(7/4/92)
   THEN
      RETURN "The date falls on a weekend."
   ELSE
      RETURN "The date falls on a weekday."
ENDIF
```

Procedures like IsWeekDay are called *user-defined functions*. They provide you with the ability to create your own extensions to the PAL language. In most cases, if PAL does not provide you with a function that meets a particular need, you can create your own with a procedure.

A procedure that returns a value can also be used following the required keyword VALUE in a pushbutton control element of a dialog box. When the pushbutton is selected, the procedure is executed. During execution, the pushbutton appears depressed on the dialog box. Such a procedure must return a value, and this value is assigned to the pushbutton variable if the dialog box is accepted.

Releasing a Procedure

Defined procedures are stored in your computer's memory. Unfortunately, this memory is a limited resource. If you continue to add procedures to memory using the PROC command, and do not remove ones already placed there, you will eventually run out of memory. This is a particularly unpleasant event. Paradox displays a message "Resource limit exceeded" and all script play comes to a halt.

Procedures are removed from memory using the PAL command RELEASE PROCS. The syntax is as follows:

Procedures and Procedure Libraries

```
RELEASE PROCS Procedure1 ...[, ProcedureN]
```

When Paradox plays the RELEASE PROCS command, it immediately releases the named procedure or procedures from memory. For example, when you no longer need the procedure IsWeekDay in your script, you issue this command:

```
RELEASE PROCS IsWeekDay
```

NOTE: The procedure name in the RELEASE PROCS command is not an expression. Instead, it is the literal name of the procedure. If you treat the procedure name as an expression, by enclosing it in quotation marks or using a variable whose value is the procedure name, a script error will result.

Defining and releasing procedures in an application is a lot of work. Fortunately, there is a very nice solution to this problem. The solution is to use procedure libraries.

Procedure Libraries

Procedure libraries are special files that store procedures. The procedures stored in libraries are identical to those stored in your computer's memory. There are, however, a number of advantages to procedure libraries that will make them an indispensable part of your Paradox usage.

- ✦ A procedure can be loaded from a library directly into memory. This defines the procedure, making it available to your scripts and other procedures.

- ✦ Although you can explicitly load a procedure from a library, you can also make Paradox automatically load your procedures.

- ✦ A procedure loaded from a library does not have to be explicitly released. If memory begins to run low, Paradox will make room by unloading the defined procedure called least recently. However, if your script then calls an unloaded procedure, Paradox will read it again from the library.

- A single library can hold as many as 640 different procedures (300 maximum in Paradox 3.5).
- You can use more than one library in an application.
- Once a procedure has been added to a library, and you no longer need to make changes to it, the script that created the procedure is no longer needed. A complete Paradox application, therefore, usually consists of tables and their families, one or more procedure libraries, and a small startup script that loads the first procedure from the library.

Creating a Library

Before you can add a procedure to a procedure library, you must create the library using the PAL command CREATELIB. The syntax is

```
CREATELIB LibraryName [SIZE MaximumNumberOfProcedures]
```

The CREATELIB command requires a single expression that defines the library name. This name must conform to DOS file-naming conventions. That is, it can begin with either a letter or number, cannot be longer than eight characters in length, and cannot contain blank spaces. For example, the command

```
CREATELIB "Mylib"
```

creates a procedure library called Mylib. This library is stored as a DOS file with the extension .LIB. (This file extension is supplied by Paradox. Do not include it in the library name expression.) You can also include a full DOS path. For example, to create a procedure library called Mylib in the directory C:\SALES, use the command:

```
CREATELIB "C:\\SALES\\Mylib"
```

Remember: You must use two backslashes to represent a single backslash in an alphanumeric constant.

Procedures and Procedure Libraries

The CREATELIB command has an optional keyword, SIZE, which must be followed by an integer between 50 and 640 (300 in Paradox 3.5). Use this keyword whenever you are creating a library that must hold more than 50 procedures. The number that follows the SIZE keyword defines the maximum number of procedures the library can hold. In most cases, you will probably store less than 50 procedures in a library, and therefore, the SIZE command is usually unnecessary.

In the following exercise, you will create a procedure library called Mylib:

1. Press [Alt]-[F10] (PAL menu).
2. Select MiniScript.
3. Type **CREATELIB "Mylib"** and press [Enter].

Paradox plays the command and creates a library called Mylib. Because you did not use the optional SIZE keyword, this library cannot hold more than 50 different procedures.

Adding Procedures to a Library

Once the library is created, you can add procedures to it by using the WRITELIB command. However, before you can write a procedure to a procedure library, the procedure must be defined. The easiest way to do this is to define the procedure and write it to the library in a single script. You can do this easily to any procedure by using the WRITELIB command immediately after the ENDPROC keyword in the script that defines the procedure. The syntax is

```
WRITELIB LibraryName Proc1 ...[, ProcN]
```

The WRITELIB command must be accompanied by both an expression that evaluates to the library name and the name of the procedure. As with the RELEASE PROCS command, the procedure name is not an expression, but the actual name of the procedure. Therefore, to add a procedure named IsWeekDay to the Mylib library, use the following command:

```
WRITELIB "Mylib" IsWeekDay
```

If you have two or more procedures that are defined, you can write them all to the library in a single WRITELIB command by supplying a comma-separated list of procedure names.

Probably the easiest way to add a procedure to a procedure library is to keep the procedure definition and the WRITELIB command in the same script. This is demonstrated in the following exercise by adding the Colors procedure to the Mylib library:

1. Select Scripts/Editor/Open.
2. Type **Colors** and press [Enter].
3. Move your cursor to the last line of the script, where the procedure call Colors( ) is located.
4. Press [Backspace] or DEL until you have deleted the statement Colors( ).
5. Type the following two lines:

   ```
   WRITELIB "Mylib" Colors
   RELEASE PROCS Colors
   ```

   Your screen should look like Figure 12-4.
6. Select Go from the Editor menu.

```
≡ File Edit Search Options Go DO-IT! Cancel
┌[■]══════════════════ C:\SALES\COLORS.SC ══════════════════[↑]┐
│PROC Colors()                                                 │
│CLEAR                                                         │
│FOR BackGround FROM 0 TO 7                                    │
│  FOR ForeGround FROM 0 TO 15                                 │
│    STYLE ATTRIBUTE BackGround * 16 + ForeGround              │
│    @ BackGround + 8,ForeGround * 5                           │
│    ?? FORMAT("W5,AR",STRVAL(BackGround * 16 + ForeGround))   │
│  ENDFOR                                                      │
│ENDFOR                                                        │
│MESSAGE "Press any key to continue."                          │
│a = GETCHAR()                                                 │
│RETURN "Thank you for using Colors"                           │
│ENDPROC                                                       │
│WRITELIB "Mylib" Colors                                       │
│RELEASE PROCS Colors                                          │
```

This script writes the procedure Colors to Mylib
Figure 12-4.

F1 Help Alt-Z Next Alt-A ReplaceNext Ctrl-A Replace | Main |

Procedures and Procedure Libraries

When Paradox plays this script, it parses the procedure Colors and stores it in memory. Next, the WRITELIB command causes Paradox to write this procedure to the library Mylib. The final command, RELEASE PROCS, causes Paradox to remove the procedure definition from memory. This last step was not essential since all procedure definitions are automatically removed when all script play ends. However, using a RELEASE PROCS command when a procedure is no longer necessary is a good habit to get into, and is useful if you ever use one script to play two or more scripts that load procedures into a library.

NOTE: Having one script play two or more scripts that each add a single procedure to a library is useful when you want to add two or more scripts to a library at once. Since the one script plays the others in sequence, script play does not terminate after each procedure is added. If the procedures are not explicitly released at the end of each script, you may run out of memory.

Changing Procedures in a Library

It is not unusual to need to make changes to a procedure stored in a library. To do so, make the necessary changes to the script you used to define the procedure, then add the changed procedure to the library using the same procedure name. When you add the updated procedure to the library using the same procedure name, Paradox marks the existing version of the procedure as obsolete and adds the new version to the library. The space the existing procedure occupied is not released, however. In fact, each time you add or update a procedure to your library, the library will grow by the size of the added procedure, even if the procedure is a revision of an existing procedure.

NOTE: Whenever you change a script that defines a procedure stored in a library, you should play that script to add the changes to the library. If you change the script but fail to update the procedure in the library, and then a script error occurs in the procedure created from it, Paradox will not be able to load the script into the Debugger.

There is no way to remove obsolete procedures from a library. In fact, if you continue to update procedures, your library will eventually grow to an unmanageable size. The solution is to re-create the library, using the CREATELIB command, and then add to it only the newest versions of each of the procedures.

There is a simple trick you can use to re-create your procedure library if each of your procedures is stored in its own script, and each of the scripts includes the WRITELIB and RELEASE PROCS commands after the ENDPROC keyword. Create a table in which you store the names of each of the scripts that add a procedure to your library. At a minimum, this table must have one field where the name of each script is stored. It can also contain additional fields where you store a description of the script, the date the script was last changed, and so on.

Assuming that the list of scripts that define your procedures is stored in a table called Scripts and a field called Script Name, and this table is in the current directory, the following script will create the library Mylib, and add all of the procedures defined by the scripts into it.

```
VIEW "Scripts"
RecordsInScripts = NRECORDS("Scripts")
;Since we must test the number of records in the table
;Scripts more than once, call the function NRECORDS()
;only once, assigning its value to a variable.
SWITCH
  CASE RecordsInScripts > 640 AND VERSION() > 3.5:
    RETURN "Too many scripts for a library. Cannot continue."
  CASE RecordsInScripts > 300 AND VERSION() < 4:
    RETURN "Too many scripts for a library. Cannot continue."
  CASE RecordsInScripts > 50:
    ;There are more than 50 records in the table, but less
    ;than the maximum. Create a library that can hold all
    ;of the procedures.
    CREATELIB "Mylib" SIZE RecordsInScripts
  OTHERWISE:
    ;Less than 50 records means you can use
    ;the default limit of 50 procedures.
    CREATELIB "Mylib"
ENDSWITCH
```

Procedures and Procedure Libraries

```
SCAN
  MESSAGE "Playing ",[Scripts -> Script Name]
  PLAY [Scripts -> Script Name]
ENDSCAN
CLEARIMAGE
```

Since each script contains the definition of one procedure plus the commands to write that procedure to the Mylib library and then release the procedure, this script will re-generate the entire library.

TIP: Instead of using an alphanumeric constant to refer to the procedure library in the WRITELIB command of each script, use a variable. Assign the name of a library to this variable prior to playing any scripts to add or update procedures to the library. (This assignment could take place in your Init script.) By using a variable instead of a constant in the WRITELIB command, you can easily change the location of the library without having to modify each script individually.

Listing the Contents of a Library

You can display a list of the procedures stored in a library using the command INFOLIB followed by the name of the library. The syntax is

```
INFOLIB LibraryName
```

When Paradox plays this command, it creates a temporary table called List. List contains two fields, Procedure and Size. The Procedure field contains the name of each procedure stored in the library. The Size field displays the number of bytes occupied by each procedure.

The following exercise makes use of the INFOLIB command to view the procedures stored in the Mylib procedure library:

1. Press [Alt]-[F10] (PAL menu).
2. Select MiniScript.
3. Type **INFOLIB "Mylib"** and press [Enter].

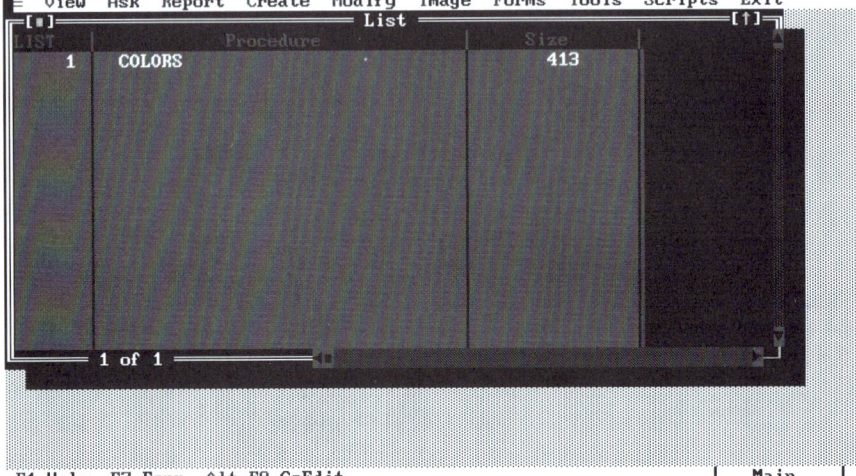

Temporary table, List, created by INFOLIB
Figure 12-5.

Paradox inspects the library Mylib and creates the table List. This table is displayed in a window on the desktop, as shown in Figure 12-5. This figure shows that Mylib contains only one procedure. If more than one procedure were stored in Mylib, these would also be displayed in List.

Using Procedures from a Library

Before a procedure stored in a library can be used, it must be read from the library and placed in your computer's memory. Only then is the procedure defined. There are two ways to read a procedure from a library. The first way is to use the READLIB command. The second is to have Paradox automatically read your procedures from one or more libraries.

NOTE: The procedure stored in an .SC2 file cannot be loaded into memory using either of these techniques. Instead, such a procedure is only loaded when the script that created the procedure is played, by selecting Play from either the PAL or Scripts menu, or by using the PAL command PLAY.

Procedures and Procedure Libraries

The READLIB Command

The syntax of the READLIB command is

```
READLIB LibraryName [IMMEDIATE] Proc1 ... [,ProcN]
```

The READLIB command requires that you define the library name and the procedure to read from it. The library name is an expression, but the procedure name is not. For example, to load the IsWeekDay procedure from the Mylib library, you would use the following command:

```
READLIB "Mylib" IsWeekDay
```

You can read more than one procedure from the library in a single command if you separate the procedure names with commas. The READLIB command also has an optional keyword IMMEDIATE. When you use this keyword, Paradox reads the procedure into memory immediately. Otherwise, the procedure may not be read until it is called.

The following exercise demonstrates the use of READLIB:

1. Press [Alt]-[F10] (PAL menu).
2. Select MiniScript.
3. Type **READLIB "Mylib" Colors Colors( )** and press [Enter].

Paradox reads the first command, READLIB "Mylib" Colors, and loads the procedure Colors into memory. The procedure Colors is now defined. The next command, Colors( ), executes the procedure. When you press any key, the procedure is exited, the MiniScript ends, the procedure is released from memory, and you return to interactive Paradox.

When your script is through using a procedure loaded using READLIB, and you no longer need the procedure, you do not need to explicitly release it, as you do when you define a procedure using the PROC command. When Paradox begins to run low on memory, it will automatically remove the procedure from memory. If the procedure is needed again later, Paradox reads it in again automatically.

NOTE: Like a procedure defined using the PROC command, any procedure read into memory using READLIB will be removed from memory when all script play ends, when it is explicitly released by the RELEASE PROCS command, or if it was loaded by a closed procedure which terminated. Unlike the PROC command, however, Paradox will also remove these procedures from memory, as needed, if memory runs low.

The Autolib Variable

Paradox can load your procedures automatically. All you need to do is tell Paradox which library you stored them in. To do so, assign the name of your procedure library to the system variable Autolib.

When the variable Autolib has a value that refers to the name of a library, you do not have to load a procedure from this library before calling it. When you call the procedure, Paradox looks at the variable Autolib, retrieves the name of your library, and loads the called procedure from that library.

Demonstrate this with the following exercise:

1. Press [Alt]-[F10] (PAL menu).
2. Select MiniScript.
3. Type **Autolib = "Mylib"** and press [Enter].

   Paradox will now automatically load any procedures stored in the library if you call one.
4. Press [Alt]-[F10] again.
5. Select MiniScript.
6. Type **Colors( )** and press [Enter].

Paradox reads the command, loads Colors into memory, and then executes it.

You can also use Autolib to define two or more libraries from which Paradox should load procedures. Do this by providing Autolib with a comma-separated list of library names. It is important, however, that you do not include any spaces in this list. If you do, Paradox will ignore all library names listed after the space. Following is the correct way to define three libraries, Mylib, Utillib, and Demo, as libraries from which Paradox should automatically load procedures.

```
Autolib="Mylib,Utillib,Demo"
```

All these examples of Autolib assume that the library or libraries are in the current directory. If you want to use a library from a directory other than the current directory, you must include the DOS path of that directory in the value of Autolib. For example, if your library is located in the directory C:\SALES, but you are not currently in that directory, you should use the following assignment statement:

```
Autolib="C:\\SALES\\Mylib"
```

Autolib is so useful that nearly every PAL application makes use of at least one, if not more, libraries from which procedures are automatically loaded. Typically, one of these libraries holds procedures that are unique to the application, and another contains general-purpose procedures you use in all your applications.

The Paradox Library

If you do not make extensive use of libraries, you can create only one, called Paradox. If you create a library called Paradox, and do not assign a value to the variable Autolib, Paradox will automatically load procedures from the Paradox library. As soon as you assign a value to the variable Autolib, Paradox will no longer automatically load procedures from Paradox.lib. If you normally only use the Paradox library, yet occasionally need to use Autolib, you should add the Paradox library to your list of libraries you assign to Autolib as follows:

```
Autolib="Mylib,Paradox"
```

This way, any useful procedures you store only in the Paradox library will always be available.

Any utilities you write in PAL for use in interactive Paradox can be turned into procedures and stored in the Paradox library. A procedure can then be called using a key macro (defined by the SETKEY command). For example, you can add the Colors procedure to the key combination  by adding the following command to your Init script (or any other script you play at the beginning of your session to initialize your SETKEY definitions):

```
SETKEY -46 Colors()
```

If you want to store these procedures in a library other than Paradox.lib, you must also assign the name of your library to the Autolib variable from within the Init script. Alternatively, use the READLIB command in the SETKEY definition to explicitly load the procedure from a library before calling it. Use this second method when another script you use assigns a value to Autolib, or uses the command RELEASE VARS ALL. For example:

```
SETKEY -46 READLIB "C:\\PDOX35\\Mylib" Colors Colors()
```

Advanced Procedure Topics

For the most part, procedures are as easy to use as scripts, and in some cases easier. The remaining topics cover special features of procedures that are important when you use them in an application.

NOTE: The issue of procedure swapping becomes moot with Paradox 4 because of the way it handles memory. Therefore, the sections "Using the SETSWAP Command in Paradox 3.5" and "Making Better Use of Memory in Paradox 3.5" do not apply to Paradox 4.

Using the SETSWAP Command in Paradox 3.5

When you use Autolib or the Paradox library, Paradox 3.5 manages the loading and releasing of procedures for you. This makes your use of procedures virtually painless. When memory runs low, Paradox swaps the procedure called least recently out of memory to make room for new procedures or the manipulation of Paradox objects.

Unfortunately, you may still run out of memory, causing an unexpected termination of your application. This is because Paradox does not actually attempt to remove procedure definitions from memory until you are almost entirely out of memory. This is often too late, since the amount of memory remaining may not even be enough to permit procedure swapping to take place.

However, the SETSWAP command permits you to define how much memory Paradox should reserve for procedure swapping. The syntax is

```
SETSWAP NumberOfBytes
```

The SETSWAP command tells Paradox 3.5 how much memory, in bytes, it should keep free. If you issue the command,

```
SETSWAP 20000
```

Paradox begins swapping procedures out of memory as soon as less than 20,000 bytes of memory remain free (about 20K). As a rule, you should never permit Paradox to let available memory fall below 10K, or about 10,000 characters of memory. A more conservative approach is to set SETSWAP to 30000. This should be done at the beginning of any application. SETSWAP will remain in effect until all script play terminates.

Making Better Use of Memory in Paradox 3.5

You will make better use of your computer's memory with your PAL application if you follow two general rules of procedure usage. First, avoid creating procedures much larger than 10K in size. Procedures larger than 10K can interfere with Paradox 3.5's ability to swap procedures from memory. To determine a procedure's size, use INFOLIB to list the procedures and the size of each procedure in your library.

Second, you should avoid other situations that disable procedure swapping. If your procedures are small, very little harm can be done. However, if you prevent Paradox from swapping larger procedures, you may run out of memory even though SETSWAP is set high enough. The following actions prevent procedure swapping:

♦ Playing a script or using EXECUTE from a procedure. While a procedure plays a script or executes PAL commands, the procedure cannot be removed from memory.

- Using the command EXECPROC to play a procedure. Like playing a script, the procedure that uses the EXECPROC command cannot be swapped out of memory.
- Defining a procedure using PROC-ENDPROC. Procedures defined this way cannot be swapped from memory.
- Using a procedure as a function in an expression.

As an example of using a procedure as a function in an expression, the following command:

```
IF IsKeyFields()
   THEN
...
```

prevents the procedure that uses it from being swapped out of memory. If the procedure is small, no harm will come of this. However, if the IsKeyFields procedure is large, use the following instead:

```
IsKeyFields()
IF Retval
   THEN
...
```

Paradox 3.5 *does* permit you to use a procedure in a simple assignment statement without preventing procedure swapping, however. This technique is useful when you do not want to use the system variable Retval. The following command, for example, does not inhibit swapping:

```
a = IsKeyFields()
IF a
   THEN
...
```

Using Closed Procedures

A *closed procedure* is a special type of procedure. When a closed procedure terminates, any variables or procedures that were defined while it was playing are automatically removed from memory. Closed procedures are particularly useful in large applications that consist of

Procedures and Procedure Libraries

two or more separate modules. If you define each of these modules as a closed procedure, your application will make more efficient use of memory.

You define a closed procedure by including the CLOSED keyword between the PROC keyword and the name of your procedure. Within that procedure, you can define variables and load procedures, just as you can in any other procedure. However, a closed procedure does not automatically know of any procedures or variables that were defined prior to its being called. You can use the optional keyword USEVARS to gain access to any variable definitions that exist outside of the closed procedure. However, you do not need to use the PRIVATE keyword with a closed procedure, since all variables defined within a closed procedure are private.

A closed procedure can only be loaded from a procedure library. This means that the script that defines a closed procedure cannot also play it. Following is an example of a script that creates a closed procedure and writes it to a library called AppProcs. This procedure is designed as the first procedure in an application. Note also that it includes calls to other procedures that must exist in one of the two libraries assigned to the variable Autolib if the procedure is to work properly.

```
PROC CLOSED MainMenu()
Autolib = "AppProcs,Mylib"
Errorproc = "CatchError"
READLIB "Mylib" CatchError
IF NOT GetPassword()
   THEN
       QUIT "Access denied"
ENDIF
SETSWAP 30000
Choice = "Add"
WHILE True
  SHOWMENU
    "Add"     :"Add a new record to the database.",
    "Edit"    :"Edit an existing record in the database.",
    "Reports" :"Display the Reports menu.",
    "Leave"   :"Return to Paradox."
    DEFAULT Choice
    TO Choice

    SWITCH
```

```
      CASE Choice = "Add":     AddRecords()
      CASE Choice = "Edit":    EditRecords()
      CASE Choice = "Reports": ReportsMenu()
      OTHERWISE:  RETURN "Have a nice day."
    ENDSWITCH
  ENDWHILE
ENDPROC
WRITELIB "AppProcs" MainMenu
RELEASE PROCS MainMenu
```

This example demonstrates one of the most common uses of a closed procedure, that is, as the first procedure in an application. It is typically loaded by a small script that does only two things: loads the procedure and then calls it. Once an application is bug free, this small script may be the only script used in the entire application. It might look like this:

```
READLIB "AppProcs" MainMenu
MainMenu()
```

Using a closed procedure as the first procedure in the application causes all variables defined and procedures loaded to be automatically released when the application terminates.

Using an Error Procedure

An *error procedure* is a special procedure that is automatically executed when Paradox encounters a script error. The error procedure should make a record of the error, and then quit to interactive Paradox, or even use the EXIT command to return to DOS. Error procedures are used from within an application so that an inexperienced or unauthorized user will never be presented with the Cancel-Debug menu. You define an error procedure by assigning the name of a procedure to the variable ErrorProc. For example, the following statement,

```
ErrorProc = "Error"
```

tells Paradox to execute the procedure named Error when a run-time error is encountered.

The trick to using an error procedure is that it must be loaded into memory explicitly using the READLIB command. Even when the error

Procedures and Procedure Libraries

procedure is located in a library assigned to the Autolib variable, the error may be so severe that it prevents Paradox from loading the procedure from the library. Therefore, at the beginning of your application you should both define the error procedure and load it into memory. The lines may look like this:

```
ErrorProc = "Error"
READLIB "AppProcs" Error
```

In some cases, your error procedure may be triggered by an event that is not fatal to your application. If you can anticipate these problems, you can program your error procedure to handle them gracefully and then return to executing the script without the user ever knowing there was a problem. Besides quitting or exiting the application, your error procedure can use the RETURN command, followed by one of three possible values. Use RETURN 0 to return to the command that was executing when the error was encountered. You use this if your error procedure was able to correct the problem that prohibited the command from being executed. RETURN 1 also returns to the script, but it skips the command that triggered the error, continuing with the command that followed it. Finally, you can use RETURN 2 to display the Cancel-Debug menu. This is what happens when there is no error procedure in the first place. You can use this return value as a development tool, preventing the error procedure from limiting your access to the PAL Debugger while you are programming the application.

Following is an example error procedure. It is short enough so that it does not require much memory. This procedure makes use of the PRINT FILE command to print information about the error to a DOS file. PRINT FILE appends a DOS file, meaning that every time the procedure is executed, the information is added to the end of the DOS file. This file, called ERROR.ERR in this example, will store a record of every script error it encounters.

```
PROC Error()
PRIVATE ErrorProc, a   ;Making ErrorProc private prevents
                       ;an infinite loop in case the error
                       ;procedure itself causes an error.
;Terminate all non-main mode activity and display a message
RESET
CLEAR
@ 10,1 ?? "An error has occurred."
```

```
@ 12,1 ?? "Please call the application administrator."
MESSAGE ERRORMESSAGE()
;Tests to make sure that there is at least 4K of space
;available on the current drive.
IF DRIVESPACE(SUBSTR(DIRECTORY(),1,1)) > 4096
   THEN
     ;There is enough disk space. Create or append a file with
     ;error information.
     PRINT FILE "ERROR.ERR" "******************************\n"
     PRINT FILE "ERROR.ERR" "The time    =",TIME(),"\n"
     PRINT FILE "ERROR.ERR" "The date    =",TODAY(),"\n"
     PRINT FILE "ERROR.ERR" "ErrorCode   =",ERRORCODE(),"\n"
     PRINT FILE "ERROR.ERR" "Error       =",ERRORMESSAGE(),"\n"
     PRINT FILE "ERROR.ERR" "Memory left=",MEMLEFT(),"\n"
     PRINT FILE "ERROR.ERR" "System mode=",SYSMODE(),"\n"
     PRINT FILE "ERROR.ERR" "The user    =",USERNAME(),"\n"
ENDIF
;Display the error message until the user presses a key.
@ 14,1 ?? "Press any key to return to Paradox."
a=GETCHAR()
;Return to Paradox. Use EXIT instead of QUIT to return to DOS
QUIT
ENDPROC
```

NOTE: The characters \n add a line feed to the end of each line appended to the file.

This example is only one possible error procedure. In many instances, error procedures are more involved than this one. You can, however, use this as a starting point for creating your own error procedure.

Quick Review

- In Paradox 4, any script you play is automatically turned into a procedure, and stored in an .SC2 file, the first time you play the script and each time you play it after editing it.

- You explicitly define a procedure using the PAL command PROC.

- You can pass zero, one, or more arguments to a procedure. These arguments are assigned to variables called formal parameters of the procedure, and are private to the procedure.

- A procedure can return a value. Procedures that do so can be used in expressions.

- A procedure is released from memory when all script play ends, when the RELEASE PROCS command is used, or, if the procedure was called by a closed procedure, when the latter terminates.

- A procedure must be defined before it can be stored in a procedure library.

- If you assign one or more procedure library names to the system variable Autolib, Paradox will automatically load your procedures as you call them.

- If you do not assign a value to the variable Autolib, Paradox will attempt to load called procedures from the library named Paradox.

CHAPTER

EVENTS AND EVENT PROCEDURES

This chapter introduces you to the advanced topics of events and event procedures. Although you can create perfectly acceptable applications without using any of the techniques described here, some of these will naturally find their way into your programming repertoire. This is because they provide you with the highest level of control, and consequently, the greatest flexibility in defining the behavior of your scripts.

This chapter is divided into two sections. In the first you are introduced to events, how they are generated, and what you can do with them. In the second, the topic of event procedures is covered.

NOTE: Paradox 3.5 does not support any of the commands described in this chapter. With a little work, however, you can simulate many of the features of event driven processing using a combination of the GETCHAR( ) function and the KEYPRESS command.

Events

An *event* is the smallest meaningful action Paradox can act on. It cannot be broken down into two or more discrete components, it is a whole. For example, a single keypress is an event; either a key is pressed or it is not. The entry of an entire word, however, is not an event. Instead, it is a series of events—the individual keypresses.

As events occur, Paradox processes them on a first come, first processed basis. As each new event occurs, it must line up behind any events that have occurred but have not yet been processed. This queue is called the *event stream.* Paradox takes each event from the front of the event stream, one at a time, and either acts on it or discards it. Paradox acts on the event if it is meaningful within the current Paradox context, and discards it if it is not. Discarded events disappear, as if they never occurred.

In all, there are five types of events: key, mouse, message, trigger, and idle. Key events and mouse events originate from the user. Message events are generated internally by Paradox to manipulate windows and menus. Trigger events occur during a SHOWDIALOG or WAIT command to signal user interaction with an object. Idle events are generated by your computer, and recognized by Paradox. They occur at regular, frequent intervals (many times a second) during an absence of activity from the keyboard or mouse.

Whenever the user presses a key, or moves or clicks the mouse, one or more events are generated. For example, if a window is open on the desktop, and the user presses (Ctrl)-(F8), at least two events result. The first one is a key event, the pressing of (Ctrl)-(F8). Since this event is relevant in the current Paradox context ((Ctrl)-(F8) is relevant when there is an open window on the desktop), Paradox acts on the keypress. In

Events and Event Procedures

this case, the action it takes is to generate another event, a CLOSE message event which closes the window. This message event is added to the end of the event stream. When Paradox processes this message event, it closes the window. If Ctrl-F8 is pressed when no windows are open on the desktop, the event is meaningless in that context, and Paradox discards it without generating a CLOSE message.

Although an event is a discrete occurrence, it is rich in context. For example, pressing a button on your mouse generates a DOWN event. However, not only does Paradox know that a button was pressed, but it also knows which mouse button (right, left, or both), the row and column position of the mouse pointer at the instant the button was pressed, and whether the Shift key was down at the moment of the mouse button press. Likewise, although pressing a key on your keyboard is a single event, Paradox also knows whether an Alt key, a Ctrl, or a Shift was down at the same time of the keypress, as well as whether Caps Lock was on or off.

Getting Events

You can intercept the event stream using the PAL command GETEVENT. The syntax of this command is

```
GETEVENT
  [{ALL |
  [KEY Key1 ... [,KeyN]]
  [MOUSE { "ALL" | ["DOWN"] ["UP"] ["MOVE"] ["AUTO"] }]
  [MESSAGE { "ALL" | ["CLOSE"] ["MAXIMIZE"]["MENUSELECT"]
                     ["NEXT"] ["MENUSELECT"]["MENUKEY"]}]
  [IDLE]}]
  TO DynamicArrayName
```

NOTE: Trigger events are specific to dialog and wait procedures; they cannot be included in the event list of the GETEVENT command. Working with trigger events is discussed in detail later in this chapter.

The GETEVENT command has two required keywords, GETEVENT and TO, and one required dynamic array name. The remaining optional keywords and expressions permit you to define an event list, which acts as a filter. If you use none of these optional keywords, or the optional keyword ALL, GETEVENT will *trap* (intercept) and hold the next event in the event stream. (Idle events are not trapped when you do not use an event list, they *are* trapped if you use ALL.) Using any of the other optional keywords permits you to specify one or more types of events to trap. Any event that does not match this type is automatically passed along to Paradox, which will act on it (if it is relevant in the current context), or discard it.

Consider the following command:

```
GETEVENT KEY "ESC" TO EventArray
```

When Paradox executes this command, it looks at the next event (the one that will normally be processed next by Paradox) and evaluates it against the event list. In this case, the event list contains only one event, an [Esc] keypress. If the event is not an [Esc] keypress, it is passed along to Paradox and GETEVENT continues to wait. If there are no events in the event stream (this is normally the case), this GETEVENT command waits until an event comes along, and passes all non-[Esc] events to Paradox.

GETEVENT continues to process events until one that matches the event list is found. When such an event is found, it is not passed to Paradox. Instead, GETEVENT assigns all of the available information about the event to the dynamic array listed after the TO keyword. Exactly what information this dynamic array contains depends on the event.

It is the responsibility of your script to decide what to do with the trapped event. In most cases, your script will inspect the contents of the dynamic array and determine what action to take.

There are three general categories of action that your script may take with a captured event:

- ◆ Pass the event on to Paradox.
- ◆ Not pass the event to Paradox, but issue alternative commands that Paradox must act upon.
- ◆ Not do anything, which is the same as discarding the event entirely.

Events and Event Procedures

GETEVENT intercepts the event stream immediately before it would normally be processed by Paradox. Therefore, if your script passes along the event to Paradox, or passes Paradox other commands, those are acted upon by Paradox immediately. They do not enter the event stream. In other words, a GETEVENT command will never intercept the event that your script passes along to Paradox.

The Event Dynamic Array

When GETEVENT captures an event, information about that event is assigned to a dynamic array. The elements of this array store a wealth of information about the specific event. In most cases your script evaluates this information and decides what to do based on it.

NOTE: You do not need to explicitly declare a dynamic array before using it in the GETEVENT command. This command implicitly declares the array before assigning values to it. Furthermore, each time you use GETEVENT, the dynamic array is created from scratch. Consequently, even if you use the same dynamic array name for two consecutive events, the array only contains information about the current event, and never information left over from a previous one.

The following exercise will show you the contents of dynamic arrays created by the GETEVENT command. Begin this exercise from the Main menu.

1. Select Scripts/Editor/New.
2. Type **Getevent** and press [Enter].
3. Enter the following script:

```
ECHO NORMAL
WINDOW CREATE @ 3,5 HEIGHT 20 WIDTH 40 TO ShowEvent
WHILE True
   GETEVENT To EventArray
   IF EventArray["TYPE"] = "KEY" AND EventArray["KEYCODE"] = 27
     THEN
        WINCLOSE
        RETURN "Done"
```

```
  ENDIF
  @ 0,0 CLEAR
  FOREACH e in EventArray
     ? e," = ",EventArray[e]
  ENDFOREACH
ENDWHILE
```

4. Select Go from the Editor menu.

This script begins by using ECHO NORMAL to drop the full-screen canvas and then creates a canvas window in which the contents of the dynamic array will be displayed. The remaining commands appear within a WHILE loop, so they may be executed repeatedly. Within the loop, GETEVENT is used to trap each event that occurs. (Since no event list is provided, all events except idle events are trapped.) As each event is captured, a description of the event is stored in the dynamic array named EventArray.

Immediately following the GETEVENT command is a test for the (Esc) key. When the event is a press of the (Esc) key (ASCII code 27), the WINCLOSE command closes the canvas window, and the RETURN command terminates the script. For each event other than (Esc), the script displays the contents of the event array in the canvas window.

When the script first begins to play, there are no events in the event stream. However, press a key on the keyboard, or use the mouse in any way, and the canvas window displays the contents of the dynamic array created by that event.

The single most important element of the dynamic array is the one that reveals what type of event the array holds. The index for this element is called TYPE, and it is an element of every event array, regardless of what event type it holds. Only by knowing the value of this element can you know what other indices are available in the array. Once you determine the type of event stored in the array, you can test other elements of the array for additional information, if necessary.

The value of the TYPE element for each event type is shown in the following table:

Events and Event Procedures

Event	TYPE Value
Idle	IDLE
Key	KEY
Mouse	MOUSE
Message	MESSAGE

The arrays created from each of these four event types are described in the following sections.

Key Event Arrays

The dynamic array elements of a key event are shown in Table 13-1. Although the information Paradox gathers concerning the key event is rich, in most cases you are concerned about only one element of this

Key Event Array Index	Description
LEFT ALT	True if the left [Alt] key was pressed during the key event, otherwise False
LEFT CTRL	True if the left [Ctrl] key was pressed during the key event, otherwise False
INS	True if the [Ins] key was pressed during the key event
CAPS LOCK	True if the keyboard [Caps Lock] was on, otherwise False
NUM LOCK	True if the keyboard [Num Lock] was on, otherwise False
SCROLL LOCK	True if the keyboard [Scroll Lock] was on, otherwise False
ALT	True if any [Alt] key was pressed, otherwise False
CTRL	True if any [Ctrl] key was pressed, otherwise False
LEFT SHIFT	True if the left [Shift] key was pressed, otherwise False
RIGHT SHIFT	True if the right [Shift] key was pressed, otherwise False
TYPE	KEY for all key events
KEYCODE	ASCII or extended IBM code of the key pressed
SCANCODE	Key code based on the system BIOS

Dynamic Array Elements of a Key Event
Table 13-1.

array, the key code. By evaluating the key code, you know what key was pressed and can take appropriate action based on that key. This *key code* is the ASCII code, or extended IBM code, for the pressed key. For example, the key code for the (Esc) key is 27, which is why the script in the preceding exercise compared EventArray["KEYCODE"] to 27.

Mouse Event Arrays

The dynamic array elements of a mouse event are shown in Table 13-2. Notice that many of these elements are similar to those stored for key events. As with key events, there is more information available in this array than you will need in most situations.

It is more difficult to program mouse interactions than key interactions. Key interactions often result in only one event; whereas mouse interactions often consist of two or more mouse events in a row. For example, a simple mouse click results in two separate events, the mouse button being pressed and that same button being released. A *drag* is more complicated still, consisting of a button down, at least one move, and finally a button up.

The element of the mouse event dynamic array that specifies what action occurred has the index ACTION. This is the most important element of the mouse event array, and can have one of four values: AUTO, DOWN, MOVE, or UP. Except when your script is processing single clicks only, once you detect a mouse DOWN event, your script should enter a loop until the remaining mouse events have been received. Only then will your script have enough information to continue. Fortunately, once a mouse DOWN event occurs, every event that follows will be a mouse event, until a mouse UP event is received.

The following exercise demonstrates one way to process these more complex mouse events. This script will permit you to draw colored boxes on the canvas. Begin this script from the Main mode:

1. Select Scripts/Editor/New.
2. Type **Drawbox** and press (Enter).

Events and Event Procedures

Mouse Event Array Index	Description
LEFT ALT	True if left [Alt] key was down
LEFT CTRL	True if left [Ctrl] key was down
INS	True if [Ins] key was active
CAPS LOCK	True if [Caps Lock] was on
NUM LOCK	True if [Num Lock] was on
SCROLL LOCK	True if [Scroll Lock] was on
ALT	True if an [Alt] key was down
CTRL	True if a [Ctrl] key was down
LEFT SHIFT	True if left [Shift] key was down
RIGHT SHIFT	True if right [Shift] key was down
TYPE	MOUSE for all mouse events
ACTION	The type of mouse action: AUTO, DOWN, MOVE, or UP
COL	The full-screen canvas column coordinate at time of mouse action; local canvas coordinates if the GETEVENT is followed by a LOCALIZEEVENT command
ROW	The full-screen canvas row coordinate at time of mouse action; local canvas coordinates if the GETEVENT is followed by a LOCALIZEEVENT command
DOUBLECLICK	True if DOWN action was a double click
BUTTONS	Button involved in an AUTO, DOWN, or UP action (LEFT, RIGHT, or BOTH; NONE if the action was a MOVE action with no button down)
WINDOW	Handle of window that will be affected by mouse event if the event is passed to Paradox; this element is only created if the GETEVENT is followed by a LOCALIZEEVENT command

Dynamic Array Elements of a Mouse Event Table 13-2.

3. Type the following commands into the Editor window:

```
PROMPT "Use mouse to draw colored boxes. Press ESC to exit."
ECHO NORMAL ECHO OFF
WHILE True
  GETEVENT KEY "ESC" MOUSE "DOWN" TO HoldEvent
  SWITCH
    CASE HoldEvent["TYPE"] = "KEY":
      RETURN "Done"
    CASE HoldEvent["TYPE"] = "MOUSE":
      R = HoldEvent["ROW"]
      C = HoldEvent["COL"]
      Color = INT(RAND()*127)+1
      WHILE True
        GETEVENT MOUSE "ALL" TO HoldEvent
        IF HoldEvent["ACTION"] ="UP"
          THEN
            QUITLOOP
          ELSE
            PAINTCANVAS ATTRIBUTE Color
                    R,C,HoldEvent["ROW"],
                    HoldEvent["COL"]
        ENDIF
      ENDWHILE
  ENDSWITCH
ENDWHILE
```

4. Select Go from the Editor menu.

This script consists of two WHILE loops. The outer loop uses GETEVENT to process only DOWN mouse and [Esc] key events. All other events are automatically passed along to Paradox. GETEVENT is followed by a SWITCH control structure that evaluates the event type. Because the GETEVENT traps for only one type of key code (ESC) and one mouse action (DOWN), the CASE commands do not need to evaluate more than the TYPE element to know exactly what event is held in the dynamic array. If more than one key or mouse action was trapped by the GETEVENT command, the CASE command would need to evaluate both TYPE and KEYCODE (key events) and TYPE and ACTION (mouse events).

If a key event is trapped, meaning that [Esc] was pressed, the script terminates. If a mouse event is detected (a DOWN action

Events and Event Procedures

occurred), the script assigns the row and column where the DOWN action occurred to variables (R and C) and enters a WHILE loop. This inner loop is exited as soon as the mouse UP event is detected. Until then, however, each time the mouse is moved (a MOVE action), the PAINTCANVAS command paints a rectangle from the mouse DOWN row and column coordinates to the current mouse coordinates. (This use of PAINTCANVAS will only draw a box if you move your cursor down and to the right while the button is held.)

5. Demonstrate how this script performs by moving your mouse to the middle of your screen and holding down the left mouse button (you can just as easily use the right mouse button if you like).

6. Holding the mouse button down, move your mouse down and to the right. As you move the mouse, a box is drawn.

7. Release the mouse button.

    The inner loop is exited and the GETEVENT in the outer loop now waits for the next [Esc] key or mouse DOWN event.

8. Try this several more times. Each time you do, a box of a different color is drawn. This is the result of the use of the RAND function to calculate a color attribute.

9. When you are finished drawing colored boxes, press [Esc].

> **NOTE:** The ROW and COL elements of the mouse dynamic array are coordinates relative to the full-screen canvas. If you want these coordinates relative to a canvas window, use the command, LOCALIZEEVENT. This command will convert the dynamic array elements ROW and COL to local window coordinates. Furthermore, it will add an element to the array. This element, indexed WINDOW, contains the handle of the window these coordinates refer to.

If your script is only interested in single mouse click events, processing these events is far easier. Simply trap only for a DOWN mouse action, and process the array created. To do this, your GETEVENT command would look something like this:

```
GETEVENT MOUSE "DOWN" TO EventArray
```

Message Event Arrays

The elements of a message event are shown in Table 13-3. Messages that relate to a window have only two elements, TYPE and MESSAGE. When the message pertains to a pull-down menu interaction, the array will have three or four elements. When a menu item is selected from a pull-down menu, the message array will also have the MENUTAG element, which contains the tag of the selected menu item. If the pull-down menu definition includes the UNTIL keyword, and a list of keys, the array will also include the same elements as those in a key event array when one of those keys is pressed. The different messages, and how they are generated, are given in Table 13-4.

Message Event Array Index	Description
TYPE	MESSAGE for all message events
MESSAGE	Type of message event: CLOSE, MAXIMIZE, MENUKEY, MENUSELECT, or NEXT
MENUTAG	The tag of the selected or highlighted menu item for MENUSELECT or MENUKEY events

Elements of a Message Event Array
Table 13-3.

Value	Description
CLOSE	User pressed Ctrl-F8 or clicked the window close icon
MAXIMIZE	User clicked the maximize icon or double clicked the title bar of a window
MENUKEY	User pressed a key associated with the UNTIL optional keyword of the pull-down menu
MENUSELECT	User selected an item from the pull-down menu
NEXT	User pressed Ctrl-F4 to select a new active window

Possible Values of the MESSAGE Element of a Message Event
Table 13-4.

Just as the ACTION element of a mouse event determines how you process the event, the MESSAGE element of a message event is used to decide what action to take. In other words, unless you are trapping for only one type of message, you must evaluate both the TYPE and MESSAGE elements to determine what course of action to take with the event.

Idle Event Arrays

An idle event generates an array with only a single element. This element, indexed TYPE, contains the value IDLE. If you want to trap for idle events, you must use the keyword IDLE in the event list.

An idle event is generated each time your computer has nothing to do. Your computer, however, is very fast, and normally has a lot of spare time on its hands. Consequently, idle events occur constantly. Except in specialized situations, you will never really care about idle events.

An idle event is an informational event; that is, Paradox does nothing with it. Therefore, it does not make any difference whether you trap and discard it, or pass it along to Paradox.

Executing an Event

After evaluating an event you trapped using GETEVENT, you may determine that you want to pass the event along to Paradox. You do this using the EXECEVENT command. The syntax of this command is

```
EXECEVENT DynamicArrayName
```

When Paradox encounters this command, it executes the command represented by the elements of the dynamic array. In most cases, this array is created by a preceding GETEVENT command. However, if the need arises, you can use EXECEVENT with an array you declared, as long as its indices and elements are consistent with a valid event.

If you use GETEVENT without a corresponding EXECEVENT, the intercepted event is never received by Paradox. Consider the following script:

```
ECHO NORMAL
WHILE True
   GETEVENT ALL TO HoldEvent
   SWITCH
```

```
    CASE HoldEvent["TYPE"]="KEY" and HoldEvent["KEYCODE"]=27:
      RETURN "Done"
    CASE HoldEvent["TYPE"] = "MOUSE":
        LOOP
    OTHERWISE:
       EXECEVENT HoldEvent
  ENDSWITCH
ENDWHILE
```

If you played this script, it would permit you to have almost any keyboard interaction with Paradox. Each and every event that occurs is intercepted by GETEVENT. Every event that is not the press of the Esc key or a mouse event is then passed on to Paradox using the EXECEVENT command. If a mouse event is detected, nothing happens. It is as though the mouse event never happened. If you press the Esc key, the script terminates.

SHOWPULLDOWN and GETEVENT

The SHOWPULLDOWN command builds a menu but does not wait for a response. Instead, Paradox continues on to the PAL commands that follow the ENDMENU command. You learned in Chapter 9 that you can use the GETMENUSELECTION command to pause Paradox until the user selects from the menu.

While GETMENUSELECTION permits you to easily use pull-down menus, it neutralizes one of the major advantages of this command. Instead of using GETMENUSELECTION, you can use GETEVENT to intercept only message events from the user, passing all other events on to Paradox, thereby permitting the user to freely interact with tables on both the desktop and the menu. The following script demonstrates a simplified version of this usage.

```
SHOWPULLDOWN
  "View":"Display the View table menu":"Viewtab"
    SUBMENU
      "Customer":"View the Customer table":"Viewcust",
      "Employee":"View the Employee table":"Viewemp"
    ENDSUBMENU,
  "Close":"Close the current window.":"Closewin"
ENDMENU
ECHO NORMAL
```

Events and Event Procedures

```
PROMPT "Press ESC to exit"
WHILE True
  GETEVENT KEY "ESC" MESSAGE "MENUSELECT" TO EventArray
  SWITCH
    CASE EventArray["TYPE"] = "KEY":
      QUITLOOP
    CASE EventArray["TYPE"] =  "MESSAGE":
      SWITCH
        CASE EventArray["MENUTAG"] = "Closewin":
          WINCLOSE
        CASE EventArray["MENUTAG"] = "Viewcust":
          VIEW "Customer"
        CASE EventArray["MENUTAG"] = "Viewemp":
          VIEW "Employee"
      ENDSWITCH
  ENDSWITCH
ENDWHILE
CLEARPULLDOWN
```

The preceding script permits the user to view one or two tables. When those tables are on the desktop, the user is free to view or edit the tables. There are some severe limitations to this script, however. It does not perform any checking of the validity of the user's requests. For example, the user is free to select Close from the displayed menu even when there are no tables on the desktop. While this causes no harm, it does not make much sense either. A similar problem, and one that does cause difficulty, is if the user enters Edit mode with one table, and then selects another table to view from the menu, a run-time error will occur.

Because of these complexities, your script rarely provides a single pull-down menu. Instead, as the user makes selections from the pull-down menu, either you use the MENUDISABLE command to make one or more of the menu selections unavailable, or you create a new pull-down menu with only those selections that are relevant to the situation.

This script suffers from another problem. In order to permit the user to see the tables placed on the desktop, the entire desktop is echoed onto the full-screen canvas. While this permits users to see the tables, it also displays all intermediate working of the script. To avoid problems like these, and to reduce the complexity of your script, user interaction with tables is often permitted within the WAIT command, rather than by using the GETEVENT command. There is a special version of the WAIT command, described later in this chapter, that permits all the flexibility of the GETEVENT command, as well as additional, table-specific features. This version of WAIT can be used in combination with a pull-down menu.

Event Procedures

While the GETEVENT and EXECEVENT command combination provides you with event-level control over the Paradox environment, it cannot be used in all situations. For instance, when your script displays a dialog box, Paradox takes over until the user either accepts or cancels the dialog box. While Paradox is in control, the GETEVENT command is useless. The same is true for a WAIT command.

Fortunately, both the SHOWDIALOG and WAIT commands give you the option of defining a procedure that can be called, under certain conditions, from within the SHOWDIALOG and WAIT commands. When used with a dialog box, this procedure is called a *dialog procedure*. When used with a WAIT command, it is called a *wait procedure*.

Dialog and wait procedures are associated with an event list much like the one you use in the GETEVENT command. Paradox knows that it should immediately call the defined procedure if one of the events in this list occurs. From within this procedure, your script can determine which event took place, and respond to it. What response is made is entirely up to you.

Trigger Events

The event list of an event procedure can include special types of events called *trigger events*. Trigger events signal certain types of user interactions specific to dialog boxes and tables. For example, a user accepting a dialog box results in an *ACCEPT trigger*. If you include the ACCEPT trigger in the event list for the dialog box, your script can make sure that the user completed the dialog box correctly before continuing. If your script determines that the dialog box is not complete, the dialog procedure can discard the ACCEPT event, display an appropriate error message, and return the user to the dialog box.

In many situations, one action by the user will result in two or more trigger events. For example, when a user presses ⬇ to move to another record in a table, no less than four trigger events occur. These are DEPARTFIELD, DEPARTROW, ARRIVEROW, and ARRIVEFIELD.

Before and After Triggers

Each trigger event can be classified as either a before trigger or an after trigger. *Before triggers* indicate that an event is about to occur. If your event list includes before triggers, you can evaluate the event, and optionally accept or discard the trigger. If you accept the trigger, the event occurs. Discarding the event prohibits the event from occurring. For example, when a user presses [Tab] to leave a field, the first trigger event generated is the DEPARTFIELD trigger. This is a before trigger. If you include the DEPARTFIELD trigger in your wait procedure event list, you can evaluate the field the user is attempting to leave, and prohibit the user from leaving it, if necessary.

After triggers indicate that an event has already occurred. You cannot prohibit an after trigger. For example, an ARRIVEFIELD trigger signals that the cursor has arrived in a new field. After triggers are often used to prepare for the next user interaction. For example, you can include the ARRIVEFIELD trigger in your event list, and upon detecting this trigger, determine which field the cursor has arrived at, and if appropriate, assign a default value to the field.

Trigger Cycles

The *trigger cycle* is a concept used to group trigger events. All trigger events that result from a single action occur within a single trigger cycle. Furthermore, the events within a given trigger cycle occur in a predictable order. For example, when a user presses [↓] to move to a new field in a table, the DEPARTFIELD trigger occurs before the DEPARTROW trigger. The last trigger in this cycle is the ARRIVEFIELD trigger.

Trigger cycles are especially important for handling situations where one user action results in two or more trigger events. If you cancel a before event, all remaining events in the same trigger cycle, both before and after events, are discarded. Canceling an after event, however, has no affect. Once the trigger cycle contains only after events, all will be processed, no matter what.

Dialog Procedures

Dialog procedures are used to process events without exiting a dialog box. To use a dialog procedure, follow your dialog box title with the optional keyword PROC, then with an expression that evaluates to the name of a defined procedure. The procedure name can be followed by an event list. (When no event list is provided, all events except IDLE events trigger the dialog procedure.) The syntax of the event list is

```
{ALL |
[KEY {"ALL" | Key1 ... [,KeyN]}]
[MOUSE {"ALL" | ["AUTO"] ["DOWN"] ["MOVE"] ["UP"]]
[TRIGGER { "ALL" | ["ACCEPT"] ["ARRIVE"] ["CANCEL"] ["CLOSE"]
                   ["DEPART"] ["OPEN"] ["SELECT"] ["UPATE"]}]
[IDLE]
```

Following the event list (or the dialog procedure name when no event list is provided), the SHOWDIALOG command continues with the required @ command, followed by the row and column position of the upper left corner of the dialog box. The remainder of this command is unchanged.

The following is an example of a SHOWDIALOG command that makes use of a dialog procedure. In this script, the dialog procedure is only called upon an open trigger, which occurs only when the dialog box is first drawn. This procedure removes the frame from the dialog box (frameless dialog boxes cannot be moved). You can use a technique like this to create unique features for all your dialog boxes.

```
PROC ChangeDialog(EventType, TagValue, EventValue,
                  ElementValue)
  PRIVATE DialogAttributes
  ;Get the handle of the dialog box
  WINDOW HANDLE DIALOG TO DialogHandle
  ;Create a dynamic array to define the dialog box attributes
  DYNARRAY DialogAttributes[]
  ;Set HASFRAME to False
  DialogAttributes["HASFRAME"] = False
  WINDOW SETATTRIBUTES DialogHandle FROM DialogAttributes
ENDPROC

SHOWDIALOG "Dialog Procedure Demonstration"
  PROC "ChangeDialog" TRIGGER "OPEN"
```

Events and Event Procedures

```
  @ 5,20
  HEIGHT 10
  WIDTH 40
  @ 3,5  ?? "This text is a canvas element"
  PUSHBUTTON
    @ 6,7 WIDTH 10
    "~O~k" OK DEFAULT
    VALUE True TAG "Okbutton" TO Retval
  PUSHBUTTON
    @ 6,21 WIDTH 10
    "~C~ancel" CANCEL
    VALUE False TAG "Cancelbutton" TO Retval
ENDDIALOG
```

When Paradox plays the SHOWDIALOG command, it constructs the dialog box. Each time one of the events listed in the event list occurs, Paradox executes the procedure named in the expression following the PROC command.

NOTE: The expression following the PROC keyword does not have the same form as a procedure call. This expression must not include parentheses or an argument list.

Table 13-5 displays a list of all dialog box triggers, what causes them, and whether they are before or after triggers.

Building Dialog Procedures

A dialog procedure must be defined prior to using it in a dialog box. In most cases, you will store the dialog procedure in a library assigned to the Autolib variable.

A dialog procedure must have four formal parameters. When one of the events in the event list of the SHOWDIALOG command occurs, Paradox passes information to the dialog procedure through these parameters. Since formal parameters are automatically private to a procedure, only your dialog procedure has access to this information.

Trigger	Cause	Before or After
ACCEPT	User accepts the dialog box	Before
ARRIVE	Cursor arrives at control element	After
CANCEL	User cancels the dialog box	Before
CLOSE	Dialog box is removed	After
DEPART	User leaves a control element	Before
OPEN	The dialog box is created	After
SELECT	User selects from a pick list using a double click	Before
UPDATE	User changes a value of a control element	Before

**Dialog Box Triggers
Table 13-5.**

The following is an example of how a dialog procedure is defined:

```
PROC ProcName(EventType, TagValue, EventValue, ElementValue)
  ;Commands to process the events in the SHOWDIALOG event list
ENDPROC
```

NOTE: You can use any names you want for the four formal parameters in your dialog procedure. However, for clarity, the following discussion will use the names shown in the preceding example.

The first formal parameter is a variable that holds the event type. If the event is a mouse, key, or idle event, the value of EventType is EVENT. If the event is a trigger event, EventType is the name of the trigger event. For example, if the dialog procedure is generated by an OPEN trigger event, the EventType is assigned the value OPEN.

The second format parameter is assigned a value only if the event is an ARRIVE or DEPART trigger event. In these instances, TagValue is assigned the tag of the control element involved. For example, if the event is the user pressing [Tab] to leave a radio button, and the radio button has the tag ButtonTag, EventType is assigned the value DEPART, and TagValue is assigned the value ButtonTag. If any events other than

Events and Event Procedures

a DEPART or ARRIVE trigger occur, the second format parameter is assigned a null value (" ").

The third formal parameter is either a variable or a dynamic array, depending on the event. If the event is a trigger event, EventValue is a variable that evaluates to the value that will be assigned to the current control element if the dialog box is accepted. If the event is a mouse, key, or idle event, EventValue is a dynamic array. This dynamic array is identical to one created by the same event captured with the GETEVENT command. The elements of this dynamic array, and their contents, are shown earlier in this chapter in Tables 13-1 and 13-2.

The fourth formal parameter is only assigned a value when a Checkbox element is involved in the event. For example, if the user is on a check box, and presses Tab, EventType is DEPART, TagValue is the tag for the check box, EventValue is the value of the current check box variable, and ElementValue is the label of the specific check box element the cursor is on.

In most cases, your dialog procedure must evaluate the values of one or more formal parameters to determine what event occurred. This is most frequently done using one or more SWITCH statements. Which formal parameters you test, and in which order, depends on the events you included in your event list.

If your event list contains several different types of events, your dialog procedure may look something like this:

```
PROC MyDialogProc(EventType, TagValue, EventValue,
                  ElementValue)
   SWITCH
     CASE EventType = "EVENT":
       SWITCH
         CASE EventValue["TYPE"] = "MOUSE":
           ;process mouse events here
         CASE EventValue["TYPE"] = "KEY":
           ;process keypresses here
         OTHERWISE:
           ;process idle events here, if desired
       ENDSWITCH
     CASE EventType = "DEPART":
       ;process depart trigger events here
     CASE EventType = "UPDATE":
       ;process open trigger events here
     ;Use additional CASE commands to evaluate any other
```

```
    ;trigger events included in the event list.
ENDSWITCH
```

You should try to make your dialog procedure as efficient as possible, for performance reasons. In other words, those events that will occur most often should be tested first. This will permit your script to process these events faster. Infrequent events should be tested later in your SWITCH control structure.

This is just one strategy, however. In your application, certain frequent events may not require a snappy response from your dialog procedure. In these cases, you place the tests for events that must be processed quickly early in your SWITCH command.

Returning from a Dialog Procedure

There are four ways to exit a dialog procedure. The first two are to either accept the dialog box or cancel it. You do this using the commands ACCEPTDIALOG or CANCELDIALOG, respectively. If Paradox encounters either of these commands in your dialog procedure, the dialog box is immediately removed from the canvas. Furthermore, Paradox behaves exactly as though the user accepted or canceled the dialog box. Specifically, using ACCEPTDIALOG causes Retval to be set to True, and values are assigned to each variable associated with a control element of the dialog box. Using CANCELDIALOG, Retval is set to False and no values are assigned to the control element variables.

Most of the time, however, you will return to the dialog procedure once your procedure is through. This will happen one of two ways: either the last command in the dialog procedure will be executed, automatically returning to the calling script or procedure, or you will use the command RETURN. When the final command in a dialog procedure has been executed, the event is accepted and Paradox returns to the dialog box. If the trigger cycle still contains one or more triggers, and those triggers appear in the event list, Paradox will immediately return to the dialog procedure. If there are no more events in the trigger cycle, Paradox will simply return to the dialog box.

Using RETURN followed by a logical expression permits you to control whether the event is accepted or discarded. If you use RETURN True, the event is accepted and Paradox returns to the dialog procedure or to the next event in the trigger cycle. If you use RETURN False, and the event is a before trigger, the event is ignored, and the trigger cycle is exited. Any triggers in the trigger cycle that have not yet been processed are discarded. If the event is an after trigger, RETURN False has no effect, and any remaining after triggers will be processed.

The following script creates a dialog box that makes use of a dialog procedure. The event list contains a single event, the CANCEL trigger (for this reason the dialog procedure does not need to test any of the formal parameters). When the dialog procedure is called, it displays another dialog box, asking the user to confirm that the dialog box should be canceled. If the user confirms, the dialog procedure returns True, meaning that the Cancel trigger is accepted. If the user does not confirm, False is returned and the cancel trigger is discarded.

```
PROC ConfirmCancel(EventType, TagValue, EventValue,
                   ElementValue)
   SHOWDIALOG "Confirm"
     @ 10,25 HEIGHT 7 WIDTH 40
     @ 1,2 ?? "Are you sure you want to cancel?"
     PUSHBUTTON @ 3,8 WIDTH 10
       "Yes" OK
       Value True
       TAG "ConfirmYes"
       TO Retval
     PUSHBUTTON @ 3,19 WIDTH 10
       "No" CANCEL
       DEFAULT
       Value False
       TAG "ConfirmNo"
       TO Retval
   ENDDIALOG
   IF Retval
     THEN
       RETURN True
     ELSE
       RETURN False
   ENDIF
ENDPROC

SHOWDIALOG "Print?"
   PROC "ConfirmCancel" TRIGGER "CANCEL"
```

```
           @ 5, 20
           HEIGHT 9 WIDTH 40
           @ 1,6 ?? "Select OK to begin printing"
           PUSHBUTTON
             @ 5,8 WIDTH 10
             "OK" OK
             Value True
             TAG "Printit"
             TO Retval
           PUSHBUTTON
             @ 5,19 WIDTH 10
             "Cancel" CANCEL
             Value False
             TAG "DoNotPrint"
             TO Retval
        ENDDIALOG
```

Controlling the Dialog Box

In addition to accepting or discarding events, you can exert other types of control over a dialog box from within a dialog procedure. Paradox provides you with a number of commands you can use in your dialog procedure to change and update the values displayed in a dialog box. These commands are shown in Table 13-6. You can find the syntax of these commands in the *PAL Reference*.

Command	Description
ACCEPTDIALOG	Accepts the current dialog box
CANCELDIALOG	Cancels the current dialog box
REFRESHCONTROL	Reevaluates expressions used in a control element
REFRESHDIALOG	Reevaluates all expressions used in all control elements
REPAINTDIALOG	Updates all canvas elements in a dialog box
RESYNCCONTROL	Updates a control element with its variable value
RESYNCDIALOG	Updates all control elements with their variable values
SELECTCONTROL	Makes a given control element the current control element

Dialog Box-Specific PAL Commands
Table 13-6.

Events and Event Procedures

Many of these commands are demonstrated in the following script, which permits a user to select a table from any directory.

```
PROC ConfirmRequest(EventType, TagValue, EventValue,
                    ElementVar)
   SWITCH
     CASE EventType = "DEPART" AND TagValue = "TheDirectory":
       ;Verify that the directory exists.
       IF DIREXISTS(DirectoryVar) = 1
         THEN
            ;Ensure that the directory name is in the correct form
            IF NOT MATCH(DirectoryVar,"..\\")
              THEN
                 DirectoryVar = DirectoryVar+"\\"
            ENDIF
            ;Display the current directory name in the ACCEPT
            ;window.
            RESYNCCONTROL "TheDirectory"
            ;Update the tables shown in the pick list.
            REFRESHCONTROL "TableList"
            ;Move to the picklist
            SELECTCONTROL "TableList"
            RETURN True
         ELSE
            BEEP
            MESSAGE DirectoryVar+" does not exist. Press any key"
            z = GETCHAR()
            MESSAGE ""
            DirectoryVar = DIRECTORY()
            RESYNCCONTROL "TableList"
            RETURN False
       ENDIF
     CASE EventType = "SELECT":
       ;The user selected a table from the picklist.
       ACCEPTDIALOG
     CASE EventType = "OPEN":
       ;Make the pick list current.
       SELECTCONTROL "TableList"
   ENDSWITCH
ENDPROC

;Initialize the directory variable.
```

```
DirectoryVar = DIRECTORY()

SHOWDIALOG "Select table to view"
PROC "ConfirmRequest" TRIGGER "SELECT","DEPART","OPEN"
@ 2,2 HEIGHT 14 WIDTH 50
ACCEPT @ 2,2
  WIDTH 45
  "A42"
  PICTURE "*!"
  TAG "TheDirectory"
  TO   DirectoryVar
LABEL @ 1,1
  "~D~irectory"
  FOR "TheDirectory"
PICKTABLE
  @ 4,8
  HEIGHT 6 WIDTH 32
  COLUMNS 3
  DirectoryVar
  TAG "TableList"
  TO TabName
LABEL @ 3,7
  "~T~able"
  FOR "TableList"
PUSHBUTTON
  @ 11,8 WIDTH 10
  "~O~K" OK
  Value True
  TAG "OKButton"
  TO Retval
PUSHBUTTON
  @ 11,30 WIDTH 10
  "~C~ancel" CANCEL
  Value False
  TAG "CancelButton"
  TO Retval
ENDDIALOG

IF Retval AND ISTABLE(DirectoryVar+TabName)
    THEN
       VIEW DirectoryVar+TabName
ENDIF
```

Wait Procedures

Wait procedures, like dialog procedures, are procedures called when an event you specify in an event list occurs. Wait procedures can only be used with a second version of the WAIT command. This version of the WAIT command has a syntax that is different from the one you learned in Chapter 10. The syntax for this second version of WAIT is

```
WAIT {WORKSPACE | TABLE | RECORD | FIELD }
   PROC ProcedureNameExpression EventList
ENDWAIT
```

The syntax of the event list is

```
[{ALL |
[KEY {"ALL" | Key1 ... [,KeyN]}]
[MOUSE {"ALL" | ["AUTO"] ["DOWN"] ["MOVE"] ["UP"]]
[MESSAGE { "ALL" | ["CLOSE"] ["MENUKEY"] ["MENUSELECT"]
                   ["MAXIMIZE"] ["NEXT"]}]
[TRIGGER { "ALL" | ["ARRIVEFIELD"] ["ARRIVEPAGE"]["ARRIVEROW"]
                   ["ARRIVETABLE"] ["ARRIVEWINDOW"]
                   ["DEPARTFIELD"] ["DEPARTPAGE"] ["DEPARTROW"]
                   ["DEPARTTABLE"] ["DISPLAYONLY"] ["EVENT"]
                   ["IMAGERIGHTS"] ["PASSRIGHTS"] ["POSTRECORD"]
                   ["READONLY"] ["REQUIREDVALUE"]
                   ["TOUCHRECORD"] ["VALCHECK"]}]
[IDLE]}]
```

There are several notable features of the wait procedure event list. The first is that unlike the dialog procedure event list, a wait procedure can be called as a result of a message event. This is not surprising if you think about it. Since a user cannot interact with windows or a pull-down menu while a dialog box is active, message events cannot coexist with a dialog box. During a WAIT WORKSPACE, however, the user is free to maximize, resize, and even close windows (only canvas windows can be closed, not object windows); that is, as long as the attributes of the windows permit these interactions. Furthermore, if a pull-down menu is displayed, the user may activate the menu and select any enabled items from it. All of these events can be included in a wait event list, and processed by the wait procedure.

The second notable feature of the wait procedure event list is that the triggers are primarily associated with table navigation and editing. These triggers provide you with the capability to control every element of the user's interaction with the table or tables on the desktop. In your event list you include each trigger that requires some checking or possible intervention. In the wait procedure, you determine which trigger occurred, and perform the desired validation or manipulation. Since many of these triggers are before triggers, your script can either accept or discard the event.

Table 13-7 displays a list of each of the wait procedure triggers, organized by the order in which they will occur. In other words, if two or more of these trigger events occur in a single trigger cycle, the triggers that appear at the top of the list will invoke the event procedure before triggers lower in the list.

Building a Wait Procedure

Like a dialog procedure, a wait procedure must be defined before you call it in a WAIT command. In most cases, the wait procedure will be stored in a library assigned to the variable Autolib.

A wait procedure requires three formal parameters. The following is an example wait procedure:

```
PROC ProcessWaitEvents(EventType, EventArray, CycleNumber]
;commands to process events in your WAIT event list
ENDPROC
```

NOTE: The name of the formal parameters to a wait procedure can be any valid variable and array names. However, to prevent confusion, the names EventType, EventArray, and CycleNumber are used in this chapter.

The first parameter, EventType, stores the trigger type for trigger events, or the value EVENT if a key, mouse, message, or idle event occurs. For example, if the DEPARTFIELD trigger is included in your wait event list, the variable EventType will be set to DEPARTFIELD when this event calls the wait procedure. If a key listed in the event list is pressed, EventType is set to EVENT.

Events and Event Procedures

Event	Description	Before or After
EVENT	Any mouse or keyboard event listed in the event list	Before
TOUCHRECORD	User attempted to change a value in CoEdit, or arrived at a record in Edit	Before
DISPLAYONLY	User attempted to change a display-only form	Before
PASSRIGHTS	User attempted to change a field without password rights	Before
IMAGERIGHTS	User attempted to change a field without sufficient rights	Before
REQUIREDVALUE	User attempted to leave a required field without providing a value	Before
VALCHECK	User attempted to leave a field without satisfying the field ValCheck	Before
READONLY	User attempted to change a write-protected table	Before
DEPARTFIELD	User action will result in leaving current field	Before
DEPARTROW	User action will result in leaving current record	Before
DEPARTPAGE	User action will result in leaving current page (form view only)	Before
DEPARTTABLE	User action will result in leaving table	Before
POSTRECORD	User action will result in an attempt to post the record	Before
ARRIVEWINDOW	Cursor arrived at new window	After
ARRIVEPAGE	Cursor arrived at different page (form view only)	After
ARRIVETABLE	Cursor arrived at different table	After
ARRIVEROW	Cursor arrived at different record	After
ARRIVEFIELD	Cursor arrived at a different field	After

Wait Procedure Trigger Events
Table 13-7.

The second formal parameter of a wait procedure is used to hold a dynamic array that contains all the relevant information about the event. This array is identical to the one generated by an event captured using the GETEVENT command. Therefore, when EventType evaluates to EVENT, EventArray["TYPE"] contains the type of event: KEY, MOUSE, MESSAGE, or IDLE. The remaining elements of EventArray contain every detail about the event. See Tables 13-1, 13-2, and 13-3 for a list of the dynamic array elements generated by each of these events.

The final formal parameter is the variable CycleNumber. This value is a unique number that identifies the trigger cycle. In most cases this number is of little interest. However, in situations where your script needs to determine if two consecutive events occurred in the same trigger cycle, CycleNumber is invaluable.

In the following exercise you create a simple wait procedure and call it for all message and trigger events. The event list for this wait also includes the (Esc) keypress, which is used to exit you from the WAIT command. In order to display the variables and array generated by the event, the SLEEP command is used to display the event information for three seconds. You can lengthen or decrease this time to suit your needs.

1. Select Scripts/Editor/New.
2. Type **Waitproc** and press (Enter).
3. Enter the following script into the Editor. If you want, you can omit any line beginning with a semicolon. These comments are provided for your information only.

```
PROC ShowTrigger(EventType, EventArray, CycleNumber)
  ;Test for an ESC and exit if it is pressed.
  IF EventType = "EVENT" AND EventArray["TYPE"] = "KEY"
    THEN
      DO_IT!
      RETURN 2
  ENDIF
  ;Display the contents of the variables and array.
  @ 0,0
  ;Recapture the desktop on the canvas.
```

Events and Event Procedures

```
      CANVAS OFF ECHO NORMAL ECHO OFF CANVAS ON
      ? "EventType = ",EventType
      FOREACH Element IN EventArray
         ? Element," = ",EventArray[Element]
      ENDFOREACH
      ? "CycleNumber = ",CycleNumber
      ;Keep this information displayed for 3 seconds.
      SLEEP 3000
      ;Return to the WAIT command
      RETURN 0
    ENDPROC

    ;Remove the Paradox menu.
    SHOWPULLDOWN ENDMENU
    ;Bring the tables onto the desktop.
    VIEW "Customer"
    COEDIT "Invoice"
    ;Display a prompt.
    PROMPT "Press ESC to exit."
    ;Enter the wait.
    WAIT WORKSPACE
       PROC "ShowTrigger" KEY "ESC" MESSAGE "ALL" TRIGGER "ALL"
    ENDWAIT
    CLEARALL
```

4. Play this script by selecting Go from the Editor menu.

   After a moment, Paradox will display the two tables, Invoice and Customer.

5. Press [Tab] to move the cursor to the first field of Invoice.

   The [Tab] results in two trigger events that call the wait procedure: DEPARTFIELD and ARRIVEFIELD. The wait procedure displays the contents of the variables and array that described the event on the canvas for three seconds each.

6. Try moving your mouse, editing fields, and changing windows. Each one of these actions will generate one or more message or trigger events. Notice the order of the events, and the wealth of information about them provided by the variables and array.

7. When you are finished, press [Esc] to exit.

NOTE: Consider replacing the SHOWPULLDOWN ENDMENU commands with the commands to create an actual pull-down menu. Then, play Waitproc again, and observe the events generated by selecting from the menu.

Wait procedures, like dialog procedures, can get quite long if you must evaluate many different events. It is important, then, to process events efficiently. In deciding which events to evaluate first, and in what order, you should consider both the frequency of an event and the need for a speedy response. The following is one example of a wait procedure skeleton that evaluates events. For each type of event, one CASE statement appears as an example. Your event procedure, however, would only test for those events that you have included in the event list of the WAIT command.

```
PROC MyWaitProcedure(EventType, EventArray, CycleNumber)
  SWITCH
    CASE NOT EventType = "EVENT":
      SWITCH
        ;Test any trigger events in the event list
        CASE EventType = "DEPARTFIELD":
          ;commands to process given a departfield event
        ;Test for any other trigger events.
      ENDSWITCH
    ;All remaining events are either key,
    ;mouse, message, or idle.
    CASE EventArray["TYPE"] = "KEY":
      SWITCH
        ;Test for any key events in the event list.
        CASE EventArray["KEY"] = 27:
      ENDSWITCH
    CASE EventArray["TYPE"] =  "MOUSE":
      SWITCH
        ;Test any mouse events in the event list
        CASE EventArray["ACTION"] = "DOWN":
      ENDSWITCH
    CASE EventArray["TYPE"] = "MESSAGE":
      SWITCH
        ;Test for any message events in event list.
        CASE EventArray["MESSAGE"] = "MENUSELECT":
      ENDSWITCH
```

Events and Event Procedures

```
      CASE EventArray["TYPE"] = "IDLE":
         ;Commands used during idle events
      ENDSWITCH
ENDPROC
```

Returning from a Wait Procedure

Unlike returning from a dialog procedure, in which you can return True, False, or no value at all, you must use RETURN to return from a wait procedure. Furthermore, the RETURN command must be followed by one of three values: 0, 1, or 2. These values and their effects are shown in Table 13-8.

Your wait procedure must include at least one RETURN 2. This is the command that will cause the wait to be terminated, and continue to the commands that follow the keyword ENDWAIT. This is different from version 1 of the WAIT command, which is automatically terminated when any one of the keys listed after the UNTIL keyword is pressed.

The two most common ways to exit the second version of the WAIT command are to trap for special keys or to trap for menu selections. If you are using a pull-down menu with your wait, you can include a selection that permits the user to exit the wait. Alternatively, you can include one or more keys in the event list that the user can press to escape. In the preceding exercise, Esc was used for this purpose. You can, however, use any key or keys you want, such as F2.

Within your wait procedure, you test for the menu selection or key(s) that signal that the user wants to leave. When one of these events occurs, your script should evaluate whether to permit the user to leave or not. For example, if the user was editing a record, you may want to

Valid Wait Procedure Return Values
Table 13-8.

Return Value	Effect
0	Accept the event and continue to the next event in the trigger cycle
1	Discard the event and exit the trigger cycle, returning to the wait
2	Discard the event, exit the trigger cycle, and exit the wait

first test that they have filled out the record appropriately. If they have, use RETURN 2 to exit the wait.

If you want the wait procedure to return to the wait, you use either RETURN 0 or RETURN 1. RETURN 0 accepts the event and returns to the wait procedure. If you do not want to accept an event, use RETURN 1. This is only effective if the event is a before event, however. If you use RETURN 1 with a before event, the event is not processed, and all remaining events in the current trigger cycle are discarded. Using RETURN 1 with an after trigger has no effect, since after triggers are simply signals that an event occurred.

Controlling the Desktop from a Wait Procedure

Unlike dialog procedures, there are no commands that are unique to wait procedures. To control the desktop from within a wait procedure, you can use any commands that normally manipulate the desktop. These commands include MOVETO, LOCATE, =, SCAN, EDIT, and so on. Using these commands is described in Chapter 10.

Creating More Efficient Event Procedures

Event procedures are some of the more useful and powerful features of Paradox 4. Unfortunately, without proper planning they can become complex and long. As a result, your scripts may become difficult to follow and your application can perform sluggishly.

There are several techniques you can use to improve the efficiency and readability of event procedures. One is to make use of procedure calls within an event procedure, and the second is to store PAL commands in a dynamic array and execute these commands as needed. Both of these methods are covered in the following sections.

Above all, proper planning will improve your use of event procedures. By weighing the need for a quick response with the frequency of events, you can produce event procedures that impose little noticeable delays while providing the greatest utility.

Calling Procedures Within Event Procedures

Although all of the event procedures included in this chapter have been self-contained procedures, this is rarely the case. In most situations, an event procedure determines the general class of event, and then either plays a script or calls a procedure that is designed to process that type of event. Designing your event procedures this way has a number of important benefits. One is that you can call the same procedure from numerous event procedures. For example, you can create a generic message handling procedure. From within each event procedure you use in your application, you can call this message procedure if you determine that the current event is a message event. There is another benefit to this approach. If you decide to modify how you want your wait procedures to respond to message events, you only need to modify a single procedure, instead of every event procedure you use.

Finally, calling procedures from within an event procedure produces shorter procedures overall. Shorter procedures permit Paradox to make more efficient use of the available memory, which leads to improved performance.

Using Dynamic Arrays to Process Events

The demonstration scripts in this chapter have all made use of a SWITCH command followed by individual CASE statements to evaluate the current event. However, there is a situation where you can skip using a SWITCH and greatly improve the responsiveness of your event procedures.

NOTE: The following is an advanced technique. If you are new to using event procedures, you may want to skip this discussion. Once you become comfortable with event procedures, consider returning to this section.

Imagine that you have a WAIT command that is combined with a pull-down menu. In the wait procedure you must evaluate the type of event. Once you determine that the event is a menu selection, you must test for each of the possible menu tags in order to know how to continue. Assuming that EditTab and ReportTab are valid procedures, this script may look something like this:

```
PROC ProcessMyWait(EventType, EventArray, CycleNumber)
  SWITCH
    CASE EventType = "EVENT" AND
      EventArray["TYPE"] = "MESSAGE" AND
      EventArray["MESSAGE"] = "MENUSELECT":
      SWITCH
        CASE EventArray["MENUTAG"] = "EditCust":
          EditTab("Customer")
        CASE EventArray["MENUTAG"] = "EditEmp":
          EditTab("Employee")
        CASE EventArray["MENUTAG"] = "EditInv":
          EditTab("Invoice")
        CASE EventArray["MENUTAG"] = "RepCust":
          ReportTab("Customer")
        CASE EventArray["MENUTAG"] = "RepEmp":
          ReportTab("Employee")
        CASE EventArray["MENUTAG"] = "RepInv":
          ReportTab("Invoice")
        CASE EventArray["MENUTAG"] = "ExitApp":
          RETURN 2
      ENDSWITCH
  ENDSWITCH
  RETURN 0
ENDPROC

SHOWPULLDOWN
  "Edit":"Select a table to edit.":
    SUBMENU
      "Customer":"Edit the Customer table.":"EditCust",
      "Employee":"Edit the Employee table.":"EditEmp",
      "Invoice":"Edit the Invoice table.":"EditInv"
    ENDSUBMENU,
  "Report":"Output a report for a table":
    SUBMENU
      "Customer":"Output the Customer report.":"RepCust",
      "Employee":"Output the Employee report.":"RepEmp",
      "Invoice":"Output the Invoice report.":"RepInv"
    ENDSUBMENU,
  "Exit":"Exit the application.":"ExitApp"
ENDMENU
```

Events and Event Procedures

```
VIEW "Customer"
VIEW "Employee"
VIEW "Invoice"

WAIT WORKSPACE
  PROC "ProcessMyWait" MESSAGE "MENUSELECT"
ENDWAIT

CLEARALL
```

As you can see, you must test for each menu item tag. Since a pull-down menu can contain as many as 2000 items, the event procedure used to process these events can get very long. Furthermore, since every CASE condition must be evaluated until a True condition is found, the farther down a menu tag appears in the SWITCH statement, the longer it takes Paradox to find the commands to execute.

Instead of a SWITCH command, you can create a dynamic array which is indexed using the same values as the menu item tags. You assign to each element of this array the PAL commands you want executed if the corresponding menu item is selected. You can then use the EXECPROC or EXECUTE command to call these procedures or execute these commands. Instead of evaluating what event occurred, you can instantly access the appropriate commands and procedures using the event variables or array elements as the indices to dynamic arrays.

The following is a small example of how this type of processing works:

```
DYNARRAY MenuArray[]
  MenuArray["EditCust"] = "EditTab(\"Customer\") RETURN 0"
  MenuArray["EditEmp"]  = "EditTab(\"Employee\") RETURN 0"
  MenuArray["EditInv"]  = "EditTab(\"Invoice\") RETURN 0"
  MenuArray["RepCust"]  = "ReportTab(\"Customer\") RETURN 0"
  MenuArray["RepEmp"]   = "ReportTab(\"Employee\") RETURN 0"
  MenuArray["RepInv"]   = "ReportTab(\"Invoice\") RETURN 0"
  MenuArray["ExitApp"]  = "RETURN 2"

PROC ProcessMyWait(EventType, EventArray, CycleNumber)
PRIVATE Retval
  SWITCH
    CASE EventType = "EVENT"
      AND EventArray["TYPE"]    = "MESSAGE"
      AND EventArray["MESSAGE"] = "MENUSELECT":
```

```
              EXECUTE MenuArray[EventArray["MENUTAG"]]
              RETURN Retval
    ENDSWITCH
ENDPROC

SHOWPULLDOWN
   "Edit":"Select a table to edit.":
     SUBMENU
       "Customer":"Edit the Customer table.":"EditCust",
       "Employee":"Edit the Employee table.":"EditEmp",
       "Invoice":"Edit the Invoice table.":"EditInv"
     ENDSUBMENU,
   "Report":"Output a report for a table":
     SUBMENU
       "Customer":"Output the Customer report.":"RepCust",
       "Employee":"Output the Employee report.":"RepEmp",
       "Invoice":"Output the Invoice report.":"RepInv"
     ENDSUBMENU,
   "Exit":"Exit the application.":"ExitApp"
   ENDMENU

VIEW "Customer"
VIEW "Employee"
VIEW "Invoice"

WAIT WORKSPACE
   PROC "ProcessMyWait" MESSAGE "MENUSELECT"
ENDWAIT

CLEARALL
```

NOTE: In the dynamic array assignments, the backslash character precedes each quotation mark within the outer quotation marks. These backslashes make Paradox include the inner quotation marks in the value assigned to the dynamic array, instead of interpreting these marks as the outer quotation marks.

Although this second script is not much shorter than the first, it executes much faster. Within the wait procedure, the script uses the menu tag of the selected menu item as the index for the dynamic array. This provides the script with instant access to the appropriate commands without having to evaluate the menu tag. Furthermore, the space and speed advantage of this method increases in direct proportion to the number of tags.

If you are willing to make extensive use of dynamic arrays in this fashion, you can avoid the use of the SWITCH command altogether. However, in most situations, you will likely use a combination of both these techniques.

Quick Review

- There are five types of events: key, mouse, message, trigger, and idle.
- You can use GETEVENT to intercept key, mouse, message, and idle events. Which of these events is intercepted depends on an event list. Any event not appearing in the event list is automatically passed along to Paradox.
- Once you get an event, you can pass it to Paradox, discard it altogether, or discard the event and pass alternative instructions to Paradox.
- Events captured using GETEVENT result in the creation of a dynamic array that holds all of the relevant information about the event.
- Use EXECEVENT to pass an intercepted event on to Paradox.
- The commands SHOWDIALOG and WAIT permit you to specify a procedure that is called if an event listed in an event list occurs.
- Dialog and wait procedures permit you to control almost every aspect of a user's interaction with a dialog box or a Paradox object.

CHAPTER

14 MULTIUSER APPLICATIONS

This final chapter introduces you to the advanced topic of multiuser applications. Unlike many of the preceding chapters, there are no exercises in this chapter. Instead, the concepts and principles of multiuser applications are discussed.

The topics covered in this chapter are among some of the most complicated in PAL. In large part this is because there is no one correct solution to the problems that arise in multiuser situations. In all instances, there is a trade-off between what the user needs and what is available. Finding a suitable middle ground often requires careful consideration of how the application will be used, how flexible it must be, and who will be using it.

A multiuser application is one in which two or more users can access the same tables at the same time. For instance, in a multiuser invoicing application, two or more users must be able to view the Customer table simultaneously. Likewise, they must each be able to enter new invoices at the same time.

A multiuser application by definition requires a local area network—it could run on a stand-alone computer, but it would not be multiuser in that case. On a network, two or more users can be given access to the same directories. If Paradox tables are in these directories, users can also access these tables at the same time.

This access is not without limitations, however. For instance, if one user is performing a Changeto query on a table, no other users can use that table—not even to view it. Paradox regulates who can access a table, and how, by using table locks, record locks, and private tables, as described in the following sections.

NOTE: Paradox users running versions earlier than Paradox 4 cannot access any directory simultaneously with a Paradox 4 user.

Table Locking

A *table lock* is a restriction placed on a table by Paradox. On a network, Paradox automatically places at least one lock on a table whenever you access it in any way, for example, when you view a table, print a report for it, query it, and so forth. The restriction imposed by the lock applies to other users, not to you.

The purpose of a lock is to ensure that you will continue to have access to the table as long as you need it. For instance, if you view a table, Paradox automatically places a lock on it. This lock prevents another user from using a Paradox feature, such as a Changeto query, that would prevent you from viewing the table.

There are four different types of table locks that Paradox can place. From most restrictive to least, they are full locks, write locks, prevent write locks, and prevent full locks. At any one time, a table may have none, one, or more than one lock placed on it. Furthermore, these locks can be placed on the table by more than one user at a time, as long as the locks are compatible with one another.

Full Lock   A *full lock* prevents any other user from accessing the table in any way. Paradox automatically places a full lock on a table when you need complete and uninterrupted access to it. For example, when you are restructuring a table, Paradox places a full lock on that table. No other users may access that table until you are done. Likewise, when you enter Edit mode, any tables you currently have on your desktop will also have full locks placed on them. For this reason, Edit mode is not commonly used in multiuser applications. CoEdit should be used instead.

Write Lock   A *write lock* prevents any other users from making changes to a table while you are using it. When you are copying a table, for example, Paradox places a write lock on it, preventing other users from making changes to it until the copy process is complete.

Prevent Write Lock   A *prevent write lock* prohibits any other users from placing a write lock on a table. For instance, when you are changing a record in a table using CoEdit, Paradox places a prevent write lock on the table to prevent any other user from placing a write lock and thus keeping you from completing the change to the record.

Prevent Full Lock   A *prevent full lock* guarantees you access to a table. When you view a table, Paradox places a prevent full lock on it. This prevents another user from trying to perform another task on the table that would revoke your access, such as restructuring it.

NOTE: In Paradox 3.5 there is a fifth type of lock, called a *form lock*. A form lock is automatically placed when a user begins CoEditing a table using a multitable form, or uses a multitable form with the FormAdd tool from the Tools/More menu. The form lock prevents other Paradox users from CoEditing any of the tables involved with any view other than the one multitable form. In Paradox 4, there is no form lock. Instead, the master table record and each of the records that appear in the restricted views of linked, embedded forms, are locked with a record lock. Record locks are described later in this chapter.

Explicit Table Locking

Although Paradox can automatically lock tables for your application, you should not rely on this feature for table locking since Paradox locks do not always succeed. For example, if your application tries to view a table, but that table already has a full lock on it, the automatic lock will fail, and the table will not be displayed. When your script continues, and attempts to use the table, a run-time error is sure to result.

In order to ensure that you will have sufficient access to the tables your application needs, you should place explicit locks on them using the LOCK command.

The syntax of the LOCK command is

```
LOCK Table1 {FL|WL|PWL|PFL}...[,TableN {FL|WL|PWL|PFL}]
```

The LOCK command requires one expression, which must evaluate to the name of a table. The table name is followed by a code signifying the type of lock you want to place on the table. Optionally, you can supply a list of tables and the desired locks for each. If you want to place more than one lock on a single table, you must list the table repeatedly, once for each lock.

When Paradox plays the LOCK command, it attempts to place the specified lock on each table listed. If all locks can be placed, Paradox sets the system variable Retval to True. If even one of the locks fails, none of the locks is placed, and Retval is set to False. For example, to place a full lock on the Invoice table and prevent a full lock on the Customer table, use the following statement:

```
LOCK "Invoice" FL, "Customer" PFL
```

NOTE: If a lock fails, you can use the functions ERRORCODE( ), ERRORMESSAGE( ), and ERRORUSER( ) to determine why.

The Retry Period

When Paradox attempts to lock a table, it doesn't necessarily give up immediately if one or more of the tables are not available. Instead, it attempts to apply the lock for a length of time called the *retry period*. The retry period can be from 0 to 30,000 seconds in length, and is defined using the PAL command SETRETRYPERIOD. The syntax is

```
SETRETRYPERIOD NumberOfSeconds
```

When Paradox plays the SETRETRYPERIOD command, it changes the retry period. The number that follows SETRETRYPERIOD is the number of seconds you want Paradox to attempt to lock a table before failing. (You can use the function RETRYPERIOD( ) to determine the current retry period.) If the retry period is greater than 0, Paradox continues attempting to lock the table until the lock succeeds or the retry period expires and the lock fails, whichever comes first.

TIP: In most applications, it is not wise to set the retry period to a length longer than about 10 seconds without displaying a message informing the user that Paradox is waiting for the table to become available. Otherwise, the user may conclude that the lack of activity means that the computer has stopped functioning correctly. However, if your application is running a batch process, one that can operate overnight, for instance, you can set a very long retry period.

Removing Explicit Locks

A table lock placed with the LOCK command lasts until one of the two following events occurs:

You exit Paradox normally
You explicitly release the locks

Locks are released explicitly using the UNLOCK command. There are two versions of the command, version 1:

```
UNLOCK Table1 {FL|WL|PWL|PFL}...[,TableN {FL|WL|PWL|PFL}]
```

and version 2, as follows:

```
UNLOCK ALL
```

When you use version 1, the UNLOCK command is followed by an expression that evaluates to a table name and a code identifying the lock type to remove. You can optionally include a comma-separated list of tables and locks. The second version uses the keyword ALL, and removes all locks explicitly placed on all tables by you. It does not, however, remove locks placed automatically by Paradox. These are removed only when you are no longer accessing a table. Likewise, it cannot remove locks explicitly placed by other users.

CAUTION: If Paradox encounters an unexpected condition and exits to DOS abnormally (not through the Main menu), any locks that were explicitly placed by the application the user was using will remain in place, unnecessarily restricting other users' access to one or more tables. If this occurs, and there is a possibility that explicit locks remain, the user should immediately reenter Paradox. Paradox will then release all locks placed by that user.

Managing Table Locks

One of the most important aspects of a multiuser application is managing table locks. If you do not explicitly lock a table before trying to use it, a script error may occur if someone else has already restricted your access to it. These script errors are particularly difficult to debug, since they happen only occasionally (only when another lock is present). On the other hand, if you place more locks on a table than are needed, you will unnecessarily restrict other users' access to that table.

The following are guidelines for using table locks in an application:

◆ Place the least restrictive lock necessary to provide the required access to the table. Placing too restrictive a lock on a table may unnecessarily limit other users' access to it.

◆ As soon as you no longer need the protection of a lock, remove it. This applies even when you have placed two or more locks on the same table. For example, if you placed both a prevent full lock and a write lock on a table, remove the write lock as soon as it is no longer necessary, even if you want to keep the prevent full lock.

Multiuser Applications

- When an operation requires two or more tables, place the needed locks on all of them with a single LOCK command. This way, you can be sure these tables are available to you. If you place the locks one at a time, problems may result. For example, imagine that two users both want to place full locks on the same two tables. If the locks are placed one at a time, each user may lock one of the tables, giving neither user access to both. This is called a *deadly embrace*. If instead, both users attempt to lock both tables each using a single LOCK command, one user will succeed, and the other will fail.

- Design your application so that as few full locks and write locks as possible are used. Furthermore, design your application so that the length of time these locks are in force is minimized.

- Design your application so that it can accommodate failures of the LOCK command. If the system variable Retval indicates that the lock failed, your script should display a message telling the user that resources are unavailable, and return to a menu where the user can make a different selection.

CoEdit Mode

When your application needs to permit two or more users to change the same table simultaneously, you must use CoEdit mode. You should not use Edit mode, since it results in an automatic full lock on the table or tables being edited. In contrast, CoEdit mode places a prevent full lock on the table and an additional prevent write lock as soon as you begin changing a record.

Under CoEdit mode, two or more users can view and even edit the same table simultaneously. However, although they can view the same record, no two users can edit the same record at the same time. This is because Paradox places an automatic lock on a record when you begin to make changes to it. This lock prohibits other users from trying to change the record.

Like the automatic locking of tables, you should not rely on Paradox's automatic locking of records when you are in CoEdit mode. If another user is already editing that record, the automatic record lock will fail. In most situations, this will cause a script error. Therefore, you should explicitly lock a record before making changes to it in CoEdit mode.

Explicit Record Locking

While in CoEdit mode, you can explicitly lock a record using the PAL command LOCKRECORD. You should do this before permitting a user to make a change to an existing record in a table. The syntax is

LOCKRECORD

When Paradox encounters the LOCKRECORD command, it immediately attempts to lock the current record. If the lock succeeds, Paradox automatically places a prevent write lock on the table and sets Retval to True. If the lock fails, Retval is set to False.

When a record lock fails, you can use the functions ERRORCODE( ) and ERRORMESSAGE( ) to determine why. For example, if the record is already locked, the function ERRORCODE( ) will return the number 9, and the function ERRORMESSAGE( ) will return "Record locked by another user." For this error, the function ERRORUSER( ) will return the name of the user who has locked the record.

NOTE: This discussion of locking and unlocking records assumes that the tables are keyed. Although most tables in applications are keyed, this is not a requirement for using CoEdit or for creating multiuser applications. If your tables are not keyed, a record lock will not fail due to a key conflict (the new record key field values conflict with an existing record's key field value) only because another user has locked that record first.

In Paradox 4 there is a very nice solution that permits your script to easily manage multiple users CoEditing a table. Include the TOUCHRECORD trigger in your wait event list. This trigger signals that the user has attempted to make a change to the current record. When your wait procedure detects the TOUCHRECORD trigger, it should attempt to lock the current record. If this record lock fails, a message should be displayed to the user indicating that the record is unavailable, and the event should be rejected with a RETURN 1. (TOUCHRECORD triggers are before triggers, and therefore can be rejected. Before triggers and wait procedures are discussed in detail in Chapter 13.)

Unlocking Records

Posting a record means adding a new or changed record to a table. When you are through making changes to a record in CoEdit mode, these changes will not be posted until you either leave the record, exit CoEdit mode (play DO_IT!), issue the UNLOCKRECORD command, or use the POSTRECORD command.

NOTE: POSTRECORD is not available in Paradox 3.5.

When a change has been made to the key field or fields of a record, attempting to leave the record or play DO_IT! will fail—and often result in a script error—if the new key conflicts with another record's key. When you are through permitting changes to a record, post it using either the UNLOCKRECORD or POSTRECORD command.

The syntax of UNLOCKRECORD is

```
UNLOCKRECORD
```

The syntax of POSTRECORD is

```
POSTRECORD [{ NOPOST | FORCEPOST | KEYVIOL }] [LEAVELOCKED]
```

When Paradox plays the UNLOCKRECORD command, it attempts to post the changed record to the table. If the key of the record has not been changed, or is still unique, the unlocking will succeed, the record will be updated in the table, and Retval will be set to True. If the unlocking fails, because the key was changed and now conflicts with an existing record, the system variable Retval will be set to False.

REMEMBER: In CoEdit mode, every time a record is posted to the table, it is placed in its appropriate location in the table based on its key. Thus, when you issue the UNLOCKRECORD command, the cursor will not necessarily stay with the record you are posting. If a change to a key field places the record in a different location within the table, the record may seem to disappear. However, it is merely moving to its appropriate location in the table.

When UNLOCKRECORD fails, a key violation exists. (If the table is not keyed, UNLOCKRECORD never fails.) As a result of the key violation, Paradox places a lock on the existing record that uses the same keys as the one you attempted to unlock. Your application can take one of three steps in this situation:

- Delete the current record—the record you are trying to post to the table. You can do this by using the DEL command, in which case all locks are removed. Alternatively, you can use KEYLOOKUP followed by LOCKKEY, which will make the existing record current and retain the lock on it.

- Change at least one of the key field values in the current record. This will remove the key violation, releasing the lock on the existing record, and returning the current record to a pre-posted state. You are then free to use the UNLOCKRECORD command again, which will succeed if the new key field values are unique, and will fail again if a new key violation results.

- Keep the current record, replacing the existing record with it by using the LOCKKEY command. In most cases, this is undesirable, unless you are certain that the existing record should be replaced.

The POSTRECORD command provides you with an easier solution. Use POSTRECORD NOPOST to add the current record only if it does not result in a key violation. If the current record's key conflicts with an existing record, the record is not posted and Retval is set to False. Before attempting to post the record again, you need to change one or more key field values.

If you use POSTRECORD FORCEPOST, the record is posted whether or not a key conflict exists. If there is an existing record that has the same key as the record you posted, that record is replaced with the posted record.

 **NOTE:** You cannot use POSTRECORD FORCEPOST on a master table record of a multitable form.

Finally, you can use POSTRECORD KEYVIOL. If this command fails, the result is the same as when the UNLOCKRECORD command fails: a key violation condition exists. You respond to this situation the same as you respond to an UNLOCKRECORD failure.

As with the UNLOCKRECORD command, you test Retval to determine if POSTRECORD succeeded or failed. If Retval is False, the posting failed. If Retval is True, the record was successfully added.

POSTRECORD permits you to specify an additional keyword, LEAVELOCKED. When you include LEAVELOCKED in the POSTRECORD command, the record you are adding remains locked if the command succeeds. This is particularly valuable if you want to continue to use the record even after posting it.

Adding a New Record During CoEdit

Adding a new record to a table during a CoEdit session is different from changing an existing record. For starters, a new record does not belong to the table until it has been posted. There are three ways to post a new record (without simply leaving the record or playing the DO_IT! command). You can use LOCKRECORD, UNLOCKRECORD, or POSTRECORD.

When you use LOCKRECORD to post a new record, the record is both posted and locked. The cursor will stay with the record when it moves to its appropriate location in the table based on the key. This also happens when you use POSTRECORD LEAVELOCKED. When you use UNLOCKRECORD, the record is posted, but the cursor does not stay with it. Therefore, the record may seem to disappear.

When the UNLOCKRECORD or LOCKRECORD command fails due to a key conflict, you must change a key field value before attempting the command again. If you do not change a key field value before issuing the LOCKRECORD or UNLOCKRECORD command again, you will lose the existing record, the record you are adding, or a script error will occur. Therefore, after the attempt to post a record using one of these commands fails, your script should use the PAL command = to assign a value to a key field, which will cancel the key violation state. Alternatively, you can use the POSTRECORD NOPOST LEAVELOCKED command to achieve this same result.

This is demonstrated in the following script, which is designed to add new records to a keyed table in a multiuser environment:

```
;Lock the customer table.
LOCK "Customer" PWL
;If the lock failed, return and display the error message.
IF NOT Retval
  THEN
    RETURN ERRORMESSAGE()
ENDIF
;The lock worked. Enter the CoEdit mode.
COEDIT "Customer"
;Insert a new record.
PICKFORM 1
INS
WHILE True
  WAIT RECORD
    PROMPT "Adding a new record. Press F2 when done. "+
           "Press ESC to cancel."
    UNTIL "F2", "ESC"
  SWITCH
    CASE Retval = "ESC":
      ;Delete the unposted record.
      DEL
      ;Exit the CoEdit mode.
      DO_IT!
      QUITLOOP
    CASE Retval = "F2":
      IF VERSION() > 3.5
        THEN
          POSTRECORD NOPOST LEAVELOCKED
        ELSE
          LOCKRECORD
      ENDIF
      IF NOT Retval
        THEN
          MESSAGE "Press any key to continue."
          a = GETCHAR()
```

Multiuser Applications

```
              IF VERSION() > 3.5
                THEN
                  MESSAGE ""
                ELSE
                  ;Change a key field value to its own value.
                  [Customer Code] = [Customer Code]
              ENDIF
              LOOP
          ENDIF
          ;The lock worked and the record is posted.
          ;Insert a new record and loop back.
          INS
          LOOP
     ENDSWITCH
ENDWHILE
;Remove the table from the desktop.
CLEARIMAGE
;Remember to release the lock on Customer.
UNLOCK "Customer" PWL
```

NOTE: You can create a more flexible record-editing script in Paradox 4 by using the WAIT command in conjunction with a wait procedure. The event list of such a command should include the triggers TOUCHRECORD and POSTRECORD, and the wait procedure should issue the appropriate LOCKRECORD and POSTRECORD commands in response.

Private Directories

On a local area network, not all Paradox tables are stored in shared directories. Some are stored in a user's private directory. These tables cannot be accessed by any other users on the network. Therefore, it is unnecessary to lock these tables.

Each Paradox user on a network has a private directory (usually assigned by the network administrator). This directory is used to store the user's Paradox configuration as well as any temporary tables. It is because your temporary tables are stored in your own private directory that other users on a network cannot access them. If this were not the case, another user's query could replace your Answer table.

In a multiuser application, you can store tables you do not want other users to have access to in a private directory. These tables are called *private tables*.

Declaring Private Tables

If your application will create a table, and other users should not have access to it, declare the table as private before creating it. Then, when it is created, Paradox will store it in your private directory. Thereafter, any reference to that table name will refer to the table stored in the private directory. The syntax is as follows:

```
PRIVTABLES Table1 ... [,TableN]
```

The PRIVTABLES command tells Paradox that each of the tables listed are private tables. From that time forward, Paradox will look to the private directory to access any of these tables. You can only use the PRIVTABLES command once for a given table within your application. Therefore, it is best to use this command at the beginning of your application.

TIP: You should restrict your use of private tables to those that hold temporary information only needed by one user.

Other Multiuser Application Topics

The final sections in this chapter describe some additional topics you might want to consider in your multiuser applications. These topics include the use of DataEntry to add new records to a shared table, testing your multiuser applications, and the security needs of a multiuser application.

Using DataEntry in a Multiuser Application

Instead of using CoEdit to permit more than one user to enter data into a table, you can use the DataEntry feature of Paradox. When you use DataEntry, Paradox asks you which table you want to add data to.

Paradox then creates a temporary table, called Entry, that has the same structure as the table into which you want to add the records. When you are through adding records, the records in Entry are added to the original table.

One of the nice features of DataEntry is that the Entry table is stored in your private directory. This means that no other users will see this table. Furthermore, DataEntry uses DataEntry mode, which is similar to Edit in that you can undo changes repeatedly. (In CoEdit only the last record can be undone.)

If the original table has one or more forms, you can use PICKFORM on the Entry table to select one of these forms. If the form is a multitable form, DataEntry will create a family of tables, named Entry1, Entry2, and so on. When you issue the DO_IT! command, these tables will be added to their respective tables.

No PAL command exists to use DataEntry. Instead, you use braced menu selections. To enter DataEntry mode, use

```
MENU {Modify} {DataEntry} SELECT TableName
```

In this statement, TableName must be an expression that evaluates to a table name (alternatively, you can replace SELECT TableName with the literal table name in curly braces).

When using DataEntry in a multiuser application, consider the following:

- ◆ You must place a prevent full lock on the original table before entering Entry mode. If this lock fails, do not continue. This lock can be released once you have entered Entry mode, since Paradox's automatic prevent full lock will be enforced during the entire data entry session.

- ◆ When the entry session is through, you must place a prevent write lock on the original table before issuing the DO_IT! command. If this lock fails, you cannot DO_IT!. Your script can save the Entry table, using the KeepEntry selection on the DataEntry menu, but this will require additional programming by you. At a minimum you will want to rename the Entry table, since it is a temporary table. Furthermore, you will need to program a means for adding the saved table to the original table.

◆ If you used a multitable form, you must place a prevent write lock on all tables used in the multitable form before using DO_IT!. If the lock fails, you need to rename all the Entry tables created when you use the KeepEntry selection from the DataEntry menu. One Entry table (named Entry1, Entry2, and so on) will be created for each detail table in the multitable form. You must also rename the temporary table, List, which contains a map specifying the corresponding shared table name for each Entry table. Later, you should use {Tools} {FormAdd} to add these saved tables to their original tables.

◆ Always test for the existence of the KeyViol table after using DO_IT! to end a DataEntry session. If the KeyViol table exists (assuming that you deleted it before entering DataEntry), your script should take appropriate action to avoid losing the data. Remember that the KeyViol table, like the Entry table, is a temporary table.

Testing Multiuser Applications

Testing multiuser applications is particularly time-consuming because you need to simulate the competition for resources that occurs in a multiuser environment. In many instances, this may require coordinating two or more people on different computers on the same network. In this testing, one user should access a resource, and the other user(s) should attempt to use it, to verify that the application can handle any conflicts. For example, one user should CoEdit a record, and another user should try to change that record.

Adding Security to an Application

While the topic of security is not unique to multiuser applications, it is far more important to maintain security when more than one person will access the data. There are three places where security is normally applied: to the tables, to the scripts, and to entry into the application.

Table Protection

All tables in an application should be password protected to prevent changes to them by unauthorized persons. This password protection is applied using either the Paradox Protection Generator (described in the

Multiuser Applications

Paradox *Network Administrator's Guide*) or by using the Password tool in interactive Paradox.

In order to maintain security, users should only have access to an auxiliary password. This will prevent them from accidentally changing the master password. If there is only one level of access provided by an application, all tables used in that application should make use of the same auxiliary password. If an application has two or more levels, two or more auxiliary passwords should be used, each one conferring the rights necessary to carry out the tasks at each level.

Within an application, you use the PASSWORD command to present the table passwords to Paradox. The syntax is

```
PASSWORD Password1 ...[,PasswordN]
```

When Paradox plays the PASSWORD command, any table that uses the password or passwords as a master or auxiliary password may be accessed. This access, however, is limited to the rights conferred by these passwords. For example, if your application will permit a user to add a record to a table, the PASSWORD command must be followed by a password that at least confers entry rights to the table.

A password issued by the PASSWORD command will be valid until the Paradox session ends or the command UNPASSWORD is used to revoke the password. The syntax of the UNPASSWORD command is

```
UNPASSWORD Password1 ...  [,PasswordN]
```

When Paradox plays the UNPASSWORD command, the passwords listed are no longer valid and rights conferred by those passwords are revoked. If you fail to clear one or more passwords before returning to Paradox, users will be able to access any table that uses those uncleared passwords without first entering a password for the remainder of the current session.

TIP: At the end of an application, if you use the EXIT command to return to DOS, the Paradox session ends and all passwords are cleared.

Caution: In Paradox version 3.0, the UNPASSWORD command does not work correctly. If you are using that version, use the braced menu selections,

{Tools} {More} {Protect} {ClearPasswords}

to remove all passwords before returning to Paradox.

Script Protection

Most applications are played entirely from a procedure library, with the exception of a small "starter" script that loads the first procedure from the library and calls it. Procedure libraries have the advantage that they are stored in binary form on your hard disk and cannot be easily changed.

If scripts of an application are stored in a shared directory on a network, they should be encrypted to prevent unwanted changes by unauthorized persons. When a script is encrypted, it can be played without a password but not changed. Scripts are encrypted using the Tools/More/Protect/Password/Script selection in interactive Paradox.

Caution: Do not forget any password you use to encrypt a script. If you are unable to remember a password, you will never be able to change the script again. This also applies to encrypting tables.

Application Protection

If you want to prevent unauthorized persons from using your application, users should be required to enter a password before they can continue. In order to make this effective, the tables and scripts should also be encrypted.

At a minimum, you should prompt users for a password and then use the STYLE ATTRIBUTE command to set the foreground and background

Multiuser Applications

colors to the same color. Then an ACCEPT statement is used to receive the password. Your script can then compare the password to a constant that it stores, or it can issue the password and then attempt to access one of the tables to verify that the password is valid, before continuing.

For example, the following script displays a prompt and tests for a valid password. If one is not supplied within three tries, the user is denied access. If the correct password is given, then the first procedure in the application is loaded and called.

```
CLEAR
;Initialize the first try.
Count = 1
;Give the user three tries.
MESSAGE "Enter a password."
WHILE Count <=3
   ;Set the foreground and background colors to black.
   @ 0,0 ?? "Password :"
   STYLE ATTRIBUTE 0
   ACCEPT "A15" TO PassValue
   ;reset the colors
   STYLE
   IF NOT Retval
      THEN
         ;ESC was pressed.
         QUIT "Application cancelled."
   ENDIF
   ;Test the value of PassValue
   IF PassValue = "LET ME IN"
      THEN
         ;Issue one or more passwords that give the
         ;necessary rights to the tables of the application.
         PASSWORD "AUXPASSWORD"
         ;Load the application main menu and call it.
         READLIB "YourLib" MainMenu
         MainMenu()
         ;If the Main menu returns here, exit to Paradox.
         RESET
         QUIT
      ELSE
         ;Increment the variable Count
         Count = Count + 1
```

```
                MESSAGE "Password not valid. Try again."
    ENDIF
ENDWHILE
;This is only played if the password failed three times.
QUIT "Access denied."
```

Note: It is essential that this script be encrypted.

The preceding script is only one example of a password script. You can create better and more sophisticated password scripts. This one is presented simply as a demonstration. No guarantees about its adequacy are made or implied.

Instead of writing your own password validation script, you can also use the Paradox Password Generator to create one for you.

Quick Review

- Multiuser applications permit two or more users to access the same data simultaneously.
- Paradox automatically places locks on tables. These locks restrict other users' access to the tables.
- You should not rely on Paradox's table locks. Instead, you should explicitly lock the required tables using the LOCK command.
- You can place two or more locks on the same table.
- Two or more users can place locks on the same table.
- You should try to use the least restrictive lock, and remove it when you are through.
- Use CoEdit to permit two or more users to change records in a table simultaneously.
- Use LOCKRECORD to lock a record before attempting changes to it.
- Use UNLOCKRECORD or POSTRECORD to post a changed record to a table in CoEdit.
- When posting a new record to a table, you can use LOCKRECORD, UNLOCKRECORD, or POSTRECORD.
- When posting a record to a table, always test the success of the posting.
- DataEntry is a viable means of adding new records to a table in a multiuser environment.
- Security of data, scripts, and the application itself should be considered in any multiuser situation.

APPENDIX

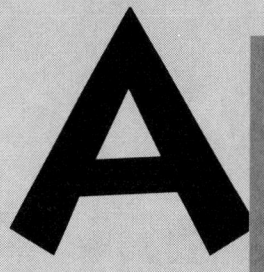

ASCII CODES AND KEY NAMES

This appendix consists of two tables. Table A-1 contains a list of every key and key combination, and their associated key names, that you can produce from your keyboard. These key names are used in PAL commands and functions such as SETKEY, WAIT, SHOWMENU, and so on.

Table A-2 contains the standard IBM ASCII Character Set. You can produce any character whose

ASCII code is greater than 127 by holding down the [Alt] key, typing the three-digit ASCII code, and then releasing the [Alt] key.

Key Command	Action	
1	REPLACE	Ctrl-A
2		Ctrl-B
3		Ctrl-C
4	DITTO	Ctrl-D
5	MINIEDIT	Ctrl-E
6	FIELDVIEW	Ctrl-F
7	GOKEY	Ctrl-G
8	BACKSPACE	Ctrl-H, Backspace
9	TAB, \t	Ctrl-I, Tab
10	\n	Ctrl-J
11		Ctrl-K
12	RESYNCKEY, \f	Ctrl-L
13	ENTER, \r	Ctrl-M, Enter
14		Ctrl-N
15	DOS	Ctrl-O
16		Ctrl-P
17		Ctrl-Q
18	ROTATE	Ctrl-R
19		Ctrl-S
20		Ctrl-T
21	UNDO	Ctrl-U
22	VERTRULER	Ctrl-V
23		Ctrl-W
24		Ctrl-X
25	DELETELINE	Ctrl-Y
26	ZOOM	Ctrl-Z

Table A-1. ASCII Codes and Key Names Used in PAL Commands

ASCII Codes and Key Names

ASCII Code	Key Name	Keypress
27	ESC	Ctrl-[, Ctrl-Esc, Esc
28		Ctrl-\
29		Ctrl-]
30		Ctrl-6
31		Ctrl--
32		Spacebar, Shift-Spacebar, Ctrl-Spacebar
33	!	!
34	\"	"
35	#	#
36	$	$
37	%	%
38	&	&
39	'	'
40	(	(
41	)	)
42	*	*
43	+	+
44	,	,
45	-	-
46	.	.
47	/	/
48	0	0
49	1	1
50	2	2
51	3	3
52	4	4
53	5	5
54	6	6

ASCII Codes and Key Names Used in PAL Commands (*continued*)
Table A-1.

ASCII Code	Key Name	Keypress
55	7	7
56	8	8
57	9	9
58	:	:
59	;	;
60	<	<
61	=	=
62	>	>
63	?	?
64	\@	\@
65	A	A
66	B	B
67	C	C
68	D	D
69	E	E
70	F	F
71	G	G
72	H	H
73	I	I
74	J	J
75	K	K
76	L	L
77	M	M
78	N	N
79	O	O
80	P	P
81	Q	Q
82	R	R
83	S	S

ASCII Codes and Key Names Used in PAL Commands (*continued*)
Table A-1.

ASCII Codes and Key Names

ASCII Code	Key Name	Keypress
84	T	T
85	U	U
86	V	V
87	W	W
88	X	X
89	Y	Y
90	Z	Z
91	[	[
92	\\	\
93	]	]
94	^	^
95	_	_
96	`	`
97	a	a
98	b	b
99	c	c
100	d	d
101	e	e
102	f	f
103	g	g
104	h	h
105	i	i
106	j	j
107	k	k
108	l	l
109	m	m
110	n	n
111	o	o
112	p	p

ASCII Codes and Key Names Used in PAL Commands (*continued*)
Table A-1.

ASCII Code	Key Name	Keypress
113	q	q
114	r	r
115	s	s
116	t	t
117	u	u
118	v	v
119	w	w
120	x	x
121	y	y
122	z	z
123	{	{
124	|	|
125	}	}
126	~	~
127	CTRLBACKSPACE	Ctrl-Backspace
–2	ALTSPACE	Alt-Spacebar
–3		Ctrl-2
–4	CLIPCOPY	Ctrl-Ins
–5	CLIPPASTE	Shift-Ins
–7	CLIPCUT	Shift-Del
–15	REVERSETAB	Shift-Tab
–16		Alt-Q
–17	WHEREAMI	Alt-W
–18		Alt-E
–19	REFRESH	Alt-R
–20		Alt-T
–21		Alt-Y
–22		Alt-U
–23		Alt-I

Table A-1. ASCII Codes and Key Names Used in PAL Commands (*continued*)

ASCII Codes and Key Names

ASCII Code	Key Name	Keypress
–24	DOSBIG	Alt-O
–25		Alt-P
–30	REPLACENEXT	Alt-A
–31	ORDERTABLE	Alt-S
–32	DELETEWORD	Alt-D
–33		Alt-F
–34		Alt-G
–35		Alt-H
–36		Alt-J
–37	KEYLOOKUP	Alt-K
–38	LOCKKEY	Alt-L
–44	ZOOMNEXT	Alt-Z
–45	CROSSTABKEY	Alt-X
–46	TOGGLEPALETTE	Alt-C
–47		Alt-V
–48		Alt-B
–49		Alt-N
–50		Alt-M
–59	HELP, F1	F1
–60	DO_IT!, F2	F2
–61	UPIMAGE, F3	F3
–62	DOWNIMAGE, F4	F4
–63	EXAMPLE, F5	F5
–64	CHECK, F6	F6
–65	FORMKEY, F7	F7
–66	CLEARIMAGE, F8	F8
–67	EDITKEY, F9	F9
–68	MENU, F10	F10
–71	HOME	Home

Table A-1. ASCII Codes and Key Names Used in PAL Commands (*continued*)

ASCII Code	Key Name	Keypress
−72	UP	↑
−73	PGUP	Pg Up
−75	LEFT	←
−77	RIGHT	→
−79	END	End
−80	DOWN	↓
−81	PGDN	Pg Dn
−82	INS	Ins
−83	DEL	Del
−84	F11	Shift-F1
−85	F12	Shift-F2
−86	F13	Shift-F3
−87	F14	Shift-F4
−88	WINMAX, F15	Shift-F5
−89	GROUPBY, F16	Shift-F6
−90	F17	Shift-F7
−91	F18	Shift-F8
−92	F19	Shift-F9
−93	F20	Shift-F10
−94	F21	Ctrl-F1
−95	F22	Ctrl-F2
−96	F23	Ctrl-F3
−97	WINNEXT, F24	Ctrl-F4
−98	WINRESIZE, F25	Ctrl-F5
−99	CHECKDESCENDING, F26	Ctrl-F6
−100	GRAPHKEY, F27	Ctrl-F7
−101	WINCLOSE, F28	Ctrl-F8
−102	F29	Ctrl-F9
−103	TOQPRO, F30	Ctrl-F10

Table A-1. ASCII Codes and Key Names Used in PAL Commands (*continued*)

ASCII Codes and Key Names

ASCII Code	Key Name	Keypress
−104	F31	Alt-F1
−105	SHOWSQL, F32	Alt-F2
−106	INSTANTRECORD, F33	Alt-F3
−107	INSTANTPLAY, F34	Alt-F4
−108	FIELDVIEW, F35	Alt-F5
−109	CHECKPLUS, F36	Alt-F6
−110	INSTANTREPORT, F37	Alt-F7
−111	CLEARALL, F38	Alt-F8
−112	COEDITKEY, F39	Alt-F9
−113	PALMENU, F40	Alt-F10
−114		Ctrl-Prt Sc
−115	CTRLLEFT	Ctrl-←
−116	CTRLRIGHT	Ctrl-→
−117	CTRLEND	Ctrl-End
−118	CTRLPGDN	Ctrl-Pg Dn
−119	CTRLHOME	Ctrl-Home
−120		Alt-1
−121		Alt-2
−122		Alt-3
−123		Alt-4
−124		Alt-5
−125		Alt-6
−126		Alt-7
−127		Alt-8
−128		Alt-9
−129		Alt-0
−130		Alt-−
−131		Alt-=
−132	CTRLPGUP	Ctrl-Pg Up

ASCII Codes and Key Names Used in PAL Commands (*continued*)
Table A-1.

IBM ASCII Character Set Table A-2.

ASCII Value	Character	ASCII Value	Character
0	Null	29	Cursor left
1	☺	30	Cursor up
2	☻	31	Cursor down
3	♥	32	Space
4	♦	33	!
5	♣	34	"
6	♠	35	#
7	Beep	36	$
8	◘	37	%
9	Tab	38	&
10	Linefeed	39	'
11	Cursor home	40	(
12	Form feed	41	)
13	Carriage return	42	*
14	♫	43	+
15	☆	44	,
16	►	45	-
17	◄	46	.
18	↕	47	/
19	‼	48	0
20	¶	49	1
21	§	50	2
22	▬	51	3
23	↨	52	4
24	↑	53	5
25	↓	54	6
26	→	55	7
27	←	56	8
28	Cursor right	57	9

ASCII Codes and Key Names

ASCII Value	Character	ASCII Value	Character
58	:	87	W
59	;	88	X
60	<	89	Y
61	=	90	Z
62	>	91	[
63	?	92	\
64	@	93	]
65	A	94	^
66	B	95	_
67	C	96	'
68	D	97	a
69	E	98	b
70	F	99	c
71	G	100	d
72	H	101	e
73	I	102	f
74	J	103	g
75	K	104	h
76	L	105	i
77	M	106	j
78	N	107	k
79	O	108	l
80	P	109	m
81	Q	110	n
82	R	111	o
83	S	112	p
84	T	113	q
85	U	114	r
86	V	115	s

IBM ASCII Character Set *(continued)*
Table A-2.

ASCII Value	Character	ASCII Value	Character
116	t	145	æ
117	u	146	Æ
118	v	147	ô
119	w	148	ö
120	x	149	ò
121	y	150	û
122	z	151	ù
123	{	152	ÿ
124	|	153	Ö
125	}	154	Ü
126	~	155	¢
127	⌂	156	£
128	Ç	157	¥
129	ü	158	Pt
130	é	159	*f*
131	â	160	á
132	ä	161	í
133	à	162	ó
134	å	163	ú
135	ç	164	ñ
136	ê	165	Ñ
137	ë	166	ª
138	è	167	º
139	ï	168	¿
140	î	169	⌐
141	ì	170	¬
142	Ä	171	½
143	Å	172	¼
144	É	173	¡

IBM ASCII Character Set (*continued*)
Table A-2.

ASCII Codes and Key Names

ASCII Value	Character	ASCII Value	Character
174	<<	203	╩
175	>>	204	╠
176	░	205	=
177	▓	206	╬
178	█	207	╧
179	│	208	╨
180	┤	209	╤
181	╡	210	╥
182	╢	211	╙
183	╖	212	╘
184	╕	213	╒
185	╣	214	╓
186	║	215	╫
187	╗	216	╪
188	╝	217	┘
189	╜	218	┌
190	╛	219	█
191	┐	220	▄
192	└	221	▌
193	┴	222	▐
194	┬	223	▀
195	├	224	α
196	─	225	β
197	┼	226	Γ
198	╞	227	π
199	╟	228	Σ
200	╚	229	σ
201	╔	230	μ
202	╩	231	τ

Table A-2. IBM ASCII Character Set (*continued*)

IBM ASCII Character Set (*continued*)
Table A-2.

ASCII Value	Character	ASCII Value	Character
232	φ	244	⌠
233	θ	245	⌡
234	Ω	246	÷
235	δ	247	≈
236	∞	248	°
237	∅	249	•
238	∈	250	·
239	∩	251	√
240	≡	252	η
241	±	253	²
242	≥	254	■
243	≤	255	(blank 'FF')

APPENDIX

B

COLOR CODES

Color codes are numbers that refer to foreground and background color combinations. For example, the command STYLE can be followed by the keyword ATTRIBUTE and a color code, to define the color of text to be printed to the current canvas. Color codes are also used by the commands GETCOLORS, PAINTCANVAS, SETCOLORS, WINDOW GETCOLORS, and WINDOW SETCOLORS, as well as the function SYSCOLORS ( ).

Color Monitors

To define a color attribute for color monitors, add the background color number to the foreground color number. To create blinking text, add 128 to the color attribute number.

Background Color	Number
Black	0
Blue	16
Green	32
Cyan	48
Red	64
Magenta	80
Brown	96
Light gray	112

Foreground Color	Number
Black	0
Blue	1
Green	2
Cyan	3
Red	4
Magenta	5
Brown	6
Light gray	7
Dark gray	8
Light blue	9
Light green	10
Light cyan	11
Light red	12
Light magenta	13
Yellow	14
White	15

Color Codes

Monochrome Monitors

To define a display attribute for monochrome monitors, use the numbers from the following table. For blinking characters, add 128 to the monochrome attribute number.

Monochrome Attribute	Number
Blank	0
Underlined	1
Normal	2
High-intensity, underlined	9
High-intensity	10
Reverse video	112

APPENDIX

ERROR CODES

The following are the error codes returned by the PAL function, ERRORCODE( ). In most cases, the corresponding error message is returned by the ERRORMESSAGE( ) function. However, when your script uses these functions to handle errors, you should rely on the error code returned by ERRORCODE( ) to determine the error. Do not rely on the text returned by ERRORMESSAGE( ).

Error Code	Error Message
0	(no error message)

File or Directory Errors

Error Code	Error Message
1	Drive not ready
2	Directory not found
3	Table in use by another user
4	Full lock placed on table by another user
5	File not found
6	File corrupted
7	Index file corrupted
8	Object version mismatch
9	Record locked by another user
10	Directory in use by another user
11	Directory is private directory of another user
12	No access to directory at operating system level
13	Index inconsistent with sort order
14	Multiuser access denied
15	PARADOX.NET file conflict

Script Errors

Error Code	Error Message
20	Invalid context for operation
21	Insufficient password rights
22	Table is write-protected
23	Invalid field value
24	Obsolete procedure library
25	Insufficient image rights
26	Invalid PAL context
27	Operation not completed
28	Too many nested closed procedures
29	Table is remote

Error Codes

Error Code	Error Message
Argument Errors	
30	Data type mismatch
31	Argument out of range
32	Wrong number of arguments
33	Invalid argument
34	Variable of procedure not assigned
35	Invalid menu command
36	Missing command parameter
37	Nested complex expression
Resource Errors	
40	Not enough memory to complete operation
41	Not enough disk space to complete operation
42	Not enough stack space to complete operation
43	Printer not ready
44	Low memory warning
Record-level Errors	
50	Record was deleted by another user
51	Record was changed by another user
52	Record was inserted by another user
53	Record with that key already exists
54	Record or table was not locked
55	Record is already locked by you
56	Lookup key not found
57	Record and group lock dependencies on this table lock
Multitable Errors	
60	Referential integrity check
61	Invalid multitable form

Error Code	Error Message
Multitable Errors (continued)	
62	Form locked
63	Link locked
64	Group locks applied to table with different key
65	Group of records locked
66	Cannot read file due to incompatible file version

APPENDIX

EXERCISE TABLES

Throughout this book, step-by-step exercises are provided so that you can use PAL features. The following tables are referred to in those exercises. By creating these tables and entering the sample data into them, you can compare the results you obtain from doing the exercises to the descriptions in the book.

NOTE: You will want to create a directory to store all of the scripts you create as a result of the exercises. (C:\SALES is used in the examples, but you can call it anything you wish.) When you first load Paradox to perform these exercises, remember to first move to this directory.

Tables

The tables are created by following these steps:

1. Select Create from the Main menu.
2. Enter the name of the table at the prompt.
3. Enter the appropriate field names and field types into the Struct table.
4. Press F2 (Do-It!) to complete the creation of the table.

Sample data for each table is provided. This is the same data that appears in the figures in this book. You should enter this data into the tables you create so you can compare your results with those described.

Customer Table Structure

```
Customer Code          A4*
Company Name           A10
Address                A25
City                   A12
State                  A2
Zip                    A7
```

Customer Table Contents

```
Customer  Company
Code      Name      Address            City          State   Zip
------    ------    -------            ----          -----   ---
A100      Company A 535 Seventh Street Houston       TX      77002
B100      Company B 2000 Century Blvd. Atlanta       GA      30308
C100      Company C 11543 Main Street  Seattle       WA      98211
D100      Company D 4624 West Road     Los Angeles   CA      91348
E100      Company E 10021 Lake Drive   New York      NY      01260
F100      Company F 983 First Street   Chicago       IL      60606
```

Exercise Tables

Employee Table Structure

```
Employee Code           A4*
Last Name               A15
First Name              A10
Position                A10
```

Employee Table Contents

```
Employee Code   Last Name         First Name   Position
-------------   ---------------   ----------   ----------
1000            Barrez            Cecelia      Manager
2000            Williams          Joseph       Sales Rep.
3000            Luciano           Peter        Manager
4000            Johnson           Cindy        Sales Rep.
```

Invoice Table Structure

```
Invoice #               A4*
Date                    D
Employee Code           A4
Customer Code           A4
```

Invoice Table Contents

```
Invoice #   Date        Employee Code   Customer Code
---------   --------    -------------   -------------
1000        8/31/92     2000            F100
1001        9/01/92     1000            A100
1002        10/15/92    4000            D100
1003        11/05/92    1000            A100
1004        12/18/92    3000            B100
1005        1/22/93     2000            E100
1006        2/04/93     4000            C100
1007        3/11/93     2000            A100
```

Indetail Table Structure

```
Invoice #              A4*
Product Code           A4*
Quantity                S
Unit Price              $
```

Indetail Table Contents

```
Invoice #   Product Code   Quantity   Unit Price
---------   ------------   --------   ----------------
1000        1002           1            499.00
1000        1004           3            495.00
1000        1005           2            199.00
1001        1001           1            369.00
1001        1002           4            499.00
1002        1003           1            799.00
1002        1005           5            199.00
1003        1001           2            369.00
1003        1002           1            499.00
1003        1003           5            799.00
1004        1005           1            199.00
1005        1003           2            799.00
1006        1002           1            499.00
1007        1003           1            799.00
```

Product Table Structure

```
Product Code           A4*
Product Description    A15
Unit Price              $
```

Product Table Contents

```
Product Code   Product Description   Suggested Retail Price
------------   -------------------   ----------------------
1001           Word Processor                369.00
1002           Spreadsheet                   499.00
1003           Database                      799.00
1004           Graphics                      495.00
1005           Utilities                     199.00
```

Exercise Tables

Creating a Form for the Exercises

In order to complete the exercises in this book, you must create a single form for the Customer table, called form 1. If you have experience creating forms, design one according to your own preferences. If you do not have this experience, or are short on time, use the following steps to have Paradox create a default form for the Customer table:

1. Select Tools from the Main menu.
2. Select Copy from the Tools menu.
3. Select Form from the Copy menu.
4. Select SameTable.
5. Type **Customer** and press .
6. Select F to copy the standard form.
7. Select 1 to create form 1.

INDEX

@, 118, 174
@ operator, 253
{ } (braced menu selections), 104-105
=, 75-78, 120, 287-288
?, 118, 176-177
??, 118, 176-177
" " (quoted strings), 106-108, 286-287.
    See also Constants, alphanumeric
* operator, 96
\+ operator
    in alphanumeric expressions, 92,
        95-96
    in date expressions, 97
    in numeric expressions, 96
; (comment), 129-130
= operator, 98
\- operator
    in date expressions, 97
    in numeric expressions, 96
.. operator, 253
/ operator, 96
< operator, 98
<= operator, 98
<> operator, 98

\> operator, 98
\>= operator, 98
~ character
    for control element hot keys, 228
    for menu hot keys, 204-205
    using with variables in queries,
        304-306
\\, 73
\\f, 406
\\n, 340, 406
\\r, 406
\\t, 406

A

Abbreviated menu commands, 109-112
    advantages of, 112-113
    table of, 110-111
ABS( ), 94
ACCEPT, 118, 214-218
ACCEPTDIALOG, 119, 364, 366
ACOS( ), 93
ADD, 110
After triggers, 359

Alphanumeric constants, 71-73
ALTSPACE, 114, 248, 410
AND operator, 99
APPENDARRAY, 120, 288-289
Application layer, 172
Application Workshop, 15
Applications defined, 4-5
ARRAY, 120
Arrays, 79-80
   assigning values to, 81-82
   declaring, 80-82, 347
   dynamic, 79-82, 345, 377-381
   event arrays, 345-355
   fixed, 79-82
   using in menus, 205-206
ARRAYSIZE( ), 93
ASC( ), 94
ASCII codes
   getting keyboard input as, 218
   table of, 406-418
ASIN( ), 94
Assignment, 286-289
ATAN( ), 94
ATAN2( ), 94
ATFIRST( ), 94
ATLAST( ), 94
AutoIndent, 30
Autolib, 332-333

B

BACKSPACE, 114, 292, 406
BANDINFO( ), 94
BEEP, 118
Before triggers, 359
BLANKDATE( ), 93
BLANKNUM( ), 94
Blinking colors, 183, 422-423
BOT( ), 94

C

CALCDEBUG, 119
Calculations in queries, 300-301
Calling procedures, 314
CANCELDIALOG, 119, 364, 366
CANCELEDIT, 110, 268
CANVAS, 118
Canvas elements, 224
Canvas, 19-21, 170-172
   attributes, 182-186
   clearing, 175
   controlling, 172-173
   echoing, 186-187
   full-screen, 19-20, 136, 171-172
   position of cursor on, 174
   printing to, 176-182
   raising and dropping, 19, 65-66
   selecting, 195
   windows, 20, 171, 187-194
CaseSensitivity, 29-30
CAVERAGE( ), 94
CCOUNT( ), 94
CHARWAITING( ), 93, 222
CHECK, 115, 299, 411
Check boxes, 232-235
CHECKDESCENDING, 115, 299, 412
Checking fields in queries, 299-300
CHECKMARKSTATUS( ), 94
CHECKPLUS, 114, 299, 413
CHR( ), 93
CLEAR, 118, 123, 175-177, 248
CLEARALL, 114, 247-248, 413
CLEARIMAGE, 116, 247-248, 411
CLEARPULLDOWN, 118, 212-213
CLIPCOPY, 26, 115, 410
CLIPCUT, 27, 116, 410
CLIPPASTE, 27, 116, 410
CLOSE PRINTER, 118
Closed procedures, 315, 336-338
Closing windows, 193-194

Index

CMAX( ), 94
CMIN( ), 94
CNPV( ), 93
COEDIT, 110, 278-281, 389
COEDITKEY, 114, 278-281, 413
COL( ), 95
COLNO( ), 95
Colors
   color attributes, 184, 421
   displaying, 220-222
   monochrome attributes, 423
   on screen, 182-186
Commands. *See also* specific command names
   abbreviated menu commands, 109-113
   arranging in scripts, 125-126
   braced menu selections, 104-105
   branching commands, 150-155
   control structures, 149-166
   keypress interactions, 104-108
   looping commands, 156-165
   programming commands, 117-121, 250
   quoted strings, 106-108
   special key commands, 113-117, 248-249
   syntax, 121-124
   system commands, 135-147
   using in scripts, 124
Commenting scripts, 129-133
Comparison operators, 98-99
Conditions in queries, 300-301
Constants, 71
   alphanumeric, 71-73
   date, 74
   logical, 74
   numeric, 73
Control elements, 224-225, 227-235, 322
Control structures, 150
   branching control structures, 150-155
   controlling loops, 164-165
   looping control structures, 156-165
   nesting, 164-165
CONTROLVALUE( ), 95
CONVERTLIB, 119
COPY, 110, 123
COPYFORM, 110
COPYFROMARRAY, 120, 288
Copying scripts, 39
COPYREPORT, 110
COPYTOARRAY, 120, 288
COS( ), 94
CREATE, 110
CREATELIB, 119, 324-325, 327
CROSSTABKEY, 114, 411
CSTD( ), 94
CSUM( ), 94
CTRLBACKSPACE, 114, 292, 410
CTRLBREAK, 28, 114
CTRLEND, 114, 249, 413
CTRLHOME, 115, 249, 413
CTRLLEFT, 115, 249, 413
CTRLPGDN, 115, 249, 413
CTRLPGUP, 115, 249, 413
CTRLRIGHT, 115, 249, 413
Current field, 85
Current record, 83-85
Current table, 83
CURSOR (command), 118
CURSORCHAR( ), 95
CURSORLINE( ), 95
CVAR( ), 94

D

DataEntry, 396-398
Date constants, 74
DATEVAL( ), 93
DAY( ), 93

DEBUG, 119, 138-139
Debugger. *See* PAL Debugger
Debugging, 31-32
Debugging scripts, 132. *See also* PAL Debugger
DEL, 115, 292, 412
DELETE, 110
DELETELINE, 26, 115, 406
DELETEWORD, 114, 411
Deleting scripts, 39
Desktop, 170
    clearing, 247-248
    navigating, 248-256
    placing tables on, 240-242
Dialog boxes
    canvas elements in, 224
    check boxes, 232-235
    control elements in, 224-235
    creating, 222-235
    dialog procedures, 224
    example of, 5
    pick lists, 230-232
    planning, 226-227
    pushbuttons, 227-230
    radio buttons, 232-235
Dialog procedures, 224, 358, 360-368
    controlling a dialog box from, 366-368
    returning from, 364-366
DIRECTORY( ), 93
DIREXISTS( ), 93
DITTO, 114, 292, 406
DOS, 110, 115, 406
DOSBIG, 114, 410
DOW( ), 93
DOWN, 116, 249, 412
DOWNIMAGE, 115, 249, 411
DO_IT!, 110, 115, 268, 295-296, 411
    adding to a saved query, 64-66
DRIVESPACE( ), 93
DRIVESTATUS( ), 93
Dynamic arrays. *See* Arrays
DYNARRAY, 120
DYNARRAYSIZE( ), 93

E

ECHO, 118, 186-187, 246
Echo layer, 171-172
EDIT, 110, 267
Edit menu, 28-29
Editing tables, 267-281, 285-293
EDITKEY, 116, 267, 411
EDITLOG, 119
Editor. *See* Paradox Editor, Script Editor
EDITOR EXTRACT, 120
EDITOR FIND, 110
EDITOR FINDNEXT, 110
EDITOR GOTO, 120
EDITOR INFO, 120
EDITOR INSERT, 120
Editor menu, 27-28
EDITOR NEW, 110
EDITOR OPEN, 110
EDITOR READ, 110
EDITOR REPLACE, 110
EDITOR SELECT, 120
EDITOR WRITE, 110
EMPTY, 110
Encryption, 398-402
END, 115, 249, 412
ENTER, 115, 406
EOT( ), 95
Erasing the screen, 176
Error codes, 426-428
Error messages, 426-428
Error procedures, 338-340
ERRORCODE( ), 93, 386, 390, 425-428
ERRORINFO, 120

Index

ERRORMESSAGE( ), 93, 386, 390, 425-428
Errors in script logic, 33, 35-36
ERRORUSER( ), 93, 386, 390
ESC, 115, 406
Event procedures, 358-381
Event stream, 344
Events, 344-345
   executing, 355-356
   getting, 345-355
   stream, 344
   trapping. *See* getting
EXAMPLE, 115, 411
Example elements in queries, 301-304
EXECEVENT, 120, 355-356
EXECPROC, 119, 336
EXECUTE, 119, 335
Executing an event, 355-356
Exercise form, 435
Exercise tables, 431-433
EXIT, 110
EXP( ), 94
Expressions, 69-71
   arrays, 79-82
   constants, 71-74
   data types of, 70
   elements used in, 70-71
   field specifiers, 82-89
   functions, 89-95
   operators, 92, 95-100
   using procedures as, 321-322, 336
   variables, 74-79

F

FAMILYRIGHTS( ), 93
Feedback, 292-293
Field specifiers, 82-83
   using, 86-89
   using with MOVETO, 250-251

FIELD( ), 95
FIELDINFO( ), 95
FIELDNO( ), 95
FIELDRIGHTS( ), 93
FIELDSTR( ), 95
FIELDTYPE( ), 95
FIELDVIEW, 114, 406, 413
File menu, 28
FILEREAD, 120
FILESIZE( ), 93
FILEVERSION( ), 93
FILEWRITE, 119
FILL( ), 93
FIRSTSHOW, 120
Fixed arrays. *See* Arrays
Floating windows, 172, 189, 192
FOR, 118, 156-159
FOREACH, 118, 159-161
Form lock, 385
FORM( ), 95
Formal parameters, 320-321
FORMAT( ), 93
FORMKEY, 115, 245, 411
Forms
   creating for exercises, 435
   getting handles of, 245
   picking, 242-246
   uses for, 222, 242-246
FORMTABLES, 120
FORMTYPE( ), 95
FRAME, 119
Full lock, 385
Full-screen canvas. *See* Canvas
Functions, 89-90. *See also* specific function names
   complete list of, 93-95
   types of, 91-92
   user-defined, 321-322
   using, 90-91
FV( ), 93

G

GETCANVAS( ), 95, 196
GETCHAR( ), 95, 218-222, 344
GETCOLORS, 120, 421
GETEVENT, 120, 345-358
GETKEYBOARDSTATE, 120
GETMENUSELECTION, 119, 212-213
GETWINDOW( ), 95, 196
Global canvas. *See* Canvas, full-screen
Global variables, 317-318
Go, 37-38
GOKEY, 26, 115, 406
GRAPHKEY, 115, 412
GRAPHTYPE( ), 93
GROUPBY, 116, 412

H

Handles, 188-190, 196, 242
Headers, 131-132
HELP, 110, 115, 411
HELPMODE( ), 95
HOME, 116, 249, 411
Hot keys
    in dialog boxes, 228
    in menus, 204-205

I

Idle events, 344, 355
IF, 118, 151-153
IIF( ), 93
IMAGECAVERAGE( ), 94
IMAGECCOUNT( ), 94
IMAGECMAX( ), 94
IMAGECMIN( ), 94
IMAGECSUM( ), 94
IMAGENO( ), 95
IMAGERIGHTS, 120
IMAGETYPE( ), 95
INDEX, 110
INFOLIB, 119, 329-330
Indenting, 127-128
Init script, 18
Input from the user, 199-236
INS, 116, 292, 412
Instant scripts, 14, 54
    creating, 18, 54-56
    limitations of, 58-59
    playing, 16, 56
INSTANTPLAY, 114, 412
INSTANTRECORD, 114, 413
INSTANTREPORT, 114, 413
INT( ), 94
ISASSIGNED( ), 93
ISBLANK( ), 95, 276
ISBLANKZERO( ), 93
ISEMPTY( ), 93
ISENCRYPTED( ), 93
ISFIELDVIEW( ), 95
ISFILE( ), 93
ISFORMVIEW( ), 95, 245
ISINSERTMODE( ), 95
ISLINKLOCKED( ), 95
ISMASTER( ), 93
ISMULTIFORM( ), 95
ISMULTIREPORT( ), 95
ISRUNTIME( ), 93
ISSHARED( ), 93
ISTABLE( ), 93
ISVALID( ), 93
ISWINDOW( ), 95

K

Key commands. *See* Special key commands
Key events, 344, 349-350
Key names, 145, 269, 406-413
Key violations, 279-281, 391-393
Keyboard buffer, 221-222

Index

Keyboard input, 214-222
Keyboard state. *See* GETKEYBOARDSTATE
KEYLOOKUP, 114, 392, 411
KEYPRESS, 119, 344
Keyviol table, 398
Keyword operators, 99-100

L

LEFT, 116, 249, 412
LEN( ), 93
Libraries. *See* Procedure libraries
LINKTYPE( ), 95
LN( ), 94
LOCALIZEEVENT, 120, 351, 353
LOCATE, 120, 250, 252-256
LOCATE INDEXORDER, 120, 256
LOCK, 110, 386, 388-389
LOCKKEY, 114, 392
LOCKRECORD, 119, 279-281, 390, 395
LOCKSTATUS( ), 95
LOG( ), 94
Logical constants, 74
Logical error in scripts, 33, 35-36
Lookup. *See* ACCEPT
LOOP, 118, 164
LOWER( ), 93

M

MATCH( ), 93
MAX( ), 94
MEMLEFT( ), 94
MENU, 116, 411
MENUCHOICE( ), 95
MENUDISABLE, 119, 357
MENUENABLE, 119
MENUPROMPT( ), 95
Menus, 200-210
    Edit, 28-29
    Editor, 27-28
    File, 28
    Options, 29-30
    PAL, 22-23
    Scripts, 21-22
    Search, 29-30
    SHOWARRAY, 119, 200, 205-206
    SHOWFILES, 119, 200, 206-208
    SHOWMENU, 119, 200, 202-205
    SHOWPOPUP, 119, 200, 208-210
    SHOWPULLDOWN, 119, 200-201, 210-213, 356-358
    SHOWTABLES, 119, 200, 206-207
MESSAGE, 119, 178-179, 273, 292
Message events, 344, 354-355
MIN( ), 94
MINIEDIT, 22, 114, 406
MOD( ), 94
MONITOR( ), 93
MONTH( ), 93
MOUSE CLICK, 119
MOUSE DOUBLECLICK, 119
MOUSE DRAG, 119
Mouse events, 344, 350-353
MOUSE HIDE, 120
MOUSE SHOW, 120
MOVETO, 110, 120, 250-252
MOY( ), 93
Multiuser applications, 383-402

N

Naming
    arrays, 79
    procedures, 314
    scripts, 17-18
    variables, 78
Nested control structures, 164-165
NETTYPE( ), 94

NEWDIALOGSPEC, 119
NEWWAITSPEC, 119
Next, 37
NFIELDS( ), 95
NIMAGERECORDS( ), 95
NIMAGES( ), 95
NKEYFIELDS( ), 95
NOT operator, 99
NPAGES( ), 95
NRECORDS( ), 95
NROWS( ), 95
Numeric constants, 73
NUMVAL( ), 94

O

OPEN PRINTER, 119
Operators
   *, 96
   +, 92, 95-97
   -, 95-97
   /, 96
   <, 98
   <=, 98
   <>, 98
   =, 98
   >, 98
   >=, 98
   AND, 99
   comparison, 98-99
   date, 97
   keyword, 99-100
   logical, 97
   NOT, 99
   OR, 99
   order of evaluation, 96, 100
Options menu, 29-30
OR operator, 99
ORDERTABLE, 114, 411

P

PAGENO( ), 95
PAGEWIDTH( ), 95
PAINTCANVAS, 119, 184-186, 352-353, 421
PAL defined, 1-9
PAL Debugger, 31-32
   features of, 36-39
   invoking, 33, 35, 138
   using, 33-39
PAL menu, 15-16, 22-23
PALMENU, 114, 413
Paradox Editor,
   creating scripts with, 15, 24-25
   editing scripts, 25-27
   keys used in, 26-27
   loading from Debugger, 39
   using, 22-30
   using an alternative, 11
   using AutoIndent, 29-30
   using CaseSensitivity, 29-30
   using WordWrap, 29-30
Paradox.lib, 333-334
PASSWORD, 119, 399
Password protection, 398-400
Pattern operators, 253
Pausing. *See* SLEEP
Pausing a script, 221-222. *See also* SLEEP
PAW. *See* Application Workshop
Personal Programmer, 15
PGDN, 116, 249, 412
PGUP, 116, 249, 412
PI( ), 94
PICKFORM, 110, 242-246
Pick lists, 230-232
PLAY, 16, 119, 139-142
Playing scripts, 15-16
PMT( ), 93
Pop, 39
POSTRECORD, 119, 391-393

Index

POW( ), 94
Prevent full lock, 385
Prevent write lock, 385
PRINT, 119
PRINTER, 119
PRINTERSTATUS( ), 94, 265
Printer readiness, 256
Printing
   reports, 264-265
   to screen, 176-182, 195
Private directories, 395-396
Private tables, 396
PRIVDIR( ), 94
Private variables, 317-319
PRIVTABLES, 119, 396
PROC, 119, 313-317, 336
Procedure libraries, 323-324
   adding procedures to, 325-327
   changing procedures in, 327-329
   creating, 324-325
   listing contents of, 329-330
   loading procedures from, 330-334
Procedures, 312-313
   advantages of, 313
   calling, 314
   closed, 315, 336-338
   creating, 314-317
   dialog procedures, 358, 360-368
   error procedures, 338-340
   event procedures, 358-381
   formal parameters in, 319-321
   loading from a library, 330-334
   private variables in, 317-319
   releasing, 322-323
   returning values from, 321-322
   swapping, 334-336
   using in a dialog box, 228-229
   wait procedures, 358, 369-376
Programming commands, 117-118. *See also* specific command names

   categories of, 120-121
   for desktop movement, 250-256
   table of, 118-120
PROMPT, 119, 212
Prompting for input, 216-217
PROTECT, 110
Pushbuttons, 227-230, 322
PV( ), 93

Q

Queries
   calculations in, 300-301
   changing, 298-308
   checking fields in, 299-300
   conditions in, 300-301
   creating, 293-295
   displaying a query form, 294-295
   example elements in, 301-304
   operators in, 300-301
   processing, 295-297
   removing, 296
   underscore character in, 303-304
   user-defined, 306-308
   variables in, 304-306
   verifying success of, 296-298
QUERY, 120
QUERYORDER( ), 94
QUIT (command), 118, 142-144
Quit, Ctrl-Q, in Debugger, 38
QUITLOOP, 118, 164

R

Radio buttons, 232-235
RAND( ), 94
READLIB, 119, 330-332
RECNO( ), 95
Record level processing, 289-291

Recorded scripts, 14, 44. *See also* Instant scripts
  contents of, 50-52
  creating, 46-47
  limitations of, 58-59
  playing, 47-48
  uses for, 45-46
Records
  adding a new record, 275-281
  current record, 83-89
  editing a specific record, 273-275, 289-292
  locating, 252-256
  locking, 279-281, 390
  selecting. *See* Queries
  unlocking, 391-393
RECORDSTATUS( ), 95
REFRESH, 114, 410
REFRESHCONTROL, 119, 366
REFRESHDIALOG, 119, 366
RELEASE, 119, 120, 322-323, 328, 332
RENAME, 110
Renaming scripts, 39
REPAINTDIALOG, 119, 366
REPLACE, 26, 114, 406
REPLACEFIELDS, 120, 289
REPLACENEXT, 26, 114, 411
REPORT, 110
Reports
  printing, 264-265
  report previewer, 266
  using, 264-266
  verifying printer readiness, 265
REPORTTABLES, 120
REQUIREDCHECK, 120
RESET, 119
RESYNCCONTROL, 119, 366
RESYNCDIALOG, 119, 366
RESYNCKEY, 115, 406
Retry period, 387

RETRYPERIOD( ), 94, 387
RETURN, 118, 135-136
  with dialog procedures, 364-365
  with expression, 321-322
  with wait procedures, 375-376
Retval, 203, 218
  with ACCEPT, 229
  with LOCATE, 254-256
  with WAIT, 261-262
REVERSETAB, 116, 249, 410
RIGHT, 116, 249, 412
RMEMLEFT( ), 94
ROTATE, 115, 406
ROUND( ), 94
ROW( ), 95
ROWNO( ), 95
RUN, 119
Run-time script error, 33-34

S

Saved queries, 59. *See also* Queries
  automating, 64-66
  creating, 60-62
  playing, 62-63
  processing, 63-64
SAVETABLES, 119
SAVEVARS, 120
Savevars script, 19
SCAN, 118, 163-164, 290-292
Screen attributes, 182-186, 217, 422
Script Editor (Paradox 3.5), 31
  keys used in, 32
  loading from Debugger, 39
Script menu in Script Editor, 31-32
Scripts, 14
  adding comments to, 129-130
  blank lines in, 128-129
  commenting, 129-130
  copying, 39

Index

creating, 14-15
creating headers for, 131
creating procedures from, 314-317
deleting, 39
documenting, 130-131
errors in, 21
execute, 18-19
indenting, 127-128
init, 18
instant, 14, 18
menu, 21-22
mini, 18-19
naming, 17-18
playing, 15-16, 139-142
playing when loading Paradox, 16
recorded, 14, 44-53
renaming, 39
terminating, 16-17, 136, 142-144
using blank space in, 126-129
value, 18-19
Scripts menu, 15
SCROLLPRESS, 120
SDIR( ), 94
Search menu, 29-30
SEARCH( ), 93
SEARCHFROM( ), 93
Security, 7, 398-402
SELECT, 120, 295
SELECTCONTROL, 119, 366
Separator. *See* SHOWPOPUP, SHOWPULLDOWN
SETAUTOSAVE, 119
SETBATCH, 119
SETBW, 119
SETCANVAS, 119, 195
SETCOLORS, 119, 421
SETDIR, 110
SETKEY, 16, 119, 144-146, 333-334, 405
SETKEYBOARDSTATE, 120
SETMARGIN, 119
SETMAXSIZE, 120
SETNEGCOLOR, 120
SETPRINTER, 119
SETPRIVDIR, 110
SETQUERYORDER, 120
SETRECORDPOSITION, 120
SETRESTARTCOUNT, 119
SETRETRYPERIOD, 119, 387
SETSWAP, 119, 334-335
SETUIMODE, 120
SETUSERNAME, 110
SHIFTPRESS, 120
SHOWARRAY, 119, 205-206
SHOWDIALOG, 119, 222-235, 344
SHOWFILES, 119, 206-208
SHOWMENU, 119, 200, 202-205, 405
SHOWPOPUP, 119, 208-210
SHOWPULLDOWN, 119, 210-213, 356-358
SHOWSQL, 114, 413
SHOWTABLES, 119, 206-207
SIN( ), 94
SKIP, 120
SLEEP, 120, 137-138
SORT, 110
SORTORDER( ), 94
SOUND, 119
SPACES( ), 93
Special key commands, 113
    for desktop movement, 248-249
    table of, 114-116
SQRT( ), 94
Status bar, 212
Step, 36-37
STRVAL( ), 93
STYLE, 119, 182-183, 185, 217, 421
Submenus. *See* SHOWPOPUP, SHOWPULLDOWN
SUBSTR( ), 93
SUBTRACT, 110

Swapping procedures, 334-336
SWITCH, 118, 153-155
SYNCCURSOR, 120
Syntax, 121-122
    notation for, 122-124
    script errors, 33-34
SYSCOLOR( ), 94, 421
SYSINFO, 120
SYSMODE( ), 94

T

TAB, 116, 406
Table locks
    automatic locks, 384-386
    explicit locks, 386-387
    managing, 388-389
    removing, 387-388
    retry period, 387
TABLE( ), 95
TABLERIGHTS( ), 94
Tables
    coediting, 278-281
    current table, 83-89
    editing, 267-281, 285-293, 389
    handles, 241-242
    keyed tables, 278-281, 285
    Keyviol, 398
    locking, 384-388
    navigating, 248-256
    picking form for, 242-246
    private, 396
    querying, 293-308
    scanning, 163-164
    selecting, 250-252
    using, 239-240
    viewing, 240-242, 256-264
    waiting, 257-264
Tags
    in dialog boxes, 228, 231

    in menus, 208, 212
TAN( ), 94
Terminating scripts, 16-17
TEXT, 119, 179-182
TICKS( ), 93
Tildes
    for control element hot keys, 228
    for menu hot keys, 204-205
    using with variables in queries, 304-306
TIME( ), 93
TODAY( ), 93
TOGGLEPALETTE, 114, 411
TOQPRO, 115, 412
Trace, 37
Trapping keypresses, 263
Trigger cycles, 359, 372
Trigger events, 358
    before and after triggers, 359, 361-362, 371
TYPE( ), 94
TYPEIN, 120, 287

U

Underscore character in queries, 303-304
UNDO, 110, 115, 406
UNLOCK, 110, 387-388
UNLOCKRECORD, 119, 391-393
UNPASSWORD, 110, 399
UP, 116, 249, 412
UPIMAGE, 115, 411
UPPER( ), 93, 291
USDATE( ), 93
User-defined functions, 321-322
USERNAME( ), 93

V

Variables, 74-75
    assigning values to, 75-78

Index

global, 317-318
naming, 78-79
private, 317-319
in queries, 304-306
VERSION( ), 94, 273
VERTRULER, 115, 406
VIEW, 110, 240-242, 256-257, 267

W

WAIT, 119, 123, **257-264**, **268-269**, 344
  with wait procedures, 369-370, 395
Wait procedures, 358, 369-376
  controlling a table from, 376
  creating, 370-375
  returning from, 375-376
Where?, 38, 319
WHEREAMI, 26, 114, 410
WHILE, 118, 162-163, 263-264
Wildcard operators, 253
WINCLOSE, 115, 194, 248, 412
WINDOW( ), 95, 296-297
WINDOW CLOSE, 120, 194, 248
WINDOW CREATE, 120, 188-189
WINDOW ECHO, 119
WINDOW GETATTRIBUTES, 120, 190-191
WINDOW GETCOLORS, 120, 421
WINDOW HANDLE, 120
WINDOW LIST, 120, 242
WINDOW MAXIMIZE, 120
WINDOW MOVE, 120
WINDOW RESIZE, 120

WINDOW SCROLL, 120
WINDOW SELECT, 120, 245, 252
WINDOW SETATTRIBUTES, 120, 194, 246-247
WINDOW SETCOLORS, 120, 421
WINDOWAT( ), 95
Windows
  canvases for, 188-190
  closing, 193-194, 247-248
  creating, 188-190
  on desktop, 171, 188-190
  floating, 172, 189, 192
  getting attributes of, 190-192
  getting handle of, 196, 245
  handles, 188-190, 196, 242, 245
  selecting, 245
  setting attributes of, 192-194, 246-247
WINMAX, 116, 412
WINNEXT, 114, 249, 412
WINRESIZE, 115, 412
WordWrap, 29-30
Workshop. *See* Application Workshop
Write lock, 385
WRITELIB, 119, 325-329

Y

YEAR( ), 93

Z

ZOOM, 26, 100, 115, 254, 406
ZOOMNEXT, 114, 411

 ▷ *Expand* **Your Skills Even More**
*with help from our expert authors. Now that you've gained greater skills with **PAL for Paradox 4 Made Easy**, let us suggest the following related titles that will help you use your computer to full advantage.*

Paradox 4 Made Easy
by Edward Jones
Get a fast start with Borland's newest relational database. Jones will turn you into a savvy Paradox 4 user as you follow step-by-step instructions. You'll learn all the basics of creating a database and manipulating data before discovering how to use the Query by example facility and other exciting features.
$19.95, ISBN: 0-07-881766-8, 512 pages, 7 3/8 x 9 1/4

Paradox 4: The Complete Reference
by Carole Boggs Matthews and Patricia Shepard
With this outstanding reference, you'll have the best and most complete resource available on Borland's widely used relational database for the IBM PC and compatibles. All Paradox commands, functions, and features are described clearly for beginners and in detail for experienced users.
$29.95, ISBN: 0-07-881794-3, 896 pages, 7 3/8 x 9 1/4

FoxPro 2 Made Easy
by Edward Jones
This book will have you using FoxPro 2.0 the latest version of this popular database and compiler in just a few chapters. Database expert Ed Jones quickly takes you from basic database creation to intermediate-level applications.
$24.95, ISBN: 0-07-881721-8, 694 pages, 7 3/8 x 9 1/4

▶ ── Osborne **McGraw-Hill** ■ Available at local book and computer stores

FoxPro 2: The Complete Reference
by Edward Jones and David Nesbitt
Take full advantage of everything FoxPro 2.0 has to offer with this well-organized, information-packed volume containing detailed descriptions of every command, function, and parameter. Jones and Nesbitt also cover features that include Screen Painter, Menu Builder, SQL access and more.
$29.95, ISBN: 0-07-881688-2, 819 pages, 7 3/8 x 9 1/4

dBASE IV 1.5 Inside & Out
by Edward Jones
With *dBASE IV 1.5 Inside & Out*, you'll find complete coverage of this software, from an overview of beginning procedures, such as how to create a database, manipulate data, and use a mouse with dBASE, to a discussion of advanced topics, including programming and using dBASE on a network.
$27.95, ISBN: 0-07-881817-6, 752 pp., 7 3/8 x 9 1/4
Covers dBASE IV Versions 1.0, 1.1 & 1.5

Liskin's dBASE IV 1.1 Handbook
by Miriam Liskin
Renowned dBASE expert, Miriam Liskin has completely revised her bestselling book, *dBASE IV Made Easy* to cover dBASE IV 1.1. Liskin provides an exceptionally comprehensive handbook that assumes no prior knowledge of dBASE IV 1.1, yet covers all aspects of the program without requiring previous programming experience.
$34.95, ISBN: 0-07-881016-7 928 pages 7 3/8 x 9 1/4

Liskin's dBASE IV 1.1 Programming Book
by Miriam Liskin
Miriam Liskin, nationally recognized dBASE expert, has spent years training dBASE users. Now in her Programming Book, she puts her keen insights to work covering the kinds of practical applications and hands-on programming skills users really need to take full advantage of this database.
$34.95, ISBN: 0-07-881681-5, 1337 pages, 7 3/8 x 9 1/4

▶ ——— Osborne **McGraw-Hill** ■ Available at local book and computer stores

Teach Yourself dBASE III Plus
by Charles Ackerman
Ackerman quickly instructs you in all the fundamentals of this widely-used database program. Each chapter is organized into a 15-minute presentation of easy-to-use material containing hands-on exercises and skill checks at the end of each chapter.
$19.95, ISBN: 0-07-881680-7, 435 pages, 7 3/8 x 9 1/4

Using dBASE III Plus
by Edward Jones
With Jones' expertise you'll be in full command of all the features of this powerful database software. Learn to design, create, and display a dBASE III Plus database, devise entry forms with the Screen Painter, generate reports, use Query files and much more.
$22.95, ISBN: 0-07-881252-6, 530 pages, 7 3/8 x 9 1/4

dBASE III Plus Made Easy
by Miriam Liskin
Learning dBASE III Plus couldn't be simpler. You'll install and run the program, enter and edit data. Discover all the features of using dBASE III Plus at the dot prompt. Each concept is clearly explained and followed by examples and exercises that you can complete at your own speed.
$19.95, ISBN: 0-07-881294-1, 350 pages, 7 3/8 x 9 1/4

dBASE III Plus: The Pocket Reference
by Miriam Liskin
This handy guide provides a concise summary of all the important elements of the dBASE III Plus command language. Miriam Liskin gives you the information you need so you can quickly check the exact syntax of a command or confirm the available options.
$9.95, ISBN: 0-07-881831-1, 115 pages, 4 3/4 x 8

▶──── Osborne **McGraw-Hill** ■ Available at local book and computer stores

Q&A 4 Made Easy
by Carole Boggs Matthews
This is the best introduction to the newest version of Symantec's widely used Q&A database software. After introducing you to database principles, Matthews teaches you how to organize your data into files. Within a few chapters, you'll be creating reports, documents, macros and much more.
$19.95, ISBN: 0-07-881697-1, 426 pages, 7 3/8 x 9 1/4

Clipper Programming
by Brett Oliver
This outstanding guide provides novice and expert database programmers with a solid, fast-paced introduction to the capabilities of Clipper releases 5.0 and 5.01. Oliver, founder of Nantucket, moves quickly from database programming to designing stand-alone applications, and more.
$29.95, ISBN: 0-07-881758-7, 512 pages, 7 3/8 x 9 1/4

Using SQL
by James Groff and Paul Weinberg
Whether you're a database user, manager, consultant, or programmer, you'll benefit from this no-nonsense, jargon-free discussion of SQL's strengths and weaknesses, and comparisons of the leading SQL-based databases.
$26.95, ISBN: 0-07-881524-X, 686 pages, 7 3/8 x 9 1/4
Available in Spanish: ISBN: 0-07-104082-X

ORACLE: The Complete Reference
by George Koch
Koch gives every user and application developer the essential ORACLE in a single volume. This book features an alphabetical listing of all ORACLE commands with detailed explanations and cross-references, plus invaluable practical chapters with extensive examples on using, designing, and managing databases effectively.
$34.95, ISBN: 0-07-881635-1, 1045 pages, 7 3/8 x 9 1/4
Covers Versions 5 & 6

▶ —— Osborne **McGraw-Hill** ■ Available at local book and computer stores